The middle years of the twentieth century marked a particularly intense time of crisis and change in European society. During this period (1930-1950), a broad intellectual and spiritual movement arose within the European Catholic community, largely in response to the secularism that lay at the core of the crisis. The movement drew inspiration from earlier theologians and philosophers such as Möhler, Newman, Gardeil, Rousselot, and Blondel, as well as from men of letters like Charles Péguy and Paul Claudel.

The group of academic theologians included in the movement extended into Belgium and Germany, in the work of men like Emile Mersch, Dom Odo Casel, Romano Guardini, and Karl Adam. But above all the theological activity during this period centered in France. Led principally by the Jesuits at Fourvière and the Dominicans at Le Saulchoir, the French revival included many of the greatest names in twentieth-century Catholic thought: Henri de Lubac, Jean Daniélou, Yves Congar, Marie-Dominique Chenu, Louis Bouyer, and, in association, Hans Urs von Balthasar.

It is not true — as subsequent folklore has it — that those theologians represented any sort of self-conscious "school": indeed, the differences among them, for example, between Fourvière and Saulchoir, were important. At the same time, most of them were united in the double conviction that theology had to speak to the present situation, and that the condition for doing so faithfully lay in a recovery of the Church's past. In other words, they saw clearly that the first step in what later came to be known as *aggiornamento* had to be *ressourcement* — a rediscovery of the riches of the whole of the Church's two-thousand-year tradition. According to de Lubac, for example, all of his own works as well as the entire *Sources chrétiennes* collection are based on the presupposition that "the renewal of Christian vitality is linked at least partially to a renewed exploration of the periods and of the works where the Christian tradition is expressed with particular intensity."

In sum, for the *ressourcement* theologians theology involved a "return to the sources" of Christian faith, for the purpose of drawing out the meaning and significance of these sources for the critical questions of our time. What these theologians sought was a spiritual and intellectual communion with Christianity in its most vital moments as transmitted to us in its classic texts, a communion that would nourish, invigorate, and rejuvenate twentieth-century Catholicism.

The *ressourcement* movement bore great fruit in the documents of the Second Vatican Council and deeply influenced the work of Pope John Paul II.

The present series is rooted in this renewal of theology. The series thus understands *ressourcement* as revitalization: a return to the sources, for the purpose of developing a theology that will truly meet the challenges of our time. Some of the features of the series, then, are a return to classical (patristic-medieval) sources and a dialogue with contemporary Western culture, particularly in terms of problems associated with the Enlightenment, modernity, and liberalism.

The series publishes out-of-print or as yet untranslated studies by earlier authors associated with the *ressourcement* movement. The series also publishes works by contemporary authors sharing in the aim and spirit of this earlier movement. This will include any works in theology, philosophy, history, literature, and the arts that give renewed expression to Catholic sensibility.

The editor of the Ressourcement series, David L. Schindler, is Gagnon Professor of Fundamental Theology and dean at the John Paul II Institute in Washington, D.C., and editor of the North American edition of *Communio: International Catholic Review,* a federation of journals in thirteen countries founded in Europe in 1972 by Hans Urs von Balthasar, Jean Daniélou, Henri de Lubac, Joseph Ratzinger, and others.

RETRIEVAL & RENEWAL

Ressourcement

IN CATHOLIC THOUGHT

VOLUMES PUBLISHED

Mysterium Paschale
Hans Urs von Balthasar

The Heroic Face of Innocence: Three Stories
Georges Bernanos

The Letter on Apologetics and *History and Dogma*
Maurice Blondel

Prayer: The Mission of the Church
Jean Daniélou

On Pilgrimage
Dorothy Day

We, the Ordinary People of the Streets
Madeleine Delbrêl

The Discovery of God
Henri de Lubac

Medieval Exegesis, volumes 1 and 2:
The Four Senses of Scripture
Henri de Lubac

Letters from Lake Como:
Explorations in Technology and the Human Race
Romano Guardini

Divine Likeness: Toward a Trinitarian Anthropology of the Family
Marc Cardinal Ouellet

The Portal of the Mystery of Hope
Charles Péguy

In the Beginning:
A Catholic Understanding of the Story of Creation and the Fall
Joseph Cardinal Ratzinger

In the Fire of the Burning Bush:
An Initiation to the Spiritual Life
Marko Ivan Rupnik

Love Alone Is Credible:
Hans Urs von Balthasar as Interpreter
of the Catholic Tradition, volume 1
David L. Schindler, ed.

Hans Urs von Balthasar: A Theological Style
Angelo Scola

The Nuptial Mystery
Angelo Scola

LOVE ALONE IS CREDIBLE

Hans Urs von Balthasar
as Interpreter of the Catholic Tradition

VOLUME 1

Edited by

David L. Schindler

WILLIAM B. EERDMANS PUBLISHING COMPANY
GRAND RAPIDS, MICHIGAN / CAMBRIDGE, U.K.

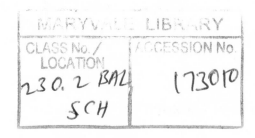
© 2008 Wm. B. Eerdmans Publishing Co.

Published 2008 by
Wm. B. Eerdmans Publishing Co.
2140 Oak Industrial Drive N.E., Grand Rapids, Michigan 49505 /
P.O. Box 163, Cambridge CB3 9PU U.K.

Printed in the United States of America

12 11 10 09 08   7 6 5 4 3 2 1

Library of Congress Cataloging-in-Publication Data

Love alone is credible: Hans Urs von Balthasar as interpreter of the Catholic tradition,
    vol. l / edited by David L. Schindler.
        p.   cm.
    Includes bibliographical references.
    ISBN 978-0-8028-6247-1 (pbk.: alk. paper)
    1. Balthasar, Hans Urs von, 1905-1988.
    2. Catholic Church — Doctrines.   I. Schindler, David L., 1943-

    BX4705.B163L68   2008
    230'.2092 — dc22

                                            2007045768

www.eerdmans.com

Contents

PREFACE   xi

CONTRIBUTORS   xiii

Toward a Renewal of Theology

The Eucharist and Mission in the Theology
of Hans Urs von Balthasar   3

    Roch Kereszty

Love Alone: Hans Urs von Balthasar as a Master
of Theological Renewal   16

    Adrian J. Walker

What Does Triunity "Add" to the Reality of God — and to the Structure of the Cosmos?

Trinity, Creation, and Aesthetic Subalternation   41

    Michael Hanby

Eternal Happening: God as an Event of Love   75

    Antonio López

What Does Trinity "Add" to the Reality of the Covenants?   105

    Richard Schenk

Contents

Motion and the Body: Does "Love Make the World Go 'Round"?

God's Labor, Novelty's Emergence: Cosmic Motion
as Self-Transcending Love   115
    Stephen Fields

Love and the Organism: A Theological Contribution
to the Study of Life   141
    José Granados

Love Makes the World Go 'Round: Motion and Trinity   176
    Simon Oliver

Sources of the Christian Mystery

Balthasar as Interpreter of the Catholic Tradition   191
    Jacques Servais

Descensus ad inferos, Dawn of Hope: Aspects of the Theology
of Holy Saturday in the Trilogy of Hans Urs von Balthasar   209
    Juan M. Sara

Movement Toward God: The Relation of Natural and Supernatural Love, of *Erōs* and *Agapē*

Love, Action, and Vows as "Inner Form" of the Moral Life   243
    David S. Crawford

"Husbands, Love Your Wives as Your Own Bodies":
Is Nuptial Love a Case of Love or Its Paradigm?   261
    Margaret H. McCarthy

Being Fruitful: Personal Agency and *Communio*

On Moral Theology   297
    Romanus Cessario

The Other and the Fruitfulness of Personal Acting   303
    Stefan Oster

Dialectic and Dialogic: The Identity of Being as Fruitfulness
in Hans Urs von Balthasar   318
    Emmanuel Tourpe

Can a Christian Be a Good Citizen?

Can a Christian Be a Good Democrat, a Dedicated
Member of the *Polis,* in a Time of War?   331
    Roberto Graziotto

Can a Christian Be a Democrat? A (Devoted) Member
of the *Polis?* Or, The Common Good and the Modern State   339
    V. Bradley Lewis

Heartfelt Grief and Repentance in Imperial Times   349
    William L. Portier

Preface

On the centenary of Hans Urs von Balthasar's birth, Pope Benedict XVI said of the Swiss theologian, "I am convinced that his theological reflections preserve their freshness and profound relevance undiminished to this day and that they incite many others to penetrate ever further into the depths of the mystery of the faith, with such an authoritative guide leading them by the hand." The present volume, the first of two, brings together numerous contributions first given at the anniversary conference organized in April 2005 in Washington, D.C., by the English-language editors of *Communio: International Catholic Review.* April 2005 was a momentous month in the recent history of the Church; our gathering to honor one of the twentieth century's great theologians took place scarcely two weeks after the death of the century's great pope, John Paul II, who had honored Balthasar with a cardinal's hat. The planned keynote speaker, Marc Cardinal Ouellet, primate of Canada, was unable to attend the conference because of his presence at the consistory. Our efforts to "penetrate ever further into the depths of the mystery of the faith," then, took place in an intense atmosphere of expectation for the whole Church, and on the eve of the election to the papacy of Balthasar's friend Joseph Ratzinger, who, along with Balthasar, Henri de Lubac, and others, was a co-founder of *Communio* following the Second Vatican Council. The reflections by an international gathering of scholars, among whom are numerous students, colleagues, friends — and also critics — of Balthasar, were all the more memorable because of the remarkable moment in which they took place.

The task of our extended conversation was to engage fundamental questions of faith and reason in light of Balthasar's contribution to Catholic thought. Balthasar's Trinitarian theology, Christology, and theology of creation served as the impetus for papers, both friendly and critical, on a variety of themes, including metaphysics and causality, the nature of rationality, the relationship between God and the world, fruitfulness and states of life, and the meaning of the body. *Communio* remains grateful for the seriousness of the engagement of these themes and for the collegiality and fruitfulness of the conversation, a collegiality maintained in the face even of occasional vigorous disagreement.

The conference, the collection of papers following the conference, and the final editing of the papers for this book are the fruit of the labors above all of Emily Reilley, Managing Editor of *Communio,* and Lesley Rice, Editorial Assistant for *Communio* and Research Assistant at the John Paul II Institute. The participants at the conference are deeply grateful to Emily for the execution of what was a beautiful three days of common reflection, and to Lesley for her careful and intelligent editorial review of their papers in preparation for publication.

Communio also expresses its gratitude to the Knights of Columbus and to Our Sunday Visitor for their generous support for the conference.

DAVID L. SCHINDLER
Washington, D.C.
March, 2008

Contributors

ROMANUS CESSARIO, O.P., is professor of systematic theology at St. John's Seminary School of Theology in Brighton, Massachusetts.

DAVID S. CRAWFORD is associate professor of moral theology and family law at the John Paul II Institute for Studies on Marriage and Family at The Catholic University of America, Washington, D.C.

STEPHEN FIELDS, S.J., is associate professor of theology at Georgetown University, Washington, D.C.

JOSÉ GRANADOS, D.C.J.M., a priest of the Disciples of the Hearts of Jesus and Mary, is assistant professor of patrology and systematic theology at the John Paul II Institute for Studies on Marriage and Family at The Catholic University of America, Washington, D.C.

ROBERTO GRAZIOTTO teaches religion, history, and philosophy at the Jugenddorf-Christophorusschule in Droyßig, Germany.

MICHAEL HANBY is assistant professor of biotechnology and culture at the John Paul II Institute for Studies on Marriage and Family at The Catholic University of America, Washington, D.C.

Fr. ROCH KERESZTY, O.Cist., is head of the theology department of the Cistercian Preparatory School in Irving, Texas, and adjunct professor of theology at the University of Dallas.

V. BRADLEY LEWIS is associate professor of philosophy at The Catholic University of America, Washington, D.C.

Contributors

ANTONIO LÓPEZ, F.S.C.B., a priest of the Fraternity of St. Charles Borromeo, is assistant professor of theology at the John Paul II Institute for Studies on Marriage and Family at The Catholic University of America, Washington, D.C.

MARGARET H. McCARTHY is assistant professor of theology at the John Paul II Institute for Studies on Marriage and Family at The Catholic University of America, Washington, D.C.

SIMON OLIVER is Senior Lecturer in Theology at the University of Wales, Lampeter.

STEFAN OSTER, S.D.B., teaches philosophy at the Philosophisch-Theologische Hochschule in Benediktbeuern, Germany.

WILLIAM L. PORTIER is Mary Ann Spearin professor of theology and professor of religious studies at the University of Dayton.

JUAN M. SARA holds a doctorate in philosophy from the Pontifical Gregorian University in Rome and is director of the Fundación San Juan in Rafaela, Argentina.

RICHARD SCHENK, O.P., is professor of philosophy and theology at the Dominican School of Philosophy and Theology in Berkeley, California.

JACQUES SERVAIS, S.J., teaches systematic spiritual theology at the Gregorian University and is rector of the Casa Balthasar in Rome.

EMMANUEL TOURPE teaches at the Institute d'Études Théologiques in Brussels, Belgium.

ADRIAN J. WALKER is an associate editor of *Communio.*

Toward a Renewal of Theology

The Eucharist and Mission in the
Theology of Hans Urs von Balthasar

Roch Kereszty

After a tumultuous self-analysis in the post-conciliar phase of Church reform, debate, and confusion, a new generation of Catholic laity and clergy
is emerging with a fresh outlook and priorities. They reject an *aggiornamento* without *ressourcement* and are wary of an "openness to the world"
without fidelity to the truth of the gospel.[1] They realize that the two fash-
ionable ways of presenting the gospel in the seventies and eighties, either
as a set of truths (the approach of conservative Catholics) or as an experience of God through a loving community (an approach preferred by the
so-called "progressive" Catholics), have fallen short of grasping what is in-
comparably new and central in Christianity. They are now discovering,
perhaps instinctively or through theological reflection, the "heart of the
Church," the source and center of her mission, in the mystery of the Eucharist. They perceive with increasing clarity that the mission of the
Church is not merely to convey a message or an experience, but more importantly, to draw all humankind into full participation in the eucharistic
mystery.

This spontaneous grassroots process of discovery has been confirmed and given shape and direction by the Magisterium; the last encyclical of John Paul II, *Ecclesia de Eucharistia*, as well as his promulgation of
the year of the Eucharist, bring to light the centrality of the Eucharist. For

---

1. The word "ressourcement" (a return to the sources of Christian faith and life) was
coined by Y. Congar and became the motto of biblical, patristic, and liturgical renewal in the
Church before Vatican II. In the first decades following the Council, however, it was largely
forgotten at the expense of a one-sided opening to the world.

3

this renewed understanding of the Church's mission as centered on the Eucharist, the theology of Hans Urs von Balthasar provides new insights and a powerful impetus. A comprehensive analysis of Balthasar's eucharistic theology would exceed the purpose of this essay; I will only present here some of the insights and implications of Balthasar's thought on the theme "Eucharist and Mission."

Though explicitly eucharistic writings or chapters form a small portion of his monumental *Lebenswerk*, Balthasar's theological synthesis is profoundly eucharistic, in that the mysteries of the Trinity, Creation, Revelation, Incarnation, and Redemption include an essential eucharistic dimension that defines our Christian existence. Looking at the mystery from three different angles (those of theological aesthetics, theo-drama, and theo-logic), we will investigate the Eucharist as form, our participation in the divine-human drama through the Eucharist, and finally the logic of divine love that reveals itself in this mystery.

From the Perspective of Theological Aesthetics

For Balthasar, theological aesthetics is very different from aesthetical theology. By the latter he understands the uninvolved spectator's subjective approach, which separates beauty from truth and goodness.[2] Balthasar nevertheless articulates a helpful analogy between what aesthetes perceive as beauty and the beauty of revelation. Worldly beauty is the radiance, that is, the splendor or light of the form of any particular being that is both good and true. It calls the beholder not simply to passive enjoyment but to embrace the beauty and seek the richness of being and goodness that the beautiful form expresses. Theological beauty, on the other hand, discloses the ultimate ground of worldly beauty; it is the splendor that radiates from God's revelation, endowing every created thing with meaning and value by centering them on the form of Jesus Christ. This beauty draws one even more powerfully beyond passive contemplation than worldly beauty does. If combined with a grace-inspired desire *(eros)* within us, the visible, perceptible form of Jesus the man draws us into be-

---

2. Hans Urs von Balthasar, *The Glory of the Lord: A Theological Aesthetics* (= *GL*), vol. I: *Seeing the Form* (San Francisco: Ignatius Press, 1985; Edinburgh: T. & T. Clark, 1985), pp. 50-51. Note that, with the exception of *Theologik* III, all quotes are from the English editions.

ing conformed to him by participating in his passion and resurrection. This form, which is Jesus Christ himself, has been given over to the Church in the form of the Eucharist for that period of salvation history stretching from the end of Jesus' earthly life to his Parousia.[3] We need to examine this "form" in greater detail.

Balthasar's synthesis of Johannine and Pauline theology provides the background to understanding the eucharistic form of Jesus' self-donation. As in John, the mission of the Son reaches its consummation on the cross when blood and water flow out of his pierced side and, with his last breath, he hands over the Spirit. The water and blood that flow from the pierced, sacrificed body of Jesus are the sources of the sacramental life of the Church, in particular, Baptism and the Eucharist. Through the latter the once-for-all event of Jesus' Passover sacrifice becomes the sacrifice of the Church. As in Paul, Jesus' sacrifice consists in his total self-emptying, his total gift of self to the Father in the form of giving himself to us.[4]

Balthasar starts from the assumption that the economic Trinity reveals the immanent Trinity. The Father's self-emptying into Jesus at the time of the incarnation reflects the Father's analogous self-emptying into the Son from all eternity. This self-emptying is the Father's total gift of self to the Son. The Son's return of self to the Father also takes place from all eternity in the Holy Spirit, the Spirit of both Father and Son. In the economy of salvation, however, the Son's return to the Father takes place in historical events through his incarnation, earthly life, passion, death, descent into hell, and resurrection. At every step this return takes place in the Holy Spirit: the Spirit prepares the womb of the Virgin for the incarnation and leads Jesus in obedience to the Father step by step through his earthly life, passion, and death, up to his final self-emptying on the cross, by constantly reminding him of the common decision that all three Persons have reached from all eternity. Jesus goes through this process in order to carry out his mission of universal redemption. In the lowly form of a servant, he is enabled by the Holy Spirit to carry out his mission of taking upon himself all our sins and descending to the ultimate abyss of death and hell, while at the same time returning his love to the Father in the state of total

3. Hans Urs von Balthasar, *The Glory of the Lord: A Theological Aesthetics*, vol. VII: *Theology: The New Covenant* (San Francisco: Ignatius Press, 1985; Edinburgh: T. & T. Clark, 1989), pp. 148-52.

4. *GL* VII, pp. 253, 406.

abandonment by the Father. In this way, he lives out his divine sonship in our fallen world.

By the end of Jesus' obedient fulfillment of his mission, the Holy Spirit has so fully penetrated Jesus' flesh that in his pneumatic body Jesus has become both the sender of the Spirit and the giver of his body and blood, in such a way that the three (flesh, blood, and Spirit) form one reality (cf. 1 Jn 5:6-7). His gift of self in the Spirit on the cross is eternalized in the resurrection and, through the Spirit, penetrates every moment of our history, both in its past and future dimensions. The effective sign of his gift of self to the Father is the transubstantiated bread and wine in the form of food and drink; they express and communicate the gift of self of Jesus to his Church.[5]

Understood in this way, then, the Eucharist is the form, or *Gestalt*, of divine self-communication at our stage of salvation history, the glory and splendor of divine trinitarian love in the crucified and glorified humanity of Jesus Christ under the humble signs of bread and wine. The contemplation of this form, if accompanied in our hearts by God's grace, stirs up our *eros*, the desire to be taken up into it.

In the history of the Church some explicitly eucharistic conversions have taken place; we might say that the "form" of the Eucharist broke these persons' resistance to grace and led them into the Catholic Church. Simone Weil, a searching agnostic, was led by Christ into a Catholic church and was told to kneel down before the tabernacle. She wrote later that the simplicity of the form of Christ's presence was a most decisive sign of its authenticity and allowed her to realize, "Here is the Truth." According to his own words, André Frossard, a well-known Catholic intellectual, entered a church as an agnostic, saw the adoration of the Eucharist by people in that church, and emerged as a believing Catholic.

From the Perspective of Theo-Drama

The form itself, however, is not simply the person of the crucified and risen Christ under the sign of bread and wine; it includes the entire drama of Christ's life, death, and resurrection. Thus, his entire life (as the gradual gift of self to God in the form of serving us) becomes contemporaneous to

5. Cf. Hans Urs von Balthasar, "The Mass: A Sacrifice of the Church?" *Explorations in Theology,* vol. III: *Creator Spirit* (San Francisco: Ignatius Press, 1993), pp. 185-243, at 241.

us in the eucharistic celebration.[6] The contemplation of what is revealed to us, therefore, is only the first step; the liturgy of the Eucharist consists precisely in Jesus' bestowal of his sacrifice upon the Church, in order that the Church may offer it as her own. But how can this appropriation take place? How can the weak, sinful disciples make Jesus' sacrifice their own, the disciples who are so obtuse and reluctant to perceive, let alone enter into the mystery of Jesus' passion?[7] Balthasar's answer elaborates on a widely forgotten connection between Mary and the Eucharist, a connection that is nevertheless firmly based on biblical data and patristic theology:

> Christ is entrusted to the hands of Mary at birth and at his death: this is more central than his being given into the hands of the Church in her official, public aspect. The former is the precondition for the latter. . . . [S]he alone utters the Yes that is necessary if the incarnation of the Word is to take place. It is from this archetypal Yes that the faith — more or less weak, more or less strong — of the other members of the Church is nourished.[8]

Long before the disciples (the official hierarchical Church) received the command to perform the eucharistic action in memory of Jesus, Mary had already uttered her *fiat,* implicitly yet wholeheartedly accepting, in faith, all that had been said to her by the Lord as she accepted the Word made flesh into her womb. Her initial acceptance of the sacrifice of her Son becomes explicit at the foot of the cross. Her consent, by which she allows the self-donation of her Son to the Father to take place in our stead and for our sake, is full and wholehearted because she is the *Immaculata,* the one fully redeemed in advance by her Son's sacrifice, and therefore conceived without original sin and full of grace. Thus, her Yes, her acceptance, is not weakened or divided by any sinful tendency. She alone has been able to make the sacrifice of her Son fully her own. Since Mary is the archetype and the beginning of the Church, the sacrifice of Christ has fully become the Church's sacrifice in her. Balthasar elucidates the consequences of his thesis for ecclesiology:

---

6. See more on the dramatic dimensions of the Eucharist in Hans Urs von Balthasar, *Theodrama: Theological Dramatic Theory* (= *TD*), vol. IV: *The Action* (San Francisco: Ignatius Press, 1994), pp. 389-406.

7. Cf. Balthasar, "The Mass," pp. 223-24.

8. *TD* IV, p. 397.

The patristic phrase *"personam Ecclesiae gerens," "in persona Ecclesiae,"* denotes a kind of representation that is truly valid only when the role that is played *(persona)* portrays precisely the subjectivity of the Bride-Church. But how could a sinner be capable of playing this role, which demands spotless love? The disposition he would have to portray would necessarily always be something high above him, an ideal that had not been realized, so that it would not be possible anywhere for the Church to play the role assigned to her in Christ's sacrifice in keeping with what was expected. This is why the dogma of the Immaculate Conception is a strict postulate of ecclesiology. . . . The assent of the *Ekklesia* to the sacrifice of the Son must press on until it reaches Mary's perfect selflessness, so that this agreement may not retain any stain of the egotism that allows Jesus the Paschal Lamb to be slain for one's own redemption and perfection.[9]

The fact that Mary offers her Son to the Father does not minimize her offering of herself; on the contrary, in the same act in which Mary offers her Son, she most effectively offers herself. This, then, is that original *admirabile commercium* in which Mary accepts her Son's sacrifice into her heart and in the same act of consenting to it gives herself over to God's will. This "real life" exchange, the unity between the sacrifice of Jesus and that of Mary, is the archetype and condition for the Church's eucharistic liturgy. In every Mass the liturgical assembly participates in Mary's acceptance of her Son's sacrifice, and with Mary the assembly unites her own gift of self to that of the Son. In this perspective we see how well the motto of John Paul II's pontificate *("Totus tuus")* expresses the very center of Balthasar's marian and eucharistic spirituality: by emptying ourselves of ourselves, we should strive to belong more and more to Mary and enter into the dispositions of her heart. To the extent that we succeed in this, we make the sacrifice of Mary our own. As we receive the Body and Blood of the Lord, it is precisely by sharing in Mary's sacrifice that we appropriate Christ's loving obedience to the Father and thereby offer ourselves to the Father in union with his Son. We never achieve the full identity-in-difference that has been realized between Jesus' act and Mary's selfless reception of Jesus' act in faith; that is the reason why the Church renews daily (or rather, unceasingly) the eucharistic

---

9. Balthasar, "The Mass," pp. 239-40.

sacrifice and, in Augustinian terms, learns to offer herself in the sacrament of the Son's sacrifice.[10]

Against this background we understand better why the Eucharist so eminently embodies the mission of the Church. As we are drawn into the unfathomable depth of Christ's love, we become conformed to Him so that we can empty ourselves of our own self-centered existence and learn to love our fellow human beings with the very love of Christ. In this way we share in the life-giving and life-nourishing mission of the Word made flesh. The common mission of the ecclesial Body of Christ includes every member's unique mission, which participates in the universal redemptive mission of the Son. This mission of ours is not something accidental and external to us; to the extent that we accept it, it makes us persons in the full (theological) sense of the word. Mission thus makes persons out of those who, before accepting their mission in Christ, were mere individual rational subjects *(Geistessubjekte)*.[11] Moreover, we need to keep in mind that the mission of Christ is the "quoad nos" aspect, the reaching out into history of the eternal generation of the Son by his loving Father. Analogously, the mission of the Church and of each individual member within the Church is not a mere legal mandate, but springs from Christ's love, a love that in the power of the Holy Spirit engenders us who become unique persons in the one corporate Marian Person which is both Christ's Body and his Bride. This unity of Body and Bride is built up and strengthened by the Eucharist.

Being built up by the Eucharist into the Body and Bride of Christ, however, is not an automatic process but an essential part of the theo-drama that calls for a series of free decisions on our part. As we offer ourselves with Mary through Christ to the Father, we ourselves are called to become a gift for others. Our mission, then, includes works of social justice, but is not reducible to such works. The love that springs from the Eucharist respects the autonomy of the created order, as well as the moral obligations that stem from our common humanity, and calls for all the activity that makes our society more civilized and humane. It cooperates with all people of good will in building a "civilization of love," but does not stop at the mere building of the new civilization, for this eucharistic love

---

10. Balthasar, "The Mass," pp. 185-243.

11. Cf. Hans Urs von Balthasar, *Theo-Drama: Theological Dramatic Theory*, vol. III: Dramatis Personae: *Persons in Christ*, trans. Graham Harrison (San Francisco: Ignatius Press, 1992), pp. 149-259, 282.

both transforms our motivation and transcends the limits of any possible civilizational activity. It includes interceding in Christ for others, both for members of the Church and for the whole world; it entails sharing their burden, standing in their place, suffering and atoning for them, all by way of sharing in the infinite love of Christ.[12] In other words, our life for others includes both action and suffering, since the redeeming love of Christ in which we share has, in fact, become most effective after he passes beyond activity by freely surrendering himself to vicarious passion and death.

Finally, we need to explore the cosmological dimension of Balthasar's eucharistic theology. Balthasar reflects at length on the role of the Son in creation as taught in the Pauline Letters to the Colossians and Ephesians. The universe has been created in Christ and for Christ. God "creates room" for the world in its relative autonomy of non-divine, created being, yet fulfills the world by making a gift of the world to his Son, summing it up under one head, Christ. This gift of the world to his Son, which begins in the incarnation, finds its hidden anticipatory completion in the Eucharist. The material world and humankind are given over to Christ by the Father so that he may return it, redeemed and transformed, to the Father in the thanksgiving which is the Eucharist:

> If the mission of the incarnate Son involves receiving all of creation as a gift from the Father only to return it back to the Father, but now redeemed by his death, then the Son only accomplishes and completes his mission through the Holy Spirit and the Church by bestowing on the Church the mission through the Spirit of continuing to transform the world through her celebration of the Eucharist.[13]

After reviewing the theo-dramatic perspective on the Eucharist, I would like to highlight four most fruitful yet largely forgotten insights that I have gained from Balthasar's thought:

1. Balthasar shows that the marian Church's active reception of the sacrifice of Jesus through Mary's *fiat* is prior to the official church's celebration of the Eucharist. The eucharistic liturgy, presided over by the

---

12. See more on this theme in David L. Schindler, "Towards a Eucharistic Evangelization," *Communio: International Catholic Review* 19, no. 4 (1992): 549-75.

13. Nicholas Healy and David L. Schindler, "Balthasar on the Church as Eucharist," in *The Cambridge Companion to Hans Urs von Balthasar*, ed. E. T. Oakes and D. Moss (Cambridge: Cambridge University Press, 2004), p. 55.

bishop or priest who represents Christ, presupposes Mary's *fiat* at the Annunciation and at the foot of the cross. The hierarchical church makes present the sacrifice of Christ by virtue of this marian faith.

2. In our age even the best representatives of eucharistic theology are, to some extent, caught up in emphasizing its subjective, anthropological aspect. It is obviously legitimate to concentrate within the eucharistic action upon our gift of self as united to that of Christ, yet we often forget the awesome and fearful mystery of Christ's own sacrifice to which we intend to unite our imperfect gift of self. If we really mean "to do this in memory" of him, we should not shrink away from participating in the unfathomable abyss of Jesus' suffering and love, in his carrying of the burden of all our sins, and in his love for the Father while being abandoned by him. In his infinite love Jesus gives thanks to the Father for allowing him to empty himself to the final point of dying for us on the cross. We are called to take part in the frightening and awesome "pro nobis" of Jesus' gift. Briefly, Balthasar invites us to go beyond our usual view of the Eucharist, from seeing it primarily as the sacramental enactment of our gift of self in union with Christ to actively participating in the sacrifice of Christ himself.[14]

3. Balthasar's view of how the Mass is to become the sacrifice of the Church has important ecumenical implications. He shows that the liturgical assembly cannot add any redemptive value to the sacrifice of Christ. They participate in his sacrifice in a mode of active receptivity, by sharing in Mary's *fiat*, her consenting to the sacrifice of her Son. Catholics should not look at the Mass as a "good work" on the part of the Church, but an act of pure and active faith. At the same time Protestants are invited to reevaluate the role of Mary so they can see in the *Immaculata* the exemplar and fullness of the Church's faith.

Even though Balthasar himself does not explicitly point out this ecu-

---

14. "One may indeed, with M. ten Hompel, follow Augustine in indicating the element of gift of self as the center of the sacrifice and in seeing in the gift of self also the door by which the believer enters into the sphere of Christ, into his Church; but this must not lead anyone to overlook the fact that Christ's gift of self was consciously his offer of himself to bear the entire guilt of the world, i.e., the unimaginably and unsurpassably terrible state of being rejected by God, his offer to be the one 'cast out' (K. Barth) vicariously, so that the mass of his rejected brothers would become chosen" (Balthasar, "The Mass," p. 202). The Barthian notion of universal salvation needs to be interpreted in the context of Balthasar's later works, and even those later views call for criticism in this matter. Yet Balthasar's insistence on our participation in Jesus' sacrifice remains a much-needed corrective.

menical significance, he shows the intrinsic connection between the Eucharist as thanksgiving and as expiatory sacrifice. Protestants raise no objections to calling the Mass a sacrifice of praise and thanksgiving, but even today many Protestant theologians condemn the Catholic understanding of the Mass's expiatory character as an affront to the perfect once-for-all sacrifice of the cross. Balthasar demonstrates that the two aspects are inseparable: Jesus gives thanks to the Father that he may offer himself in the form of food and drink for us as the universal sacrifice of expiation and atonement. His praise and thanksgiving envelop and define his gift of self unto the forgiveness of sins; the Eucharist cannot participate in one aspect of his sacrifice without implying the other.[15]

Similarly, the mission of Christians who intend to pattern their lives in this world on the Eucharist must also consist inseparably of thanksgiving and praise, as well as atonement and expiation. They thank God not only for the good things of his creation and for the gift of participation in God's own trinitarian life, but they also unite their sufferings to that of Christ so that his atoning and expiatory sacrifice may become effective for them and for those entrusted to their care, as well as for the whole world.

4. Balthasar's thought on the cosmic aspect of the Eucharist (as a return in thanksgiving by the incarnate Son of all creation in himself to the Father) has some important seminal insights that Balthasar himself — to my knowledge — has not developed. Here I would like to offer some tentative suggestions for further reflection.

In the average post-Tridentine approach to the Eucharist, such a return of creation to the Father that would include the material universe appears hardly conceivable, if not impossible. This theology denied any level of reality to the material species of the consecrated bread and wine; it taught that what appears as bread and wine is not bread and wine in any sense of the word. False material appearances, however, could not symbolize the return of the material universe to the Father. In contrast, Balthasar's metaphysics of being, if further developed, may provide a better articulation of the cosmic aspect of the mystery. If being, analogously on all levels, entails both a richness and a poverty or, rather, a richness consisting in its poverty (in the sense

---

15. Balthasar, *TD* IV, pp. 400-402. See also Balthasar, *Theologik*, vol. III: *Der Geist der Wahrheit* (Einsiedeln: Johannes Verlag, 1987), p. 316 (my translation from the German original): "Sacrifice of praise and *logikē thysia* are not innocuous spiritual exercises, but they mean a consecration of the self, the fulfillment of a vow, a thanksgiving that calls for the total gift of self."

that, on different levels in different ways, being empties itself of itself for the sake of new being), and it is in this self-emptying that all beings reach their perfection,[16] then the eucharistic consecration and subsequent offering can indeed symbolize the return of material creation on a new transcendent level to the Father. Then the ontological "poverty" of the bread and wine would also be the metaphysical condition for the miracle of transubstantiation to take place. In other words, through the creative words of Christ and in the power of the Holy Spirit, the bread and wine on the altar will no longer exist in themselves; they will, rather, become the real communicative signs of the crucified and risen body of Jesus Christ. In the divine-ecclesial act of transubstantiation, the bread and wine are not annihilated or deprived of all reality; on the contrary, they are elevated above themselves so as to become the "bread of life" and "the cup of eternal salvation." As the crucified and risen Body and Blood of the Lord, they are now *the* "real food" and *the* "real drink." The fact that their empirical qualities of bread and wine remain is not a pious deception on the part of God; it signifies, rather, that Jesus Christ is present for us as food and drink. It is in this sense that the Eucharist symbolizes and anticipates the transfiguration of the whole material universe and its return to the Father in Christ.

This cosmic aspect of the Eucharist sheds light on another aspect of the mission of Christians in the world, an aspect that was first articulated in *Gaudium et spes* and later quoted by Pope John Paul II in his encyclical *Sollicitudo rei socialis:* Along with all people of good will, we Christians must work on human progress (improving the human condition of poverty, sickness, armed conflicts, and other forms of evil).[17] Even our greatest efforts, however, will only produce the material for the new heaven and new earth that God will bring about at the end of history, just as in the Eucharist our contribution can only consist in preparing the gifts of bread and wine for the divine act of consecration.

From the Perspective of Theo-Logic

To my knowledge, Balthasar himself did not develop an explicit treatise on the "theo-logic" of the Eucharist but did consider the divine logic of the

---

16. See more on this in Nicholas J. Healy, "The World as Gift," in vol. 2 of this collection.
17. Cf. John Paul II, *Sollicitudo rei socialis,* 32.

Eucharist within the global process of incarnation and redemption. What we must do here, then, is explicate what is already implicit in Balthasar's thought. The divine love that manifests itself in the Eucharist exceeds the limits of any human understanding; yet, for those who surrender to the inner working of the Holy Spirit in their hearts, the Eucharist illumines the ultimate depth of God's creating and redeeming love, as well as the meaning of all reality. Beginning with the disciples' reaction to Jesus' eucharistic discourse in Capernaum, through the centuries and up to our present day, the Eucharist has always remained "a continental divide": it becomes either a stumbling block to faith or the most compelling evidence for the reality of God's love. The Eucharist is a stumbling block because it shows the ultimate depth of God's humility: he hides not only his divine majesty, as he did in his earthly life and crucifixion, but his humanity as well. He appears as an "object," a piece of bread or a few drops of wine, the greatest imaginable degradation for a person. In his eucharistic state he becomes totally vulnerable and totally dependent on us. He has handed himself over to the Judases and Peters of his Church, allowing himself to be either trampled upon and blasphemed, or loved and adored. Ponder Calvin's remark: "[I]f we would place him under the corruptible elements of this world . . . we annihilate the glory of the Ascension."[18]

If we accept, however, the logic of God's love, which transcends the limits of human logic and at the same time fulfills the deepest yearnings of human love, we see in the Eucharist precisely the hidden light of God's love and the glory of the Ascension, a glory that is revealed only to the eyes of faith. The resurrection and ascension of Jesus, the full transformation of his flesh by the Holy Spirit, enables him to be with us in a way that both transcends the limitations of time and space and assures his presence to us at any given time and place wherever the Eucharist is celebrated. He is not only present with us but also enters into us in his human-divine reality, in his state of gift to the Father so that, in the words of Ignatius of Antioch, our union with him may become both bodily and spiritual.

Human logic cannot explain how this is possible; it can, however, show that this infinitely simple and intimate presence of the whole being of Christ within us is what human love in its loftiest moments aspires to but is unable to fulfill. Lovers try in vain to give not just symbols of themselves to the beloved but their very psychosomatic selves. Only the God-

---

18. John Calvin, *Short Treatise on the Supper of Our Lord*, n. 42.

man, however, can truly give the totality of himself to every member of his Bride, the Church.

The truth that the material elements of bread and wine are changed into the crucified and glorified humanity of the Lord has a special relevance for today's intellectual climate, in which the material universe (of which our own bodies are a part) may appear to unbelievers as a mortal threat to their personal existence. Global warming, storms in the sun, comets on a possible collision course with planet Earth, the inevitable aging of our universe which will result at a certain point in the fiery death of all living creatures, are prospects we do not like to face but, even when suppressed, still work in our unconscious. Moreover, all material things that enter our body from outside may carry with them the danger of a lethal disease. The material world thus seems to be totally indifferent, if not hostile, to our personal fate. Relying only on the data of natural science, a philosopher can affirm the existence of an all-powerful creative intellect but not the existence of a loving God who guides our personal lives to a blessed consummation. In this context of existential "angst," the cosmological aspect of the Eucharist appears in a new light. Not only Christ's bodily resurrection, but also his presence radiating through the transubstantiated material elements, reveals and guarantees for us that our material universe and our own bodies are not excluded from God's plan of salvation. The risen, spiritualized, and yet material body of Christ reveals and communicates to us God's personal presence precisely through the signs of bread and wine. Then, at the consummation of history, our bodies will be transformed through Christ and find a home in a transformed material universe, the new, eschatological creation, where Christ will be all in all (Col 3:11).[19]

---

[19]. This last paragraph, with some changes, is taken from my book, *Wedding Feast of the Lamb: Eucharistic Theology from a Historical, Biblical and Systematic Perspective* (Chicago: LTP Hillenbrand Books, 2004), p. 218.

Love Alone: Hans Urs von Balthasar as a Master of Theological Renewal

Adrian J. Walker

Introduction: Re-Theologizing Theology

Catholic theology is in the throes of an identity crisis, because Catholic theologians work under no overarching consensus about the first principle of theological intelligence.[1] I take it for granted that this fissiparous pluralism is a bad thing. This is not to deny, of course, that truth is "symphonic," as Balthasar puts it in the title of one of his books.[2] Nevertheless, the "sym" of the "sym-phony" presupposes a unitary principle. Otherwise, legitimate theological plurality would not be symphony, but cacophony. Such cacophony, moreover, would both reflect and result in what might be called "theological emotivism." As Alasdair MacIntyre explains in *After Virtue*, "[e]motivism is the doctrine that all evaluative judgments and more specifically all moral judgments are *nothing but* expressions of preference, expressions of attitude or feeling, insofar as they are moral or evaluative in

---

1. By "first principle" I mean not just a non-negotiable commitment, as when someone says that Jones is a "man of principle," but the permanent source and governing architectonic of all the things falling within a certain order (here the order is "theology"). This source-architectonic is such that what comes from it processes from it, remains within it, and reverts to it, as Proclus says effects do with respect to their cause in his *Elementatio Theologica*, proposition 35. At the same time, the reversion is not simply a repetition of the procession, but includes a novel enrichment that testifies to the fecundity of the principle.

2. Hans Urs von Balthasar, *Die Wahrheit ist symphonisch. Aspekte des christlichen Pluralismus* (Einsiedeln: Johannes Verlag, 1972); Eng. trans., *Truth Is Symphonic: Aspects of Christian Pluralism* (San Francisco: Ignatius Press, 1987).

character."[3] Similarly, what I am calling theological emotivism is the conviction, expressed or unexpressed, that theological judgments are essentially expressions of incommensurable, pre-rational commitments that, as such, cannot be impartially evaluated according to universally recognized standards, viz., in the light of a single, overarching principle of theological intelligence. Theological emotivism thus obscures the reasonableness of the Catholic tradition and thereby calls into question the very existence of theology as "faith seeking understanding."

Of course, sheer pluralism is actually impossible,[4] and the pluralism of contemporary Catholic theology is in reality not quite so diverse as it first appears to be on the surface. For example, the ever more numerous "contextual theologies" that dominate Catholic theology departments in the United States today — feminist theology, *mujerista* theology, gay theology, liberation theology, and so on — actually do share a single, unifying principle: the appeal to so-called *"experience."* In one sense, this reliance on experience is nothing new. The great tradition of Catholic theology has always known that faith is not just assent to propositions (while also insisting that it is not less than that), but includes a lived conformation to the theological realities which the propositions assented to are about.[5] The current appeal to experience departs from this venerable tradition, though, in that it tends to make untutored experience an *a priori* measure of all truth-claims purporting to be drawn from divine revelation. However much contextual theologians might thunder against "Enlightenment rationalism," their own appeal to experience in truth continues the Enlightenment project of confining "religion within the limits of reason alone." The only difference is that they have replaced the objectivist "reason alone" of Kant with a subjectivist "experience alone." Contextual theologies are merely the latest offspring of Liberal Protestantism, distinguished from their stodgy ancestor only by the attitudes of 1968. Like much of multiculturalism, current American Catholic theological plural-

3. Alasdair MacIntyre, *After Virtue,* 2nd ed. (Notre Dame: University of Notre Dame Press, 1984), p. 12 (emphasis in the original).

4. To cite Proclus again: "every manifold participates somehow in the one" (Proclus, *Elementatio Theologica,* proposition 1).

5. See Hans Urs von Balthasar, *Herrlichkeit. Eine Theologische Ästhetik. I: Schau der Gestalt* (Einsiedeln: Johannes Verlag, 1961), pp. 211-410, for a very positive and rich account of the role of experience in the act of faith. Eng. trans., *The Glory of the Lord: A Theological Aesthetics,* vol. 1: *Seeing the Form* (San Francisco: Ignatius Press, 1982), pp. 219-425.

ism turns out to be merely the same old liberal monism decked out in colorful funky costumes.

Contrarily to what it may seem at first, then, the crisis of Catholic theology today boils down to a conflict between two and only two possible first principles: experience and divine revelation. Or, to be more precise: between the *logos* of what John Milbank calls "secular reason" and the *logos* contained in divine revelation itself.[6] This contest, it is important to see, is an unequal one. Of the two alternative principles, in fact, divine revelation has the greater integrative power: it can comprehend all that is true in "secular reason," whereas the converse is far from being the case. Recognizing this poverty of mainstream liberal theology, with its captivity to the secular social sciences as the oracles of all-judging experience, a growing number of voices on the English-speaking Catholic theological scene have begun to call for what William L. Portier has felicitously termed the "re-theologization of theology."[7] These theologians have found confirmation and support in the pontificates of John Paul II and Benedict XVI, who, contrarily to the stale clichés propagated endlessly by the media, have not been conservative "restorationists," but faithful expositors of Vatican II's attempt to reawaken in the Church a living awareness of its all-embracing catholicity — not on the basis of liberal cosmopolitanism, but on the basis of Christ who, in revealing the Father, also reveals man to himself (see *Gaudium et spes,* 22).

As encouraging as this re-theologization of theology may be, it is insufficient by itself. For theology must not only have a distinctive principle that sets it apart from other forms of knowing, but this principle must also be capable of illumining all of reality. Without abandoning the platform of its unique, non-negotiable commitment to the Creed, theology must also be universally relevant — and not just an in-house "grammar" by which the Christian community "parses" what happens to be its peculiar worldview. A re-theologized theology worthy of the name will therefore be neither "liberal" in the sense of mainstream American Catholic theology's

---

6. See John Milbank, *Theology and Social Theory: Beyond Secular Reason* (London: Blackwell, 1993). On the difficulties generated in post–Vatican II Catholic theology by the failure to understand this alternative, see David L. Schindler, *Heart of the World, Center of the Church:* Communio *Ecclesiology, Liberalism, and Liberation* (Grand Rapids: Eerdmans, 1995); Tracey Rowland, *Culture and the Thomist Tradition: After Vatican II* (London: Routledge, 2003).

7. William L. Portier, "Here Come the Evangelical Catholics," *Communio: International Catholic Review* 31, no. 1 (Spring 2004).

Babylonian captivity to the secular social sciences, nor again merely "post-liberal" in the sense of a tendentially historicist valorization of the peculiarity of Christian tradition without a corresponding emphasis on how this peculiarity vehicles a universal revelation addressed to all men by a God who wants them to be saved and to come to a knowledge of the truth (see 1 Tim 2:4).[8] A re-theologized theology, if it is to measure up to the Christian tradition it claims to recover, must go beyond the opposition between Christian uniqueness and universal relevance that both liberal and post-liberal theology assume, in order to re-learn that the distinctive principle of theology is itself what is most universally relevant, "so that holy teaching," as Aquinas puts it, "is a sort of impression of the divine knowledge, which embraces all things in its simple oneness."[9]

With that we come to Hans Urs von Balthasar, whom I would like to propose in the following pages as a master of theological renewal able to teach us how to re-theologize theology without sacrificing its hallmark claim to speak to universal human reason. To be sure, Balthasar clearly distinguishes himself from most other contemporary Catholic theologians by the radical consistency of his commitment to starting theology from, and letting it be normed by, the uniquely Christian revelation of God's trinitarian love in Christ.[10] This Balthasarian commitment to "love alone" is, however, anything but an un- or anti-philosophical theological positivism. Balthasar's project, particularly in the Trilogy, is to maintain christological love as the first principle of theology, while simultaneously developing a philosophy of a "truly metaphysical range"[11] whose intrinsic openness to

---

8. By historicism I mean a metaphysic that makes becoming simply prior to being, the temporal simply prior to the eternal. I do not deny that historicism reflects a concern that, *rightly understood*, is also a Christian one. But that is just the point: the qualifier "rightly understood" points to a synthesis in which the static and the dynamic, the eternal and the temporal both receive their full due. From the point of view of this synthesis, we can critique raw historicism, without having to subscribe to a one-sided "a-historicism," either. What I would like to suggest is that this synthesis is the form of Christian revelation — indeed, that it is Jesus Christ himself as the revelational *Gestalt par excellence*.

9. Thomas Aquinas, *Summa theologiae* (= *ST*) I, 1, 3 ad 2.

10. This — and not simply that theologians also have to be holy in addition to being smart — is the main claim of Balthasar's famous essay, "Theologie und Heiligkeit," in *Verbum Caro. Skizzen zur Theologie. I* (Einsiedeln: Johannes Verlag, 1960), pp. 195-225; Eng. trans., "Theology and Sanctity," in *Explorations in Theology*, vol. 1: *The Word Made Flesh* (San Francisco: Ignatius Press, 1989), pp. 181-209.

11. John Paul II, *Fides et ratio*, 83.

that love secures the connection between the uniqueness of Jesus Christ and universal human reason in its quest for first principles.[12] Balthasarian "love alone," far from adding up to a one-sided "theologism," is really another name for what is sometimes called the "Catholic 'and,'" which embraces both the "from above" and the "from below," grace and nature, theology and philosophy in a differentiated unity that is plural without being pluralist and one without being uniform.

In what follows, I will attempt to illustrate and defend Balthasar's claim that "love alone" — meaning the trinitarian love revealed in Jesus — is not just an *object* of theological reflection, but is the very *principle* of theological intelligence itself *as intelligence*. In particular, I will emphasize how Balthasar reconciles this claim with theology's character as a *logos* having a purchase on universal reason. I will proceed in three steps of unequal length, all of which aim to bring home the unity-in-distinction of *logos* and love, and of *ens* and *caritas,* that undergirds this reconciliation. First, I will explain how the love revealed in Christ has to do with the very *logos* of being. Second, I will argue that christological love, reflected in the whole existence of the theologian, plays an intrinsic role in the constitution of theological discourse as such. This will give us

12. See, for example, Hans Urs von Balthasar, "Philosophie, Christentum, Mönchtum," in *Sponsa Verbi. Skizzen zur Theologie. II* (Einsiedeln: Johannes Verlag, 1961); Eng. trans., "Philosophy, Christianity, Monasticism" in *Explorations in Theology*, vol. 2: *Spouse of the Word* (San Francisco: Ignatius Press, 1991), pp. 333-72; idem, "Das Wunder des Seins und die Vierfache Differenz," in *Herrlichkeit. Eine theologische Ästhetik. III. 1: Im Raum der Metaphysik* (Einsiedeln: Johannes Verlag, 1965), pp. 943-57; Eng. trans., "The Miracle of Being and the Fourfold Distinction" in *The Glory of the Lord: A Theological Aesthetics,* vol. 5: *The Realm of Metaphysics in the Modern Age* (San Francisco: Ignatius Press, 1991), pp. 613-27. The philosophical dimension of Balthasar's thought has been splendidly retrieved by three recent works that set the standard for what I hope is a new period in Balthasar scholarship that will free the Swiss theologian from the grip of one-sided interpretations: Juan Manuel Sara, *Forma y amor. Un estudio metafísico sobre la triología de Hans Urs von Balthasar* (Privatdruck, 2000); D. C. Schindler, *Hans Urs von Balthasar and the Dramatic Structure of Truth: A Philosophical Investigation* (New York: Fordham University Press, 2004); Nicholas J. Healy, *The Eschatology of Hans Urs von Balthasar: Being as Communion* (Oxford: Oxford University Press, 2005). The philosophy underlying Balthasar's work is also found to a large extent in other authors to whom Balthasar often refers; prominent among them are the German Thomists Gustav Siewerth and Ferdinand Ulrich, who are unfortunately as yet little known in the English-speaking world. For Siewerth, see Gustav Siewerth, *Das Sein als Gleichnis Gottes* (Heidelberg: Kerle, 1958); for Ulrich, see Ferdinand Ulrich, *Homo Abyssus. Das Wagnis der Seinsfrage,* 2nd ed. (Freiburg: Johannes Verlag, 1998).

an occasion to reflect on how discourse and enfleshment are inseparable within the theological enterprise. Third, I will give a more technical account, and defense, of the claim that love, as constitutive of the *ratio entis*, is also able to function as the principle of theological intelligence without undermining theology's rational character. In the conclusion, I will underscore once again how Balthasarian "love alone" is not a recipe for a simplistic reduction of the *intellectus fidei* to enthusiastic piety, but is, on the contrary, a subtle and far-reaching program for a truly catholic thought that tries to think the world from God and God from the world in light of Christ, the concrete *"analogia entis,"* as Balthasar himself does in his Trilogy.[13] Because Balthasar is often unjustly perceived as exalting grace at the expense of nature, I will also use the conclusion as an opportunity to suggest how Balthasarian theology includes a recovery of the

---

13. "I have accordingly attempted," Balthasar writes at the end of his life, "to erect a philosophy and a theology on the basis of an analogy . . . of being [*Sein*] as it presents itself concretely in its (transcendental, and not categorial) properties" (Hans Urs von Balthasar, "Eine letzte Rechenschaft," in *Hans Urs von Balthasar. Gestalt und Werk*, ed. Karl Lehmann and Walter Kasper [Cologne: Communio, 1989], p. 15; Eng. trans., "Retrospective," in *My Work: In Retrospect* [San Francisco: Ignatius Press, 1993], pp. 115-16.). Some Thomists object that the term *"analogia entis"* is of Suarezian, rather than of Thomistic provenance. This may be the case, but there can be no doubt that, for Thomas, there is an analogical community of predication of *ens* between creatures and God based on the former's participation in the latter. Moreover, it is also clear that Thomas uses the community of predication between the creature and God to illuminate the theme of participation and *vice versa*. Similarly, by *"analogia entis,"* Balthasar means the participation of creatures in God as the foundation for, but also as illumined by, the community of predication between them. The *"analogia entis"* is thus for Balthasar a relationship of creature to God such that the former is similar to the latter (both by way of an "analogy of attribution" and an "analogy of proportionality," which are really two sides of the same analogical coin) — but within a greater dissimilarity that clearly underscores the creatureliness of the creature and the free transcendence of the Creator. Christ, as both God and man, is at once the highest instance and the foundation of this relation — and in this specific sense can be said to be or embody the *analogia entis* in his own person. By calling Christ the *"analogia entis,"* then, Balthasar means to underscore how classical Christology implies that Christ is nothing less than the ontological key to all of reality. Among Balthasar's many affirmations to this effect, see, for example, this one from his monograph on Maximus Confessor: "'Synthesis,' not 'mixture,' is from the outset the structure of all worldly being . . . ontology and cosmology are Christology in an extensive form, inasmuch as the hypostatic synthesis, as God's final idea of the world, is also his first" (Hans Urs von Balthasar, *Kosmische Liturgie. Das Weltbild Maximus' des Bekenners*, 2nd ed. (Einsiedeln: Johannes Verlag, 1961), p. 204; Eng. trans., *Cosmic Liturgy: The Universe According to Maximus the Confessor* (San Francisco: Ignatius Press, 2003), p. 207.

notion of nature, whose defense is a hallmark of the universal relevance of a truly c/Catholic theology.[14]

The Catholicity of Triune Love

Schau der Gestalt, "seeing the form." This title of the first volume of Balthasar's Trilogy indicates the source of every renewal of theology: the catching sight of, and being swept away by, the novelty of Christian revelation. Balthasar sees this novelty embodied in Jesus Christ, insofar as he is *the* revealer *par excellence* of God as trinitarian love. Among the many expressions of this Balthasarian insight is the slim volume entitled *Glaubhaft ist nur Liebe,* "love alone is credible."[15] The book opens with the question, "What is it that makes Christianity Christian?"[16] and goes on to show that the answer to this question is also the answer to another: What is it that makes Christianity *credible?* Balthasar's response to this double question is

---

14. While acknowledging the importance of philosophy for theological reflection, many proponents of re-theologized theology often evince a certain hesitation about the philosophical concept of nature. In a sense, this reticence is understandable, given the nature-grace dualism typical of the so-called "manualist" Neo-scholasticism that held undisputed sway in Catholic theology from the mid-nineteenth century to Vatican II. That said, there can be no c/Catholic re-theologization of theology without a retrieval of nature. This retrieval is all the more urgent today because of the breakdown in the culture of the distinction between the artificial and the natural, the made and the born. Catholic theology is called upon today to defend the naturalness of the natural, but without insisting on a Neo-scholastic "separated philosophy" as the only means of doing so. Such a project will require re-integrating the Aristotelian philosophy of nature within a metaphysics of creation as gift that is in turn embedded in a christocentric and trinitarian theology. Balthasar's thought, especially as articulated in the Trilogy, seems to me to be a fruitful resource for this re-integration, as I will suggest briefly in the conclusion. Of course, such a re-integration must also proceed in dialogue with Thomas, on whom Balthasar builds to an extent that is not often recognized either by Thomists or by Balthasarians. Nevertheless, it is not just Balthasarians who need to learn from Thomists; Thomists need the *ressourcement* tradition to remind them of the full breadth of Aquinas's thought and to help them avoid the temptation to reduce Aquinas to a catechetical handbook, reliance on which quickly becomes an intellectual pharisaism incapable of letting itself be interrogated by any questions formulated outside of the language of its own tradition.

15. H. U. von Balthasar, *Glaubhaft ist nur Liebe* (Einsiedeln: Johannes Verlag, 1963); Eng. trans., *Love Alone Is Credible* (San Francisco: Ignatius Press, 2004).

16. See Balthasar, *Glaubhaft ist nur Liebe,* p. 5.

that the only *"logos,"* the only principle of intelligibility, which makes Jesus' figure cohere into that single, compelling *Gestalt* whose luminous wholeness could captivate the entire existence of a Francis or a John Paul II — the only such *logos* is a love that comes uniquely from the trinitarian God.[17] Indeed, for Balthasar, Jesus is the convincing *Gestalt* he is only because he is the appearing of trinitarian love in person, which means: only because he is himself the *Logos* of divine love in the flesh. Jesus either is the incarnate *Logos* of trinitarian love, or he makes no sense at all:

> The designation of Christ as Logos in John points to the fact that the Evangelist thinks of him as occupying the place of the (Greek-Philonic) world-reason through which all things become intelligible. The sequel of the Gospel shows, however, that he does not aim to demonstrate this by projecting the life of Jesus onto the plane of Greek wisdom (or vice versa), but through the self-interpretation of the very *Logos* who has appeared in the flesh. This happens insofar as the Logos makes himself known as "gracious love" *(charis)*, and therein as "glory" (the "beauty proper to God," *doxa*) — and precisely thus as "truth" [*alētheia*]: Jn 1:14). In this way, a kind of intelligibility becomes possible whose light raises the pure facticity of the historical to the level of necessity, even as any reduction to what man might demand or (for whatever reason) expect is ruled out as impossible.[18]

This passage from *Glaubhaft ist nur Liebe* claims that divine love is more than just a principle for interpreting the Christian Creed, more than just the in-house "grammar" we in the Christian community use when we speak *entre nous*. It claims, over and above this, that divine love occupies

---

17. One would have to add, in light of other affirmations of Balthasar, that Christ is the incarnation of both God's love for us and of our love for him — the covenant in person. See, for example, the following passage: "the One, whose name is Jesus Christ, has to descend into the absolute contradiction against the Lord's sovereign majesty, into the night of Godforsakenness and the amorphous chaos of sin. He must do this in order to set up and to be, beyond what man can imagine as form, *the* form that overcomes all futility, the intact and indivisible form that unites and reunites God and the world in the New and Eternal Covenant" (Hans Urs von Balthasar, *Herrlichkeit. Eine Theologische Ästhetik. III, 2, 2. Neuer Bund*, 2nd ed. [Trier: Johannes Verlag, 1988], p. 12; Eng. trans., *The Glory of the Lord: A Theological Aesthetics*, vol. 7: *Theology: The New Covenant* [San Francisco: Ignatius Press, 1989], p. 14).

18. Balthasar, *Glaubhaft ist nur Liebe*, p. 35.

the *"place of (Greek-Philonic) world-reason" itself.* Balthasar can advance this claim because he knows that by dying, sojourning among the dead, and rising to new life, Jesus has made trinitarian love *the* Reality that holds sway throughout all the realms of being — and so has set this love up as the principle that keeps the world together as a meaningful whole and guarantees that it can be interpreted meaningfully in the first place (see Col 1:17: "all things hold together [*synestēken*] in him"). By the same token, the Christian experience concerns the whole of being, and so forces, by its very nature, fresh thinking about everything: motion, reason, personal agency, causality, technology, war and peace — all in the light of love as the *logos* of being:

> Only a philosophy of free love can justify our existence, but it cannot do so unless at the same time it exegetes the essence of finite being in terms of love. In terms of love and not, in the end, of consciousness, or spirit, or knowledge, or power, or pleasure, or utility, but of all these things only insofar as they are modes of, or first steps towards, the one act that really fulfills them, the act which shines forth superabundantly in the sign of God. And beyond existence as such and the constitution of essence as such the constitution of being as such comes to light, in the sense that it "is" in no way other than by "not clinging to itself," in expropriating itself of itself, into finite concretion. At the same time, finite essences can in turn receive and grasp being as it is in itself only if they do not try to protect themselves, but are trained by being in the love that gives away: consciousness, and the possession of oneself and of being, grow only and precisely in the measure that one increasingly breaks out of one's being by and for oneself into communication, exchange, sympathy with humanity and with the cosmos.[19]

19. Balthasar, *Glaubhaft ist nur Liebe*, p. 95. Note the connection Balthasar makes in this passage between the structure of the Thomistic real distinction between *esse* and essence, on the one hand, and christological love, on the other. In order to illumine Balthasar's understanding of this connection, we can recall a key text in which Thomas Aquinas, speaking of *esse*, says that it is "something complete and simple, but not subsistent" (Thomas Aquinas, *Quaestiones Disputatae de Potentia Dei*, I, 1, ad 1). While insisting with Thomas that creaturely essences have no actuality without the *actus essendi*, Balthasar also points out that these essences, while depending *de facto* on *esse creatum* for their very existence, nonetheless have their *ultimate* origin in God. If creaturely essence is not absolute, neither is creaturely *esse*, and the latter depends in its own way on the former as much as the former does on the latter. Created *esse*, then, is just that: created. Putting it somewhat paradoxically, we might say that *esse*

"Love Alone" as the Principle of Theological Intelligence

So far, we have briefly sketched how the love revealed in Christ has made trinitarian love *the* Reality that determines the *logos* of all being. The task we now face is to give a brief account of how this ontological foundation

---

creatum would have been God's being, except that it is always already given away as the "pure mediation" (Ferdinand Ulrich) of God's self-communication — and so is one with its Archetype only within this radical "given awayness," which makes it wholly transparent to God only at the moment it perfectly distinguishes created *esse* from him as ultimate origin of essences (and of created *esse* itself). The result is the following structure: *esse* makes essences be as their quasi- or supra-formal cause and, in so doing, depends on them; essences, thus affirmed in their otherness from *esse*, are caught up into the dynamic of gift carried in *esse* as "dependent actualization," so that the creature's exercise of *esse*, its subsistence, is a "having-received-oneself-from-God-into-a-dynamic-of-self-gift."

Now, according to Thomas, in the incarnation the Son's hypostatic *esse* is communicated to the assumed humanity at the same point where created *esse* normally would be, "taking over" from created *esse* all the functions that created *esse* normally would perform for it, realizing it as a subsisting, individual, complete, fully operational human nature — in which the person of the Son of God can then subsist for the temporal expression of his eternal personal being in the context of his visible mission (see, for example, *ST* III, 17, 2). Developing this Thomistic position, Balthasar adds that the Son's hypostatic *esse* "stands in" for created *esse*, not only in its completeness and simplicity, *but also in its non-subsistence*, insofar as this non-subsistence is an expression of divine liberality in the sense explained above. The Son's hypostatic *esse* therefore makes his assumed humanity subsist constitutively in the dynamic of gift, as even *created esse* would, while simultaneously transforming that subsistence-as-gift into a temporal expression of the Son's eternal act of letting himself be generated.

In becoming man, then, the Son "relives" creaturely genesis from both sides — from the side of the "given awayness" of non-subsistent *esse* and the side of its reception by the creature — but from the platform of his eternal generation. By the same token, the incarnation, while remaining for us a temporal event that occurs after the world is created, presupposes, on the part of the *persona assumens*, a timeless (albeit free) act that precedes the divine act of creation "in the order of intention." Only this intention is the person of the Son himself as he stands before the Father's face at the timeless "moment" when the Father first conceives, and resolves on, the creation of the world. In this sense, the Son's becoming man not only relives the "given-awayness" of non-subsistent *esse* and its reception by the creature; it also precedes, justifies, and defines the structure of the communication of creaturely being in the interplay of essence and *esse* as described here. The incarnation not only presupposes the real distinction, but also grounds it — so that "the ultimate mystery of God's *kenosis* in Christ," without losing for an instant its character as a singular event deriving from an unanticipatable free divine grace, "is analogically prepared in the metaphysical mystery of being," as Balthasar is suggesting in this passage from *Glaubhaft ist nur Liebe*.

plays out epistemologically in the theologian. The first thing to be said is that theology, as Balthasar understands it, is either configuration to the christological *Gestalt* of trinitarian love, in strict obedience to its normative pattern, or it is simply not theology in the first place. Christ, as *the* Figure of the trinitarian love *par excellence,* is not only theology's chief content, but also its primary method. Once again, "love alone" is the principle of theological intelligence in the strongest possible sense.

One surprising corollary of the primacy of christological love as the principle of theological intelligence is that theology is not just a matter of discourse, but also of the enfleshed display of what that discourse is about. The theologian can explain Christ's claim over the *logos* of all being, and prove its truth, only to the extent that he himself lets that claim be the Reality that determines all of *his* being — including his body — all of the time. It is important to stress that Balthasar is not encouraging the theologian to exhaust himself in a moralistic effort to "imitate" Christ, however. The theologian's enfleshed person becomes a statement and a demonstration of the truth of Christianity, not through his solitary initiative, but by being borne along by the already-flowing stream of ecclesial tradition. Precisely because ecclesial tradition is the ever-renewed presence *hic et nunc* of Jesus' eucharistic "traditioning,"[20] it is not a screen that comes between the theologian and his object, but is the concrete being caught up by, and indwelling in, Christ as the *Gestalt* of love *in actus exercitu* that, as I said in the previous section, is the principle of all true theological renewal.[21] Conversely, the

20. Paul suggests this connection in a particularly dense passage in 1 Corinthians that links Christ's *paradosis,* his sacrificial handing over of himself, the institution of the Eucharist, and the apostolic *paradosis* about the Eucharist: "For I received from the Lord what I have also handed over [*paredōka*] to you, that the Lord Jesus, on the night in which he was handing himself over [*paredideto*], took bread, gave thanks, broke it, and said, This is my body, which is for you. Do this in memory of me. And in the same way also the chalice after the meal, saying, This chalice is the new covenant in my blood, do this, as often as you drink, in memory of me. For as often as you eat this bread and drink this chalice, you proclaim the death of the Lord until he comes" (1 Cor 11:23-26).

21. Christ's eucharistic *paradosis,* by which he hands himself over for our salvation, and the *paradosis* of ecclesial tradition are strictly correlative. So much so, that tradition can be seen as the Eucharist spread out in time and space, even as the Eucharist can be seen correspondingly as the time and space of the tradition gathered up into the risen eternity of the Lord where past, present, and future interpenetrate beyond the fragmentation of earthly spatio-temporality. This suggests the distinctive feature of Balthasar's way of reading the Catholic tradition: the "reduction" (in the sense of "leading back" to the principle) of the

theologian's being "handed over to the pattern of doctrine" (Rom 6:17) is itself an act of ecclesial traditioning that makes quasi-sacramentally present the christological traditioning by which Jesus' body reveals and enacts the all-encompassing catholicity of trinitarian love — and it is just so that the theologian can be said to theologize in the first place.

Although Balthasarian "love alone" builds what might be called the theologian's "eucharistic enfleshment" into the theological enterprise itself, we would be fundamentally misreading Balthasar's intentions if we imagined that he were proposing this eucharistic enfleshment as an alternative to discourse, or as a mere instrument for putting it into action (for "practicing what one preaches"), or even as a "liturgical consummation" of it that comes "*after* writing," as Catherine Pickstock puts it.[22] Eucharistic

---

multiple expressions of Catholic tradition to its simple core, which is nothing other than Christ as the revelation of the catholicity of trinitarian love. We could say that he interprets the Catholic tradition by trying to catch its various expressions in their native transparency to what he calls in *Glaubhaft ist nur Liebe* the "self-exegeting revelational form of love" (p. 36). It is as if Balthasar, in his interpretive practice vis-à-vis the Catholic tradition, were attempting to relive, say, the origin of the *Summa theologiae* from the core of the tradition with Thomas, or the origin of the dogma of Chalcedon from the same core with the Council Fathers. Balthasar's "formula" for interpreting the Catholic tradition, then, is this: to begin anew from *the* Beginning — together with all those who have done so in the past — in a creative fidelity that brings out treasures new and old from the heritage that they have left us. This formula strives to combine the greatest fidelity to tradition (the expressions of the tradition that have been handed down to us are not just monumental fossils, but living vehicles through which the core of the tradition binds us to itself authoritatively here and now) with the greatest freedom (the interpreter not only sees the core of the tradition through its expressions, but, so to say, *with* them, in the same direction, out of the same spirit in which they took shape, and so is free to draw creatively from them without any fundamentalistic slavery to the letter). This is not to say, of course, that Balthasar thinks that familiarity with the canonical texts of the tradition is unimportant, or that one may play fast and loose with them so as to try to force them to mean something other than what they in fact mean. His point is simply that, insofar as these canonical texts emerged from the same tradition in which we stand today, they are not a death-dealing letter, but life-giving sources that flow here and now, participating in, and making bindingly present, the tradition's inexhaustible fecundity. The art of the interpreter of Catholic tradition is from this point of view to let himself be surprised by what that fecundity still has to reveal when held up to the burning light of *the* Source. The offspring of this fecundity will never contradict binding claims inherited from the past, but it will place them in new constellations that bring out hitherto unsuspected riches of meaning from them.

22. Catherine Pickstock, *After Writing: On the Liturgical Consummation of Philosophy* (London: Blackwell, 1997).

enfleshment, it is true, is not itself a discourse, and yet it is not so much *beyond* speech and writing as it is *the* beyond *of* speech and writing, which pervades them as the concentration and ground of their own proper intelligibility. Indeed, as we saw in the first section, the *Gestalt* of Christian revelation, as a Word-made-flesh, is in the first instance a *beautiful form* possessing a unique kind of intelligibility able to unite both the good and the true, concept and existence, word and deed, speech and silence[23] in a luminous, intact unity without confusion. Only such a luminous form, in fact, can adequately exposit the unique identity-in-difference of the Word-made-flesh, and state convincingly the claim that christological love determines the *logos* of all of being.[24] Replicating in miniature the essential gesture of the Church's tradition, the theologian's body is not dumb, meat-like "flesh" that "profiteth nothing" (Jn 6:63), but, in the Spirit, acquires all the force of a life-giving *logos,* at the precise point where Christ's *kenosis* and the structure of created being mutually confirm and enlighten each other in the universality of their reciprocal belonging.

Being as Love

Balthasar's claim that "love alone" is the principle of theological intelligence, as we have seen, not only makes Christ's love an *object or theme* of theological discourse, but also gives it intrinsic relevance to theological discourse as such, which in turn acquires a constitutive relation to the flesh. But, an objector might ask, does not Balthasar's attempt to make "love alone" the principle of theological discourse therefore run the risk of mixing incommensurables, of confusing loving and knowing, enfleshed

---

23. This presupposes that the lived body and the word are two sides of one and the same mysterious intimacy with, and distance from, the world that defines the structure of human existence as such. On the one side, the word refers to a world that is not itself, and does so by means of a reference that is not another word, but a kind of transparency that allows the world to appear, to be intimately present even, but as what is other than the spoken word. On the other side, the lived body enables us to be in the world, and so to need no bridge to reach it, and, at the same time, to stand over against the world as something other than ourselves. There is thus a convergence between word and embodied presence that allows them to interpenetrate without any undue confusion.

24. The foregoing paragraph is indebted to D. C. Schindler's account of the foundation of reason in *Hans Urs von Balthasar and the Dramatic Structure of Truth.*

existence and conceptuality? Is not Balthasar's "love alone" a huge "category mistake"? If so, then his well-intentioned effort to exalt love actually destroys the very possibility of speaking coherently about love at all. Given this objection, incarnate love can at most be an object of theological discourse, but it cannot reasonably be elevated to the status of the objective principle of theological discourse *as a discourse* without undermining theology as a rational enterprise altogether.

Let me reformulate this objection more technically. According to Aquinas, being is the deepest and most comprehensive foundation of all intelligibility: as we read in Thomas's *De Veritate*, "*all other* conceptions of the intellect are gotten by adding something to being [*ens*]."[25] Pre-eminent among these "conceptions" are the so-called transcendentals, which, though all substantially identical with *ens*, are nonetheless rationally distinct from it. But if we follow Aquinas in assuming that love emerges as such only with the transcendental *bonum*, then it looks as though Balthasar's claim that "love alone" is the principle of theological intelligence makes two crucial errors. First, it seemingly amounts to an illicit inference that, because the *bonum* and *ens* are substantially one, they are also therefore rationally one as well, that is, it confuses the *ratio entis* with the *ratio boni*. Second, by re-defining the *ratio* of being from the *ratio* of the good in this way, Balthasar also appears to compromise the transcendental *verum*, which Thomas sees as lying *between* being and the good as the primordial articulation of being's intelligibility in relation to intellect.[26] We thus come to the core of the objection: collapsing the *ratio entis* into the *ratio boni*, Balthasarian "love alone" makes it impossible to *think* the *ratio entis* in terms of the *verum* and thereby undermines the possibility of theology as a rational enterprise.

The objection that "love alone" destroys the rationality of theology does not rest only on a general consideration of the relationship between being, the true, and the good. For Aquinas, as for Augustine before him, the interplay of these three transcendentals is the key to articulating the structure of what is theology *par excellence*, namely, the "immanent Trinity." But both Augustine and Thomas hold that the priority of the true over

25. Aquinas, *Quaestiones Disputatae de Veritate* I, 1, c; italics added.
26. Of course, Thomas also sees the good as in some sense foundational for the true. The Thomistic reciprocity of the good and the true in the interplay of intellect and will is an opening on Aquinas's side to the Balthasarian solution that I will sketch briefly in the remainder of this section.

the good in the manifestation of the intelligibility of being is necessary to account for the word-character of the Word. From this point of view, Balthasarian "love alone" seems to obscure the reason why the Son should have any special relation to the articulation of the intelligibility of the divine being as Word. Balthasar's account of the relation between the Trinity and the transcendentals, in other words, seems to deprive the Son of his word-character and, by the same stroke, of his ability to communicate anything like a *sacra doctrina* that delivers to us the objective truth about God. If "love alone" is the principle of theological intelligence, then it appears that the Word is not a Word, and theology is impossible.

In what follows, I will address this objection in three steps of unequal length. (1) First, I will deal with its ontological foundation, calling into question the reading of the transcendentals that I have just sketched. (2) Second, I will address the objection on the properly trinitarian level where the interplay of the transcendentals is brought to bear on the processions of the divine persons. (3) Third, I will return briefly to the question of how the incarnation can make the flesh that the Word assumes part of his Word-character *for us.* Before beginning to lay out these three points, however, I would like to stress that my aim in doing so is not to polemicize against Augustine or Aquinas. It is rather to show that, by grounding truth in love, Balthasar is able to recuperate the basic intuitions of these two theological giants, while at the same time allowing theology to exploit perhaps more fully than even they did the concrete *Gestalt* of Jesus Christ, and the love that is its *logos,* in order to understand both worldly and divine being in their reciprocal illumination.

(1) Much could be said in response to the ontological part of the objection we are considering here, but I will limit myself to calling into question its underlying assumption that love first emerges only with the transcendental *bonum,* understood, moreover, as constituted by a relation to the will, such that the good is *ens* insofar as it is appetible.[27] To claim that "love alone" is the principle of theological intelligence, then, is not to confuse the *ratio entis* with the *ratio* of the good[28] — or, indeed, with any of

---

27. For a thorough treatment of this point, together with a detailed engagement with the objection against the Balthasarian primacy of love, see D. C. Schindler, "Does Love Trump Reason? Towards a Non-Possessive Concept of Knowledge: An Essay on the Centenary of Hans Urs von Balthasar's Birth" (in volume 2 of these proceedings).

28. I do not wish to deny, of course, that some special connection exists between love and the good, a connection which Balthasar himself acknowledges when he makes the good

the transcendentals. It is rather to claim that love is intrinsic to the *ratio* of being, and so lies at the root, not only of the good, but also of the beautiful, the true, and the one.[29] By the same token, putting love at the heart of the

---

the thematic of the *central* panel of his Trilogy. It is important to bear in mind, however, that the aspect of love that Balthasar mainly associates with the good is not love's appetibility for a will, but what he calls its "gratuity": its uncalculating "whylessness," to borrow a term from Meister Eckhart ("without why," *âne warumbe"*; see, for example, German Homily 5b in the Quint edition). The good thematizes this gratuity, moreover, only in concert with the other Balthasarian transcendentals: the beautiful, the true, and the one. Thus, the *pulchrum*, with which Balthasar opens his Trilogy, is the primordial appearing of love's gratuity, which, as such, contains both the good (the beautiful is an appearing of *gratuity*) and the true (the beautiful is an *appearing* of gratuity, which therefore appeals to *logos*). For their part, the good and the true reciprocally ground each other, as it were, in the light of beauty: the good thematizes the gratuity that founds the *logos*-character of the true; the true emphasizes precisely this *logos*-character, without which gratuity would be irrational, and so could never be real gratuity at all. The oneness of the good and the true, already announced implicitly in the beautiful, then becomes thematic in the *unum* (which had always been present as the foundation of the other transcendentals), to which Balthasar fittingly dedicates his short recapitulation of the entire Trilogy: *Epilog* (Einsiedeln: Johannes Verlag, 1987); Eng. trans., *Epilogue* (San Francisco: Ignatius Press, 1991).

29. How can being be said to be convertible with love? As Aquinas himself explains, the *ratio entis* as such is complex, inasmuch as it reflects the "real distinction" between *esse* and essence: the name *ens*, Thomas says, "is taken from the *actus essendi*," even as it is the essence "according to which" every *ens* "is said *to be* [*esse*]" (Aquinas, *Quaestiones Disputatae de Veritate* I, 1, c; italics added). By the same token, to understand the *ratio entis* is not just to grasp a self-contained quiddity, but to co-grasp the act of being that makes it, the quiddity, be denominable as *ens* in the first place. But this means, in turn, that, intrinsic to the *ratio entis*, there is a depth that is not in- or sub-determinate, but is rather the "hyper-determinate" (to borrow a term from Kenneth Schmitz) ground of being's quidditative intelligibility. Balthasar, for his part, calls this inner depth or intrinsic ground of the *ratio entis* "love," inasmuch as the creaturely *actus essendi* that accounts for it is a pure self-diffusion: "created *esse* itself is a similitude of the divine goodness" (XXII, 2, ad 2). So much so, in fact, that created *esse* never had any "self" to diffuse in the first place, but is always already "selfless," viz. non-subsistent. Intrinsic to the *ratio entis* as such is something like a selfless being-given-away that, far from undermining the intelligibility of *ens*, actually founds it from within. We do not, of course, grasp the *actus essendi* apart from the concrete *ens* that "instantiates" it. We grasp it rather only insofar as the concrete *ens* displays to us its participated share in the richness of the *actus essendi*. But this display is in turn what the self-diffusion of *esse* "looks like" when it is "instantiated" in concrete *ens* as its subsistent supposit. For the concrete *ens*, which provides the "missing self" for *esse*'s self-diffusion, is, at the moment it does so, caught up into *esse*'s dynamic of self-diffusion, and so exists in itself only to the extent that it also exists outside of itself, and vice versa, in a reciprocity of ecstasy and enstasy. Insofar as the resulting communion of *entia*, especially of personal *entia*, pro-

ratio entis does not compromise the originality of the *verum* in favor of the *bonum*. On the contrary, it qualifies the *ratio entis* as a unity of "whylessness" *and* of sense, of freedom *and* of rational necessity, whose richness only the *interplay* of the true and the good — which first comes to light as wonder-provoking *pulchrum* and then becomes thematic in its inexhaustible fruitfulness in the *unum* — can sufficiently display.[30] In this interplay, the good goes to the root of the true, not in order to undermine its specificity and originality as truth, but to underscore the gratuity that is co-constitutive of the *verum* as an expression of the *ratio entis*[31] — just as

---

vides the selves required for self-diffusion that, to put it figuratively, created *esse* wants but cannot give itself because of its non-subsistence, it is the full display and unfolding of the *ratio entis* in its character as love. Of course, the *communio entium* and *personarum* in its own turn needs the trans-personal universality of created *esse* in order to be more than a contingent collection of individuals; in order to be just that, a communion of persons that, as such, has ontological weight and value.

30. According to Emmanuel Tourpe, Balthasar "give[s] the impression of not sufficiently expressing the in-stance or 'reflexivity' of indifference, which is immediately thrown back into the dynamic of gift" (Emmanuel Tourpe, "Dialectic and Dialogic: The Identity of Being as Fruitfulness in Hans Urs von Balthasar," in this volume. In other words, the whyless spontaneity of love seems to trump any reflexive self-mediation, and, hence, to undermine the specificity of the *logos*. Tourpe's objection (which he presents in an entirely friendly manner as responding to a one-sidedness that he thinks Balthasar has the resources to overcome) fails, however, to take account of Balthasar's claim that the whyless spontaneity of gift includes *both* gratuity and sense, ecstasy and enstasy, thought and action. It is this simultaneity of "ands" that Balthasar calls "gratuity" and to which he attributes what he calls (borrowing from Schelling) *"Unvordenklichkeit"*: a priority, both temporal and ontological, over deliberative reflection. But that is just the point: this non-deliberative, self-less character assures Balthasarian gratuity precisely the highest possible degree of intelligence and selfhood. It therefore does not undermine the specificity of the *logos*, but rather simply makes the good and the *logos* mutually implicating, without collapsing them into each other.

31. *Logos*, in fact, is a gathering of many into a one — into a "point" that one needs to "get" in order to understand *logos*. But this unitary point cannot ultimately be another *logos*, otherwise we would have an infinite regress, an endless unraveling of Derridean *différance*. It must be something that grounds without needing any further grounding. It must be in this sense "whyless" — not because it is absurd, but because its sense is to ground sense without needing to be grounded in turn. We can call this "whylessness" love because it is rooted in the gratuitous self-gift of the Creator, which is rooted, in turn, in the gratuitous self-gift of the Father. The *logoi* of creatures proceed from the abyss of paternal love together with, and in, the Word as their center and goal. The Word, for its part, makes sense, and is the quintessence of all sense, even as the sense it makes exists entirely in view of making the "point" that the Father is an abyssal fountain of love.

the true goes to the root of the good in order to underscore the sense that is co-constitutive of the *bonum* as an equi-primordial expression of that same *ratio*.

(2) Now, in Balthasar's view the three divine persons are in their circumincession the *Gestalt*, the "form," of God's being as love (although without process or complexity) — and it is to this triune form as a whole that all the transcendentals primarily and properly belong in *their* circumincession as the joint co-explication of the coincidence of being and loving in God.[32] It is on this basis that Balthasar can relativize the Augustinian-Thomistic appropriation of the true to the Son and the good to the Spirit: *both* the good and the true, in the interplay described in point (1), belong, on Balthasar's reading, to the personal properties of both the Son and the Spirit. Nevertheless, insofar as Balthasar assigns to the Son and the Spirit *distinct aspects* of the trinitarian *Gestalt*,[33] and, therefore, distinct aspects of the interplay of the true and the good as joint expressions of the *ratio divini entis,* he can do full justice to the undeniable truth contained in the Augustinian-Thomistic appropriations of the truth to the Son and the good to the Spirit — while simultaneously allowing us to take better account of the way in which the circumincession of the persons is required to unfold the *ratio* of the divine being in its fullness as love. Just as Balthasar makes the good and the true reciprocally grounding, while preserving the distinctive character of each, he can maintain the specificity of the production of the Word in the Trinity, while also showing that the co-eternity of the procession of the Spirit as the "consubstantial communion"[34] of Father and Son signifies the presence of love at the very origin of the Word — not because the Spirit is the source of the Word, but because the Word cannot manifest the *ratio* of the paternal being as love

---

32. For Balthasar, the divine being, as the *analogatum princeps* of all being, is the first, most proper "instance" of the co-extension of love and *ens,* which creaturely being accordingly only participates in. By the same token, God is also the primordial "instantiation" of the transcendentals, which are, after all, nothing other than the concrete "thickness" of being as love. God accomplishes this instantiation as Trinity, according to Balthasar: the Trinity is the concreteness of God's being as love and, therefore, of the transcendentals. For more details, see Sara, *Forma y amor.*

33. The Son stands for that *Gestalt* as an objective expression of the Father's love, the Spirit for the fruitful unity of that objective expression and of the groundless ground of the "whyless" paternal charity that comes to light therein.

34. Augustine, *De Trinitate,* VI, 5, 7.

without himself being in a loving communion with the Father, whose bond and fruit is the Spirit.[35]

(3) Balthasar's claim that "love alone" is the principle of theological intelligence, far from undermining the *logos*-character of the Word, explains it within the exigencies of the trinitarian *Gestalt* as the articulation of God's being as love. This insertion of the word-character of the Word within the triune *Gestalt* enables Balthasar to reconcile the Augustinian-Thomistic emphasis on the procession of the *verbum interius* as the analogical key to understanding the generation of the Word with the Bonaventurian-Greek emphasis on the Son as the intra-trinitarian *expressio* of the Father, who eternally manifests the Father's being in his own consubstantial *hypostasis*. Now, in light of this reconciliation, the word-character of the *Logos* appears, not only as a rational saying, but as a rational saying that is also a showing of what one says, that is as it were "embodied" in oneself. The point, of course, is not that Balthasar projects flesh back into the immanent Trinity. It is rather that, presupposing the incarnation, the Son's eternal word-character cannot be captured by verbal teaching alone, but only by verbal teaching in just the sort of *Gestaltic* reciprocity with silent, bodily presence that we described under the heading "'Love Alone' as the Principle of Theological Intelligence" above. Hence the great advantage of Balthasarian "love alone," which justifies the value of our long and somewhat circuitous explanation and defense of it: "love alone" enables theologians to use Christ's concrete *Gestalt* to illumine the logical

---

35. The Word remains the principle of *sacra doctrina,* but precisely from within the circumincession of the three divine persons, where the Son and the Spirit, existing in an inseparable reciprocity as the Father's "two hands" even in the immanent Trinity, co-manifest the *ratio* of divine being as love in their dual unity. Significantly, Augustine himself seems to come close to this view in *De Trinitate,* IX, 12, 18, when he explains that an appetitive impulse lies behind the generation of the inner word, an impulse that then "becomes" love in the fully articulated sense once the inner word is generated. If we take this affirmation seriously, then we have to say that, even for Augustine, the "self-mediation" accomplished in *logos* not only grounds love, but is also grounded by it, and that intentionality and whylessness are mutually foundational. Indeed, this seems to be the point of Augustine's doctrine of the *filioque* as expressed above all in *De Trinitate* VI and XV: the procession of the Spirit depends on the procession of the Son, but also accompanies it, as the "consubstantial communion" of Father and Son. The Augustinian model of the Trinity is not one-sidedly "psychological," but seeks to point to the reality of God as combining both intra-personal oneness and inter-personal community in a real synthesis lying beyond all human analogies — just as Balthasar, in his different way, also tries to do.

architecture of divine revelation, so that the specificity of Christian revelation can shape the rationality of theological exposition itself — without any fideistic reduction or rejection of traditional accounts of theo-logic. Balthasar's emphasis on "love alone" as the principle of theological intelligence, far from undermining the specificity of *logos,* offers a thoroughly Christian account of that specificity, which also secures the deepest insights of the philosophical account of *logos* inherited by Augustine and Aquinas, and so speaks to the universality of reason as such.[36]

Conclusion: A Theology of the "Catholic 'And'"

Contrarily to a widespread impression seemingly corroborated by the unfortunate one-sidedness of some of his disciples, Balthasar is not a fideist or a theological positivist. For Balthasar, in fact, the novelty of Christianity does not consist in God's violent invasion of an idolatrous world "from above." It consists rather in Christ, who does not overturn what Balthasar calls the *"analogia entis,"* but rather *is* the *"analogia entis,"* the "marvellous accord of man and God" (to quote the felicitous title of a dissertation on Balthasar's work)[37] in person. Precisely because of his radical christocentrism, then, Balthasar is, before anything else, a theologian of the so-called "Catholic 'and'": of the unity-without-confusion of the "from above" *and* the "from below"; of grace *and* of nature; of philosophy *and* of theology; of the radical following of Christ *and* of passionate love for the world; of tradition *and* of the development of doctrine. A theology of "love alone" in the Balthasarian style is thus catholic in the fullest sense, for it includes the guardianship not only of theological revelation, but also of worldly being, together with all of mankind's attempts to do justice to it, not only in philosophy, but also in religion, science, and art. The theologian undertakes this guardianship in the grateful awareness of how much he and all Christians *owe* to the philosophers, the sages, and the artists of the universal human tradition, including those who have lived and labored outside the visible bounds of the Church:

36. For an indirect confirmation of this point, see D. C. Schindler, *Plato's Critique of Impure Reason: On Goodness and Truth in* The Republic (forthcoming).

37. Georges de Schrijver, *Le merveilleux accord de l'homme et de Dieu: Étude de l'analogie de l'être chez Hans Urs von Balthasar* (Louvain: University Press, 1983).

> [W]e will show that the experience of glory that distinguishes the
> Christian — which, however, will have to be thought through and for-
> mulated anew for our time out of the center of revelation — places the
> Christian under an obligation to enact and to live exemplarily the ex-
> perience of being, which in any case can never be alienated. In this way,
> the Christian is to become the responsible guardian of glory as a
> whole, as indeed the Jew who sang the creation Psalms to his God was
> already the responsible guardian of the glory of the covenant *and* of
> creation.[38]

One of the things whose guardianship Balthasar entrusts to the theologian
is *nature*. Although Balthasar has relatively little to say *ex professo* about
Aristotle, no one who reads both *Theologik. I: Wahrheit der Welt* and
Herrlichkeit. I: Schau der Gestalt can miss the convergences (intended or
unintended) between Aristotelian *physis* and Balthasarian *Gestalt*. At stake
in both, in fact, is a basic, irreducible ontological unity that possesses an
original interiority out of which it manifests itself with unmistakable clarity against the background of the world. At the same time, Balthasar offers
the "meta-physical" grounding that is essential for opening *physis* up to
creation as gift and, by means of this opening, for giving it a place and an
ultimate safeguard within the christological analogy of the transcendentals
between God and the world proposed in the Trilogy.[39] Central to this project is Christ's Paschal Mystery, which can be seen as providing the deepest
foundation — the *"intimior intimo meo"* as it were — of the bottomless
abyss of self-manifesting interiority that Aristotle glimpsed in *physis:* in his
kenosis, Christ recapitulates the "noughting" of non-subsistent being, presupposing nature in its non-instrumentalizable, inalienable depth-
dimension — and, in so doing, giving nature that depth in the first place.[40]

---

38. H. U. von Balthasar, *Herrlichkeit. III. 1. Im Raum der Metaphysik* (Einsiedeln:
Johannes Verlag, 1965), p. 19 (author's italics); Eng. trans., *The Glory of the Lord: A Theological Aesthetics,* vol. 4: *The Realm of Metaphysics in Antiquity* (San Francisco: Ignatius Press,
1989).

39. See Balthasar, *Herrlichkeit. III. 1*, pp. 13-39 (Eng., pp. 11-39).

40. Christ's *kenosis* is the *concretissimum* of the non-subsistence of *esse* as a reflection
of the divine liberality that shines forth when *esse,* at the very moment it accounts for created nature as a quasi- or supra-formal cause, also "depends" on created nature as the abyssal ground out of which it, created *esse,* is to be instantiated and exercised (as the natural
thing's substantial *energeia*). Christ thus presupposes and accounts for the whole relation by
which created *esse* at once causes and depends on created nature — and in so doing both

This connection between the depth of Holy Saturday and the depth of nature deserves much more attention among Balthasarians than they have hitherto given it.

Balthasar always insisted that "without philosophy, there is no theology."[41] This lapidary dictum means that theology both presupposes, and is a renewed re-entry into, the source-point of all thinking without exception: the *thaumazein* over reality that Plato and Aristotle claim is the principle of philosophy.[42] And not just over reality in general, but also over *nature*, that "dearest freshness deep down things" (Hopkins) whose self-manifestation is the first wonder-provoking revelation of being with which we come into contact.[43] If Balthasar is a master of theological renewal, it is not just because he insists on the primacy of grace. It is also because, from the height of specifically Christian revelation, he gives us the eyes to wonder at *physis* again and the resources to stand up for its integrity. The contemplation of the Paschal Mystery, in fact, lays upon the Christian a genuine feeling for, and obedience to, the natures of things, just as Christ himself obeyed them when he received them from the Father to shepherd them up from nothingness in his rising from the "lower regions of the earth" (Eph 4:9). Care for nature is one of the chief tasks that fall to the Christian layman (to whom Balthasar primarily entrusts the theologi-

---

causes, and in causing depends on, created nature himself. Christ not only grounds *physis*, but simultaneously presupposes, and receives himself from, it — and (only) in so doing bestows on it its characteristic interiority in the first place.

41. H. U. von Balthasar, *Theologik. I: Wahrheit der Welt* (Einsiedeln: Johannes Verlag, 1985), vii; Eng. trans., *Theo-Logic: Theological Logical Theory*, vol. 1: *Truth of the World* (San Francisco: Ignatius Press, 2000).

42. Philosophy, on Balthasar's account, is not just one more or less well-paid academic discipline alongside others, or even a source of "conceptual tools" for theology; it is the falling in love with being as love — a falling in love that Plato called *eros* — that stands for the quintessence of all genuine understanding. This is not to say, of course, that Balthasar recommends setting aside hard thinking in favor of some sort of enthusiastic wordless immediacy. Balthasar knows that part of being in love means staying in love, and staying in love takes work, which in this case means a desire to do the highest justice to what one has seen by rendering the most comprehensive, subtle, and argumentatively sound account one can give of it. Balthasar's point, then, is simply that, unless hard thinking is awakened and sustained by wonderment over the splendor of being as love, it cannot ever see the point of going all the way to the bottom of any problem — and so lacks the principle that alone can found the logical stringency that distinguishes hard thinking from mush.

43. This is particularly, but not exclusively, true of personal nature.

cal exposition of the catholicity of trinitarian love)[44] in the following of Christ who, in the Paschal Mystery, went to the uttermost lengths imaginable to lay created nature, whole and intact, at the feet of the Father.[45]

44. The "lay" represents for Balthasar a fundamental "place" where the Church and the world come together to anticipate their eschatological unity already in time. The "lay," in turn, Balthasar entrusts to the new form of consecrated life in the world called the "secular institute." Indeed, as is well known, Balthasar thought that the center of his own work lay not in his books, but in the secular institute he founded in 1945 with Adrienne von Speyr: the Community of Saint John. For more information on this point, see Hans Urs von Balthasar, *Unser Auftrag. Bericht und Entwurf* (Einsiedeln: Johannes Verlag, 1984). For a good presentation of Balthasar's theology of secular institutes, see his *Gottbereites Leben* (Freiburg: Johannes Verlag, 1993), Eng. trans., *The Laity and the Life of the Counsels: The Church's Mission in the World*, trans. Brian McNeil, C.R.V., with D. C. Schindler (San Francisco: Ignatius Press/Communio Books, 2003); and Juan M. Sara, "Secular Institutes in the Theology of Hans Urs von Balthasar," in *Communio: International Catholic Review* 29, no. 2 (Summer 2002).

45. One could express this by saying that Balthasar's theological aesthetics has enormous potential for the development of a sound theology of the environment and the natural world. See Connie Lasher, *"The Contemplative Glance of Faith": Hans Urs von Balthasar's Contribution to a Catholic Theology of Ecological Identity* (unpublished Ph.D. dissertation, UMI number 3135966: 2004).

What Does Triunity "Add" to the Reality of God — and to the Structure of the Cosmos?

Trinity, Creation, and Aesthetic Subalternation

Michael Hanby

The Trinitarian formulation of Nicaea serves to identify the self-offering of Jesus Christ and the delight the Father takes in him with the very being of God. It is in the light of this identification that we understand St. John's assertion that "God is love" as properly a claim about God, that is, a claim first about how God is in himself, and only secondarily — and at an analogical distance — a claim about how God is for us. Even so, the second claim is the basis of the first. It is only because of Christ that we can say God is Trinity, but it is because God is Trinity that we can say that it is *God* who so loved the world in Christ, because God is love before the foundation of the world.

Richard of St. Victor held that it is only due to this love, this eternal generosity, reciprocity, and shared delight between the Father, Son, and Spirit that we can predicate supreme goodness of God.[1] I would add that this convertibility of divine love and divine being also implicates the other transcendentals in dynamic circumincession with one another inasmuch as the intentional *ecstasis* of one divine *persona* toward repose in the goodness of another is prompted by delight in the other's beauty, and inasmuch as this very *ecstasis* acknowledges the authority of an "evidentiary" claim and therefore affirms the true.[2] It is precisely this internal gift and provocation among the trinitarian *personae*, wherein each simultaneously gives

---

1. Richard of St. Victor, *De Trinitate*, III.

2. Augustine, *De Trinitate*, VI.10.12, "For in that Trinity is the supreme source of all things, and the most perfect beauty, and the most blessed delight. Those three, therefore, both seem to be mutually determined to each other and are in themselves infinite." See my "These Three Abide: Augustine and the Eschatological Non-Obsolescence of Faith," *Pro Ecclesia* 14 (Summer 2005): 340-60.

to, seeks, and delights in the other, that allows us to say of the transcendentals what Augustine says of the *personae* themselves in their infinite determination to one another: "Each are in each, and all in each, and each in all, and all in all, and all are one."[3]

Setting aside for now the convertibility of the transcendentals, we might follow Richard further in adding that we can only properly predicate even *divinity* of God in predicating love *essentially* of God. For a proper understanding of divinity requires an adequate conception of God's difference from the world, beyond every opposition of Being and beings, Being and non-being, or presence and absence. We can only think this difference from the world along with God's "indifference" *to* the world; and only the fullness of love sufficient unto itself — which is to say, the simultaneity of free generosity, reciprocity, and delight — secures this freedom for thought. Of course, by "indifference" I do not mean that unpremised *arbitrium* of late scholastic voluntarism which Descartes employs in order to launch his *epoche*. This un-trinitarian understanding severs the will from its formal object and thus leaves God undetermined with respect to his own essence. Rather, by "indifference" I mean something like what Aquinas meant when he denied that God had a real relation to the world. I mean God's freedom, co-extensive with his self-determination as love, with respect to the world's existence. This difference and indifference are intrinsic to the unique relation which Judeo-Christian tradition calls creation, which establishes the world in the utter contingency of a free gift, and grounds the "what" and "why" of creatures in the intelligibility of a "whyless" delight that seeks no end beyond itself, without — for all that — becoming merely arbitrary. Only with the conceptual advent of this relation and this contingency do we arrive at a genuine thinking of transcendence, beyond even the ontological difference of Being and beings or the abyssal difference between Being and nothing; and only within the ambit of this transcendence is it possible to grasp a finite incarnation of this infinite love that does not diminish or contradict it.[4] Yet the importance of this category is not restricted to theology proper. It does not leave the world unaffected. For creation renders the world as a gratuitous effect of this love and a reflection of the divine beauty.

---

3. Augustine, *De Trin.*, VI.10.12.

4. David Bentley Hart, *The Beauty of the Infinite: The Aesthetics of Christian Truth* (Grand Rapids: Eerdmans, 2003), pp. 125-51.

It is, of course, the incarnation of Christ which reveals this love and recalls the world to union with it and to its own integrity. So we must insist that the christological manifestation of God "interprets" and conditions what we may say about God's immanent triune nature. And yet it is just as true that the revelation of God's triunity interprets the economic revelation of God — and the innermost meaning of the world — in Christ.[5] ("But when he comes, the Spirit of truth, he will guide you to all truth" [Jn 16:13].) The Trinity allows us to see in the events of Christ's life, and creation's sacrificial "return" to God in Christ, the unity of a love sufficient to encompass its own rejection and the emphatic affirmation of Genesis's original judgment of creation — it is good. This judgment reaffirms and restores the original beauty of creation as gift and repose despite all appearances to the contrary, or rather, precisely in an "astonishing" contrary form: "so marred was his appearance, beyond human semblance, and his form beyond that of the sons of men" (Is 52:14).

To assert that the eternal, immanent Trinity is disclosed in the economic is to claim that the world as a whole and all of its constituents derive their innermost and decisive determination in relation to this judgment, even if they remain blind to that fact or discover it as the fulfillment of projects commenced in indifference to it. This is to say that the relation denoted by that term is not extrinsic to creatures determined to God by that relation. Just as triunity "adds" nothing to the reality of God — for God is not a subject in relation to his own goodness, and does not have love, but *is* love — so creation from the Triune God *adds* nothing to the structure of the cosmos, for it is not an event among things *in* the cosmos. Of course, this assertion is complicated by the fact that this God becomes flesh and dwells among us, but for now, let it suffice to say that if the relation of creation is intrinsic to the world, then the world is always already shot through with an intrinsic meaning that reflects this relation; a particular sort of intelligibility is part and parcel of its very structure. This means that the creation and redemption of the world — which, viewed from one angle, are but two phases of a single divine "act" — should have a real, *intrinsic* bearing on the content of our knowledge and the relationship of different branches of knowledge to each other, if we would truly know the world.

Yet the various branches of knowledge embodied institutionally in the modern university conspire to hide this relation from view. The

---

5. Aquinas, *Summa theologiae* (= *ST*), I, 1, 3 and 4.

problem here is not simply that these disciplines embody metaphysical first principles and assume corresponding models of rationality that are functionally atheistic, though this is true enough. Rather, the still deeper problem is that in rejecting the intelligibility granted to the world by the doctrine of *creatio ex nihilo,* modernity arguably undermined the intelligibility of a fundamental precondition for *any* university and indeed for education properly so-called, Christian or not: namely, a *uni-verse.* Nietzsche, undoubtedly, would have appreciated the point, and it pertains just as much to the sciences as to philosophy. Granted, some of this is the natural result of specialization and the proper, relative autonomy of the different branches of knowledge. Yet one need not look far in contemporary intellectual or political culture to see that any comprehensive sense of the world as an intelligible unity is now virtually extinguished.[6] The current attempt to make virtue of necessity by re-christening this fragmentation as a "multiversity" is an indication of the paucity of secular solutions to this puzzle.

The essay that follows will offer a roughly Thomistic conception of creation that issues in a program for a theological aesthetics more or less commensurate with Balthasar's, in both its objective and subjective dimensions.[7] I will contend that the doctrine of creation is fundamentally aesthetic in character and that it issues in a corresponding conception of reason that lays greater claim to rationality than its rivals, on the subjective

6. One might counter, as does Nicholas Boyle, that any such talk of incommensurability is betrayed by the hegemony of science, the global dominance of liberal political culture, or by the forces of production and consumption, all of which are imposing an unprecedented uniformity of global culture. I do not deny such dominance, but suggest that the success of these forces depends not upon truth, but upon ontological reductionism and political power that masks the underlying incoherence, fragmentation, and disunity of thought and life. Nicholas Boyle, *Who Are We Now: Christian Humanism and the Global Market from Hegel to Heaney* (Edinburgh: T. & T. Clark, 1998), pp. 69-93.

7. A point of clarification is in order here. I am neither a Thomist nor a Balthasarian of the strict observance, and while I am well aware that the two are susceptible to profoundly different interpretations on such questions as the processions of persons within the Godhead, the place of beauty among the transcendentals, and the theory of cognition, I am not concerned to negotiate or mediate these differences. My point in undertaking this exercise is not to offer a definitive interpretation of either Aquinas or Balthasar, much less to attempt a synthesis of the two, but rather only to draw upon what I have learned from each of them for the sake of constructing a "third thing" addressed to a very specific problem, namely, what it might mean within the current intellectual context to allow our understanding of the world to be intrinsically governed by an understanding of that world as creation.

grounds that it does greater justice to what actually occurs when we understand, and on the objective grounds that it does greater justice to the infinite complexity of its objects. This understanding will accord priority to faith not in opposition to knowledge but as inherent within knowledge and as its genuine possibility, which is to say that it is finally only the acknowledgment of creation, and the aesthetic rationality attending it, that protects the scientific character of science and holds out hope for retrieving the unity of the world from the fragmentation of a post-rational culture.

The Beautiful "Mechanics" of *Creatio ex nihilo*

The doctrine of creation, when not downright mischaracterized by those with a stake in dismissing it, is frequently misunderstood even by those who profess it.[8] There are undoubtedly many reasons for this, and not all of them vicious, though chief among them is surely the mechanistic cosmology which has penetrated so deeply into the tacit conceptual architecture of our culture, despite its precarious position in contemporary physics.[9] Despite the displacement of this cosmology by quantum mechanics,

---

8. Daniel Dennett's absurd likening of "divine intervention" to a "skyhook" comes to mind as one such malicious mischaracterization. See Dennett, *Darwin's Dangerous Idea: Evolutions and the Meaning of Life* (New York: Simon & Schuster, 1995), pp. 73-80.

9. This precariousness, of course, depends upon one's definition of mechanism. The physicist David Bohm argued that mechanism in physics should be characterized by a) the reduction of the world to its basic elements; b) the notion that the relationship between these elements is fundamentally *external,* a legacy of what is the *de facto* Newtonian position: that a thing is most fundamentally "itself" in solitude; and c) the notion that the influence of one element upon another is also external. The question of determinism is irrelevant here. He remarks, "[T]his question of determinism vs. indeterminism has little or no relationship to that of mechanism vs. non-mechanism. For the essential point of mechanism is to have a set of fundamental elements that are *external to each other* and externally related. Whether these elements obey deterministic or statistical laws does not affect the question of the mechanical nature of the basic constituents (e.g., a pinball machine or a roulette wheel that would operate according to "laws of chance" is no less mechanical than is a machine whose behavior is completely knowable and predictable)." See Bohm's "The Implicate Order: A New Approach to the Nature of Reality," in David L. Schindler, ed., *Beyond Mechanism: The Universe in Recent Physics and Catholic Thought* (Lanham, Md.: University Press, 1986), pp. 13-37, at 21. Relativity theory, says Bohm, begins to undermine these by supplanting the "atomism" of classical physics with continually spreading fields of motion, but the real breakthrough is achieved by quantum theory, which divides motion into infinitesimal quanta and disrupts the continuity

45

and the changes in the meaning of "explanation" occasioned in part by the probabilities revolution at the end of the nineteenth century, many of its most salient features — the expulsion of formal and final causality and the evacuation of the transcendentals — remain.

It is extremely difficult to make the doctrine of creation intelligible within the confines of these cosmological assumptions, for they require as their precondition that the trinitarian God of orthodox Christian under-standing had to be un-thought and forgotten, and the metaphysical gram-mar appropriate to his transcendence dismantled.[10] The subsequent "grey ontology," which filled the vacuum left by the Cartesian and Newtonian evacuation of teleology and the transcendentals, redefined the very concepts of nature and matter, denying that wholes are more than aggregates of their independent component parts and refusing formal and qualitative attribu-tions — the so-called "secondary qualities" — any ontological foothold or intrinsic relation to quanta.[11] As a consequence, the now hypothetical God

---

of movement in classical physics. Moreover, the environmental variation of the fundamental nature of an entity (its exhibition of wave or particle-like characteristics under different con-ditions of observation) further undermines the extrinsicism of the classical view. Still, if one follows David L. Schindler in defining as "methodological mechanism" theories that "ab-stract from the question about what material entities really are (in themselves), and restrict [themselves] rather to treating those entities as if they were just mechanical in their activity — treating them, that is, just so far as they manifest [themselves] in mechanical ways," then quantum physics is arguably no less mechanistic than classical physics. Schindler, "Introduc-tion: The Problem of Mechanism," in *Beyond Mechanism*, pp. 1-11, at 6; see Bohm, "The Im-plicate Order: A New Approach," pp. 14-21.

10. Simon Oliver argues that Newton's conceptions of matter and motion were predi-cated upon an un-trinitarian voluntarism and an Arian Christology, which aid and abet his nominalism and his conception of causality. Though Newton hoped his system would coun-teract what he saw as the atheistic implications of Cartesian philosophy, he and Descartes partake of similar dogmatic errors. On Newton, see Simon Oliver, "Motion According to Aquinas and Newton," *Modern Theology* 17, no. 2 (2001): 163-99, and his *God, Philosophy, and Motion* (Radical Orthodoxy) (London: Routledge, 2005), pp. 153-82. For an account of the Cartesian un-thinking of Christian orthodoxy, see Michael Hanby, *Augustine and Modernity* (London: Routledge, 2003), pp. 134-77.

11. "Grey ontology" is Jean-Luc Marion's phrase, and it describes "that which 'con-ceals itself under an epistemological discourse' thereby 'maintaining the thing in the grey-ness of the object, and . . . thus bears testimony to the intoxication . . . of the ego, 'master and owner' of the world reduced to evidence" (Marion, "Descartes and Onto-Theology," in Phillip Blond, ed., *Post-Secular Philosophy: Between Philosophy and Theology* [London: Routledge, 1998], p. 97, n. 1). On "extrinsicism," see David L. Schindler, "The Problem of Mechanism," in *Beyond Mechanism*, pp. 8-10.

could only appear to view either through extrinsic "intervention" from an irrelevant "position" beyond the circumference of the closed universe or as the homogenous medium through which the world passes.[12] Never mind that these could never be God — as the invocations of God in the work of Descartes, More, and Newton repeatedly demonstrate — for a God who is not genuinely immanent cannot be genuinely transcendent either.

From a post-seventeenth-century viewpoint, Thomas Aquinas's so-called "five ways" appear to be offering the sort of rationalist proofs for the existence of God characteristic of William Paley and the natural theology of the eighteenth century and their contemporary heirs in the so-called "intelligent design" school.[13] Odd then, that in the question on creation in the *Summa theologiae*, Thomas insists that the creation of the world in time is an article of faith. "By faith alone do we hold, and by no demonstration can it be proved, that the world did not always exist. The reason for this is that the newness of the world cannot be demonstrated on the part of the world itself."[14] This claim is neither an irrational leap of faith that commences where reason leaves off nor a mere negative resignation to the transcendental limits of our knowledge. Rather the claim is rooted in a rigorous theological grammar, and it serves to protect God's transcendence and genuine otherness to creation.

In Question 45 of the *prima pars,* Aquinas had distinguished creation from other modes of causality such as generation and alteration, which "are less perfect and excellent."[15]

> Creation is not change except according to a certain understanding. . . .
> For change means something should be different now than it was pre-

---

12. On Newton's debt to More with regard to the *sensorium dei,* see E. A. Burtt, *The Metaphysical Foundations of Modern Science* (Mineola, N.Y.: Dover, 2003), pp. 125-61; and Amos Funkenstein, *Theology and the Scientific Imagination: From the Middle Ages to the Seventeenth Century* (Princeton: Princeton University Press, 1986), pp. 72-80. The latter also provides an excellent account of the conceptual and lexical transformations required for seventeenth-century literalism about God's omnipresence and omnipotence.

13. This is not the place to address the controversy over the standard, intro-to-philosophy-textbook interpretation of Aquinas's five ways. For two accounts contesting the traditional presentation, see Eugene Rogers, *Thomas Aquinas and Karl Barth: Sacred Doctrine and the Natural Knowledge of God* (Notre Dame: University of Notre Dame Press, 1995), and Fergus Kerr, *After Aquinas: Versions of Thomism* (London: Blackwell, 2002), pp. 58ff.

14. *ST* I, 46, 2.

15. *ST* I, 45, 1.

viously. But in creation, by which the whole substance of a thing is produced, the same thing can be taken as different now and before only according to our way of understanding, so that a thing is understood as first not existing at all, and afterwards as existing.[16]

Creation, strictly speaking, refers not to a transmutation or alteration of form effected through a chain of efficient causes, though I will argue that only creation makes such causal transactions intelligible.[17] Rather, creation refers to the gratuitous generation of being and beings from nothing. Creation in the strict sense is the passage from potency in the mind of God to actuality, which, incidentally, is what it means for Aquinas to say in the first of the so-called "five ways" that God is the first efficient cause of motion, also defined as the reduction from potentiality to act.[18] "Since God's being is his actual understanding, creatures preexist there as held in his mind, and so, as being comprehended, do they proceed from him."[19]

Thomas's understanding of motion as the passage from potency to act does not require anything we would normally consider as movement or change from God's side. This is because God as *esse* is already pure actuality.[20] God ineffably subsists beyond the ordinary juxtaposition of motion and rest in his impassible, immutable plenitude. Thus, as David Burrell says, "Whatever is itself in act in the relevant aspect need not do anything further to become a cause."[21] In creation, properly speaking, causing an effect is construed not as a quantum of force, but simply as a non-reciprocal *relation* of the effect to the cause. As Aquinas says in Q. 45, "Creation places something in the thing created according to relation only; because what is created is not made by movement or change."[22]

---

16. *ST* I, 45, 2, ad. 2.

17. See also my "Creation Without Creationism: Toward a Theological Critique of Darwinism," *Communio* 30 (Winter 2003): 654-94, from which portions of this section are drawn.

18. *ST* I, 2, 2 and 3.

19. *ST* I, 19, 4.

20. I would argue that God is *actus purus* in virtue of being infinite love; but precisely insofar as infinite love is at once active and receptive, this must be conceived not in juxtaposition to potency, but rather as containing its own potency within what is nevertheless always undiminished actuality. Hence the subsequent claim that this designation transcends the contrasting pairs.

21. David B. Burrell, *Aquinas: God and Action* (Notre Dame: University of Notre Dame Press, 1979), p. 133.

22. *ST* I, 45, 3: ". . . For what is made by movement or by change is made from

The act of creation therefore differs in kind from all other causes. And therefore the doctrine of creation, which understands the fact of our having been created as a relation, posits no causal mechanism by which God as the active agent and creatures as passive recipients might be conjoined. Thus against both the philosophical charge of an ontotheological reduction that projects onto God an immanent causality for which God is then declared responsible, and the scientific charge that the doctrine of creation offers a flawed alternative to rival accounts of natural origins, we see instead that creation is at bottom an *apophatic* — one might even say agnostic — doctrine. It refuses to specify a causal mechanism, though this refusal should not be seen as resulting from a current state of ignorance about the totality of causal factors or from the transcendental limitations to our understanding. Rather, the negative, *apophatic* refusal to specify a causal mechanism is rooted in the positive, *kataphatic* insistence upon God's simplicity and actuality, and the nature of any "action" resulting therefrom. Strictly speaking, there can be no mechanism for the movement from nothing to something, because prior to the movement, there is nothing upon which the mechanism might act. Causality here is simply said to have occurred whenever something genuinely *new* appears and when the activity of the novelty can be described in terms similar to those describing the primary "agent."[23] Since the primary agent is God, the transcendent, immutable act of being who encompasses all the similarities of creation within the ever-greater difference that he is and who surpasses our understanding by definition, this "description," of course, can proceed only by analogy insofar — a crucial qualifier — "as existence is common to all."[24]

This is no "skyhook theory" of creation, a crude and uncomprehending metaphor for divine action which likens God to a piece of stage ma-

---

something pre-existing. And this happens, indeed, in the particular productions of some beings, but cannot happen in the production of all being by the universal cause of all beings, which is God. Hence God by creation produces without movement. Now when movement is removed from action and passion, only relation remains, as was said above (2, *ad* 2). Hence creation in the creature is only a certain relation to the Creator as the principle of its being; even as in passion, which implies movement, is implied a relation to the principle of motion."

23. Though it remains to ask in what sense something could be genuinely new to God, given that no creature can add to his sum. See fn. 36 below.

24. *ST* I, 4, 3.

chinery "intervening" in nature like Aphrodite to restore Paris to his bed-chamber.[25] Rather, because it has no real relation to its effects, the divine action of creating — inseparable from the divine being itself — is *intrinsic* to its effects and the immanent causal processes that produce them, in the very fact of their existence and irreducible novelty.

> Now since God is very being *(ipsum esse)* by His own essence, created being *(esse creatum)* must be His proper effect; as to ignite is the proper effect of fire. Now God causes this effect in things not only when they first begin to be, but as long as they are preserved in being. . . . Therefore as long as a thing has being, God must be present to it, according to its mode of being. But *being is innermost in each thing and most fundamentally inherent in all things since it is formal in respect of everything found in a thing. . . . Hence it must be that God is in all things, and innermostly.*[26]

There can be no visible "mechanism" apart from the existence and activity of things themselves, for the passage from nothing to something. Creation, which is really the presence of things in God and God in things entirely dependent upon the gratuity of this presence, is thus simultaneously utterly distinct from those things, irreducible to them, and yet not neatly separable from them, since it would compromise divine transcendence to delineate, in Pelagian fashion, the respective contributions of creature and Creator in the being of the creature or its immanent causal processes. This is what it means when Burrell says that the relationship named by creation "makes its appearance within the world as we know it and yet does not express a difference within that world."[27] And it is why the newness of the world cannot be demonstrated from the world itself. The greatest "proof" for the creation of the world is not

25. See Dennett, *Darwin's Dangerous Idea*, pp. 73-80.

26. *ST* I, 8, 1, emphasis mine. "Cum autem Deus sit ipsum esse per suam essentiam, oportet quod esse creatum sit proprius effectus eius; sicut ignire est proprius effectus ignis. Hunc autem effectum causat Deus in rebus, non solum quando primo esse incipient, sed quamdiu in esse conservantur. . . . Quamdiu igitur res habet esse, tamdiu oportet quod Deus adsit ei secundum modum quo esse habet. Esse sutem est illud quod est magis intimum cuilibet, et quod *profundius omnibus inest: cum sit formale respectu omnium quae in re sunt, ut ex supra dictis patet,* **unde oportet quod Deus sit in omnibus rebus, et intime.**"

27. David B. Burrell, *Knowing the Unknowable God: Ibn-Sina, Maimonides, Aquinas* (Notre Dame: University of Notre Dame Press, 1986), p. 20.

some change within the world, or some mechanism for it, but simply the beautiful, good, and true existence of a manifold of things not God, which is to say that the doctrine of creation is less an account of *how the world came to be* than of *what the world is,* as apprehended through that tutored regard which Christians call faith, hope, and charity.[28] The movement from non-existence to existence is infinite, and thus the one motion that only God can account for. Its "mechanism" remains inaccessible by definition.

There are both *apophatic* and *kataphatic* consequences to this understanding of creation. On the negative side of the ledger, we have seen that the doctrine of creation does not supply a mechanism for the being of the world, and it does not provide a theory in the sense demanded by science (at least in its Newtonian conceptions). One often hears in this regard that creation simply answers a different question from that of physics, biology, and the sciences more generally: not "Why this rather than that?" but "Why something rather than nothing?" But is this so? For as Balthasar notes, the existence of the world becomes almost *more* mysterious when God is admitted than when he is denied.[29]

It seems better to say that theology *refuses* to answer even this question, just as it refuses to specify a causal "mechanism" for the being of the world. Certainly Thomas thinks so. Following Augustine and the tradition,

---

28. An understanding reflected in the medieval conception of *scientia* and its coexistence with the symbolic realism contained in the bestiaries. Peter Harrison echoes Aquinas (*ST* I, 1, 10) when he writes, "Strictly, allegorical interpretation is not the wresting of multiple meanings out of words which, properly considered, are unequivocal. Multiple meanings emerge from allegorical readings of texts because the things to which the words refer have themselves further multiple references. . . . When, in the sixteenth century, the Protestant reformers began to dismantle this fertile and fecund system of allegorical interpretation, they were unwittingly to precipitate a dramatic change in the way in which objects in the natural world were conceived" (Harrison, *The Bible, Protestantism, and the Rise of Natural Science* [Cambridge: Cambridge University Press, 1998], pp. 28-29).

29. Hans Urs von Balthasar, *Love Alone Is Credible* (San Francisco: Ignatius Press 2004), p. 143. "Why in fact is there something rather than nothing? The question remains open regardless of whether one affirms or denies the existence of an absolute being. If there is no absolute being, what reason could there be that these finite, ephemeral things exist in the midst of nothing, things that could never add up to the absolute as a whole or evolve into it? But on the other hand, if there is an absolute being, and if this being is sufficient unto itself, it is almost more mysterious why there should exist something else. Only a philosophy of freedom and love can account for our existence, though not unless it also interprets the essence of finite being in terms of love."

he insists that God, who lacks nothing, does not act for an end in creation. Implying that God could somehow gain from the existence of the world would compromise the fullness of the divine plenitude and desecrate God's transcendence, simplicity, and immutability.[30] Rather, because God as Trinity subsists in the fullness of self-giving love, we can posit no motive for creation beyond the Father's self-gift to and sheer delight in the knowledge and beauty of his Image, the Son, in whom all the perfections of being dwell in superlative splendor.[31] Insofar as God knows creation in knowing himself, creation as a reflection of this knowledge comes imbued with intrinsic intelligibility. And yet, precisely because God's love is sufficient unto itself, creation is in another sense profoundly *pointless*, possessed of a beauty and a goodness of its own, existing not as some means to an end, but only so that God may "communicate his perfection, which is his goodness," to it.[32]

In short, those qualifications that we employed to protect the genuine transcendence peculiar to the doctrine of creation, qualifications that led us to reject a causal mechanism for creation and to deny that this doctrine is a "theory" in any conventional sense, lead us to assert that at the very heart of reality is an almost reckless gratuity, the mystery of beauty, goodness, and delight.[33] This gratuity and its transcendent self-sufficiency prevent us from "showing" creation as a separate causal mechanism. Still, we may nevertheless claim that this movement from non-existence to existence must be intrinsic to *every* causal transaction, even those that would seem to involve merely a transmutation of form.[34]

---

30. "But it does not belong to the First Agent, who is agent only, to act for the acquisition of some end; he intends only to communicate his perfection, which is his goodness; while every creature intends to acquire its own perfection, which is the likeness of the divine perfection and goodness. Therefore the divine goodness is the end of all things" (*ST* I, 44, 4). See also *ST* I, 18, 4.

31. See *ST* I, 18, 4.

32. Concerning the convertibility of truth and love, I would want to shift the definition of truth in a Balthasarian (or perhaps Augustinian) direction such that it names *both* idea, inasmuch as the Son is *logos* or *verbum* of the Father, and a deed, insofar as this word is always already both "spoken" by the Father, and precisely for this reason, also "speaking" in response to the Father.

33. On the claim that transcendence is only truly thought with *creatio ex nihilo*, and not, for instance, in various contemporary philosophical articulations of the ontological difference, see Hart, *The Beauty of the Infinite*, pp. 125-51.

34. This claim is not to be confused with those of the intelligent design school, that

For a causal transaction to occur, there must be a genuine *difference* between cause and effect; otherwise the result is not the production of an individuated effect that is "other" to the cause, but simply a replication of the cause. Yet for there to be genuine *difference* in the cause-and-effect relationship, there must be genuine *novelty* in that relationship.[35] The exis-

---

integrated systems such as the eye, being too complex for natural selection, warrant the inference of a designer. Whatever the merits of such claims, they do not yet ascend to a proper understanding of "creation" and, without serious theological qualifications, they lend themselves to theological misunderstandings that ultimately make a finite object of God. See Michael Behe, *Darwin's Black Box: The Biochemical Challenge to Evolution* (New York: Touchstone Books, 1996), pp. 210-16.

35. The question here is whether and in what sense there can be any real ontological novelty inasmuch as God, containing all the perfections of created being within himself and standing in no need of creation, is not increased by it. On the traditional view, novelty is registered only with respect to us, and not to God. As Dionysius the Areopagite puts it, "In reality there is no exact likeness between caused and cause, for the caused carry within themselves only such images of their originating sources as are possible for them, whereas the causes are located in a realm transcending the caused. . . ." Insofar as all the perfections of being and the first principles of everything subsist in the self-knowledge of God that causes them, the created world would seem merely to reflect these perfections in diminished form, neither adding to nor subtracting from God, nor altering the divine knowledge. Hence it would seem that we cannot talk of novelty *simpliciter*, but only from the side of the world. There is, of course, an important sense in which theology must maintain this claim in order to articulate God's transcendence, indifference, and immutability, and I wish to reaffirm all these. Still, there is a tension here, insofar as this requires us to think of effects simply as a deficient reflection of their cause and not as genuinely additive. For this would seem to deny real novelty in immanent cases of efficient causality and to make problematic the Father's reception of Christ's offering. The issue really turns, then, on whether it is possible to ascribe receptivity, and therefore the possibility of "surprise," to God without thereby negating the traditional affirmations of immutability, impassibility, plenitude, and simplicity. This is more than I can accomplish here, but I would suggest that Denys himself seems to have the resources to remedy the difficulty, when he conflates *eros* and *agape*, which then signifies "a capacity to effect a unity, an alliance, and a particular commingling of the Beautiful and the Good" (*The Divine Names*, trans. Colm Luibheid [New York: Paulist Press, 1987], 709d). It seems to me that only a rigorous articulation of the convertibility of the transcendentals with the *actus* of divine love and a recuperation of beauty as the transcendental that surprises and delights in proportion to the degree that it is grasped and "possessed" is sufficient to extricate us from this problematic. It is then possible to ascribe an inherent "surprise" to the divine being which is not the mark of a lack in the divine plenitude, but rather of its superlative beauty, but this then requires us to deepen our incorporation of the Father's delight in the beauty of the Son into our articulation of the logic of the trinitarian processions, and it requires us to understand hope and faith, not as lacks to be resolved by a knowledge

tence of individuated effects cannot therefore be reduced to the sum of their antecedent causes, nor can formal wholes be reduced to the mere sum of their component parts. Effects, rather, must bear an *analogical* relationship to their causes: being simultaneously similar to and different from their antecedents in ways that cannot be accounted for simply by adding their sum. And this analogy of being obtains not only between God as cause and the world as an effect of God's creative act that variably and remotely manifests the "traces" of its Creator, but between immanent causes and effects and between each level of their organization. Otherwise one's account of efficient causality suppresses the very difference upon which causality as such depends.

Modern physics and biology both seem to *deny* this "ontological novelty" in principle. On this view, every transmutation of form — and it matters not which forms — is merely a rearrangement of pre-existing bits effected through the conversion of energy, whose sum is constant, to entropy through work.[36] Yet this denial arguably trades on a double reduction and suppression, first of the aforesaid difference inherent in any causal transaction, but secondly and more to the point, of the formal specificity of wholes in relation to their aggregate parts. Hence physics and biology alike decline from what things actually are in their variety in order to treat them homogenously, to "treat them, just so far as they manifest

---

extrinsic to them, but rather as intrinsic to knowledge and perfected in knowledge's acquisition. See Pseudo-Dionysius, *The Divine Names*, 645c. I have attempted this argument in Hanby, "These Three Abide: Augustine and the Eschatological Non-Obsolescence of Faith."

36. The first law of thermodynamics states that the "total energy of a closed and isolated system is conserved; the energy of the universe, closed and isolated as it is, is constant." The second states that "the entropy [the disorder created when the energy in molecules is used, whereby no more energy can be converted into work] of an isolated system never decreases; the entropy of the universe strives to a maximum." R. A. Fisher, intellectual forefather of Richard Dawkins, reconceived the equilibrium of genetic fitness in terms analogous to these, which he called his "Fundamental Theorem." Notice how particular forms drop out of the equation. "It will be noticed that the Fundamental Theorem . . . bears some remarkable resemblances to the Second Law of Thermodynamics. Both are properties of populations, or aggregates, *true irrespective of the nature of the units which compose them*; both are statistical laws; each requires the constant increase of a measurable quantity, in the one case the entropy of a physical system and in the other the fitness . . . of a biological population" (R. A. Fisher, *The Genetical Theory of Natural Selection*, 2nd rev. ed. [New York: Dover, 1958], pp. 36-37, quoted, along with the laws of thermodynamics, in David J. Depew and Bruce H. Weber, *Darwinism Evolving: Systems Dynamics and the Genealogy of Natural Selection* [Cambridge, Mass.: MIT Press, 1997], pp. 252-61; emphasis added).

[themselves] in mechanical ways."[37] The quiddity, the actual formal and particular whatness of things in their variety, drops out of the equation altogether, along with the world itself.[38] Surely only a perverse and dangerous aesthetic could fail to see the genuine novelty, the self-transcending *more*, that *is* the rearrangement of bits.[39] In the maturation of an embryo into a person or the assembly of stones into a cathedral there intrudes a novel element denoting something real that did not previously exist: namely, a person or a cathedral, a whole composed of but transcending its component parts.[40] And this whole is possessed of a form — the why, rationale, or *logos* — that makes this collection of cells or this arrangement of stones intelligible and distinguishes it from some other arrangement in its generic, specific, and particular dimensions.[41]

37. David L. Schindler, "The Problem of Mechanism," p. 6.

38. Wolfgang Smith, *The Wisdom of Ancient Cosmology: Contemporary Science in Light of Tradition* (Oakton, Va.: Foundation for Traditional Studies, 2004), p. 143.

39. Balthasar, *The Glory of the Lord*, vol. I: *Seeing the Form* (San Francisco: Ignatius Press, 1982), p. 19. "In a world without beauty — even if people cannot dispense with the word and constantly have it on the tip of their tongues in order to abuse it — in a world which is perhaps not wholly without beauty, but which can no longer see or reckon with it: in such a world the good also loses its attractiveness, the self-evidence of why it must be carried out. Man stands before the good and asks himself why it must be done and not rather its alternative, evil. For this, too, is a possibility, and even the more exciting one: Why not investigate Satan's depths? In a world that no longer has enough confidence in itself to affirm the beautiful, the proofs of the truth have lost their cogency."

40. "We know the very forms that subsist in the object, the very forms, in fact, that *constitute* the object. However, we must not interpret this doctrine simplistically; it does not mean that we know the object 'without residue.' On the contrary: In the very act of knowing, we know the object to be 'more' than what is given, more than we are able cognitively to possess. In a word, we perceive the object as a *transcendent* entity. The object is transcendent, moreover, not simply because it has an existence of its own, but because it conceals within itself an immensity, an unfathomable depth" (Smith, *The Wisdom of Ancient Cosmology*, p. 62).

41. In different terms, Marjorie Grene makes a similar point with regard to evolutionary biology and the inclinations of its current orthodoxy, made explicit by Ernst Mayr, to favor "population" over "typological" thinking. She asks, "This view seems to undercut the very starting-point of any biological science, including the theory of evolution. How does one tell which 'individuals' (in the everyday sense) are parts of which larger 'species-individuals' except by noticing some kind of likeness among some and not others?" (Grene, "Introduction," in Marjorie Grene [ed.], *Dimensions of Darwinism: Themes and Counter-Themes in Twentieth Century Evolutionary Theory* [Cambridge: Cambridge University Press, 1983], p. 5).

My point here is not to propose a rationalist inference from intelligible species to "substantial form," to the forms residing in the mind of God as craftsman.[42] Rather, my point is to stress that the doctrine of creation is inextricably *aesthetic* in character, in both the objective and subjective dimensions of that term, precisely because it is inextricably *apophatic* in character. So far I have mostly stressed the negative, *apophatic* dimensions of the doctrine: the infinite difference between God and the world that surpasses any similarity between them, and by extension, what neither the doctrine of creation nor any of our scientific theorizing can properly say about God or the world. Indeed, this difference is primary, and to this extent, creation is simply another name for this unnamable difference between God and all that is not God. But if indeed God has no real relation to the world, as orthodox theology has always held, then the difference between the Father and the Son *in* God must be infinitely greater than the difference between God and the world.

Yet the *apophasis* of Christian theology, properly understood, is always a function of the determinate fullness of its positive *kataphatic* dimension. As Denys puts it, just because God is "the cause of all and as transcending all, he is rightly nameless and yet has the names of everything that is"; and Thomas follows him in insisting that those terms taken from creation which signify perfections — such as "life" and "goodness" — apply most properly to God, albeit in a fashion that exceeds our knowledge.[43] I wish now to claim that it is precisely this unspecifiable and immeasurable difference *from* God, the difference which frees *esse ipsum* from a real relation to *esse creatum*, that is the "basis" for the analogical similarity of effects *to* God. Put differently, just as God is unfathomably and thus *apophatically* mysterious precisely as a function of the *kataphatic* fullness of his determination as gratuitous, trinitarian love, so too is each thing inherently mysterious, as the finite effect and reflection of that same gratuity.[44] Our preced-

42. One might complain in this vein that my two examples are misleading in the manner of Paley's extrapolation from the design of a watch — which, like the cathedral, is evidently a piece of human artifice — to organic being, even if it is true that distinguishing the form of watches (and cathedrals) requires attention to purpose. Rather, my point — and it holds for both examples — is that we implicitly judge things as instances of this or that by virtue of what I am here calling their form.

43. See *ST* I, 13, articles 3, 5, and 6. See Pseudo-Dionysius, *The Divine Names*, 596c.

44. See *ST* I, 44, 4; 47, 1: "For he brought things into being in order that His goodness might be communicated to creatures, and be represented by them; and because His good-

ing discussion registered the *apophatic* dimension of this mystery in two ways: in the irreducibility of effects to causes and in the irreducibility of wholes to parts. Yet this very same irreducibility can be put positively, as an index of beauty and an overflowing excess of determinate form, and consequently is susceptible to an innumerable range of true predications.

To talk of form is necessarily to talk of something that transcends discrete particulars. At this point, one need not make the metaphysical commitment either to static, atemporal entities in a crudely Platonic sense or even to intelligible species in Thomas's Aristotelian sense to recognize that we cannot but invoke forms and thus transcendence in talking. And inasmuch as transcendent form is encountered only in particular discrete instantiations and in punctiliar instances of time, each of which bears an analogical relationship to all others, it seems necessary at any rate to maintain that the revelation of form, like Balthasar's *Gestalt,* has the character of an event comprised of, but irreducible to, its component parts.[45] It is precisely in this "event" character that "the truth and goodness of the depths of reality itself are manifested" from within the form itself, in all its concrete specificity.[46] The "transcendence" of particular forms is an inherent part of their immanence.

For example, earlier I suggested that it is the form of a person, a cathedral, a tree, or a game that determines these as meaningful wholes, and thus provides the why, rationale, or *logos* for designating them as such. We do not simply determine that something is a tree or a game from its material elements. While there may be a finite limit to the materials from which these can be composed, games and even trees can be composed from a vast array of materials, and other things that are not trees or games can be composed of these same materials. Moreover, the formal element of trees and games remains open to further, analogical elaborations in future encounters with trees and games yet unanticipated. So the form of a game is

---

ness could not be adequately represented by one creature alone, He produced many and diverse creatures, that what was wanting to one in the representation of the divine goodness might be supplied by another. For goodness, which in God is simple and uniform, in creatures is manifold and divided; and hence the whole universe together participates in the divine goodness more perfectly, and represents it better than any single creature whatever."

45. See D. C. Schindler's magnificent book, *Hans Urs von Balthasar and the Dramatic Structure of Truth: A Philosophical Investigation* (New York: Fordham University Press, 2004), pp. 163-254.

46. Balthasar, *The Glory of the Lord* I, p. 118.

not reducible to its matter, and yet in apprehending its formal element — the gameness, if you will, by which we identify this game as an instance of a kind — we do not isolate any discretely definable or fully knowable feature common to all games.[47] "Gameness," which transcends any discrete instance of game, is presupposed, even as it is concretely instantiated among games only as an analogical proportion between instances of games that is neither fully specifiable nor predictable. In unfolding the "meaningfulness" of superficial wholes, form is inherently self-transcending, and thus inherently receptive to a vast range of predications that unveil it. It is thus simultaneously concrete and elusive, and ever more the one for being the other. It is partly in this that its radiance and beauty consist.

When Balthasar refers to the beauty of form as the "primal phenomenon," he means that this encounter, in which all the advance preparation of the subject is drawn forth into the world by the intelligible splendor of the object, is the basis of all other activity. This insight is corroborated in quite different ways by figures as diverse as Polanyi and Wittgenstein, each of whom sees much tacit "stage-setting" coming to the fore in the event of meaning.[48] More simply, some pre-scientific intuition, some apprehension of form, some latent aesthetic judgment of meaningful patterns and wholes elicited by the things of the world themselves is always a precondition of scientific inquiry into their parts.[49] As a consequence, I would concur with Hart that "subjective certitude is an irreparably defective model of knowledge; it cannot correspond to or 'adequate' a world that is gratuity rather than ground."[50] Nevertheless, my contention for this excess, this "more" that escapes our grasp precisely in its concreteness and specificity,

47. See Wittgenstein, *Philosophical Investigations* (Oxford: Basil Blackwell, 1958), n. 66.

48. Balthasar, *The Glory of the Lord* I, p. 20. "Whoever insists that he can neither see it nor read it, or whoever cannot accept it, but rather seeks to 'break it up' critically into supposedly prior components, that person falls into the void and, what is worse, he falls into what is opposed to the true and the good." See also p. 26: "Our first principle must always be the indissolubility of form, and our second the fact that such form is determined by many antecedent conditions." For the "stage-setting" necessary for the simple act of naming, see Wittgenstein, *Philosophical Investigations,* n. 257.

49. Julius Kovesi maintains that, in all of the terms through which we know there is a formal element, a "why?" — strikingly similar, at least logically, to Aquinas's intelligible species — it is irreducible to the material elements out of which the objects of our knowledge are composed. Kovesi, *Moral Notions* (London: Routledge, 1967), pp. 7-12.

50. Hart, *The Beauty of the Infinite,* p. 138.

is not an *epistemological* or even phenomenological claim about the provisional and incomplete status of our scientific knowledge of things or their causal factors, as if improved knowledge could someday render this ignorance obsolete. This is rather an ontological claim about the very nature of how things must be if the world is created, and how our actions in living in the world "assume" it to be. Why shouldn't we affirm that "I," as a meaningful whole constituted no less biologically than socially through my relationships with nature and the artifices of convention, am just as real — indeed more real — than the DNA, or the various systems, of which I am composed?[51] Why shouldn't we insist that a cathedral, precisely as a cathedral, is just as real as the stones from which it is built, which are themselves composites of elemental and particular structures? Isn't it only a perverse aesthetic, and one that would in fact be impossible to maintain in practice with any consistency, that would require me to claim otherwise?[52]

Theological virtue and Christian faith train us to regard this excess as a reflection of the fact that each thing is always and intrinsically more than itself, and that it thus dispossesses itself of its own criterion of intelligibility, an indication of the analogical relationship of the world to God which is the watermark of creation's gratuity. To recognize this analogous character is to recognize a unity of aesthetics and teleology — not the ham-fisted teleology of Paley and the natural theologians who infer "purpose" from every biological "function" — but the teleology of de Lubac and the *nouvelle théologie*, who understand "nature" as *intrinsically* ordered and constituted precisely in relation to the excess of the supernatural.[53]

To say this is not to say that this God-world relationship can be *proved*. For as we have seen, God is no cause in the ordinary sense, and on these terms there can be no way to step "outside" of God to survey the God-world creation. Aquinas himself acknowledges this much: "This doctrine does not argue in proof of its principles, which are the articles of faith, but from them it goes on to prove something else."[54]

---

51. After all, while I may speak of "my DNA," my DNA cannot speak of its "me."

52. For all of his ranting against the aesthetic limitations of Christian thought, isn't it really Richard Dawkins's reduction of human beings to "gigantic lumbering robots" that is aesthetically bereft? See Dawkins, *The Selfish Gene* (Oxford: Oxford University Press, 1989), p. 18.

53. Henri de Lubac, *The Mystery of the Supernatural* (New York: Crossroad Herder, 1998), pp. 53-100.

54. *ST* I, 1, 8.

It would be a mistake, however, to interpret this conclusion as a sort of fideistic retreat. What it suggests, rather, is an alternative conception of rationality co-extensive with these ontological acknowledgments. To grasp this point is to begin to grasp how the unity of *apophasis* and *kataphasis,* the not-knowing that is theological knowing, might be integral to a genuine — indeed even properly scientific — grasp of reality. It is to begin to see how faith, along with the hope that expects gratuity, and the love that holds the world in a proper regard are both the ground and consummation of genuine knowledge. And it is to begin to grasp how only a knowledge grounded in faith may properly adequate a world whose gratuitous beauty, reflecting the beauty of God, resists being devoured by our ravenous gaze. It is to this understanding that we now turn.

Divine *scientia* and the Order of Science

Something like this "metaphysics of creation" underlies Thomas's remarks on the nature and order of knowledge in the very first question of the *Summa theologiae.* Article One asks "whether besides philosophy, any further doctrine is required." Thomas's response recapitulates this metaphysics.

> It was necessary for man's salvation that there should be a knowledge revealed by God, besides philosophical science built up by human reason. Firstly, indeed, because man is directed to God, as to an end that surpasses the grasp of his reason. . . . But the end must first be known by men who are to direct their thoughts and actions to the end.[55]

Nature — and especially sentient human nature — is intrinsically ordered, completed, and even defined not by its own immanent finality and so not, ultimately, by a static and fully graspable essence, but by its relation to one who always and forever exceeds our knowledge, even as he and the meaning of everything else are revealed in the life of Christ.[56] Our discussion in the previous section considered the aesthetic character of this doctrine

---

55. *ST* I, 1.

56. *ST* I, 44, 4, also ad 3. The matter of "definition" requires qualification since Aquinas insists (*ST* I, 6, 4) that a thing is good both from the divine goodness and by "the similitude of the divine goodness belonging to it," which is its own goodness.

primarily in its objective dimensions. We can now begin to make more apparent the "subjective" consequences of this understanding of creation and its implications by considering briefly Thomas's response to the query of article 2: whether *sacra doctrina* is knowledge *(scientia).*[57]

> We must bear in mind that there are two kinds of sciences. There are some which proceed from a principle known by the natural light of the intelligence, such as arithmetic, geometry and the like. There are some which proceed from principles known by the light of a higher science: thus the science of perspective proceeds from principles established by geometry, and music from principles established by arithmetic. So it is that sacred doctrine is a science, because it proceeds from principles established by the light of a higher science, namely the science of God and the blessed. Hence, just as the musician accepts on authority the principles taught him by the mathematician, so sacred science is established on principles revealed by God.[58]

There is a great difference, of course, between Thomas's *scientia* and modern science, which is largely indifferent to the metaphysical presuppositions inherent in its theorizing. Were we to try to mediate between them, we would have to negotiate this difference in much more rigorous terms than I can do here.[59] However, I am less concerned to recover the doctrine of subalternation in strictly Thomistic terms than to glean insights garnered from Thomas for the purpose of situating the practice of scientific inquiry within the context of a theological aesthetics commensurate with the doctrine of creation.

Thomas appropriates an Aristotelian conception of a science as that which proceeds from first principles in both propositional and real aspects, and he seems to mean by "higher" sciences those that are actually more fundamental and thus the basis for a subsequent knowledge dependent upon and yet irreducible to this basis. One mark of a "higher" science,

---

57. For an excellent account of Aristotelian *epistēmē* and Thomist *scientia,* and in what sense divine science, which is apprehended by faith, qualifies as *scientia,* see Rogers, *Thomas Aquinas and Karl Barth,* pp. 21-70.

58. *ST* I, 1, 2.

59. With regard to Aquinas's difference from Balthasar, from whom I have taken many cues here, I would want to develop within Thomas's account the aesthetic dimension which is typically only latent in it. For a controversial attempt at this, see John Milbank and Catherine Pickstock, *Truth in Aquinas* (London: Routledge, 2001).

in other words, is its asymmetrical relationship to those that are "beneath" it.[60] In Aquinas's example, music, insofar as it is measured, depends upon conclusions derived from the principles of arithmetic.[61] Mathematics, by contrast, does not depend upon music in the same way. Its principles are indifferent to those of music. One might say that mathematics has no real relation to music, while the reverse is not true.

For Aquinas, the pre-eminent case of this asymmetry occurs, of course, in our relationship to the *scientia divina,* the principle of *sacra doctrina* and the highest science by definition. *Scientia divina* is God's own self-knowledge, disclosed "really" in the incarnation of the Word which is *in principio* and "propositionally" in Scripture and *sacra doctrina,* which mediate *scientia divina* to the blessed — "*Sacra doctrina est impressio divinae scientiae.*" Because *scientia divina* is convertible with the divine *esse,* this claim is more than epistemological. It asserts the dependence of all truth on the intrinsic intelligibility of the divine being, "through which all our knowledge is set in order."[62] Yet what is most certain and intelligible in itself exceeds by definition the capacities of our reason and thus insinuates a caesura between the orders of being and knowledge.[63] Hence the principles of *sacra doctrina* — such as the fact of our creation — must be apprehended by faith.

Within a modern, residually rationalist juxtaposition of reason and faith, this point is almost inevitably misunderstood, and Thomas himself is somewhat ambiguous here, sometimes treating faith simply as a deficient form of knowing, despite the claim that faith is a form of participation in the divine mind and the *via* to the first truth. Thomas's view of faith is complex, and it is not my purpose here to resolve it.[64] For my part, I

60. We should add a distinction, however, between this order considered in an absolute sense, in which *sacra doctrina* is "higher" than any other science, and the relative order that obtains when an inquiry is undertaken for a particular purpose.

61. Though as Victor White notes, part of the point of the analogy is that the musician need not be a mathematician; nor conversely, is the latter a musician. Rather, inasmuch as the musician depends upon the truths of mathematics, he accepts the conclusions of the mathematician on authority — and often enough, we may assume, implicitly. Victor White, O.P., *Holy Teaching: The Idea of Theology According to St. Thomas Aquinas: A Paper Read to the Aquinas Society of London* (London: Blackfriars, 1958), pp. 3-21.

62. *ST* I, 1, 6, ad. 1.

63. *ST* I, 1, 5, ad. 1.

64. It is true that Aquinas, speaking of our knowledge, juxtaposes faith and the activity of knowing proper to *scientia* (see II-II, 1, 5), namely *scire* (he uses *cognoscere* for those

would contend that if one takes the divine *scientia* and our beatific participation in it as the paradigm case for *scientia* as such, and if one recognizes the integral place of beauty as both the object and "motive" of the intertrinitarian *kenosis* convertible with God's *scientia* (thus noting the circumincession of all the transcendentals in the circumincession of triune love), then a conception of rationality emerges to view in which it is possible to maintain both a distinction between faith and knowledge *and* their co-extension, so that an increase in knowledge does not eliminate faith *simpliciter,* but rather deepens and perfects it as it supplies what was heretofore lacking. There are once again both subjective and objective reasons for this. Subjectively speaking, if the *act* of faith is an act of responsive selfabandonment to another, then one's full possession of truth in the beatific vision marks the perfection of one's self-abandonment in wholehearted assent. Objectively, if "beauty" names a mysterious excess of form that delights and thus calls forth the *ecstasis* of assent, then as knowledge of the truth that is beauty increases, so too does mystery, and so too does faith, understood as the form of our assent to this mystery. Beauty grants to both mystery and faith a positive dimension in the apprehension of truth, rather than simply treating mystery as something to be overcome as the

---

cognitions of God obtained through "natural" reason). He insists that the *object* of faith cannot be an object of science and claims, on the basis of an understanding of faith as deficient knowing, that "faith and bliss are incompatible in one and the same subject" (*ST* I-II, 67, 3). Still, this faith is not merely the assent given to "supernatural" information about God in propositional form, as it appears from a rationalist perspective, and it is not juxtaposed to an un-graced reason, sufficient to itself as its own ground. Faith, after all, is also an act of the intellect moved by the will, a divine gift and a habit, a theological virtue, and to this degree, denotes a deeper participation in the mind of God, than "natural" reason, which even in its most elemental operations is also a participation (see *ST* I, 79, 2 and 4). Given the Aristotelian definition of a science as proceeding from first principles, which are real, unitary beings that "make both things and ideas work" by inhering in those things as forms and in the mind as intelligible species, and given that knowledge for Aquinas is a certain identity between the form and the mind, to say that we are united to the first principles of *sacra doctrina* through the habit of faith is simply to say that the intellect, while elevated, is not yet perfected through active union with the divine intellect. It is simply to note, manifestly, that we are not yet beatified. Such an interpretation might well be corroborated by *ST* I-II, 67, 3, ad 2, where Aquinas holds that "faith is the foundation inasmuch as it is knowledge: consequently when this knowledge is perfected, the foundation will be perfected also," and in his interesting claim that there was faith in the angels and in Adam in their original state (*ST* II-II, 5, 1). I develop all this in more detail with regard to Augustine in Hanby, "These Three Abide: Augustine and the Eschatological Non-Obsolescence of Faith."

vagaries of faith are resolved.[65] Here again, we see the coincidence of the *apophasis* and *kataphasis,* not simply because of the weakness of the intellect, but because of the inherently beautiful character of its object.

Given Aquinas's insistence that *scientia divina* sets all our knowledge in order and so is finally the key to the world's intelligibility, one must expect, on the one hand, that the refusal of faith is the refusal of something that should be apparent in some sense without faith and that the accounts of the world offering themselves as self-sufficient will be found wanting, on the other hand.

God, in the fullness and knowledge of his being, knows all the perfections of being, be they actual or potential. Consequently, God's self-knowledge in the generation of the Son from the Father is the origin and basis of all other truth, in both the "hard" sense of the "correspondence" of things to their divine archetypes, and in the derivative, "soft" (though epistemically prior) sense of the adequacy of our minds to those things. As we have seen, though, the inherently excessive and mysterious character of form marks a *caesura* between these two senses of truth, making our judgments of truth dependent upon analogical, "aesthetic" judgments of *adequatio* under the aspect of transcendentals: truth, unity, goodness, and beauty. This aesthetic character of truth is refused when faith is refused. More importantly, though: lost with it is also the *uni-verse* itself as an assemblage of analogically related motions and forms, constituted in themselves precisely as a function of their intrinsic relationship to each other and to their transcendent source.[66] In other words, the assertion of the pre-eminence of the *scientia divina* is not simply an extrinsicist dogmatic assertion of the juridical primacy of Christian doctrine over other fields of

65. It seems to me that D. C. Schindler is right to insist in "Does Love Trump Reason? Towards a Non-Possessive Concept of Knowledge" (in vol. 2 of these proceedings) that beauty, as the mutual coinherence of the good and the true, is the objective correlate of the circumincession of intellect and will, which must be understood in more Augustinian fashion as distinct and yet intrinsically inherent in one another, such that the will also knows, the intellect desires, and each, we might say, remembers, without any losing their proper distinction and identity. For Augustine, this is eminently true of God — "Your essence knows and wills immutably, and your knowledge is and wills immutably, and your will is and knows immutably" — and analogously of us. See Augustine, *Conf.,* XIII.16.19, 11.12.

66. Oliver, "Motion According to Aquinas and Newton," pp. 163-99. Oliver shows how after Newton, things are understood to be constituted intrinsically only in relation to themselves, and are most properly themselves in respect of their solitude. Relation becomes an extrinsic and "accidental" category, governed by force.

knowledge, but rather an ontological claim for the possibility of a single world to which our knowledge, in all its variegation, might intelligibly correspond.[67] Hence the *sacra doctrina* that issues from *scientia divina* differs from other sciences in that it does not have a discrete subject, distinct from other sciences, but rather treats the same objects as other sciences under the aspect of revelation: their relationship to God as origin and end that we recognized as creation.[68] The subject matter of *sacra doctrina* is simply God and everything else, because only such a *scientia* is properly capable of gathering the whole world in both its quantitative and qualitative dimensions into an ordered and intelligible unity without depriving it of *either* its specific and particular differences *or* its inherently gratuitous and mysterious character. To forsake this *scientia,* as Nietzsche understood, is either to refuse the possibility of this ordered unity, "to unchain the earth from its sun," or to attempt to impose unity through the power of a science that falsifies itself and the world by exercising a reductive tyranny over its objects.

While this might tell us what it means to refuse faith in *sacra doctrina* as integral to knowledge, it tells us little as yet about what it might mean to accept it. To say first that things are constituted in relation to one who exceeds them and whose self-knowledge is the ultimate truth about them is to say that this *scientia divina* is in some sense assumed and presupposed by rational inquiry as such, even if it is not apprehended (which, of course, it cannot be) or acknowledged. To suggest how that might be so, we might momentarily take recourse to an earlier point: that all inquiry begins from an infinitely tacit, pre-scientific apprehension of formal, meaningful wholes. This apprehension is inherently aesthetic and moral as well as indicative, or rather moral and aesthetic precisely in being indicative.[69]

67. As Eugene Rogers puts it, "The sublation of other sciences in sacred doctrine means not only that it may use them in manuductions. It means that they are deficient until taken up into it . . . things are intelligible just as they are under God; they are not under God in virtue of their being intelligible" (Rogers, *Thomas Aquinas and Karl Barth,* p. 51).

68. "Sacred doctrine, being one, extends to things which belong to different philosophical sciences, because it considers in each the same formal aspect, namely so far as they can be known through divine revelation" (*ST* I, 1, 4). See John Montag, "Revelation: The False Legacy of Suarez," in Milbank, Ward, and Pickstock, eds., *Radical Orthodoxy: A New Theology* (London: Routledge, 1999), pp. 38-63.

69. "Beauty, because it is to do with harmony, fittingness, and proportion, including that between being and knowing, is at once invisible and hyper-visible for Aquinas; it is oblique and yet omnipresent. But how does Beauty mediate? First of all, insofar as Being is

These apprehensions fall under the aspect of unity or oneness simply in the fact that they are the apprehension of *wholes,* and under the true insofar as they are intelligible and indicative. They fall under the good first, to the degree that they are imbedded in intentional action and are subsumed within historic intentional activity; second, to the degree that a "good" or "typical" *x* is entailed in the very notion of *x;* and third, insofar as we are moved to attend to these objects by desire.[70] These apprehensions fall under the beautiful to the degree that our intentions are elicited by the objects themselves and that the objects remain irreducible to those intentions, and insofar as such indicative judgments imply discriminations of *proportio, adequatio,* and *convenientia* in relation to the greater wholes in which the apprehended forms are a part or the analogical determination of instances of a kind.[71] Consequently, one can argue that our pre-scientific

---

something which resides in itself by a kind of integrity, Beauty is apparent as the measure of that integrity; secondly, insofar as Beauty is involved in the manifestation of things in their integrity, without which there could be no visibility, it is fundamental to knowledge; and thirdly, insofar as Beauty is linked with desire (Beauty being defined by Thomas as that which pleases the sight), it is crucial to the outgoings and ecstasies of the will and the Good. This role of Beauty, although little explicitly averred to by Aquinas, is actually essential to grasping the character of his theory of understanding. For when he speaks of a proportion between Being, knowledge and willing (of the Good), and not mathematical *proportionalitas* which would denote a measurable visible ratio, it is clear that Aquinas alludes to the ineffable harmony between the *transcendentals,* whereby in the finite world they coincide and yet are distinguished. Thus Beauty shows Goodness through itself and the Good leads to the True, yet we could never look at these relations as at a measurable distance. And this sense of something immanently disclosed through something else in an unmeasurable way, but in a fashion experienced as harmonious, is precisely something aesthetic. Every judgment of truth for Aquinas is an aesthetic judgment" (John Milbank and Catherine Pickstock, *Truth in Aquinas,* pp. 7-8).

70. Alasdair MacIntyre calls these "functional concepts," though he seems to restrict their range. See Alasdair MacIntyre, *After Virtue* (Notre Dame: University of Notre Dame Press, 1981), p. 58. See also Lesslie Newbigin, *Foolishness to the Greeks: The Gospel and Western Culture* (Grand Rapids: Eerdmans, 1986), pp. 65-94. The concept is implicit, less restrictively, in Augustine as well. See Augustine, *De Civitate,* XI.17, XII.1-2.

71. Newbigin, *Foolishness to the Greeks,* p. 81. "All science develops by the recognition of significant patterns, and the power to recognize them is a skill developed only through practice. There are no mathematical rules for deciding whether any configuration is a significant pattern or simply an accident. Our recognition of a significant pattern is an act of personal judgment for which there are no rules. It is a judgment of value: the pattern that represents something a human being finds meaningful in terms of intrinsic beauty or purpose. And although rules have been devised for quantifying the regularity in a series that may or

apprehension of those things which are to become the objects of our scientific knowledge occurs under those formal aspects which are the transcendental "properties" of being super-eminently contained and convertible with God's own self-knowledge and love, wherein essence and existence perfectly coincide, amounting to something like an intuition of the universal — and dare we say, a participation in the divine light — in the apprehension of the particular.[72]

I would nevertheless insist upon a twofold caesura built into the very structure of knowledge as constituted in relation to *scientia divina*. First, Thomas is adamant, for reasons we have rehearsed repeatedly now, that the *scientia divina*, though inherently intelligible, is unknowable to us in this life, a claim that once again warrants a return to sensible effects. Moreover this *scientia divina*, mediated discursively by *sacra doctrina*, is not simply the mysterious origin of being and knowledge, but also their last end and *telos*. And while, as Thomas says elsewhere, the last end is first in the order of intention — that is, while it is the principle of all our actions — it is last in the order of execution. It is achieved as the conclusion of a history of rightly ordered actions, through the medium of the habit of faith, and concretized in the sacramental life of the Church.[73] Thus, whereas on the one hand the constitution of things in relation to God means that God's knowledge of them is their ultimate truth and the source of our apprehension of truth, this truth, on the other hand, doubly exceeds our grasp: both by its very nature and as an end which is (for us) as yet unrealized. That is, there is a "gap" between the truth, understood as "correspondence" between our mind and its objects, and the constitutive truth of those objects as they are known in and issue from the *scientia divina*, where the distinction between being and knowledge vanishes. Truth in the latter sense is always more than can be captured by truth in the former

---

may not be random, the application of these rules by the scientist to a particular case is a matter of personal judgment that depends on skills acquired by practice and is not capable of quantification or verbal definition."

72. Though I think there are good grounds for doing so, I am not here attributing this formulation to Aquinas, as I recognize that this is a controversial point that would require a greater defense than I am prepared to mount in this essay.

73. *ST* I-II, 1, 1, ad. 1. I trust that this distinction is sufficient to protect the participatory character of human knowledge while simultaneously avoiding the conflation of the order of logic and the order of being. See David Burrell, *Faith and Freedom: An Interfaith Perspective* (Oxford: Blackwell, 2004), pp. 112-26.

sense, which means that the very objects constituted by the truth of *scientia divina* always exceed our knowledge of them, true though this knowledge may be, and always retain an element of "surprise" in their self-revelation. This "gap," in other words, is both the gap of an unknowing and of faithful expectation intrinsic to our knowing, but also of an excess of form generative of a surfeit of predication — not simply for the subjective reason that faithful expectation is intrinsic to judgment, but for the objective reason that the truth of things reveals itself in the splendor of a gratuitous beauty that the things themselves cannot contain.

Contrary, then, to the perennial modern concern that the incorporation of faith into knowledge would impose dogmatic strictures on the pursuit of knowledge, we can see, rather, that it is precisely this unity of faith and knowledge and the intrinsically supernatural character of nature, that would protect against such strictures and prevent human knowledge from reductively tyrannizing its objects. For it is precisely the doctrine of creation and the theological aesthetics attending it that insist that the truth of things is a beauty that can never finally be mastered or even fully apprehended, and indeed is not truly apprehended except in the *apophatic* knowledge of faith, hope, and love.

Creation, as an *apophatic* and aesthetic doctrine, thus provides inoculation against the disordered reductionism that ensues whenever any science arrogates to itself the mantle of "highest science," which it will inevitably do when it fails to acknowledge a just order of knowledge issuing from *scientia divina*. It is against this backdrop that we should seek to recover Aquinas's insistence that "[*sacra doctrina*] has no concern to prove the principles of other sciences, but only to judge them," and that "whatsoever is found in other sciences contrary to any truth of this science, must be condemned as false."[74]

We can now see that the order Aquinas envisions between the sciences is co-extensive with the understanding of creation I have tried to outline. We should understand this order, not in the sense of a univocally hierarchical order of knowledge mirroring the hierarchical dependence of all things on God. This is a sure conflation of the orders of being and logic and a violation of the *apophatic* character of creation. Rather we should understand that the irreducibly formal and aesthetic character of the created order is reflected in the irreducibility of the forms of our

74. *ST* I, 1, 6, ad. 2.

knowledge to each other. Indeed it is the distinction between forms, and thus between first principles, that generates the distinction in sciences for Aquinas, as it was the *esse* of God, which is formal in respect of every form, that made possible a science, through the habit of faith, of *omnia quaecumque*.

In other words, we are now prepared to say that the irreducibility of one branch of knowledge to the other, even or perhaps especially when they regard the same object, reflects the excessive character of the forms of composite things. This would be most especially true for Aquinas at the point where he would invoke the real distinction between a thing's being and essence, but the point holds for each level of a thing's organization, and for the greater wholes of which they themselves are parts. Each composite, existent thing is both one and many several times over; none of the ways that it is one is reducible to the ways in which it is many, and we are hard-pressed for a way to specify either this unity or this excess, except in judgments of aesthetic "adequacy" whose ineffable measure remains hidden. We cannot *explain* a bird, much less its activity in building a nest, through the language of physics, chemistry, or mechanics — even though each of these may give us true descriptions of the bird and its activity — without implicit reliance upon what are effectively formal and final causes and thus without recourse to aspects of reality that simply cannot be translated into the languages of the quantitative sciences.[75]

Similarly, drawing on Aquinas's own familiar illustration, it is not possible, as Newbigin elsewhere notes, to render an entirely "quantitative" account of a musician's art, to account for her every movement, and the external effect of every sounded note in terms of mechanical, chemical, and electrical principles.[76] These accounts would indeed be valid, as far as they go, but they do not go far enough to attain to the level of *understanding* the music as music. It will not suffice to treat music merely as event rather than action, but the elimination of final causality is not the only deficiency in such reductions. One must also grasp the music's form, which is unfolded "internally" by themes, tones, and note sequences, and informed "externally" by thematic and even textual antecedents which constitute the

---

75. I owe this example to Lesslie Newbigin, *Foolishness to the Greeks*, p. 83.

76. And examples could be compounded. Consider the question of how my DNA translates into "me" or the neurobiological attempts to resolve the so-called mind-body problem.

intelligibility of this form in relation to others.[77] (One thinks of Bach's *Mass in B Minor* or *St. John's Passion* here.) All of these facets occur in the interchange between the intentions and circumstances of the composer, the performers, the circumstances surrounding the performance, and the audience's encounter with it. And yet for this reason, the "meaning" of the music as music is not reducible to any of these facets, and is not patient of quantitative reduction.[78] Indeed, the more fully one has understood all of

---

77. Recall again Balthasar's remark: "Our first principle is the irreducibility of form, and our second the fact that such form is determined by many antecedent conditions" (*Glory of the Lord* I, p. 26).

78. Many critics, including David Berlinski and Michael Behe, have famously criticized Richard Dawkins's attempt to generate a computer algorithm simulating the effect of natural selection in preserving a piece of genetic code, an experiment that has spawned a rash of computer-generated genetic algorithms and endless debates over their viability. In Dawkins's version of the experiment, a computer program would sort through successive rounds of typing, saving the random characters until they achieved a Shakespearean target phrase — ME-THINKS IT IS LIKE A WEASEL. In Dawkins's version the experiment obviously fails because it smuggles back into its processes the design which it excluded by selecting figures one at a time as they approached the "target phrase," but it seems to me that this line of criticism (and the counter-attempt to generate a better algorithm) misses the more fundamental point. The mere aggregation of letters is not enough to make this assemblage an intelligible phrase, much less a *Shakespearean* phrase, each of which depends on a certain intelligible form constituted partly by its antecedent conditions. First as a simile, the meaning of the phrase is intrinsically dependent on the relation between two extrinsic objects referred to, but not contained within the phrase: the antecedent to "it" (which is a cloud) and the weasel, whose meaning is alluded to but not expressed. Its *Shakespearean* meaning within the context of the play depends not only upon the repartee between Hamlet and Polonius (*Hamlet*, act iii, scene 2), and Shakespeare's intention in placing them there, but also upon a complex interchange between the director, the venue, the actors, and the audience. "Reading the text of *The Winter's Tale*, for example, makes an impression that is vastly different from the one received in seeing it performed. The meaning of the play in this case becomes different, as it would if it were played by different actors, under a different director, or even before a different audience. In short, drama presents a complex phenomenon: an overall meaning is given (which does not mean an obvious or univocal meaning), but it is not "dropped in" simply from above. Rather, this meaning is conditioned in surprising ways by the concrete medium or media that communicate it. At the same time, these media are not scattered and formless; they are gathered into a unity by the very meaning they mediate" (D. C. Schindler, *The Dramatic Structure of Truth*, p. 18). If the characters in Dawkins's example are supposed to serve as an analogue for genetic code, then the meaning of these characters should presumably serve as the analogue for the phenotypic trait expressed by the code. But inasmuch as the meaning of the characters is intrinsically constituted in relation to something not contained within them, one suspects that this analogy, carried through to its conclusions, leads to places Dawkins does not want to go.

these aspects of music — the more one has actually heard it — the more fully one is cognizant of just how much the music by its very nature exceeds what we call understanding, and that its intelligibility is not reducible to a singular "meaning," separate from its unfolding.

Whenever one form of knowledge elevates itself above its perspectival station to the position of *sacra doctrina,* as sciences inevitably tend to do whenever they fail to recognize a "just order" of knowledge, the science becomes disordered. In so doing that science falsifies both itself and its object, and to just that degree, ceases to be scientific in any sense of the word. For what the object of knowledge actually is will most certainly drop out of the equation altogether.[79] "Obliterate ontological distinctions — obliterate hierarchy — and nothing at all remains; in a word, ontological homogeneity is tantamount to non-existence. . . . At the end of the physicist's analysis, what remains is not one substance, but no substance at all."[80]

It is precisely in its ability to account for the aesthetic "whatness" and the supernatural *telos* of things — that is, the irreducible splendor and glory of things that points beyond those things in their very shimmering — that the peculiar manner of knowing that is Christian faith, and the world which it believes to be creation, can lay greater claim to rationality than its immanentist, naturalistic rivals, incoherently instantiated in a fragmented and disordered university curriculum wherein each discipline vies with the other to reduce the world to its special province. For this faith completes as the last truth about things what we inchoately perceive to be the first truth about them, and in so doing does greater justice to the nature of mundane things as *revelabilia* which are resistant, by virtue of their beauty, to the immanent closure we would impose upon them, and insistent, by virtue of this same beauty, upon the surplus of predications this faith calls forth. This faith — ordered to this revelatory glory — is therefore truer than its rivals to the ways we mundanely live, and move, and have our being. For unlike them, Christian faith does not trade on the self-contradictory suppression of purpose and form that would be obvious, had we eyes to see and ears to hear.[81]

---

79. That is, the algorithms of natural selection, like the laws of thermodynamics or of the so-called free market, are utterly indifferent to the things they organize.

80. Wolfgang Smith, *The Wisdom of Ancient Cosmology,* p. 143.

81. "What then, are living things? They are things that defy this crumbling into dust [of entropy], at least for awhile . . ." (Dennett, *Darwin's Dangerous Idea,* p. 69).

This, I think, is how we should interpret Aquinas's remark that "[*sacra doctrina*] has no concern to prove the principles of other sciences, but only to judge them."[82] Because creation is not an event *in* the world, but rather the gratuitous event *of* the world in the splendor of its difference in unity, it does not fall to Christian theology to establish the first principles of physics or biology. Each form of knowledge, quite properly, retains a certain measure of autonomy appropriate to its specific subject matter, its perspectival location, and the ends informing the inquiry. And the academic disciplines need not fear that a deep recovery of the Christian imagination would result in any simple, fideistic judgment of their conclusions.

It does not follow from this, however, that Christian theology must be silent regarding those things about which physics or biology speaks. And in a world where God's triunity is an irrelevant piece of theological arcana, a world not yet ready to hear — perhaps no longer even capable of comprehending — the doctrine of creation and its implications for knowledge and truth, the preponderance of Christian scholarly energies may be directed to exercising this critical function. Still, this is not to say that Christian faith cannot make positive contributions to scientific inquiry as well, and indeed it does fall to Christians working within scientific disciplines as well as the humanities to seek to restore the physical sciences to metaphysical integrity, and thus to account for the physical evidence — all the complications of that term notwithstanding — in manners consistent with the latent implications of a trinitarian understanding of being as the unfolding and exchange of love, a prospect destined to transfigure the meaning of that evidence from the inside out.[83] This remains a remote

---

82. *ST* I, 1, 6, ad. 2.

83. David L. Schindler offers the work of David Bohm in physics, not as an example of "Christian physics" but of a physics that asks what are, from the Christian point of view, the right kinds of questions — and that appears to account for "the data" as well as its rivals within an alternative framework. (Alister McGrath makes a similar point with regard to Bohm.) As another case in point, we might return to the *a priori* Malthusianism of Richard Dawkins. Dawkins appears to take great pleasure in telling us that "during the minute it takes me to compose this sentence, thousands of animals are being eaten alive; others are running for their lives, whimpering with fear; others are being slowly devoured from within by rasping parasites; thousands of all kinds are dying of starvation, thirst and disease." True enough, but surely many of these and other animals are mating and caring generously, even sacrificially for their young, a fact that remains a philosophical puzzle for evolutionary theory for reasons that I cannot elaborate upon here. The point is that it is possible to accommodate this "data" within two different registers. And it is only an *a priori* — and perverse

practical possibility given the material, financial, and institutional impediments facing such ambitions. Yet this proposition is not at all fantastic, theoretically speaking. There is some hope with regard to physics, though the results have yet to prove satisfactory.[84] And there is ample precedent for hope in the patristic appropriation of Neoplatonism and the medieval retrieval of Aristotle, both of which arguably served less to synthesize the language of philosophy and faith than to put the language of philosophy in the service of its true master.[85]

— "aesthetic" judgment that prizes violence and scarcity over love as the context of these events. See Schindler, *Heart of the World, Center of the Church*, p. 173, fn 51. See Alister McGrath, *Dawkins' God: Genes, Memes, and the Meaning of Life* (London: Blackwell, 2005), p. 56. Dawkins, *River Out of Eden: A Darwinian View of Life* (New York: HarperCollins, 1995), p. 132.

84. Though physics, too, undoubtedly has its hubris, I find it to be much more agreeable in this regard than the more virulent strains of evolutionary biology. In particular, the controversial concept of "emergence," which stipulates that physical principles of organization have collective origins, and that systems operate as a function of their component parts while simultaneously transcending them, seems to hold particular promise for theological dialogue. For instance, the following remarks by Robert Laughlin, Stanford professor and 1998 Nobel laureate in physics, are at least superficially congruent with the conclusions drawn by Newbigin and argued in this paper, though I would not want to overstate this congruency.

> I think primitive organizational phenomena such as weather have something of lasting importance to tell us about more complex ones, including ourselves: Their primitiveness enables us to demonstrate with certainty that they are ruled by microscopic laws but also, paradoxically, that some of their more sophisticated aspects are insensitive to the details of those laws. In other words, we are able to prove in these simple cases that the organization can acquire meaning and life of its own and begin to transcend the parts from which it is made.

> What physical science thus has to tell us is that the whole being more than the sum of its parts is not merely a concept but a physical phenomenon. Nature is regulated not only by a microscopic rule base but by powerful and general principles of organization. Some of these principles are known, but the vast majority are not. New ones are being discovered all the time. At higher levels of sophistication the cause-and-effect relationships are harder to document, but there is no evidence that the hierarchical descent of law found in the primitive world is superseded by anything else. Thus if a simple physical phenomenon can become effectively independent of the more fundamental laws from which it descends, so can we. I am carbon, but I need not have been. I have a meaning transcending the atoms from which I am made.

Robert B. Laughlin, *A Different Universe: Reinventing Physics from the Bottom Down* (New York: Basic Books, 2005), pp. xiv-xv.

85. See Hart, *The Beauty of the Infinite*, pp. 125-51.

Michael Hanby

Perhaps most importantly, it does fall to theologically literate Christians working across the spectrum of academic disciplines to speak out when physics, biology, or any other discipline, denying the finite and perspectival character of their own takes upon the infinite, begin to *become* theology, as they inevitably intend to do when they deny their reliance upon metaphysics and when they fashion as a foil for themselves a "god" who is less than the self-sufficient love revealed in the incarnation. In revealing the divine nature as the fullness of love, the incarnation also reveals the world as the utterly gratuitous fruit of divine generosity, possessed of a fullness of its own which ultimately defies the absolutizing claims of mechanistic or reductive explanation. I have attempted to show that all of our theorizing presupposes such fullness even as, left to our own devices, we would exclude and suppress it. The recovery of this fullness, and the faith in its generous origin, which allows us properly to grasp it, is the key to the recovery not only of the unity of the world, but also of any knowledge of it that finally deserves to be called science.

Eternal Happening:
God as an Event of Love

Antonio López

Introduction

In order to ponder anew the mystery of love, without which man's "life re-mains senseless" and "incomprehensible,"[1] I would like to appeal in this essay to Balthasar's understanding of God as an "eternal happening." This insight attempts to bring together what the Triune God reveals of himself in Jesus Christ: he reveals himself as love (1 Jn 4:16), and as a love that is both an eternal being *(esse)* and an eternal event *(Ereignis, Geschehen).*[2] In Christ, man has come to learn that love is not a transient emotion, but rather the mystery that encompasses all of being: from the moment when there was nothing but God (Gen 1:1) to the present instant in which man lives out his existence (2 Cor 5:14-15). The essence of being is love. Every-thing and everyone finds its proper place within this eternal mystery. At the same time, the Incarnate Word has disclosed that the mystery of love that constitutes us (Jn 1:3; Col 1:15-20) is pure gift of himself. Divine love is an ever-new gift of himself to himself *(Hingabe)* and an undeserved gift of himself to us (Eph 2:4; Rom 8:32). God *is* an *event* of love.[3]

---

1. John Paul II, *Redemptor hominis*, 10.

2. Hans Urs von Balthasar, *Theo-Drama: Theological Dramatic Theory* (= *TD*), vol. 5: *The Last Act*, trans. Graham Harrison (San Francisco: Ignatius Press, 1983), p. 67.

3. The centrality of this concept in Balthasar's thought is indicated by, among others, Gerard F. O'Hanlon, S.J., *The Immutability of God in the Theology of Hans Urs von Balthasar* (Cambridge: Cambridge University Press, 1990); Karl J. Wallner, "Ein trinitarisches Strukturprinzip in der Trilogie Hans Urs von Balthasars?" *Theologie und Philosophie* 71 (1996): 532-46; Guy Mansini, "Balthasar and the Theodramatic Enrichment of the Trinity,"

To better perceive the richness of Balthasar's proposal, this article has been divided into five parts. After an introductory philosophical analysis of the term "event," which indicates the main characteristics of this complex term, attention shifts to the person of Christ in order to delineate what he reveals of the "eventful nature" of God.[4] The third part of the paper attempts to elucidate a notion of person that is fitting for the portrayal of the divine love Christ revealed as an agapic threefold donation. This understanding of the divine hypostases will then enable us in the fourth part to approach the richness indicated by the mysterious unity of *esse* and event. This section shows in what sense the divine being is "ever-greater." The final section offers some remarks on the implications for human existence that emerge from this understanding of God as event.

A Preliminary Approximation

In our common parlance, the term "event" stands for "the possible or factual happening of anything."[5] The association of "event" with "happening" indicates that an event is the presentation of a phenomenon to someone as a living "pro-vocation," which, without predetermining his answer, requires man to acknowledge it, that is to say, not simply to take notice of it, but rather to welcome it. In comparison to what took place before it, the

---

The Thomist 64 (2000): 499-519; Stephen Fields, S.J., "The Singular as Event: Postmodernism, Rahner, and Balthasar," *American Catholic Philosophical Quarterly* 77, no. 1 (2003): 93-111; Angelo Scola, *Hans Urs von Balthasar: A Theological Style* (Grand Rapids: Eerdmans, 1995), pp. 53-64.

4. On the importance of the category of event see, among others, Martin Heidegger, *On Time and Being,* trans. Joan Stambaugh (New York: Harper & Row, 1972); Heidegger, "Postscript to 'What Is Metaphysics?'" in *Pathmarks,* ed. William McNeill (Cambridge: Cambridge University Press, 1999), pp. 231-38. Jean-Luc Marion offers an interesting analysis of the meaning of "event," which, in contrast to the one presented here, aims to illustrate how the given phenomenon, and givenness as such, needs to be considered apart from any logic of causality. See Jean-Luc Marion, *Being Given: Toward a Phenomenology of Givenness,* trans. Jeffrey L. Kosky (Stanford, Calif.: Stanford University Press, 2002); Luigi Giussani, *He Is If He Changes,* Supplement no. 7/8 to *30 Days* (Rome, 1994); Luigi Giussani, Stefano Alberto, and Javier Prades, *Generare tracce nella storia del mondo* (Milan: Rizzoli, 1998); Joseph Ratzinger, *The God of Jesus Christ: Meditations on God in the Trinity,* trans. Robert J. Cunningham (Chicago: Franciscan Herald Press, 1979).

5. Oxford English Dictionary, s.v. "event."

event is unforeseeable and unpredictable; its unexpected occurrence does not seem to respect the chain of cause and effect that was previously in place. In this regard, although the event is never completely alien to what came before it, its appearance can seem remarkably close to chance.[6] The ostensible indeterminacy of its origins undergirds the event's incomprehensibility. Although no one can ever give a full account of the entire event, this incomprehensibility does not leave an interlocutor facing an absolute void of meaning. On the contrary, the incomprehensibility itself places its addressee in relation to the whole because through its form, the event introduces him into a deeper, richer dimension of the landscape of being. This is why the "ungraspability" of the event should not be perceived as an objection to or jettisoning of reason, but rather as the possibility for reason to discover truth. It is its connection to the whole that enables the event, by its sheer appearing, to reshape and enrich the present and to sharpen human expectations. Once it has come to pass, the event cannot be either undone or called back. What the event bears in itself makes wonder and gratitude its most fitting reception.[7]

Although some events have a greater subjective and objective significance, all events, even those that have fallen under the shadow of what is (always regrettably) written off as "obvious," have this eventful character. In fact, the most important events in life — like encountering the beloved, the birth of a child, or being granted an undeserved forgiveness — always refresh one's own gaze and allow human memory to rediscover the depth of every being (one's very self included) and its surprising and permanent coming-to-be, coming-to-itself.[8] As Guardini

6. Severinus Boethius, *De consolatione philosophiae*, V, 1.

7. To ascribe this importance to "wonder" distances our reflection from the negative Heideggerian question, "Why are there essents rather than nothingness?" (Martin Heidegger, *An Introduction to Metaphysics*, trans. Ralph Manheim [New Haven: Yale University Press, 1975], p. 1). Wonder originates within the surprise that the other *is*, and not that that which is could *not* be. Cf. Aristotle, *Metaphysics* 982b, 11-19. To answer Heidegger's question, Balthasar writes that "only a philosophy of freedom and love can account for our existence, though not unless it also interprets the essence of finite being in terms of love" (Hans Urs von Balthasar, *Love Alone Is Credible* [= *LA*], trans. D. C. Schindler [San Francisco: Ignatius Press, 2004], p. 143).

8. Although for obvious reasons we cannot delve into this matter, we need to indicate that *memory* is neither a simple "looking back" nor an attempt to bring into the present that which has already come to pass. Without denying the understanding of memory as "recollection," we would like to highlight a eucharistic conception of memory as the retrieval of

states, "in the experience of great love . . . all of what takes place becomes an event within it."[9]

The Latin root of the term, *ex-venio*, reminds us that event means "that which comes out from." Unless one wishes to maintain the Heraclitean reduction of what appears to sheer phenomenality, it is necessary to recognize that in every e-vent there is a distinction between an appearance and a "whence" — what Balthasar calls "form" *(Gestalt)*. The event brings into the present both its contingent manifestation and, in it, its grounding depth. This depth, however, should not be identified with another particular being, but rather with the transcendent ground (being itself) that freely discloses itself without losing itself in the process. To say that beings do not "come from" themselves requires the recognition of a mysterious and real distinction between the essence and existence of every being, "between the unity of all existing beings that share in being and the unity of each individual being in the uniqueness and incommunicability of its particular being," and, ultimately, between beings and a transcendent being, which philosophy calls the absolute, and theology, God.[10] It is this final distinction that both prevents us from conceiving the transcendent ground as another being among beings — thus collapsing metaphysics into ontotheology — and allows us to discover the co-extensiveness of being and freedom without, on the one hand, welding being to history, or, on the other, abandoning beings to a capricious, undetermined, absolute free-

---

interiority. Memory is then the capacity of the human gaze to rest on the dual movement of being and appearance, which, beginning with the form, is led on to the ground of the form, a ground that is older than the one who remembers. It is in this sense that "recollection" is included in memory.

9. Romano Guardini, *Das Wesen des Christentums* (Würzburg: Werkbund Verlag, 1949), p. 12: "In der Erfahrung der grossen Liebe sammelt sich die ganze Welt in das Ich-Du, und alles Geschehende wird zu einem Begebnis innerhalb dieses Bezuges."

10. *TD* 5, pp. 67-68. Cf. Aquinas, *De Ver.* q. 27, a. 1, ad 8, for his understanding of *"compositio realis."* For Balthasar the ontological difference can be unfolded into four parts: the first between the I and the Thou; the second between being and that which exists; the third between essence and existence; the last one, a "theological difference," between beings and being itself, which freely and gratuitously puts everything into existence. Cf. Balthasar, *The Glory of the Lord,* vol. 5: *The Realm of Metaphysics in the Modern Age,* trans. Oliver Davies et al. (San Francisco: Ignatius Press, 1991), pp. 429-50. See also Martin Heidegger, *Identity and Difference,* trans. Joan Stambaugh (Chicago: Chicago University Press, 2002); John D. Caputo, "Heidegger's 'Dif-ference' and the Distinction Between Esse and Ens in St. Thomas," *International Philosophical Quarterly* 20 (1980): 161-81.

dom.[11] Beings, then, can be considered events inasmuch as they appear proceeding from being itself, the ever-greater ground that does not have a "beyond itself."

If the "coming-from" of the event brings to light a distinction between the phenomenon and its origin, it also indicates that being is an event of inexhaustible disclosure. The self-manifestation of being is always richer, not only in the sense that there is always something new (this would reduce the infinity of the ground to a quantifiable dimension and reduce being to beings), but, more deeply, in the sense that it is a gratuitous, absolutely free manifestation.[12] If this self-presentation were simply mechanical or haphazard, then being would never surprise the way it in fact does, nor would this be an act of being's entrusting itself to finite freedom.[13] At

---

11. To think of the theological difference in these terms implies rooting the ontological difference in a theological difference, i.e., a difference in God. In order to preserve the difference between God and beings, however, the difference in God needs to be thought in terms of positivity and not, as is the case of Hegel, in terms of negativity. This positive differentiation is not adequately conceived unless it is posed in personal terms, i.e., to talk about difference in the absolute requires talking about personal difference. We shall return to this argument later.

12. This is why Balthasar considers truth as both *alḗtheia* and *'emeth;* see *Theo-Logic* (= *TL*), vol. 1: *Truth of the World*, trans. Adrian J. Walker (San Francisco: Ignatius Press, 2000). See David C. Schindler, *Hans Urs von Balthasar and the Dramatic Structure of Truth: A Philosophical Investigation* (New York: Fordham University Press, 2004). Studies on Balthasar's use of analogy and his speech about God should bear in mind that for the Swiss theologian, the propositional understanding of truth, and of truth as correspondence *(adequatio),* needs to be viewed within the perception of being as unveiling *(alḗtheia)* — although this term shares some resonances with Heidegger's, their elucidations cannot be (simply) equated. Any attempt to characterize Balthasar's style as "allegorical," "metaphorical," "poetic," and thus "imprecise," should simultaneously take account of his ontological understanding of truth to avoid any hasty conclusions. Cyril O'Regan clarifies that Balthasar, like Heidegger, sees that the overcoming of ontotheology is also a matter of language. Nevertheless, unlike Heidegger, Balthasar tries to find "forms of theological language that let Being be, that allow for and celebrate the gratuitousness and mystery of disclosure." Cf. Cyril O'Regan, "Von Balthasar's Critique of Heidegger's Genealogy of Morality," in *Christian Spirituality and the Culture of Modernity,* ed. Peter J. Casarella and George P. Schner, S.J. (Grand Rapids: Eerdmans, 1998), p. 47.

13. This seems to be the limitation of Plotinus, for whom the One generates without freely willing it, and of every pantheistic understanding of the relation between God and the world. See Plotinus, *The Enneads* V, 1, 6; VI, 8. It is worth noting that Balthasar entitles the section dedicated to the ontological difference in *Glory 5,* "The Miracle of Being and the Fourfold Distinction" (*GL* 5, pp. 613-27).

the risk of being rejected or cast into oblivion, being, through the phenomenon, gives itself and waits for the addressee to let itself be introduced by the hand of beauty into an unexpected, unforeseen new region of being. In order to grasp the nature of the freedom proper to the event's "coming-to-be" from a luminous and mysterious ground, it is necessary to see that the event's occurrence owes its appearance to its very ground. The freedom that characterizes this manifestation does not only entail that whatever has come or is coming to be could have not taken place. It also indicates that what comes to be is, radically and totally, given. In this respect one could say that gift and e-vent are co-extensive. This perichoresis, therefore, resists the interpretation of event as simply a "gift" for the person to which it happens. Rather, it suggests a real identification between the being-given of every phenomenon and its ontological structure.[14] Hence, the e-vent does more than demand acknowledgment of its unknown origin, and of its difference from and unity with that origin and with all other beings. Since this "coming-from" is understood not in terms of necessity or emanation, but rather of gratuitous freedom, the coming-to-be of the event also discloses its own constitutive givenness.

Events — whose historical singularity can have either a positive or a negative meaning, bear a greater or lesser importance, and involve a single phenomenon or a great many — are the free and ever-fruitful manifestations of being. The event, unexpectedly coming out from something other than itself, is that phenomenon in which being shows itself, gives itself, and speaks itself in order to call the human being into its own infinite beauty.[15] Thus, the infinitely rich variety of the phenomena indicates both an "exuberance" and a certain disclosure of the nature of their origin. As every musical composition evokes its composer in the concrete-

14. For the relation between being and gift, see Kenneth L. Schmitz, *The Gift: Creation* (Milwaukee: Marquette University, 1982); Claude Bruaire, *L'être et l'esprit* (Paris: PUF, 1986); Klaus Hemmerle, *Thesen zu einer trinitarischen Ontologie* (Einsiedeln: Johannes Verlag, 1976); Gisbert Greshake, *Der dreieine Gott* (Freiburg: Herder, 1997); *La Trinità e il pensare. Figure, percorsi, prospettive,* ed. Piero Coda and Andreas Tapken (Rome: Città Nuova, 1997); *Abitando la Trinità. Per un rinnovamento dell'ontologia,* ed. Piero Coda and L'ubomír Zák (Rome: Città Nuova, 1998); and Jean-Luc Marion, *De surcroît* (Paris: PUF, 2001), in addition to the work already mentioned.

15. Balthasar, *Epilog* (Freiburg: Johannes Verlag, 1987), pp. 45-66. The ontological difference briefly mentioned in the preceding pages precludes any pantheistic interpretation of being's showing, giving, and saying itself.

ness of his or her existence, phenomena also bear traces of their own unfathomable, transcendent ground. Their "e-ventful" dimension, always within a *maior dissimilitudo,* resembles in a certain way the nature of that being, that ultimate source, God, who is always infinitely interior and infinitely transcendent.[16]

A Unique Presence

The challenge facing any discourse on God that attempts to go beyond the simple affirmation of his existence is to avoid either, on one side, ascribing to human logic the capacity to express adequately the divine logic — as Hegel tried to do — or, on the other, upholding an extreme apophatic theology, which, in striving to free God from the clumsy web of human concepts, ends up not in the Gregorian "radiant darkness," but in the Plotinean opacity within which nothing can be said about the One because the One is not.[17] To be able to say something about God's eventful nature without claiming first to hollow out its mystery and then to explain

---

16. Augustine, *Confessions* III, 6, 11: "*Tu autem eras interior intimo meo et superior summo meo.*" Augustine expressed the existential and pedagogical implications of this statement in another equally famous aphorism: "*noli foras ire, in te ipsum redi; in interiore homine habitat veritas*" (*De vera religione,* XXXIX, 72). The principle of similitude, as Kenneth L. Schmitz suggests, needs to be thought of as the communication of being for what being is, act. Undoubtedly, one needs to recognize that "the co-presence of agent and recipient (determined by the axiom of agency) need not require the same isomorphic formality in both, as when an organism reproduces another of its own kind and likeness" (Schmitz, *The Gift,* p. 124). Bearing this in mind, the daunting and ever-present task of thinking what the *actus essendi* proper to the absolute is and how it can be conjugated with the *act of being* proper to finite beings could benefit significantly if also approached from a theological standpoint. See *TD* 5, pp. 61-109; Hans Urs von Balthasar, *Theo-Logic: Theological Logical Theory,* vol. 2: *Truth of God,* trans. Adrian J. Walker (San Francisco: Ignatius Press, 2004), pp. 81-85.

17. Plotinus, *The Enneads* V, 3, 13; V, 4, 1; VI, 9, 6; Gregory of Nyssa, *Life of Moses,* trans. Abraham J. Malherbe and Everett Ferguson (New York: Paulist Press, 1978), II, 163, 10; *TL* 1, p. 34. Jean-Luc Marion, *L'idole et la distance: Cinque études* (Paris: Grasset, 1977). It is worth noting that the main philosophical systems of Schelling and Hegel are secularized philosophical reflections on the triune mystery, as some have already illustrated. See Claude Bruaire, *Logique et religion chrétienne dans la philosophie de Hegel* (Paris: Le Seuil, 1964); Albert Chapelle, *Hegel et la religion,* 3 vols. (Paris: Éditions universitaires, 1964-1967); Cyril O'Regan, *The Heterodox Hegel* (New York: State University of New York Press, 1994).

it away, all by the sole means of the fragile tool of human logic, it is necessary to approach the divine mystery by way of the access the divine mystery itself grants: that is, by way of the only mediator between God and humankind, Jesus Christ (1 Tim 2:5-6).[18] There can be no speech about God
apart from what the person of Christ reveals of God. What theology manages to express about the godhead, then, will be adequate only if it is
rooted in his self-manifestation and not in conceptual logic.[19] Although
God remains always greater, if he has truly revealed himself in history,
what the eyes of faith contemplate in Christ refers both to God's salvific
action and to his very being. We can now turn to the person of Christ in
order to see what he reveals of the eventful nature of God.

If we consider St. Paul's experience, in an attempt to catch a glimpse
of the mystery of Jesus Christ's divine personality, it is possible to realize
that the very person of Christ presents himself as an event, i.e., as the unexpected, overabundant gift of himself to us (Rom 5:15; Heb 1:1-2; 9:14).
The man Christ Jesus is the one who, while we still were enemies of God
(Rom 5:10), "has given himself for our sins" (Gal 1:4) "as a ransom for all"
to purify for himself a people of his own, to form the Church (Titus 2:14;
Eph 5:25). His death and resurrection are the sign that he "loved me and

18. See Hans Urs von Balthasar, *The Glory of the Lord: A Theological Aesthetics* (= *GL*),
vol. 1: *Seeing the Form*, trans. Erasmo Leiva-Merikakis (San Francisco: Ignatius Press, 1983),
pp. 463-525; Balthasar, *Theo-Drama: Theological Dramatic Theory*, vol. 3: *Dramatis Personae:
Persons in Christ*, trans. Graham Harrison (San Francisco: Ignatius Press, 1992), pp. 250-58.

19. Rahner's *Grundaxiom*, "The 'economic' Trinity is the 'immanent' Trinity and the
'immanent' Trinity is the 'economic' Trinity," has been thoroughly discussed in recent theology. With L. Ladaria, it is important to notice, however, that although most of the critiques
agree with the first part of the axiom but reject the second because it jeopardizes God's transcendence, it is important not to discard the second part altogether. In fact, in order for the
economic Trinity to be the immanent Trinity, there has to be an (analogical) sense in which
the immanent Trinity "is" the economic Trinity. If, in the wholly correct attempt to avoid
confusing God with the historical process, a distinction is required between the economy
and the theology (and thus there is a sense in which the theology is much "more" than the
economy), this distinction cannot be affirmed to the extent of severing any relation between
the immanent and the economic Trinity. See Karl Rahner, *The Trinity*, trans. Joseph Donceel
(New York: Crossroad, 1997), p. 22; Luis F. Ladaria, *La Trinità: Mistero di comunione*, trans.
Marco Zappella (Milan: Paoline, 2004), pp. 13-86; Javier Prades, "'From the Economic to the
Immanent Trinity': Remarks on a Principle of Renewal in Trinitarian Theology (part 1),"
Communio 27, no. 2 (2000): 240-61; Prades, "'From the Economic to the Immanent Trinity':
Remarks on a Principle of Renewal in Trinitarian Theology (part 2)," *Communio* 27, no. 3
(2000): 562-93.

gave himself for me" (Gal 2:20). Jesus' self-gift (Phil 2:7) is, at the same time, also the consoling gift of the Father, who "did not spare his own Son but gave him up for us all" in order to give to us, with him, "all things" (Rom 8:32, 39; Phil 2:8). Christ's gift of himself is contemporaneous with man's present time because Christ, the Lord of the Spirit (2 Cor 3:17), gives man his own spirit (Rom 5:5) so that he, the Spirit, may expose the whole truth (1 Cor 2:5-13) and introduce the human being into the eternal life whose fruits are already experienced (Gal 5:22). It is the presence of the crucified, risen Lord that sets Paul — and every Christian — in motion because it is the presence that gives life. The dynamic force that governs *(synechō)* his spirit, holding it in unity by orienting all of his person towards one end, is the insurmountable fact that Christ has given himself and died for all (2 Cor 5:14-15).[20]

Paul's description of the mystery of Christ's person as the one who gives himself "for me" finds a correlate in John, who illustrates Christ's self-perception as the lucid awareness that he, while remaining with God (Jn 15:10), is the sent one (Jn 5–7).[21] The understanding of this "sending" is fleshed out by Christ in terms of an eternal life which is an absolute loving relation between him and God. We cannot get at what this love means, however, by measuring it against the human concept of love. We can only understand the latter from within and by means of divine love (Jn 3:16; 1 Jn 4:10).[22] The divine love that is disclosed in Jesus of Nazareth pertains first and foremost to his very being, and then to an action towards us. Looking

20. See also Hans Urs von Balthasar, *Theologik. Dritter Band. Der Geist der Wahrheit* (Freiburg: Johannes Verlag, 1987), pp. 76-80 (= *TL* III); Balthasar, "The Unknown Lying Beyond the Word," in *Explorations in Theology*, vol. 3: *Creator Spirit*, trans. Brian McNeil, C.R.V. (San Francisco: Ignatius Press, 1993), pp. 105-16; Balthasar, "The Holy Spirit as Love," in *Explorations in Theology*, vol. 3: *Creator Spirit*, pp. 117-34.

21. As is well known, Balthasar's Christology is built upon the concept of mission. See *TD* 3, pp. 149-259. On Christ's awareness, see also "The Consciousness of Christ Concerning Himself and His Mission," in *International Theological Commission: Texts and Documents 1969-1985*, ed. Michael Sharkey (San Francisco: Ignatius Press, 1989), pp. 305-16; Marcello Bordoni, *Gesù di Nazaret. Signore e Cristo*, vol. 2, *Gesù al fondamento della cristologia*, 2nd ed. (Rome: Herder; PUL, 1985); Herman Schell, *Katholische Dogmatik* (Munich: F. Schöningh, 1968), 3 vols; *Catechism of the Catholic Church* (Rome: Libreria Editrice Vaticana, 1994), nn. 471-73.

22. "If God wishes to reveal the love that he harbors for the world, this love has to be something that the world can recognize, in spite of, or in fact *in*, its being wholly other. The inner reality of love can be recognized only by love" (*LA*, p. 75).

at the mystery of Christ's divine personhood, we see that he himself expresses it in terms of a unique filial relationship with God whom he calls Father (Mk 14:36; Lk 3:22).[23] The Father is at the very center of his person because he is the Father's total self-bestowal. In this generation, however, the Father does not cease being himself (Jn 3:35; Mt 11:27). Christ knows himself to be sheer gift who has been given to himself, and who would not exist without the Father who remains himself while giving himself completely. The Father has loved the Son from the beginning and has given him everything, his own glory (Jn 17:24-26). Their unity (Jn 10:30) can be seen in the fact that Jesus does and says only what he sees the Father doing (Jn 5:19-20); moreover, he wishes only to affirm the Father, to do what pleases him (Jn 12:27; 8:29; 14:31), and to receive all and only what the Father gives him (Jn 2:4; 12:23). Their relation of love is one of absolute, mutual immanence; Jesus is in the Father and the Father is in him (Jn 14:10-11; 10:38). In this sense, their being in each other is a relation of sheer love: the Father loves Christ without measure (Lk 3:22; Jn 10:17) and Christ loves the Father (Jn 14:31) within and above everything (Mk 12:30).

To grasp the nature of divine love requires seeing that this love between the Father and Christ cannot be conceived as involving only two: one who gives and another who receives and gives in return. It suffices to look at Christ's mission — to love human beings to the extent of giving himself up to death on the cross (Jn 12:27; 13:1) — to perceive that the *pro nobis* of Christ's sacrificial death is also the offer of the eternal "we." Christ's gift of himself on the cross, which overturns the meaning and the reality of death and finds its fulfillment in the resurrection (Jn 10:17), and the breathing forth of the Spirit are also the communication in history of the divine loving communion.[24] In fact, the overabundant nature of the love uniting the Father and the Son, which in history can also be seen in the universality and the absolute unlimitedness of Jesus' mission, is not just a "quality" of his mission; it is Another.[25] The Holy Spirit is the one of whom Christ speaks in his promise that "we will come to them who love me and keep my word" (Jn 14:23, 26; 17:21). Christ promises the Spirit of truth (Jn 16:12-13), the Spirit of the Father (Jn 15:26), his own Spirit (Jn 19:28-30), the one who is

---

23. Joachim Jeremias, *The Prayers of Jesus* (Philadelphia: Fortress, 1978).

24. Bernard Sesboüé, *Jésus-Christ dans la tradition de l'église: Pour une actualisation de la christologie de Chalcédoine*, 2nd ed. (Paris: Desclée, 2000).

25. It is relevant to note that Christ, who acts in the power of the Holy Spirit, always enters into relation with the Father through the Holy Spirit (Lk 10:21).

asked to guide man to the fullness of truth. He breathes it forth (Jn 20:19-23) and gives it without measure (Jn 3:34), so that his disciples may remain in his love (Jn 15:9) and thus be able to experience an unheard-of fruitfulness (Jn 15:1-17; Mk 4:20), which is not so much a measure of something that the human being can possess, as, for example, he owns the fruit of his labor, but is rather communion with God. The gift of the Holy Spirit is the gift of the unity that God is (Jn 17:21), a unity that is also the incorporation into his own risen body (Rom 6:4), the Church (Eph 5:25).[26] It is the friendship with God, originally given to Moses (Ex 33:11), which, in Christ, is offered to every human being (Jn 14:2; 15:14-15).

As witnessed to by Paul's and John's perceptions of Christ's divine personality, Jesus' historical life reveals that the divine "I am" is an absolute love, a "communion of persons," which can be neither anticipated nor explained. This eternal life is so fruitful that it is offered to us "from the beginning" and, when rejected by man, it is moved by pity for man's condition and gives itself to him again overabundantly (for-gives). Through the person of Jesus Christ, God presents himself as an astonishing gift (Jn 5:20) of himself to himself, in which one wishes only that the other be, and wishes to respond to what pleases the other. In the unique presence of Christ, God discloses himself in history as an infinitely rich and mysterious communion of love in which one exists only for and in the other (Jn 10:30; 14:26). He reveals himself as one who carries out his decision to make the human being a full and free participant in his eternal life.

An Unforeseeable Love

The relation of love between the Father, Christ, and the Holy Spirit just described compels us, Balthasar contends, to perceive God as a triune mys-

---

26. For the relation between Christ and the Holy Spirit, see Heribert Mühlen, *Der Heilige Geist als Person. In der Trinität bei der Inkarnation und im Gnadenbund. Ich-Du-Wir* (Münster: Aschendorff Münster, 1963); Yves Congar, *Je crois en l'Esprit Saint* (Paris: Éditions du Cerf, 1995); François-Xavier Durrwell, *Holy Spirit of God*, trans. Sr. Benedict Davies, OSU (London: Geoffrey Chapman, 1986); Durrwell, *Jésus fils de Dieu dans l'esprit Saint* (Paris: Desclée, 1997); Marcello Bordoni, *La cristologia nell'orizzonte dello Spirito*, Biblioteca di teologia contemporanea, vol. 82 (Brescia: Queriniana, 1995); Sergej K. Bulgakov, *Il Paraclito* (Bologna: Edizioni Dehoniane, 1987); John Paul II, *Dominum et Vivificantem* (Boston: Pauline Books and Media, 1986).

tery of love, a love that is both an eternal being *(esse)* and an eternal *event (Geschehen, Ereignis)* of absolute donation.[27] To qualify the divine essence in terms of event may seem a little too daring if we insist on including all the various connotations this term can have. As the first section of this article clarified, "event" refers to the unpredictable taking place of something, whose historical coming-to-be out of a transcendent ground that is different from itself first causes wonder and then sets in motion a process of expectation and fulfillment. Moreover, events appear and come to pass: this temporal finitude is yet another sign of the ontological difference that both separates them from and unites them to their source. The concept of event is broad enough to include also that which is not necessarily positive: in fact, since it appears legitimate to think of event from the point of view of real donation, it seems difficult to exclude the possibilities of risk, loss, and even rejection. As we have seen, on the one hand, one could describe creation, historical occurrences, and phenomena as such as events; on the other hand, one could rightly claim that Christianity itself is most adequately understood as an event (Jn 1:14). Can this term also refer to divine love itself? After a painstaking passage from the missions of the Son and the Holy Spirit to the immanent Trinity, Balthasar contends not only that it can, but, even more radically, that every other event is to be understood in light of the trinitarian event, i.e., the absolute mystery whose life is an agapic threefold donation in which each one wants the other to be, lets the other be, consents to its generation or inspiration, prays to the other and lives with the other an eternal conversation of expectation and fulfillment, unfathomable gratitude and surprise.[28] For Balthasar, it is precisely this *agapē* that is not only the home from which creation has come and to which it longs to be brought back, but it is also what is able to provide a coherent account of how the world is the way it is.[29]

By characterizing the Trinity as an "event," Balthasar claims to go beyond a simplistic, romantic emphasis on the liveliness proper to the trini-

27. *TD* 5, pp. 66-98; *TL* 2, pp. 81-85, 125-49; also see *Theo-Drama*, vol. 2: Dramatis Personae: *Man in God*, trans. Graham Harrison (San Francisco: Ignatius Press, 1990), pp. 243-84; *TD* 3, pp. 505-35; *Epilog*, 69ff.; *Mysterium Paschale*, trans. Aidan Nichols (Edinburgh: T. & T. Clark, 1990).

28. In his *TD* 5, Balthasar follows Adrienne von Speyr very closely. See Adrienne von Speyr, *The World of Prayer* (= *WP*), trans. Graham Harrison (San Francisco: Ignatius Press, 1985), pp. 28-74.

29. *LA*, pp. 143-45.

tarian processions. At the same time, it is not true to say that Balthasar envisions God as an undetermined love that tends toward another, gives itself to another equal to itself, and thus determines itself. Balthasar rejects thinking of God in terms of one abstract essence, e.g., "pure love" or "absolute being," from which the divine persons gush forth (DS 804).[30] This position could easily lead to representing the three moments of the donation of love not as distinct persons but, as Sabellius did, as different manifestations of the same essence.[31] Like Barth, Balthasar claims that to think of the agapic donation as taking place out of an undetermined absolute would be nominalistic.[32] In order, then, to give an account of the divine event of threefold donation, Balthasar must articulate his own approach to the delicate issue of the relation between the essence and the three persons.

Without ever confusing "happening" *(Geschehen)* with becoming, he contends that it does not do justice to the exchange of gifts in God to think, with Anselm, that the one absolute spirit produces the Son, and thus becomes Father, when it knows itself, and the Holy Spirit when it loves it-

---

30. Balthasar does not critique Gregory the Great's elucidation of the nature of love. He rejects the idea of conceiving love as an undetermined reality that must subsequently determine itself by means of itself. Gregory the Great's explanation of the nature of love, which later became the fundamental intuition undergirding Richard of Saint Victor's *De Trinitate*, is also important for Balthasar's understanding of love. "Minus quam inter duos caritas haberi non potest. Nemo enim proprie ad semetipsum habere caritatem dicitur, sed dilectio in alterum tendit, ut caritas esse possit" (Gregory the Great, *In Evangelia hom.* 17 [76, 1139]).

31. Aquinas also rejected this abstraction very forcefully. See Thomas Aquinas, *I Sent.*, d. 26, q. 1, a. 2; Aquinas, *Quaestiones disputatae de Potentia Dei* (= *DPD*) (Turin-Rome: Marietti, 1965), q. 8, a. 4. The assertion that the divine essence and the persons must be held in unity does not disregard the teaching of the Council of Florence, which, inspired by Anselm's doctrine, decreed that in God everything is one where relations of opposition do not stand in the way (DS 1330). For a discussion on personalism and essentialism in Aquinas, see, among others, A. Malet, *Personne et amour dans la théologie trinitaire de Saint Thomas d'Aquin* (Paris: Vrin, 1956); Gilles Emery, O.P., *Trinity in Aquinas* (Ypsilanti, Mich.: Sapientia Press of Ave Maria College, 2003).

32. *TL* 2, p. 138. This affirmation should not lead the reader to conclude that Balthasar upholds the same understanding of "person" as Barth does. Barth, who in this regard is followed very closely by Rahner, regards the concept of person with suspicion and, in order to bypass what seems to him the unacceptable and insurmountable modern understanding of person, proposes interpreting the hypostases as "ways of being." Cf. Barth, *Church Dogmatics*, vol. 1, Part 1: *The Doctrine of the Word of God,* trans. G. T. Thomson (Edinburgh: T. & T. Clark, 1963), pp. 400-441; Rahner, *The Trinity.* For Balthasar's concept of person, see "On the Concept of Person," *Communio* 13, no. 1 (1986): 18-26; *TD* 3, pp. 149-230; *TL* 2, pp. 128-34; *TL* 3, pp. 99-150.

self.[33] Although Aquinas, like Augustine and Anselm, also proposes an elucidation of the triune mystery starting from the one God, Aquinas wishes to correct Anselm's position by clarifying that the hypostases are to be understood in terms of relation. Thus, he illustrates that the first procession does not stand for God's self-understanding, but for God's speaking *(dicere)*, and that the second does not mean self-love, but rather that in God the act of love *(diligere, amare)* stands for "to spirate love proceeding."[34] In this way, while stating that the processions of the Son and the Holy Spirit are thus an interior action, the difference between the three hypostases can be adequately understood in terms of relation of opposition. Balthasar accurately points out that Aquinas determines that the relations are "subsisting" by distinguishing between the *esse* and the *ratio* in the concept of "relation." Since the *esse* is that of the divine essence, relations are nothing but God himself. What makes the hypostases distinct, then, is their referentiality, their being *ad aliquid,* and what constitutes them as real persons is their identity with the divine essence.[35] Nevertheless, as in Augustine, given that the processions that ground the relation, and thus the persons, are still explained in terms of the spiritual faculties, Balthasar still wonders whether it might be possible to find a way in which the "personhood" of the hypostases could be better elucidated.

Following Aquinas, Balthasar reminds us that "processions" are not really distinct from the relations in God, only notionally so. Relation, claims Aquinas, is "notionally multiple," and thus can be understood both in itself and insofar as it constitutes the person. Relation "as such" *(ratio)* refers to that orientation *ad aliquid* of the hypostases (relation of opposi-

---

33. Cf. Anselm, *Monologion* 63, in *Anselm, Monologion and Proslogion: with the replies of Gaunilo and Anselm,* trans. Thomas Williams (Indianapolis: Hackett, 1996). Although attracted more by the trinitarian doctrine of Richard of Saint Victor, Balthasar also distances himself from it. Balthasar, in fact, critiques Richard because, in his attempt to give an account of the existence of three persons beginning from the one essence conceived in terms of *summa caritas,* Richard seems to add the *condilectus* from "outside," thus disregarding the movement from the economy to the theology. This is also evident in the lack of any reference to the economy and the *ordo expositionis* of the argument.

34. *ST* I, q. 34, a. 1, ad 3; q. 37, a. 1.

35. In this way Aquinas manages to unravel Augustine's perplexities regarding the term "person." See Augustine, *De Trinitate,* V, 9, 10; *ST* I, q. 29; *DPD,* q. 10, aa. 1-2. For an interesting presentation and critique of Aquinas's understanding of person, see Ghislain Lafont, *Peut-on connaître Dieu en Jésus-Christ? Problématique* (Paris: Éditions du Cerf, 1969).

tion). Formally, relation thus means the "bond between the termini." At the same time, thanks to the fact that relation's *esse* is one with the divine essence, it constitutes a divine hypostasis.[36] If we take relation as such, then "procession" is presupposed. If relation is the positing of the hypostasis, then "the relation that constitutes the *producing* person is logically prior to the procession." Bearing in mind that "the proceeding person is the goal at which the procession aims," we see that the relation that, instead, constitutes the person *produced*, "is logically posterior to the procession"; in this sense "sonship is logically posterior to being born." Thus, without forgetting that these two senses of relation cannot be separated, it is possible to say that the procession of the Son is (also) the positing of the Son.[37] While accepting Aquinas's understanding of person as subsisting relation, Balthasar, by contrast, prefers to emphasize the second sense of relation clarified by Aquinas, and thus to conceive "hypostasis" as that which is posited by a relation.[38] With this Balthasar not only hopes to show that the divine persons "are" in relation, but he also wishes to incorporate within this concept what the Triune God has revealed of himself in Jesus Christ, without, all the while, either blurring the distinction between the economy and the theology or forgetting that the *"ad se"* of the hypostases does not fracture the divine unity. "The Father," says Balthasar, "generates the Son as God, that is, out of his substance, but precisely as Father, not as substance."[39] Hence, since, according to him, the one divine essence cannot be the agent of the processions, and the exposition of the latter in terms of spiritual faculties "cannot give an adequate picture of the real and abiding face-to-face encounter of the hypostases," it is necessary to refer to the mystery of the Father. Turning to the Father, the primal source, allows us, according to Balthasar, to give an account of the triune

36. Gilles Emery, O.P., makes a very lucid presentation of this issue in his *Trinity and Aquinas*, pp. 165-208.

37. *DPD*, q. 10, a. 3; *TL* 2, pp. 133ff.

38. In this regard, Balthasar will say, e.g., that "he in God whom we call 'Father' is the 'fruit' of his self-giving to the one we call 'Son'; he exists as this self-giving, and the Son exists as receptivity, gratitude, and giving-in-return. Again, this giving-in-return does not close the Two in on themselves but opens them to the fullness of the 'with' (the 'co-' of 'communion'), which is made absolute in the Spirit who is common to both" ("God Is Being With," in *You Crown the Year with Your Goodness*, trans. Graham Harrison [San Francisco: Ignatius Press, 1989], p. 144).

39. *TL* 2, p. 130.

event without leaving behind what the immanent Trinity has revealed of itself in the economy and to steer clear of the problems that emerge when setting out from the one essence.[40]

Divine revelation has a fundamental claim in our representation of the immanent Trinity: it enables us to perceive that, as we delineated, the Father's identity, from all eternity, is that of giving himself to the beloved Son, and, along with and through the Son, to the Holy Spirit. For Balthasar, then, both processions are to be understood in terms of love, and not only the second procession, as for Aquinas and Augustine. While not losing sight for one instant of the equal rank of the hypostases, one must hold firm to the fact that the origin of all of the divinity is not a divine abstract essence, but the Father, who generates the Son, and who, in union with him and through him, spirates the Holy Spirit.[41] Therefore, the Father's divinity is possessed by him only as completely given away (DS 528). His divinity is seen precisely in the fact that, in the total gift of himself, he remains himself (DS 805).

Drawing from Bulgakov's Christology, while at the same time avoiding any grafting of Good Friday onto the immanent Trinity, Balthasar describes the totality of the self-donation in terms of handing-over *(Hingabe; Übereignung)* and an agapic emptying out of oneself for and in the other.[42] Thus, for Balthasar, the omnipotence of the Father implies, first and foremost, a power of self-donation (which is also that of self-expression), an

---

40. *TL* 2, p. 38. Balthasar is obviously aware that Augustine's *De Trinitate* concedes this limit. Balthasar is also aware of the limits of his own position and tries to keep the impenetrable unity of "the one God" together with "the three hypostases." This is why we think that Balthasar's model should be seen as complementary to rather than in opposition to the intrapersonal model.

41. Augustine, *De Trinitate* XV, 17, 29; DS 490.

42. For studies on the relation between Balthasar's and Hegel's thought, see Ben J. Quash, "Between the Brutely Given, and the Brutally, Banally Free: Von Balthasar's Theology of Drama in Dialogue with Hegel," *Modern Theology* 13, no. 3 (1997): 293-318; Michael Stickelbroeck, "Trinitarische Prozessualität und Einheit Gottes — Zur Gotteslehre H. U. v. Balthasars," *Forum Katholische Theologie* 10 (1994): 124-29; Bertrand de Margerie, "Note on Balthasar's Trinitarian Theology," *The Thomist* 64 (2000): 127-30; Brian J. Spence, "The Hegelian Element in von Balthasar's and Moltmann's Understanding of the Suffering of God," *Toronto Journal of Theology* 14, no. 1 (1998): 45-60; Michael Schulz, *Sein und Trinität. Systematische Erörterungen zur Religionsphilosophie G. W. F. Hegels im ontologiegeschichtlichen Rückblick auf J. Duns Scotus und I. Kant und die Hegel-Rezeption in der Seinsauslegung und Trinitätstheologie bei W. Pannenberg, E. Jüngel, K. Rahner und H. U. v. Balthasar* (St. Ottilien: Eos Verlag, 1997).

original kenosis.[43] The Father is, from all eternity, the one who pours himself forth to another, first to the beloved, *homoousios* Son, and, with and through him, to the Spirit. The Father is that inexhaustible beginning which has always surrendered himself without losing himself, and hence, from all eternity he is with the Son and the Holy Spirit (Lk 6:36; Eph 2:4; Rom 8:32). The Father's donation, in order to be a real donation, requires giving the other two hypostases to themselves; that is to say, the Father is the one who wishes to let the Son and the Holy Spirit be. At the same time, Balthasar claims that since the taxis of the trinitarian processions is not only irreversible but also eternal, the processions are not only "bringing forth," or "positing the other" (second connotation of "relation"), but the presence of the other hypostases who "let themselves be brought forth" is also required ("relation" understood as such).[44] In fact, Balthasar states that the Son and the Holy Spirit respond to the Father's surrender with an equal surrender *(Hingabe)* that is an acceptance to proceed from the Father, a giving in return (the Son), and an ever-new possibility of gratuitous love and surrender (the Holy Spirit). The "gift" of the Son and the Holy Spirit, then, is both their "consequent" surrender to the initiative of the Father and their "antecedent" consent to be begotten by or to proceed from the Father.[45]

The eternity of the divine processions, however, which requires holding together both senses of relation in God (understood in Balthasar as a

43. *TD* 5, p. 84. Although the terminology of "kenosis" and "surrender" may lead to thinking that the trinitarian donation could be caused by an ultimate negativity in God (à la Hegel), for Balthasar divine generosity is utter freedom whose grounds for existence can be found only in itself and not in any type of arbitrariness (DS 71, 526). See Balthasar, *Theo-Drama*, vol. 4: *The Action*, trans. Graham Harrison (San Francisco: Ignatius Press, 1994), 313-314; Sergei Nikolaevic Bulgakov, *L'agnello di Dio. Il mistero del Verbo Incarnato* (Rome: Città Nuova Editrice, 1990) — this edition contains the "Introductory Note" and the "Introduction" to the dialectics of the idea of theanthropy in the Patristic Age that are omitted in the French translation; Margaret M. Turek, *Towards a Theology of God the Father: Hans Urs von Balthasar's Theodramatic Approach* (New York: Peter Lang, 2001); Turek, "'As the Father Has Loved Me' (Jn 15:9): Balthasar's Theodramatic Approach to God the Father," *Communio* 26, no. 2 (1999): 295-318.

44. *TD* 5, p. 85.

45. It is in this way that Balthasar intends to preclude any possible subordinationist presentation of the triune mystery. The Father is never without a Son, and they are never without the Holy Spirit. For a concordant explanation of the "role" of the persons in their being generated or spirated, see *WP*, 58. One cannot lose sight of the fact that the divine "being-with" is that of the one God.

gift given, received, and consented to), cannot be viewed as a coalescence of "the process of being generated" and "having been generated already." Such a dichotomy can only end up sounding like an oxymoron. If it is not clear from the start that divine procession is unlike the production of beings (which eventually is called to come to an end) the result is inevitably a concept of eternity as an atemporal *nunc stans,* informed at base by a sequential idea of history and thus proposing the untenable figure of a divine procession that has lost both its beginning and end but whose outcome has already taken place. Instead, Balthasar claims that eternity, when approached from Christ's self-awareness, is better understood as an event of relation: the Son, for example, always receives himself from the Father "in a *presence* that includes both his always-having-been and also his eternal future (his eternal 'coming') from the Father."[46] The divine persons are present to each other in their coming from another and being with and in the other. The "being for and with" the other and the "coming from" another of the divine persons is not then a sign of transiency but is rather their own subsistence. In this sense, unlike in the created world, the "coming from" does not have an ephemeral nature. Their "eternity," conceived in terms of presence, consists then of an immemorial past that is always poured forth in the present, a present that is receptivity and grateful giving in return, and a future that is both eternal confirmation of the gift of love and ever-new response. Divine communion is both from eternity and "created afresh" at every instant. If this is the case in God's own being, then "history" needs to be seen in terms of God's faithfulness in fulfilling his covenant, and not merely as the succession of separate occurrences that can be reconciled only with difficulty. When eternity is thus understood as an event of relation, it is possible to discover that eternity is the plenitude of time. Eternity is, in fact, the eternal confirmation of the original creation and the victory over man's resistance to God's faithfulness — a faith-

---

46. *TD* 5, pp. 91-93. See also Hans Urs von Balthasar, *A Theology of History* (San Francisco: Ignatius Press, 1994); Balthasar, *A Theological Anthropology* (New York: Sheed & Ward, 1990); Balthasar, *Heart of the World,* trans. Erasmo S. Leiva (San Francisco: Ignatius Press, 1979); David L. Schindler, "Time in Eternity, Eternity in Time: On the Contemplative-Active Life," *Communio* 18, no. 1 (1991): 53-68; Kenneth L. Schmitz, "Traces of Eternity," *Communio* 15, no. 3 (1988): 294-304. It is also worth mentioning that Schelling's understanding of eternity could be fruitfully used if corrected by a principle of positivity. See Friedrich W. J. Schelling, *The Ages of the World,* trans. Jason M. Wirth (Albany, N.Y.: State University of New York Press, 2000).

fulness with such a powerful fascination that it can elicit a grateful but free adhesion by the human being. It is this understanding of eternity that prevents Balthasar from confusing event with historical becoming.[47]

Undoubtedly, Balthasar's illustration of the divine hypostases may sometimes give the impression that for him the persons are endowed with, so to say, a life of their own. Balthasar's methodology, which understands the divine hypostases in personalistic terms, considers the persons as "subjects."[48] In fact, if in the economy the three persons appear as having their own personhood, their own "self," then, in a mysterious way, this must also be the case for the immanent Trinity.[49] For this reason, the communication of the divine nature *(agapē)* must not be understood in terms of a mechanical transfer of some-thing, i.e., the whole of the divine essence, motivated by love. Instead, as indicated before, the gift of the Father is the free positing of some-one with whom the other hypostases are eternally in communion.[50] In giving all of himself without losing himself, the Father gives the other to himself, and thus gives him the capacity to be a self whose uniqueness is that of being the same absolute love, as received and reciprocated in thankfulness (Son), or as given from both of them and surrendered to them as an ever-new love *(Je-Mehr-Sein der Liebe)* who

47. Commenting on Gregory of Nyssa, Balthasar writes: "We believed that becoming and Being were opposites, two forms, as it were, analogous without a doubt, but irreducible. Through the incarnation we learn that all the unsatisfied movement of becoming is itself only repose and fixity when compared to that immense movement of love inside of God: Being is Super-Becoming. In constantly surpassing ourselves, therefore, by means of our love, we assimilate ourselves to God much more intimately than we could have suspected" (*Presence and Thought: An Essay on the Religious Philosophy of Gregory of Nyssa,* trans. Mark Sebanc [San Francisco: Ignatius Press, 1995], p. 153). This "Super-Becoming," as he states later on in *TD* 5, pp. 91-93, is coming-to-be and not historical developing.

48. For a concordant exploration of the meaning of hypostasis, see François Bourassa, S.J., "Personne et conscience en théologie trinitaire," *Gregorianum* 55 (1974): 471-93, 677-720; Luis Ladaria, *La trinità: Mistero di comunione,* pp. 161-78. Both Barth and Rahner distrusted the concept of person because, tending as it does to mean almost exclusively a center of consciousness and freedom, it could very easily lead to tri-theism. For Rahner, then, being conscious of oneself is not an element that distinguishes the divine persons.

49. Balthasar thus does not hesitate to adopt the personal pronouns to refer to the divine persons: I and Thou refer to the Father and the Son, and We refers to the Holy Spirit. As is well known, Balthasar here refers to the work of Heribert Mühlen, *Der Heilige Geist als Person,* and Matthias J. Scheeben, *The Mysteries of Christianity,* trans. Cyril Vollert (St. Louis: B. Herder, 1961).

50. *WP,* p. 58.

"searches the depths of God" (1 Cor 2:10) and makes God be absolute gift (Holy Spirit).[51] In God, the "totality" of the gift, therefore, does not mean only that the persons enjoy the same identity; it also means "otherness." Fatherhood is, indeed, the generation of another. Incorporating the richness of the reflection on the Father's original surrender, together with his emphasis on personhood, Balthasar conceives the triune mystery of love as a "communion of persons."[52] For Balthasar, then, the "self-awareness" and "actions" of the divine persons cannot be perceived as an un-originated, independent consciousness or deed, but rather as that of being *(esse)* God and of being a God who is a communion *(Mit-sein, Gemeinschaft, Geschehen)* of persons who are different from each other. Since each divine subject is the gift received or given, each one has the awareness and freedom of the divinity that is communicated or received. The awareness of the divine self is possessed and exercised by each one of them in a perfect unity with the other divine persons. In fact, without falling prey to the illusion of introducing space in God, Balthasar suggests that every person "'makes room' ('space') for one another, granting each other freedom of being and action."[53] According to Balthasar, the unity of essence in the circumincession of the persons does not eliminate but on the contrary makes possible and preserves the difference of the divine hypostases. Difference in God, however, does not indicate pure distinction but precisely that exuberant, overflowing, rich unity which is identical in each

51. *Dominum et Vivificantem,* n. 10.

52. From its beginning the Fathers of the Church understood "communion" as that which the hypostases share together, i.e., the divine substance. See, for example, Gregory of Nyssa, "Quod non sint tres dii," in *Gregory of Nyssa: Dogmatic Treatises,* ed. Philip Schaff and Henry Wace, trans. H. A. Wilson, vol. 5 of *Nicene and Post-Nicene Fathers* (Peabody, Mass.: Hendrickson, 1999), pp. 331-36; Basil, *Ep.* 38, n. 4. With Balthasar's reflection there is a new connotation: communion is of persons, and hence it is a being-from, -with, -for, and -in the other. It is worth noticing that other trinitarian doctrines like those of the Eastern Fathers, which, before the development of the Latin reflection, followed what today is called the "social model" of the Trinity, always rejected the possibility of going any further than stating that God is one and three. See for example, Gregory of Nazianzus, *Theological Oration* XXXI, 32, in *Faith Gives Fullness to Reasoning: The Five Theological Orations of Gregory Nazianzen,* ed. Frederick W. Norris, trans. Lionel Wickham and Frederick Williams (Leiden: E. J. Brill, 1991).

53. *TD* 5, p. 93. It is this trinitarian space, which is another way of characterizing both the hierarchical order and the unity of the divine persons, that is the ultimate ground that allows for the existence of space in the created world — and not just the existence of matter. This entails that space is to be conceived as interiorly ordered from and to relation.

hypostasis and, at the same time, is so in a unique, radically different way. It is this difference between the persons in God that ultimately grounds the ontological difference in the finite world, a difference which is at the root of the eventfulness of creation.[54]

This understanding of personhood, along with his account of relation, spurs Balthasar's theological reflection to do its utmost to defend the uniqueness of each person in order to illustrate at that very moment that the uniqueness is so because the three persons are one God (absolute love). While recognizing that his interpersonal model encounters the opposite limit from Augustine's and Aquinas's proposals, Balthasar, with his characteristic elliptic style, attempts to preserve a harmonious balance in his account of the divine mystery by holding unswervingly to the twofold mystery yielded by faith, which cannot be synthesized by a higher concept (neither that of "person" nor that of "event"): the Father, Son, and Holy Spirit really exist as distinct persons, and these hypostases are one God.[55] Balthasar explains that the divine essence and the eternal processions are co-extensive and that the former also is "concomitantly determined by the unrepeatably unique participation of the Father, Son, and Spirit in this event [of love] and so would never exist except as fatherly, sonly, and spirit-ually."[56] Balthasar's insight, then, is that it is "love alone" which exists in the eternal personal gift of himself to himself, and in which it is absolutely good that there be another who welcomes, consents to, and, as Au-

---

54. Balthasar here concurs with Bruaire, who states that "talk of the 'ontological difference' thus undergoes a radical transformation: being does not differ *from* the supreme Being, but *in* him, since there is the Spirit *in* God, as the difference between the hypostases in himself. . . . The ontological difference is null if it signifies the being that God is not" (Claude Bruaire, *L'être et l'esprit*, 190n; quoted in *TL* 2, 135). This affirmation, written polemically against Heidegger, flows from the lucid recognition that, as Aquinas puts it: "Ex processione personarum divinarum distinctarum causatur omnis creaturarum processio et multiplicatio" (*I Sent.*, d. 26, q. 2, a. 2, ad. 2; quoted in *TD* 5, 62). See also John Milbank, "The Second Difference," in *The Word Made Strange* (Cambridge, Mass.: Blackwell, 1997).

55. Balthasar states that, "perhaps, the most adequate way to defend the unity of the godhead if one starts *only* from the economic Trinity, and thus to avoid tri-theism, is by means of the *circumincession* of the hypostases." See also *TL* 3, p. 144. See *TL* 2, pp. 133ff.; *TL* 3, pp. 110-16. It deserves mention that the "one" and "three" are not mathematical but transcendental numbers. See, e.g., *ST* I, q. 30, aa. 3-4. In this regard, Balthasar is also careful to indicate with the Greek Fathers that "person" cannot be understood as a univocal concept able to portray perfectly the differences of the hypostases.

56. *TL* 2, p. 137.

gustine and Aquinas already intuited, reciprocates the absolute love that is communicated.[57] One can never go behind this absolute love, which is the ultimate ground of which there is no beyond.

Ever-Greater Surprise

Balthasar's claim, presented above, that God's eternal "happening" *(Geschehen)* is to be characterized as a movement of agapic donation *(Übereignung)*, does not intend to propose that love is the logic undergirding the divine processions — as if love were simply their animating principle. If God *is* love, then each one of the hypostases must be perceived for what it is, love. Seeing them *as* (ontological) love is the first step towards elucidating the reasons for Balthasar's affirmation that within the event which the Triune God is, there has to be something like fulfillment, risk, letting be, expectation, gratitude, and surprise.

Without, obviously, claiming to exhaust the divine mystery, Balthasar contends that to speak of "love" requires acknowledging what is proper to it. Love, as we saw, is the utterly free affirmation (positing) of the other that, while allowing him to be himself, always generates a unity that is "considerate" *(rücksichtsvoll)* of the other's difference; that is to say, a unity able to see the other for what the other is.[58] If we turn to the incarnate Logos to understand what this divine respect (beholding the other) means, we discover that the Father's handing-over of himself to the Son is seen by the Son as "the object of infinite amazement, wonderment and gratitude."[59] The amazement expressed by the incarnate Logos is not proper only to the economy; it must echo something of the eternal hypostases who are one love. The Son is divine love as received and as grateful response because the Father is, and because the Father is an overabundant gift *(Hingabe)* to him. The paternal and filial hypostases of absolute love reveal that the *agapē* that unites the Father and the Son is more than the exchange of gifts that takes place among human beings (even if that gift were life itself). They disclose

---

57. *TL* 2, p. 38. See Augustine, *De Trinitate* VI, 5, 7. It is interesting to note some echo of Augustine's understanding of the Holy Spirit in terms of friendship in Aquinas. See, for example, *DPD*, q. 10, a. 2, ad 11.

58. *TD* 5, p. 89.

59. Hans Urs von Balthasar, *Unless You Become Like This Child* (= *Unless*), trans. Erasmo Leiva-Merikakis (San Francisco: Ignatius Press, 1991), p. 45.

that the "totality" of their love is the exuberance of yet another, who is both the unity and the fruit of their love, the Holy Spirit. If God, from the beginning, in the Father "is already the miracle of love, of being itself in the gift of himself, this miracle 'completes itself' in the Holy Spirit, who, precisely because he is the exuberance of love, in his being always ever greater, is the ungraspable and insurmountable vertex of absolute love."[60] The absoluteness proper to divine love is that of being paternal (Father), filial (Son), and spiritual (Holy Spirit) as the overabundant gift of love. The infinite "excess" of the gift, its "ever-greaterness," invites us to see the triune mystery as a communion of persons who exist in awe of and amazement at each other, as a "community of surprise *(Überraschung)*."[61] This wonderment springs, then, from the fact that, for Balthasar, God is ever-greater *(semper maior)*, not only for us but for himself, who is absolute love in three persons.[62]

The meaning of the divine "ever-greaterness" would remain beyond our grasp if explained quantitatively (there is something left to be given), or chronologically (apart from the eternally present donation there is a future donation that is yet to come), or gnoseologically (there is an unshared secret in God). Balthasar, following von Speyr, uses the comparative ever-greater as the way to express God's infinity, and thus as the "true superlative," in order not to lose sight of the fact that, in God, one is always dealing with persons whose *esse* is infinite love. God is ever-greater because he is three persons, and because these three persons are one infinite mystery of love. The comparative ever-greater is thus "the linguistic form of amazement."[63]

If one thinks of the relation between the human being and God, simultaneously with the idea of infinity, the ontological transcendence implied in the *semper maior* cannot be transposed in God (there are not three gods). Nevertheless, looking at the relation between parents and their child or between two lovers may provide an inkling into what God discloses of himself

---

60. *TL* 3, p. 146. See also Balthasar, *Creator Spirit*, pp. 105-277; Aidan Nichols, *Say It Is Pentecost: A Guide Through Balthasar's Logic* (Washington, D.C.: The Catholic University of America Press, 2001); John R. Sachs, "Deus Semper Major — Ad Majorem Dei Gloriam: The Pneumatology and Spirituality of Hans Urs von Balthasar," *Gregorianum* 74, no. 4 (1993): 631-57; Kossi K. Joseph Tossou, *Streben nach Vollendung. Zur Pneumatologie im Werk Hans Urs von Balthasars* (Freiburg: Herder, 1983).

61. *TD* 5, p. 54.

62. Along with that of von Speyr, it is worth recalling the influence of Erich Przywara. See his *Deus Semper Maior. Theologie der Exerzitien* (Munich: Herold Verlag, 1964).

63. *Unless*, p. 46.

in Jesus Christ. The human lover is in awe, first of all, at the very existence of the beloved. It is the very presence of the beloved that gladdens the lover and makes him live in a "now" of thankfulness, which is unconcerned with securing the future. At the same time, since one is dealing with love, this awe is intensified by the fact that the other is there "for me," and that this preferential relationship interiorly opens both of them up to the whole of the cosmos. Undoubtedly, human existence is unable to remain in this original position. It is thus called continuously to recover this tension and to avoid any attempt either to possess or to conquer the beloved, or to determine the future and fruitfulness of their love. Forgiveness and surprise are two of the fundamental dimensions of love that enable them to regain this awareness, this tension. While forgiveness posits a new, deeper beginning between them, surprise shows that one of them has broken through habits and preconceived ideas. Yet "surprise" indicates not only that something unforeseen has taken place, but more importantly, that a "ruse of love" has been found to allow them to see each other as they are and to rediscover the nature of the love that unites them. In this way the grateful, amazed contemplation of the other attains a depth previously unknown to them. Analogically speaking, one could say that in God himself, the surprise or wonderment comes from the fact that the persons are eternally other, different from each other, and that they are so precisely inasmuch as they are for and with the other. It is the way in which they are for each other, let each other be while always being in the other, and, so to say, "look at" each other, that sheds some light on the fact that God is an ever-greater event of love, and that the divine persons exist in grateful wonderment at each other. In this regard, as Balthasar contends, surprise is not only a human experience but also a divine one, if God is, in himself, an event of absolute triune love.[64]

64. The similarity outlined here is analogical. In this regard, one cannot identify the way in which the hypostases are the one divine nature with the unity among human beings. Nevertheless, the trinitarian communion of persons illumines the meaning of man's dual reality as male and female and as a social creature existing in communion with and for others. This being a communion of persons is informed by the dynamics of gift proper to love, which, as indicated, includes, among others, these elements: donation, risk, reciprocity, expectation, fulfillment, surprise, embrace. See, for example, *TL* 2, pp. 25-62; *TL* 3, pp. 146-49; Angelo Scola, *Il Mistero Nuziale*, vol. 1: *Uomo-Donna* (Rome: Lateran University Press, 1998), pp. 43-61, Eng. trans., *The Nuptial Mystery* (Grand Rapid: Eerdmans, 2005); Marc Ouellet, *Divina somiglianza. Antropologia trinitaria della famiglia* (Rome: PUL, 2004), Eng. trans., *Divine Likeness: Toward a Trinitarian Anthropology of the Family* (Grand Rapids: Eerdmans, 2006).

We have already indicated that if the gift of self of the Father (*Urkenosis*) is to be a real gift, it has to be a complete gift of self, and thus, although it is not made either by necessity or by will, but by nature, it has to be free. What we need to ponder now is that this absolute freedom is not simply the positing of another who enjoys the same divine freedom and who is the total surrender of himself to the other.[65] If it is a truly free donation, it cannot claim a return. The Father, Balthasar says following von Speyr, gives himself over completely to the Son ("lets him go") and "expects" that the gift of himself will be fulfilled, that is to say, accepted and reciprocated. The Father, however, "will never override the Son's filial stature" and, thus, will not demand to be loved back.[66] For Balthasar, there is no real gift of self if there is not a complete gift of self, and the gift of self is not true if it imposes or predetermines a positive answer. The "risk" entailed in the Father's insurmountable expectation, however, is eternally "surpassed" by the Son, who is both "the [Father's] primal expectation and fulfillment."[67] The Son reciprocates overabundantly the "excessive" gift that his generation is. Thus, there is nothing "undetermined" in God. For this reason, it is important to note that the Father's expectation does not signify a lack in the divinity. Absolute plenitude is, in a sense, the only word for divine love; "fulfillment" and "expectation" represent an attempt to delineate absolute love's eventful nature. The language of fulfillment and expectation reveals that the exchange of (hypostatic) gifts is not so much a "correspondence" between the divine persons; e.g., the Son "co-[r]responds" to the love of the

---

65. Balthasar also sees this primordial kenosis as a "super-death." Not so much, it seems to us, because he claims that there is something like "death" in God. Were this assumption true, one would introduce negativity in the absolute, and this is not coherent with Balthasar's trinitarian thought. By "super-death," then, Balthasar is hinting at the possibility of grounding in God what he calls "the good death" of John 15:13. In other words, Christ can ask his apostles to be ready to give their lives for their friends exactly because God is nothing but the total gift (surrender) of himself to himself. Balthasar's affirmation does not mean, then, that love begets death, which enters into the world because of sin (Wis 2:24; Rom 5:12). Rather, aided by the work of Ferdinand Ulrich, among others, he attempts to say that the readiness to die, which always takes place within the horizon of the resurrection and thus of eternal life (Jn 10:17), is the final affirmation of the other in *statu isto* and the imitation of him who loved man when man was still inimical to God (Rom 5:8). See *TD* 5, pp. 83-85; *TL* 2, pp. 141-49; Ferdinand Ulrich, *Leben in der Einheit von Leben und Tod* (Freiburg: Johannes Verlag, 1999).

66. *WP*, p. 50.

67. *TD* 5, p. 79.

Father and that balance is shattered by their gift, in turn corresponded, to the Holy Spirit. If it were a matter of correspondence, then one would have to admit a lack, or a negativity, in God. Nevertheless, since it is *absolute* and *free* love, the gift cannot but be superabundant, ever-greater, and utterly free in its offer, its reception, and its return. The exuberance that we see in the relation of love between the Father and the Son is also at play in the procession of the Holy Spirit, "when Father and Son see their mutual love surpassed as it issues forth from them as a Third Person, standing boldly before them and expressing their innermost being."[68] There is no absolute love if it does not exceed the "wildest expectations," and there is no true plenitude if it "contains itself," that is to say, if it does not exceed itself in giving itself over without any limitation, only to receive itself back overabundantly in an excess of love (the Holy Spirit).[69] Bearing in mind what we said previously regarding Balthasar's understanding of the divine persons, it is now possible to see that it is the eternal interplay of fulfillment and expectation that undergirds a divine "wonderment."

God's overabundant, ever-greater gift of himself to the other is "anything but blind." It is indeed supremely wise and provident.[70] One cannot fail to point out, however, that, for Balthasar, divine omniscience is grounded in love and that this love will never allow the wisdom of the divine persons to request an answer, or to be used, in a way that would jeopardize the exuberance proper to absolute love. If faith, for the human being, is understood as an encounter between God and the human person, mediated by the form of Christ who is contemporaneous to the human being through the Marian Church, then, in God, Balthasar contends, faith can also be perceived analogically as the opening up to the other in such a way that the "irrefragable knowledge" of God does not overrule the exuberance of love, but welcomes it (1 Cor 8:3).[71] If omniscience were synonymous with "having been exhausted," it would neglect the fact that, according to Balthasar, when the Father generates, he risks, i.e., he does not wish to determine the Son's, or the Spirit's, over-fulfillment of his "unsurpassable love." It is not a matter of what is "more" or "less" important. Rather, it is a question of seeing that the

---

68. *WP*, p. 30; cf. *TD* 5, p. 89.

69. *TD* 5, p. 79.

70. *TL* 2, pp. 140-41.

71. *TD* 5, p. 97. For Balthasar's understanding of the Christian experience of faith, see *GL* 1, pp. 219-425; Giulio Meiattini, *Sentire cum Christo. La teologia dell'esperienza cristiana nell'opera di Hans Urs von Balthasar* (Rome: Editrice Pontificia Università Gregoriana, 1998).

harmonic coming together of divine wisdom with the ever-greater absoluteness of love requires both the person's freedom to explore the infinite "realm of his own free sonship [or spirituality], of his own divine sovereignty" *and* the knowing of himself through the other. While it is true that love and wisdom are contemporaneous in God, one cannot forget that truth, for Balthasar, is essentially understood as an event of disclosure *(alētheia)*, an unfolding, which takes place according to the form proper to absolute triune love. Thus, contrary to what often happens among human beings, surprise in God does not mean that one of the persons unexpectedly discloses to the others what was previously, avariciously, kept secret. Rather, it has to do first of all with the fact that the hypostases are eternally other (person), and, second, with the mysterious nature of the reciprocal gift that the eternal happening of God is: the ever-greater, personal, gratuitous love that generates gratitude both for the gift that is eternally given and received and for the "expectation" that is always already "fulfilled."[72] This gratitude, when seen from the point of view of the eternal over-fulfillment of the divine expectation, is a fundamental element of what Balthasar calls surprise. Surprise, then, could be seen as the subjective (hypostatic), grateful response to the (objective) ever-greater donation of divine love; it is absolute love gratuitously and gratefully given and reciprocated.

Eternal Fruitfulness

After having explored in what sense the Triune God can be represented in terms of "event," this essay concludes with some remarks intended to illustrate the usefulness of this concept for understanding the newness of Christianity and of human existence.

The incarnation of the Logos is indeed an unforeseen, ungraspable event that both undoes and fulfills human expectations and preconceived ideas concerning God and the meaning of human life and history.[73] It is the event of Christ alone that can unfold the design concealed in man's creation and reveal to man who he is and what he is called to be and enjoy as son in the Son, because Christ indeed reveals himself as the one in

---

72. In this regard, man's gratitude for God's salvific deed is only a faint echo of the reciprocity that characterizes donation in God, where there is no shadow of negativity.

73. For a description of Christianity as an event, see Giussani, *He Is If He Changes.*

whom everything consists.[74] The event of Christ also grants man the eyes of faith that enable him to catch a glimpse of the order beneath every phenomenon and historical event within the divine mystery, and to begin to respect the proper distance, as Jean-Luc Marion would say, between idols and the icon of Christ (Col 1:15-20).[75] In this sense, without unraveling its mystery, Christ enables man to behold the face of the ultimate ground that presents itself without losing itself through the different phenomena; *tam pater nemo.* God's revelation in Christ discloses the depth and meaning of the eventful nature of beings and history. Under the light of his presence they are nothing but the inexhaustible exuberance of divine creativity through which God gives himself to man and awaits his return (Heb 10:5).

The insertion into human history of the overabundant, ever-surprising movement of agapic donation is an unmerited and unexpected grace, with which God "for-gives" and "accompanies his creation in a perpetual now."[76] His bestowal of grace also demands an answer.[77] God, in

74. As is widely noted, Balthasar here reiterates Aquinas's and Bonaventure's doctrine. See *TD* 5, pp. 61-65.

75. In this regard Maximus the Confessor beautifully states: "Christ is everything in all of you. It is he who encloses in himself all beings by the unique, simple, and infinitely wise power of his goodness. As the center of straight lines that radiate from him he does not allow by his unique, simple, and single cause and power that the principles of being become disjoined at the periphery but rather he circumscribes their extension in a circle and brings back to himself the distinctive elements of beings which he himself brought into existence. The purpose of this is so that the creations and products of the one God be in no way strangers and enemies to one another by having no reason or center for which they might show each other any friendly or peaceful sentiment or identity, and not run the risk of having their being separated from God to dissolve into non-being" (Maximus the Confessor, "The Church's Mystagogy," in *Selected Writings,* trans. George C. Berthold [New York: Paulist Press, 1985], p. 187). Also see Marion, *L'idole et la distance.*

76. *TL* 2, pp. 114-45. It is interesting to note here the progression of John Paul II's trinitarian encyclicals: Christ is the redeemer of man, who shows to him that he is made for love and in love (*Redemptor hominis,* n. 10). The redemption that Christ brings is that of the Father, whose justice blossoms forth from and brings man back to his infinite mercy. That is why he is described as the one "rich in mercy" (*Dives in misericordia,* nn. 7-8). The merciful design of the Father, incarnated in Christ, becomes operative in the hearts of men because the Holy Spirit, the Lord and giver of life, convinces man of his own sinfulness so that, after having obtained the contrition for his own sins, so that man, having obtained contrition for his own sins, may be enabled by the Holy Spirit to taste the eternal life the risen Lord has gained for him (*Dominum et Vivificantem,* nn. 33-42).

77. See also Balthasar, "Is the Mass a Sacrifice of the Church?" in *Explorations in The-*

Christ, seeks to gain a free and conscious adhesion, a reciprocation similar to the one proper to God (Mt 8:10), which cannot but be rewarded with the same ever-greater overabundance of the triune mystery of love (Jn 15:1-17). In this sense, Christ reveals the heart of man's speech, which is the participation in the same ecstatic dialogue that permeates the trinitarian life. If one considers the Annunciation to the Virgin Mary, it is possible to see that the dramatic exchange of divine and human "yeses" is, of course, more than a simple exchange of entreaties and answers.[78] God's request to Mary is an offer of himself that longs to be accepted. Mary's discreet and simple response is, again, nothing but the complete offer of herself *(fiat)*. God incorporates Mary's self-offering within the offer of himself and thus becomes incarnate by taking his flesh from her. Astonishingly, in his gift of himself to man, God becomes, through Mary, "Creature of his creature," as Mary becomes virgin mother of God.[79] What God seeks and finds in Mary is nothing but grateful reciprocity. God, who loves gratuitously, only accepts being loved gratuitously. Mary's *fiat* illustrates that the life of the human being is called to become, through the gift of the Spirit of Christ, an "event." Not so much because of the significance that his or her historical existence may acquire but, more simply, because, as we see in Mary, human existence becomes a participant in, and thus a witness to, the gratuitous and grateful reciprocation of God's always new love. To every human embrace, regardless of its insurmountable precariousness, God responds with an overabundant gift of himself (Rom 5:20), which in turn elicits in the human being the desire to respond as Christ has indicated: "to the end" (Jn 15:12-13). This unending, increasingly intensifying dialogue is thus the continuous experience of eternal richness in which the gift itself is nothing but God himself and the fecundity of man's life (Lk 8:18). The fruitfulness that God bestows on man (Lk 1:49) by giving his very self to him not only involves man as an "isolated" being; it also constitutes the generation and

---

ology, vol. 3: *Creator Spirit,* trans. Brian McNeil (San Francisco: Ignatius Press, 1993) for a presentation of the role of man's freedom in Christ's salvific offer of himself.

78. In this regard, Giussani, recalling Kierkegaard's "imperative," clarifies that Christ's offer of himself with his claim to divinity sets forth man's existence as a question that cannot but be faced and solved. See Luigi Giussani, *At the Origin of the Christian Claim,* trans. Viviane Hewitt (Montreal & Kingston: McGill-Queen's University Press, 1998), pp. 33-35.

79. The prayer Dante puts on the lips of St. Bernard says: "Tu se' colei che l'umana natura/nobilitasti sì, che'l suo fattore/non disdegnò di farsi sua fattura" (*Divine Comedy. Paradiso* XXXIII, 4-6).

reconstitution of a people (Lk 1:50-55), the Church, which, in her mysterious unity, is the sacramental sign of the divine communion.[80] Precisely because human existence is inserted into God's eternal happening, the growth of human life and the fulfillment of man's desire can never cease.[81] God opens up the ever-greater mystery of his love and brings the human being into himself so that, seeing the glory of the Lord, he may be continuously transfigured "from one degree of glory to another" (2 Cor 3:18), always fulfilled and never satiated.

80. ". . . the mystery of the Church is rooted in God the Trinity, and therefore has this trinitarian dimension as its first and fundamental dimension, inasmuch as the Church depends on and lives in the Trinity from her origins to her historical conclusion and eternal destination" (John Paul II, *A Catechesis on the Creed*, vol. 4: *The Church: Mystery, Sacrament, Communion* [Boston: Pauline Books and Media, 1998], p. 76). See *Lumen gentium*, 1-9.

81. Gregory of Nyssa, *Life of Moses* II, 239; Jean Daniélou, *L'être et le temps chez Grégoire de Nysse* (Leiden: Brill, 1970); Daniélou, *Platonisme et théologie mystique. Essai sur la doctrine spirituelle de saint Grégoire de Nysse* (Paris: Aubier, 1953).

What Does Trinity "Add"
to the Reality of the Covenants?

Richard Schenk

The question to be posed in this brief panel contribution is twofold: What is the genuinely Christian understanding of the fate and state of the Older Covenant since the Revelation of Christ and the Trinity? And how can the study of the theology of Hans Urs von Balthasar advance this understanding? Let me preface my remarks by noting that both questions seem to me to be ones with many still-open aspects, about which significant clarification may realistically be expected.

The Need for Theological Clarification

Today's hermeneutical situation for interpreting the relationship of the Older and Newer Covenants and the Christian understanding of the relationship of today's Judaism to both of them is prepared by the well-known pastoral and theological developments stretching from the reform of the Good Friday intercessions by Pope John XXIII (1959) and the declaration of *Nostra aetate* (1965) down to the many interventions of the late Pope John Paul II. Although the affirmation (at least in principle) of these developments may be presumed of most or even all of those joined here in these centenary discussions, many of their most critical theological implications have yet to be clarified. As welcome as the departure from the older prayer "pro perfidis Iudaeis"[1] was, our present prayer that the "populus acquisitionis priorae"[2] might be graced "foederis fidelitate

---

1. "For the perfidious Jews" or "for the unfaithful Jews."
2. "the people you first made your own."

proficere"[3] and "ad redemptionis mereatur plenitudinem pervenire"[4] (the great petitions of Good Friday, when the Church makes clearer than ever what is most on her heart) stands in need of as much theological penetration as the mystery of Israel will allow us in our times. The need to explicate more fully the perennial *lex credendi* from this newly reformed *lex orandi* was arguably more intensified than satisfied by the reminder of *Nostra aetate* (= *NA*) 4 that "God holds the Jews most dear for the sake of their Fathers; He does not repent of the gifts He makes or of the calls He issues." The theological question was made more pressing by the Council's reminder (also in *NA* 4) that "the Church keeps ever in mind the words of the Apostle about his kinsmen: 'theirs is the sonship and the glory and the covenants and the law and the worship and the promises; theirs are the fathers and from them is the Christ according to the flesh' (Rom 9:4-5)."[5]

It might well be argued that there is widespread (but not unanimous) agreement within Christianity today to allow as much "graciousness" to the continued practice of Judaism as is consistent with belief in Christ as the eschatological mediator of all salvation. Although we are still searching today for a genuine theology of the relationship of Christianity to non-Judeo-Christian religions, there probably is widespread readiness at least among the participants gathered here (as opposed to both medieval "conservatives" and postmodern "liberals") to see in the continued practice of Judaism a "plus" of graciousness over and beyond the practices of non-Judeo-Christian religions. What seems uncertain, however, even among those who share all the presuppositions named above, is whether genuine Christianity must or at least may reject "supercessionism," the notion of the universal *cessatio legalium* or the termination of the Older Covenant, in order to affirm the continued "graciousness" of today's practice of Judaism by those who, at least notionally, reject its fulfillment in Jesus Christ.

There are at least four conceivable strategies for doing this. First, a moderately exclusivist position: Should we attempt to interpret *NA* 4 and Romans 9–11 away from the seeming impression of God's continued loy-

---

3. "to grow in faithfulness to his covenant."

4. "arrive at the fullness of redemption."

5. The same task of future theological clarification was established by other Conciliar texts as well, such as *Lumen Gentium* 6 and *Gaudium et Spes* 32.

alty toward previous covenants and, instead, speak only of loyalty to his promises, which he fulfills now only by means of a new *pactum?*

If, on the other hand, perhaps with what is most familiar today in its pluralist variant, we simply reject supercessionism (the second option), can we do so without also rejecting the notion of a consistent and genuine development of Christian doctrine in the sense of John Henry Newman's vision of the Church? Does the rejection of supercessionism, at least a rejection based, say, on non-relativistic arguments drawn from a notion of twin covenants, make possible or impossible our continuity with the New Testament and the patristic and medieval Church?

A third option, certainly typical of inclusivist interpretations but not limited to these, would attempt to blend the first two contrary attempts (viewed as non-contradictory) in somewhat the same fashion suggested, *albeit* unintentionally, by Thomas Aquinas, when he argued that a profitable Christian reading of the older cult needed complementary strategies of literal and metaphorical interpretation, matching the immanent and transcendent meanings of the *lex scripta*.[6] Can it be well argued that Christianity is an improvement upon rather than a replacement of the Older Covenant, which continues to point towards fulfillment in Jesus Christ *in obliquo,* but not *in recto?*

A final option, which need not be an expression of indifference (pace R. Kendall Soulen[7]), might be to suggest that God has revealed to us more about what it means to be blessed with explicit faith in Christ than what it means to be burdened by an explicit rejection of him.

The Contribution of Balthasar Studies

This admittedly rough and incomplete sketch of the *status quaestionis* suggests some of the dimensions of the second part of our second question as well: Do the writings of Hans Urs von Balthasar develop any of these four approaches, or do they offer an alternative? Do his writings exclude any of the approaches mentioned? What challenges do Balthasar's writings pre-

6. Cf. Beryl Smalley, William of Auvergne, John of La Rochelle, and St. Thomas Aquinas on the Old Law, in A. A. Maurer et al., eds., *St. Thomas Aquinas, 1274-1974: Commemorative Studies,* vol. 2 (Toronto: PIMS, 1974), pp. 11-71.

7. See R. Kendall Soulen, *The God of Israel and Christian Theology* (Minneapolis: Fortress, 1996).

sent to the search for an adequate theology of the Covenants and of today's Judaism?

One way to engage these questions would be through the comparison with and above all the contrast to Adolf von Harnack's reflections on the Marcionite controversies.[8] Both Harnack and Balthasar see clearly that the stance of Christianity towards the Old Testament will decide the proximity or distance of genuine Christianity to the varied traditions of the Reformation. The 1870 "Dorpater Preisschrift" of the young Harnack sought to portray Marcion as "the modern believer" and "the first reformer,"[9] just as fifty years later the monograph *Das Evangelium vom fremden Gott* would portray the opposition to Marcion pejoratively as "the foundation of the Catholic Church."[10] The contrasts between the two modern theologians will reflect much of their opposing sympathies for the Lutheran or Calvinist forms of the Reformational heritage. Like Balthasar's *Love Alone*,[11] but in ways far more radical, Harnack's Marcion begins by rejecting any cosmological reduction of genuine Scripture and affirms that the properly personal sphere of love and responsibility is the only credible one. The God of Marcion is "alien" to cosmological and ontological issues, which in Harnack's analysis is what separates Marcion from Gnosticism. Like Balthasar's *Love Alone*, but in ways far more radical, Harnack's Marcion will seek the success of the New Testament in its contrast to the failure and fruitlessness[12] of the Older Testament. *Love Alone* portrays the

---

8. A longer study would want to include the less dualistic positions of Apelles and Philomena in this contrastive comparison, as sharing more resources with Alexandrian theology, even though the outstanding disciple of Marcion and the visionary did not technically remain members of the Marcionite Church; cf. Adolf von Harnack, *Das Evangelium vom fremden Gott, Eine Monographie zur Geschichte der Grundlegung der katholischen Kirche. Neue Studien zu Marcion* (Darmstadt: Wissenschaftliche Buchgesellschaft, 1960), pp. 177ff.

9. Adolf von Harnack, *Marcion. Der moderne Gläubige des 2. Jahrhunderts, der erste Reformator* (Berlin: W. de Gruyter, 2003).

10. Adolf von Harnack, *Das Evangelium vom fremden Gott.*

11. All citations follow the fourth edition of Hans Urs von Balthasar, *Glaubhaft ist nur Liebe* (Einsiedeln: Johannes Verlag, 1975).

12. Cf. Aidan Nichols, *The Word Has Been Abroad: A Guide Through Balthasar's Aesthetics* (Washington, D.C.: The Catholic University of America Press, 1998), pp. 187-253, here 206; cf. Hans Urs von Balthasar, *Herrlichkeit. Eine theologische Aesthetik. Band III, 2. Theologie. Teil 2: Neuer Bund* (Einsiedeln: Johannes Verlag, 1969/1988), esp. pp. 29-36 of "Auftakt: Truemmer des Alten Bundes." (Balthasar, *The Glory of the Lord: A Theological Aesthetics* [= GL], vol. 7: *Theology: The New Covenant*, trans. Brian McNeil, C.R.V. [San Francisco: Ignatius Press, 1989], pp. 33-40.)

Older Covenant as missing the centrality and eternity of God's love,[13] as concluded *(abgeschlossen)*,[14] as stressing God's judgment and anger over love, more of a warning than a fulfillment,[15] while (in supposed contrast to the New Testament) suggesting the plausibility of final loss,[16] and, perhaps most importantly, while remaining within those boundaries of apparent reason that would exclude suffering from God.[17]

No doubt, the differences between Balthasar and Marcion are no less fundamental than those between K. Barth's neo-orthodoxy and Harnack's liberal Protestantism; but where are they located? At the broadest level, Balthasar does not find the picture of the Old Testament God, his creation, and his covenant (in short, the manifestation of his glory there) unfitting in principle for New Testament sensibilities; for Balthasar, they reveal God's glory precisely in many of the activities that Marcion saw as so inglorious. This allows not only the affirmation of the one God of both covenants, but the absorption of much of the older covenant with little transformation into the newer one; following roughly K. Barth's doctrine of Israel, it is in this sense that we should read Paul's image of being grafted onto the old and cultivated stock. The Church draws into itself life from the Root of Jesse.[18]

Sobald die Kirche die Gewalt, die Wucht, den Kabôd und die ungeheure prophetische Dringlichkeit des Alten Bundes einen Augenblick vergisst, sinkt sie sofort von ihrer Höhe ab, ihr Salz wird schal, ihr Christusbild nazarenisch, harnackisch, schliesslich nazistisch. Sogar wenn sie sich auf Paulus allein spezialisierte und den Juden Jakobus mit seiner prophetisch harten Forderung zur irdischen Tat der Liebe, zur Veränderung der sozialen Struktur, sein Wehe gegen die Reichen, seine Tat- und Werkreligion übersähe, dieses jüdische Element, von dem ja alle Evangelien voll sind, wäre sie nicht mehr allgemein und katholisch. Ja: es gibt einen dauernden jüdischen Auftrag an das

13. *Herrlichkeit III, 2: 2. Neuer Bund*, pp. 38, 42f.; *GL 7*, pp. 42-43, 47f.

14. *Herrlichkeit III, 2: 2. Neuer Bund*, pp. 56, 59, 85f.; *GL 7*, pp. 62, 65-66, 94f.

15. *Herrlichkeit III, 2: 2. Neuer Bund*, pp. 72f.; *GL 7*, pp. 81f.

16. *Herrlichkeit III, 2: 2. Neuer Bund*, pp. 60ff.; *GL 7*, pp. 66ff.

17. *Herrlichkeit III, 2: 2. Neuer Bund*, p. 68; *GL 7*, p. 76.

18. Cf. Hans Urs von Balthasar, "Die Wurzel Jesse," in Balthasar, *Sponsa Verbi. Skizzen zur Theologie II* (Einsiedeln: Johannes Verlag, 1961), pp. 306-16 (Eng., "The Church and Israel," in *Explorations in Theology*, vol. 2: *Spouse of the Word* [San Francisco: Ignatius Press, 1991], pp. 289-98).

Christentum, der aber kein anderer ist noch zu sein braucht, als der bleibende Auftrag des Alten Bundes an den Neuen.[19]

In this final sentence we hear again something of the theme of abrogation by absorption.[20] It suggests the deepest reason that Balthasar seems to give for the "hardening" *(Verstockung)* of the Jews, for the inability even of the youngest (inspired?) books of the Old Testament to grasp and keep hold of the glory of God, for the futility of all early and later Jewish efforts of a messianic, apocalyptic, or sapiential character to embrace the First Covenant legacy.[21] It is here that Balthasar's reasons are to be sought for minimalizing the present Jewish embrace of the Older Covenant.[22] In this interpretation, all these are attempts to embrace the glory of God without "embracing" suffering in his people or in his own self; for Balthasar, this involves necessarily the search for a *theologia gloriae* outside the *theologia crucis*.[23] In its consequence, however, this view of the fate of the Old Testament, like Marcion's opposing view, leaves Christianity with no relative "other" to which it needs to relate itself.

19. Balthasar, "Die Wurzel Jesse," p. 315 ("The Church in Israel," pp. 297-98).

20. For a non-absorptive model of relationality implicit in the rejection of Marcionism, cf. Rémi Brague, "Inklusion und Verdauung. Zwei Modelle kultureller Aneignung," in G. Figal et al., eds., *Hermeneutische Wege. Hans-Georg Gadamer zum Hundertsten* (Tübingen: Mohr, 2000), pp. 293-306; cf. also Brague, *Eccentric Culture: A Theory of Western Civilization* (South Bend, Ind.: St. Augustine's Press, 2002), p. 112: "In this way, it was religious secondarity that prevented all culture inherited from Christianity, as in the case with Europe, from considering itself as its own source. The refusal of Marcionism is thus, perhaps, the founding event of the history of Europe as a civilization, in that it furnished the matrix of the European relationship to the past and anchored it at the highest possible level."

21. Hans Urs von Balthasar, *Herrlichkeit. Eine theologische Aesthetik*. Band III, 2: *Theologie*. Teil 1: *Alter Bund* (Einsiedeln: Johannes Verlag, 1967/1989), esp. pp. 285-336.

22. Cf. Balthasar, "Die Wurzel Jesse," p. 312: "Man beachte wohl: es wird nicht gesagt, dass die Verheissung Israels anderswo lebendig sei als in der Kirche Christi. Es wird nicht gesagt, dass Israel theologisch eine von der Kirche unterschiedene geschichtliche Mission in der Menschheit zu erfüllen habe, wie immer wieder behauptet wird" ("The Church and Israel," p. 295).

23. Cf. A. Nichols, *The Word Has Been Abroad*, p. 206: "But considered as Jewish attempts to solve the 'problem' of Israel bequeathed by the major prophets, they are, Balthasar thinks, a failure — a fruitless effort to force the glory of God into the open. Messianism, apocalyptic and wisdom theology are, before incarnation and atonement, premature; they would integrate the shadow side (and the creation) at the level of insufficient depth. They are, in the sense stigmatised by Luther, *theologia gloriae* . . . they tempt us to ignore the necessary twilight which Israel endured for the half-millennium before the Christian era."

What seems to be beyond controversy here, at least for Christian reflection, is the value of Balthasar's references to the "twilight side" of both Older and Newer Testament experience. Following K. Barth's abiding dialectic, Balthasar reminds us to look for the *Verstockung* within our own hearts as we seek to embrace our share in the cross. Balthasar seems to suggest something like the retrieval of the less epochal, more "existential" reading provided by medieval theologians for the threefold distinction of *status legis naturalis, status legis scriptae,* and *status gratiae evangelicae.* Drawn especially from the writings of Augustine and Hugh of St. Victor, these typologies were applied not only to distinct epochs but to distinct aspects of existence present in all three. The *status legis naturalis,* or the *status legis scriptae,* thus describes an aspect of Christian existence as well, just as elements of gospel grace are found in Old Testament life.[24] The promise of glory is not found anywhere apart from the mystery of human suffering, and Balthasar's contribution in reminding us of this deserves lasting attention.

The more controversial, but also the more decisive question in this context may be left to other speakers at this symposium.[25] If Balthasar has replaced suffering's toleration by the Trinity or by the humanity of Christ *(voluntas in obliquo, voluntas rationis)* with an absolute and antecedent will of it *(in recto),* if he has heeded the unseparated character of Christ's natures in the hypostatic union at the price of their unmixed duality, if he has made kenotic suffering normative by deifying it, then it needs to be asked whether the retrieval of the Trinity as beyond suffering — precisely as a gospel of human hope — might not allow us to embrace with the living Jewish community their more genuine understanding of the Old Testament as a covenant of hope for salvation from suffering.[26] Such a non-

---

24. For one example of this existential reading of salvific historical epochs, cf. Quaestio 4 in Robert Kilwardby, *Quaestiones in librum quartum Sententiarum,* ed. R. Schenk, vol. 17 of *Veröffentlichungen der Kommission für die Herausgabe ungedruckter Texte aus der mittelalterlichen Geisteswelt* (Munich: Bavarian Academy of Sciences, 1993), pp. 14-26.

25. Cf. also R. Schenk, "Ist die Rede vom leidenden Gott theologisch zu vermeiden? Reflexionen über den Streit von K. Rahner und H. U. von Balthasar," in Friedrich Hermanni and Peter Koslowski, eds., *Der leidende Gott. Eine philosophische und theologische Kritik* (Munich: Wilhelm Fink, 2001), pp. 225-39.

26. Compare the third petition of the Our Father with the Chassidic saying of Rabbi Chinch of Alexander (d. 1859): "The real exile of Israel in Egypt was that they had learned to bear it," cited by M. Buber, *Die Erzählungen der Chassidim* (Zurich: Manesse, 1949), p. 838.

absorptive embrace both of the Old Testament and the *populus acquisitionis primae* might be made possible by our belief in the Holy — and ever Blessed — Trinity. The Trinity can make a difference in our lives only if it is different. Credible above all is our sharing in that Blessed Love.

Motion and the Body:
Does "Love Make the World Go 'Round"?

God's Labor, Novelty's Emergence: Cosmic Motion as Self-Transcending Love

Stephen Fields

Reason and the Religious Imagination

St. Ignatius Loyola calls the last prayer of his *Spiritual Exercises* "The Contemplation to Obtain Divine Love." It is intended to help the person making his way through the *Exercises* to recapitulate all the other contemplations done over thirty silent days. As a grand finale, the exercitant is asked to consider more deeply the nature of the love that God has instilled and awakened in his prayer. Love, Ignatius opines, consists principally in a mutual sharing of goods. As the paradigm of love, God, he says, is a laborer who works in creation by dwelling in it, filling it with life, and conserving it in being. Brimming forth love from his infinite superabundance, God issues all blessings and gifts "as the rays of light descend from the sun, and as the waters flow from their fountains." In recompense, what more can a human being who enjoys such unmerited bounty do but make his own self-offering to the divine self-offering he receives? "You have given all to me," the retreatant is counseled to pray, "to You I return it."[1] Like Socrates' dream of the goddess Diotima in the *Symposium*, Ignatius's contemplation to obtain divine love raises a perennial question: What has the religious imagination to do with philosophy? Does Loyola's vision, however poetic and panoramic, make any claim on our reason? Like Socrates, he clearly thinks so. Thinly veiled under his appeal to the commonplaces of experience, like work, light, and flowing water, lies a metaphysics both sweeping

---

1. St. Ignatius Loyola, *Spiritual Exercises,* ed. and trans. Louis Puhl (Chicago: Loyola University Press, 1951), pp. 101-3.

and profound. It implies a relation between infinite and finite being structured by love. It implies that a free creation has the capacity to move transcendently. The task of the study that follows will be to warrant this metaphysics — to show, in other words, that it yields not only the well-intended sentiments of piety but also the credible insights of reason.

As a preface, let us recall that, for Paul Ricoeur, the religious image is implicitly rational. It emerges because human reason is halted at a conceptual impasse. On the one hand, reason has the ability to diagnose the fundamental enigmas of human existence, such as the need for an ultimate cause that can offer a final justice for all forms of evil. On the other hand, reason is weak and can only dimly work up conceptual solutions. Framed as logically coherent arguments, these consistently fail to satisfy. Helping us to cope with reason's conceptual impotence, the imagination offers a therapy. It generates metaphors, narratives, and myths as explanations. These, as Kant would say, "quicken" reason by using a sensuously perceptible form to stimulate deeper insights in reason.[2]

According to Ricoeur, the products of the religious imagination are properly understood, not as naïvely dispensable pseudo-explanations, but as symbols pregnant with meaning. Their imagistic guise veils a surplus of signification. For instance, the story of the fall in the third chapter of Genesis uses an apple, a snake, and various anthropomorphisms to speak about God, humanity's relation to God, and the nature of evil and temptation. The surplus of signification embedded in these images needs to be teased out by repeated interpretation. Because concepts fail to exhaust the meaning of the images, Ricoeur concludes that in religion the imagination can assume a priority over reason. Images give rise to concepts.[3] Religion, as Hegel remarks, serves as the soil in which philosophy is nourished and brought to fruition.[4]

Taking Ricoeur's analysis as a cue, let us return to Ignatius. The claim

2. Immanuel Kant, *Critique of Judgment,* trans. J. H. Bernard (New York: Hafner, 1951), pp. 157, 160.

3. The treatment of Ricoeur is indebted to Joseph Kockelmans, "On Religious Myths," in *The Challenge of Religion,* ed. Frederick Ferré et al. (New York: Seabury, 1982), esp. pp. 220, 228-30, citing Ricoeur, *The Symbolism of Evil,* trans. Emerson Buchanan (New York: Harper & Row, 1967), esp. pp. 3-9, 161-71, 347-57 (originally *Finitude et culpabilité* [Paris: Aubier, 1960]).

4. G. W. F. Hegel, *Einleitung in die Geschichte der Philosophie,* ed. Hoffmeister/Nicolin (Hamburg: F. Meiner, 1959), pp. 173-75.

that his contemplation to obtain divine love makes on our reason can be framed as follows. Impregnating being, a dynamic and infinite Love drives the finite order towards Itself in a self-transcending motion. If this axiom expresses the surplus of signification implicit in the contemplation's imaginative form, then the task opened for us is to explicate it in a comprehensive philosophical idiom. Considering the axiom's claim that the finite order is dynamic best begins this task. Accordingly, we turn to the doctrine of substance that since Aristotle has explained the finite order's basic structure.[5]

Substance, Motion, and Emergent Novelty

Substance explains the process of change or "becoming" precisely as a function of being, the universal horizon that is convertible with the intelligible. A translation of the Greek term *hypokeimenon*, substance means that which "stands under" or supports a reality. The classic definitions in Western thought, following Aristotle, offer variations on a common theme: substance is that which is apt to exist in itself and not in another. A substance embraces its accidents, those attributes such as quality and quantity that are apt to exist, not in themselves, but in another. A substance is thus a reality in itself, distinct from its accidents, which inhere within it.[6]

Aristotle tends to see a substance as the sum total of its component accidents and thus to underplay the active relation obtaining between the whole and its constituents.[7] Descartes imports this tendency into modern thought. Although he contends that substances need nothing except God to exist, he tends to posit substances as isolated entities that exist "by" themselves rather than "in" themselves.[8] Norris Clarke observes that this isolation causes Whitehead, the Anglo-American process thinker, to reject the notion of substance altogether, because it fails to account for the mu-

5. Aristotle, *Metaphysics* 1029a, 1-2.

6. W. Norris Clarke, "Central Problems in Metaphysics" (course notes, Philosophy Department, Fordham University, mimeographed), section 7, pp. 7-8.

7. Clarke, "Central Problems in Metaphysics," p. 8.

8. W. Norris Clarke, "Central Problems in the History of Metaphysics" (course notes, Philosophy Department, Fordham University, mimeographed): notes on Descartes, 2. See Descartes, *Principles of Philosophy,* trans. Valentine Rodger Miller and Reese P. Miller (Dordrecht and Boston: D. Reidel, 1983), 1.51.

tual engagement among entities.[9] By contrast with the inert and reclusive model that descends from Aristotle through Descartes, recent Thomist thought aims to retrieve the incipient dynamism in Aquinas's view of substance. It seeks to understand a substance as a system within a system. Accordingly, substance, although grounding the unity of an entity through change, is intrinsically energetic. As such, it explains the vitality of the processes of the finite order.[10]

Substance as Dynamic

Making an especially important contribution to this understanding, Karl Rahner conceives finite substances as dynamic ontological events. Harnessing a theme at the core of his thought, he interprets them as "real-symbols."[11] This means that substances necessarily express themselves in order for their essential nature to become constituted.[12] They are symbols because their accidental qualities are the media in which the identity of substances manifests and realizes itself.[13] Rahner, like Ricoeur, thus adverts to a rich notion of symbol that is to be distinguished from a sign. In a real-symbol, the reality that the symbol represents is contained within the symbol itself. In a sign, this reality is not given but only pointed to. Thus, the human person is a real-symbol, because the person's spiritual essence is mediated immediately in and through the body.[14] A flag, however, is a sign, because it merely reminds us of our country and its values. So also is a traffic light, because it indicates, but does not itself embody, a positive law that must be obeyed.[15]

9. Clarke, "Central Problems in the History of Metaphysics," notes on Descartes, 2.

10. Clarke, "Central Problems in Metaphysics," sections 8-10, advances this understanding and lists a bibliography.

11. For fuller treatments of this notion, see Stephen M. Fields, *Being as Symbol: On the Origins and Development of Karl Rahner's Metaphysics* (Washington, D.C.: Georgetown University Press, 2000), and Joseph H. P. Wong, *Logos-Symbol in the Christology of Karl Rahner* (Rome: Libreria Ateneo Salesiano, 1984).

12. Karl Rahner, "The Theology of the Symbol" (= "ToS") in vol. 4 of *Theological Investigations,* trans. Kevin Smyth (Baltimore: Helicon, 1966), p. 224; originally "Zur Theologie des Symbols," in vol. 4 of *Schriften zur Theologie,* 16 vols. (Einsiedeln: Benzinger, 1954-84).

13. Rahner, "ToS," p. 231.

14. Rahner, "ToS," pp. 246-47.

15. Rahner, "ToS," p. 225.

Holding the doctrine of hylemorphism, Rahner posits that matter structured by form constitutes all finite substances. Following Aristotle, Rahner holds, on the one hand, that form is the cause of the essence or "what-ness" of any existent.[16] On the other hand, he holds that matter is the cause of individuation and change.[17] Matter is thus the principle of potency. The form of chair, for instance, has the potential to become any number of chairs not yet made. Once made, any of these has the potential to change in size, color, weight, and so forth, while still remaining recognizably the same substance. Also consistent with Aristotle, Rahner views form and matter as distinct but inseparable metaphysical co-principles.[18] But he adds new life to Aristotle by interpreting matter and form as reciprocally engaged partners. In so doing, Rahner borrows from Hegel's logic of the "notion." When Hegel posited it, the notion was a new concept knowing no counterpart in traditional realism.[19] Because of its importance for Rahner and the argument of this study, let us briefly describe it.

The Notion

According to Hegel, the notion is "the very heart" of the dynamic creativity inherent in reality.[20] "Becoming" is the fundamental, or primal notion, that originates all other ontological dynamisms.[21] It is becoming, not being, that constitutes and generates the real order. True to its dynamic nature, becoming emerges from the mutual engagement of its two constituent partners, being and nothing. Considered separately, these are not concrete realities but pure abstractions that exist only as components of the notion that embraces them. It is thus becoming, as the primal notion, that for Hegel is the first concrete thought.[22] Nonetheless, the abstract concept of being is the origin of the dynamic becoming that structures re-

16. Aristotle, *Metaphysics*, 983a, 27.

17. Aristotle, *Metaphysics*, 1042a, 25f.

18. Aristotle, *Metaphysics*, 1042a, 25f.

19. W. T. Stace, *The Philosophy of Hegel* (London: Constable, 1955), p. 223.

20. G. W. F. Hegel, *Hegel's Logic*, ed. and trans. William Wallace (Oxford: Clarendon, 1975), p. 232; originally part 1 of *Enzyklopädie der philosophischen Wissenschaften* (= EL) (1830).

21. *EL*, p. 132.

22. *EL*, p. 132.

ality. This is so because being deductively entails the concept of nothing. Because being is the highest possible abstraction, it is therefore empty of any concrete reality. As a result, it is equivalent to nothing. Because nothing is deduced from being, nothing can be considered being's "own other," into which being "passes." For its part, nothing, because it is the equivalent of being, may be said to pass into being.[23]

It is this reciprocal "passing into" that, for Hegel, is the defining principle of the notion. It means that one concept generates another concept that, because of its opposition to the concept from which it ensues, is equivalent to the generating concept.[24] In their "passing into" each other, the two concepts constitute a unity-in-difference. Most importantly, this dynamic unity-in-difference produces a genuine ontological advance. In their opposition, the two concepts parent the birth of a third concept. In turn, this concept emerges in reality as something concretely new.[25] Hegel calls it a sublation. It represents a self-perfection or self-consummation of the reciprocal passing-into of the two concepts that produce it.[26] In the case of the unity-in-difference that is being and nothing, this self-consummation is *becoming*. Because becoming is the fundamental notion, reality is thus conceived by Hegel as dialectically driven at its core.

Concerned about the deeper cause of this dialectic, Hegel's idealism asserts that the notion is embraced by Spirit. The notion is Spirit's heart. Spirit, not being, is thus for Hegel the universal horizon. Spirit reconciles all oppositions because it includes them in its own infinite act. Because Spirit is the generating source of reality's immanent dialectic, the notion's successively eternal sublations progressively disclose Spirit. Accordingly, Spirit fully enfolds within itself the finite order, which constitutes an accident within Spirit's own absolute substance. The finite and the infinite are not qualitatively different, or analogously related, as they are in Thomist realism. On the contrary, they constitute a unity-in-difference that is fundamentally univocal. For the purpose of this study, what is important is Hegel's insight that the notion's dynamic motion requires an infinite cause as its driving source. Because this infinite source embraces the notion just

---

23. *EL*, pp. 127-28.

24. *EL*, p. 218.

25. John E. Smith, "The Relation of Thought and Being: Some Lessons from Hegel's Encyclopedia," *New Scholasticism* 38 (1964): 36-37.

26. *EL*, p. 129.

as a substance embraces an accident, it is the notion's formal cause. The importance of this point will become clearer as our analysis proceeds.

Substance and the Notion

In his use of Hegel, Rahner wants to lodge becoming within the core of substance without at the same time devolving into Hegel's idealism. First, he asserts that form and matter are self-mediated within a substance in order for the substance to become perfected or consummated as a distinctive entity. This self-mediation obtains when form actively passes into the substance's matter. Rahner calls this "passing-into" form's "emanation" of itself. By means of it, form "gives itself away," as it were, to a substance's matter, which thus becomes form's own "other." Form's passing-into matter confers on matter meaning and intelligibility. Second, Rahner contends that form, having been emanated into matter, passes back into itself in order to consummate the substance precisely as distinct.[27] Form thus "returns" to itself. This return is necessary because form, as a dynamic principle, is not perfected until it is reunited with itself through its self-donation in matter.[28]

Rahner thus conceives substances as active ontological events. They are constituted by the emanation and return of form in and through matter. Substances are real-symbols, because their fundamental reality, their meaning and intelligibility, is grasped in and through matter. Matter is the means by which a substance's accidents are perceived by the senses. The accidents thus incarnate and express form, which is the principle of the substance's identity.[29]

Substance and Emergent Novelty

Especially original in Rahner's assimilation of Hegel is his understanding of how a substance gives birth to ontological novelty — how, in other words, a substance produces a genuine ontological advance. Rahner's originality becomes clear when his theory of substance is interpreted in light of

27. Rahner, "ToS," pp. 231-32.
28. Rahner, "ToS," p. 231.
29. Rahner, "ToS," p. 244.

his theory of motion, change, and becoming. In the realism of Aristotle and St. Thomas, motion is the transition from potency to act. It occurs when a substance concretely embodies any change that is possible for it to undergo. Traditionally, this transition has not been understood to produce any indeterminate or spontaneous novelty in the real order. Change brings forth no new being. Becoming merely modifies the mode in which the substance exists. In short, change simply explicates those determinations already latent in the substance.[30]

Rahner finds this traditional view untenable. Because change alters the accidents of a substance, he asserts that an entity clearly possesses a newness. Change produces increments in reality heretofore undetermined.[31] These cannot be due, he argues, to the finite substance alone. On the contrary, undetermined increments in reality emerge when substances change, precisely because substances transcend themselves.[32] In other words, the new increments effected in change entail a substance's exceeding the limits of its essence or nature. Consequently, some other cause both superior to, and independent of, the substance in motion is required.[33] But this cause cannot merely be another finite substance. When any substance acts on another, it too undergoes a change that produces in itself a new self-transcending ontological determination. Because an infinite regress obtains if an adequate cause is sought only among finite realities, Rahner reasonably infers that this cause must be infinitely self-subsisting.[34] In this he agrees with Hegel, for whom the dialectic of the notion is driven by Spirit as a formal cause.

The Infinite as Final Cause

Rahner parts company with Hegel, however, in two important respects. First, the infinite does not constitute finite substances as its own accidents. It

---

30. Karl Rahner, *Hominization: The Evolutionary Origin of Man as a Theological Problem* (= *H*), trans. W. T. O'Hara (Freiburg-im-Breisgau: Herder, 1965), pp. 87-88; originally "Die Hominisation als theologische Frage," in Paul Overhage and Karl Rahner, *Das Problem der Hominisation* (Freiburg-im-Breisgau: Herder, 1958).

31. Rahner, *H*, p. 73.

32. Rahner, *H*, pp. 76-77.

33. Rahner, *H*, pp. 75-76.

34. Rahner, *H*, p. 75.

cannot therefore be defined as Spirit, the infinite substance of Hegel's idealism.[35] Rahner follows St. Thomas in affirming that the infinite is both self-subsisting and the cause and ground of the world's unity.[36] As the world's ground, it is thus immanent in empirical processes. As self-subsisting, it is also transcendent to them. Because it exists prior to the duality of form and matter, it cannot be encountered among substances and their processes as one of them. Nor can its effects within them be categorically isolated.[37]

Second, Rahner differs with Hegel in the mode of immanence of the self-subsisting infinite in finite substances. This mode is due to final causality, not formal causality. As a final cause, the self-subsisting infinite evokes in changing substances a new end or goal. This goal is the realization of their newly determined increments. But these increments do not emerge with any mechanistic necessity. They are not fully predicable on the basis of the substance's potential. On the contrary, Rahner asserts, they embody genuine spontaneity. The infinite cause functions in tandem with the randomness of empirical process.[38] As a result, changes as such may randomly emerge in substances. That they result in real increments is a necessity, however, because the transcendent infinite draws these forth in and through the random changes.[39]

Although the immanence of the infinite causes changing substances to exceed the strict limits of their essence, it should not be understood as empowering them to mutate from one essence to another. It does not effect a substantial change. It accounts for the novelty produced in accidental change, insofar as substances realize new determinations that are spontaneous increments in being.

Critique

Rahner's analysis raises an important question. Given that an infinite cause is needed to explain change, can the manner of its immanence in substances be further specified? Although Rahner does not directly supply

---

35. Rahner, *H*, pp. 75-76.

36. Rahner, *H*, p. 50.

37. Rahner, *H*, p. 51.

38. Rahner, *H*, pp. 64-65, 75-76, 80.

39. Rahner, *H*, pp. 90-91. The relation between the infinite cause and the randomness of empirical process is an important issue that cannot be taken up here.

an answer, one can be developed based on his argument. If the dynamism that intrinsically consummates a substance can itself be considered an instance of ontological motion, then this dynamism should follow the apriori law of motion: that is, it should produce a new increment in reality. Consistent with Rahner's analysis, and with his debt to Hegel's notion, this increment should be due to the immanence of the infinite in the motion that produces it. It therefore follows that the infinite should be immanent in the ontological motion by which a substance is constituted. In other words, the infinite should be immanent in the passing of form into matter and its return through matter to itself. It should further follow that this immanence is the reason why a substance can realize any new determination when it undergoes accidental changes. Let us pursue this line of thought in greater detail.

Substance, Motion, and the Infinite

Rahner affirms that a substance is constituted by the mutual engagement of form and matter. This engagement entails four moments that structure a substance as a real-symbol: the original unity of form and matter, which is the source of their difference; their explicit differentiation within their unity; their mediation, which obtains when form is emanated or passes into matter, its own other; and their consummation, which obtains when form passes back into itself, and thus returns through its material mediation. The movement from the first moment of unity to the second moment of explicit differentiation introduces contingency into the core of a substance's structure. When form and matter are actively differentiated within the substance's unity, they necessarily entail negation. To be differentiated means that form and matter are determined in contradistinction to one another. On the one hand, "all determination is negation," as Hegel's quotation of Spinoza reminds us.[40] On the other hand, all negation entails contingency, because what is determined is dependent on its not being something else.[41]

---

40. *EL,* p. 135.

41. Kenneth L. Schmitz, "Postmodernism and the Catholic Tradition," *American Catholic Philosophical Quarterly* 73 (Spring 1999): 250, observes that contingency involves two aspects: lack of necessity and dependence.

Contingency is thus lodged in the heart of a substance's structure. It is the basis of the differentiation of form and matter. This differentiation, we recall, entails the mediation of form and matter, and their consummation precisely as a substance. Paradoxically, because contingency becomes a necessity within the motion that structures a substance as a dynamic event, it raises an important question: What carries this event beyond the negation, the contingency, that initiates it? The answer can only be the immanence of the infinite in the event. If it be acknowledged that, in moving beyond negation, the mediation of form in and through matter consummates the substance as a self-transcending event, then the cause of this event should be the same as the cause of self-transcendence in any motion. This cause is the infinite's immanence, which spontaneously generates increments in finite reality whenever new determinations obtain.

It is precisely because of the infinite's immanence in a substance's constitutive event, an event entailing motion, that novelty can appear in the empirical processes of the world. The infinite's immanence endows the substance with what might be called a surplus of reality. Because this surplus is derived from an infinitely creative source, it is able to carry the substance's constitutive dynamism beyond the contingency that initiates it. In doing so, the surplus of reality causes form to return to itself after its emanation in and through matter. This surplus thus explains how real increments can obtain when a substance undergoes accidental change. These are simply the newly determined manifestations of the surplus that is dynamically immanent in the substance's own ontological constitution. If, as Rahner says, a substance transcends itself in motion, this self-transcendence is due to a prior self-transcendence. This is defined by the immanence of the infinite that renders the core of finite substances spontaneously creative. It therefore follows: when substances interact within the empirical processes of the world, the changes they undergo produce new increments in reality. Substance, the basic structure of finite being, is thus the locus and seedbed of the novelty emergent in the cosmos.

The Causality of the Infinite's Immanence

A second question raised by Rahner's analysis of change concerns the mode by which the infinite is immanent in the dynamism constituting a substance. Rahner claims that this immanence results from final causality. This is only partially adequate, because a final causality is a necessary but not a sufficient explanation. As Aristotle remarks in *Metaphysics,* a final cause "is the end of every generation and every motion."[42] Final causality would be a sufficient explanation if the motion of change were defined by the traditional realism that Rahner criticizes. As we recall, traditional realism asserts that motion is merely equivalent to the potential in the substance undergoing the change. In this case, the final cause would sufficiently explain how change draws forth a substance's potency and converts it into an equivalent actuality, however novel this may be understood to be.

The situation is different, however, when motion is defined as producing an ontological increment. In this case, substances must embody an excess of potency. It is this excess that accounts for spontaneous creativity in the cosmos. Positing the infinite as the final cause of motion is insufficient to account for the existence of this excess. Final causality accounts, not for this potency's existence, but for how this potency is drawn forth in motion and converted into an actual ontological increment. We are thus left with a question that Rahner's analysis raises but does not answer: What cause explains the surplus ontological potency in finite reality?

To answer this question, let us return to the relation between Rahner's definition of substance and Hegel's notion. Rahner lodges the logic of the notion's reciprocal "passing-into" in the heart of substance. This means that an immanently dynamic motion constitutes finite reality. As we have seen, Hegel accounts for this dynamism by the immanence of the infinite in the finite as a formal cause. The essence of the ontological novelty produced by the notion's sublations is sufficiently explained by Spirit. This is the infinitely dynamic substance that embraces and drives the notion as its accident. By contrast, Rahner does not posit finite substances as accidents of the infinite being. Nonetheless, if emergent novelty in the cosmos is to be sufficiently explained, it seems necessary to posit the immanence of infinite being in finite substances, not only as a final cause, but also as some mode of formal causality.

We are thus brought to an aporia. On the one hand, the infinite must relate to the finite order as a mode of formal causality. On the other hand, this relation cannot be so construed as to make the finite order the accidents of the infinite substance. It is not possible, therefore, to use Rahner's understanding of the reciprocity between form and matter in a finite sub-

---

42. Aristotle, *Metaphysics,* 983a, 32-33.

stance as a model for understanding God's relation with the world. God does not emanate himself forth into the matter of the world and return to himself through the world to constitute himself. In order to qualify the mode of formal causality that obtains between God and the world's emergent novelty, we need to turn to another theme in the metaphysical axiom of Ignatius Loyola's contemplation: the relation between being and love, first in God, and then between God and the world. If it be possible to infer from reason that God is love, then it should be credible to claim that love is the mode of God's relation with the finite order. If this be so, then love should explain the dynamism of emergent novelty in the cosmos.

Freedom, God, and Love

Our first question therefore concerns whether it be possible, from reason, to infer that God is the subject of love. In his categorical denial, Aristotle has perhaps set the West's philosophical agenda. Early in *Metaphysics*, alluding to Parmenides and Hesiod, he avers that love is the cause of all motion and the reason for the coherence of the cosmos.[43] But his subsequent discussion of the prime mover makes it clear that, however necessary divinity is, it is not the subject of love. Love would imply that the infinite being desires something it does not have. This cannot be, since the prime mover is pure actuality, immune to all change, and perfect because it contemplates its own infinite self-knowledge. Were this not the case, the prime mover could not be the necessary and sufficient explanation for finite motion. This is caused precisely by the love of spatio-temporal beings; they yearn for the prime mover as their ultimate object of desire. As infinitely unchangeable, the prime mover draws the motion of their loving desire towards itself. In so doing, it initiates, sustains, and completes all change. The prime mover's influence on the world does not therefore derive from its inner life. It derives only from the prime mover's infinite finality. Thus spared the passion of love, this infinite finality is also "spared" any freedom.[44]

Aristotle's position may be slightly nuanced. St. Thomas, for in-

43. Aristotle, *Metaphysics*, 984b, 24f.

44. Aristotle, *Metaphysics*, 1072bf. See also W. D. Ross's commentary, in Aristotle's *Metaphysics* (Oxford: Clarendon, 1924), vol. 1, pp. cxxx-cliv, passim.

stance, makes note of an important line in the *Ethics* where Aristotle says, "God rejoices by an operation that is one and simple."[45] Thomas interprets this to mean that God's rejoicing is a function of his intellect and hence is devoid of any passion, sensuous desire being a function of the materiality that God by definition lacks. Thomas concludes that God can love in the same way that Aristotle affirms God can rejoice. Love is the first act of the will, because it aims at the universal good. Because God has will, God therefore aims at the universal good, which is himself (*ST* I, 20, 1).

Nonetheless, Thomas's predication of love in God is merely another way of affirming Aristotle's claim that the prime mover contemplates itself. As a result, Thomas's position does not produce a significant advance. On the one hand, he assumes the existence of God as infinite being endowed with intellect and will and then infers God's love from these assumptions. On the other hand, he does not relate God's love to the finite order. Two pressing issues thus remain. They coalesce around a key question: Is it possible to infer from the reality of the finite order that being itself is loving? In other words, is it possible to show that love, and hence the freedom that it entails, are perfections of being, not defects? If so, then the finite order in its contingency could reasonably be shown to stand in relation to a loving and free first cause. As one commentator incisively remarks, St. Thomas's metaphysics of being needs restructuring in order to take more explicit account of the personal.[46] Accordingly, let us turn again to Rahner, who develops an argument that, based on the conditions of the human person's ability to know, purports to reach God as free and loving person.

Humanity as Questioner

Rahner begins this argument with the questioning nature of humanity. When we human beings inquire about the world and its causes, we already assume that answers will be delivered, often after lengthy investigation. This seek-and-find dynamic that defines the mind's quest is the principle of in-

45. St. Thomas Aquinas, *Summa theologiae* (= *ST*) I, 20, 1, citing Aristotle, *Ethics*, 8, 14 (1154b, 26).

46. Robert O. Johann, *The Meaning of Love: An Essay towards a Metaphysics of Intersubjectivity* (Westminster: Newman Press, 1955), p. 7.

telligibility. It means that what the mind endeavors to know — the reality or being of the world and its causes — is luminous. When answers resolve our questions, reality becomes present, not only to us, but also to itself, in and through our inquiring minds. The self-presence of being shines nowhere more brightly than in language. By naming and articulating the answers to our questions, language reveals and manifests the implicit intelligibility of being, together with its intrinsic expressiveness and communicability.

That questioning defines humanity is an apriori. Rahner warrants this claim by the type of argument that originates in Socrates' critique of the skeptics and that subsequently finds echoes in Augustine, Descartes, Kant, Newman, and Maréchal. To deny that we are questioners only serves to affirm that we are. In other words, to say that I am not a questioner answers an implicit question. It therefore follows that the mind is capable of affirming at least one axiom that is necessary, absolute, and indubitable. In fact, the mind must make this affirmation if it is to obey the law imposed by its own nature.

That questioning defines humanity entails another apriori claim: we are radically contingent. The mind is not immediately replete with answers to its questions. Often it must grope laboriously before being able even to frame a question. To ask questions and secure answers, the mind must turn outward from its own being to that of the external world. Thus dependent on the world, the mind confronts the world as the heteronymous cause of its questions and answers. It follows, therefore, that humanity is not self-caused, but finite.

Because the human person, in its contingency, can and must affirm eternal apriori truths, the nature of the person is revealed as a paradox. Because the objects that the mind knows are finite and mutable, they cannot be used as a sufficient explanation of the mind's capacity to posit these truths. The only other reasonable explanation lies in the mind's act of affirmation. It is this act, after all, that makes the absolute claims. As a result, it follows that the mind's act of affirmation must intend the absolute in its noetic reach, at least implicitly.

This noetic intention does not mean that the mind knows or grasps the infinite as an object of its experience. Such a claim would posit a double contradiction. The infinite would be made finite, and the contingent mind would be made infinite. Because neither is true, the mind must intend the absolute by yearning for it, just as motion in Aristotle desires the infinite object of love. By way of correcting Aristotle, however, Rahner rightly asserts a reciprocity between the contingent questioner and the absolute. If the activity of the questioner implicitly intends the absolute as a goal, end, or final cause, then the absolute must implicitly be present in the questioner's intention — not as an object of affirmation, but as any cause must be implicit in the effect that it produces.

Because of the reciprocity between infinite being and the contingent mind, a dynamic movement is revealed as the core of human knowing. The mind comes to know contingent objects by contrast with the implicit intentionality of its questioning. Because this intentionality aims at the absolute, the absolute's immanence structures the act of knowledge by which contingent objects are affirmed. As a result, knowing entails a dual motion. On the one hand, the mind's intention moves toward the absolute. On the other hand, the contrast in the mind between the intended absolute and the contingent objects it draws from the finite world moves the person to know whatever is known.

Being as Free

We now come to the inference important for the argument's claim that being is free. The dynamic core of knowing entails volition or will as a necessary cause. Because will is the mind's yearning, will explains knowing's dual movement. Where there is volition, freedom is necessarily entailed. It follows, therefore, that we freely will ourselves. In other words, when we affirm as an apriori that we are contingent beings, we necessarily use will. As a result, freedom lies in the core of existence, and thus in the heart of being's luminous self-presence. Moreover, freedom is more than a necessary condition of our own ability to render being self-present in the act of knowing. It is a necessary condition of being as such, of pure being, of being absolutely. The argument for this claim is twofold. First, the freedom of infinite being is antecedently probable. This means that, before a direct argument is put forth, the infinite's freedom is likely, based on indirect evidence. This indirect evidence emerges from the doubly dynamic nature of knowing. More precisely, it emerges from the analogy of being that this dynamism grounds. Let us pursue this further.

We have already seen that the human intellect as questioning is the locus of being's luminous self-presence. We have also seen that being cannot become luminously self-present without the immanence of the absolute in the dynamic act of affirmation. Being's luminous self-presence thus manifests the analogy between the infinite and the finite. Analogy means that one reality exists in qualitatively different modes. Accordingly, the one act of knowing that affirms any finite object implicitly affirms the infinite that is implicitly intended in any act of affirmation. Moreover, as we have seen, to be luminously self-present means that being is intelligent, self-expressive, communicative, and free. If the human being be the locus of this self-presence, and if absolute being be implicit in human knowing, then the absolute should be affirmed as intelligent, self-expressive, communicative, and free. We have clear evidence for the first three predicates. The absolute expresses and communicates itself as the qualitatively "other" that is noetically intended in the radical contingency of the human being. If the infinite be known by analogy as intelligent, self-expressive, and communicative, then by analogy it is likely that the infinite should also be the subject of freedom.

Bolstering the antecedent probability of this indirect argument from analogy is a direct argument deduced from the necessity of humanity's nature as radically contingent. As previously shown, this contingency must be claimed by us necessarily and also willed by us. From this claim another claim follows. That we will ourselves is tantamount to ratifying that we are freely posited and do not posit ourselves. In other words, because we are by nature contingent, we are not by nature necessary. We could not have existed; the same applies to the universal cosmos of finite reality. That it, together with ourselves, does in fact exist implies that we are posited by a being who is not contingent but absolute.

Our being posited by the absolute must be free. If the absolute did not posit us freely but necessarily, then we would be necessary just as our cause is necessary. In that case, we would be posited necessarily by the absolute as beings who *could or could not exist*. This is a patent contradiction. If we were posited necessarily by the absolute, we would be beings who *must exist*. However, because we are radically contingent, we could not-have-existed. It follows, therefore, that it is absurd to claim that a contingent being can be posited necessarily by absolute being. Several implications follow from this argument. Because absolute being is free as well as intelligent, the absolute is personal. Where there is free personhood, there is love. As Aristotle observes, love is the root of choice insofar as it intends an end or goal. The finite order, therefore, is lovingly intended by the absolute person. Accordingly, this person and the human person face each other in a reciprocal freedom that is analogous to their mode of being.[47]

Conclusions

It would take us far beyond our purpose to offer a critique of Rahner's argument. Like all arguments, it is not invulnerable. Still, it will serve as a sufficient warrant to proceed with our broader discussion. If it can reasonably be claimed that God is the proper subject of love, then God is the loving end intended by the motion of human knowing. Precisely as this end, God is also lovingly immanent in this motion. Accordingly, we have rendered in a philosophical idiom some key claims of St. Ignatius's contemplation. Absolute love impregnates absolute being. Because this love draws the human being towards itself, it causes humanity's self-transcendence. But this love is also immanent in human intelligence, thus impregnating the motion of questioning and answering. Because human intelligence reveals an analogy between infinite and finite being, it follows that an analogy of love also obtains between them. As a result, God's love explains not only human self-transcendence, but also the transcendence of all finite substances previously discussed. In other words, love is the mode of the infinite being's immanence in finite substances. Infinite love renders them dynamically and spontaneously creative. In sum, therefore: the divine love, as a final cause, accounts for the emergent novelty of the cosmos.

Important claims in Ignatius's axiom still need to be worked out. These concern the nature of God in whom love impregnates being. They also concern specifying the mode of formal causality obtaining between God and the world. We shall begin to explore these issues where Rahner's argument has left us.

God, Love, and Being

Rahner's argument provides a philosophical warrant for the doctrine of creation. Creation means that the radically dependent finite order could

---

47. Rahner's argument is found in *Hearer of the Word: Laying the Foundation for a Philosophy of Religion*, trans. Joseph Donceel (New York: Continuum, 1994), chapter 7. My explication involves considerable interpretation.

not have existed, but was brought into being by the free intention of a being capable of doing so. Rahner argues that the radical contingency of the finite order entails its free positing by the absolute being, who is a loving person. If this be the case, then we need to inquire more deeply into the love that initiates the infinite person's free intention to create. On the one hand, the love that St. Thomas predicates of God is inadequate, because this is the infinitely self-sufficient love that contemplates itself as the universal good. It does not move into the finite order. If it did, it would entail contemplating as a good the contingent other and thus would violate the universal good.

On the other hand, if we posit in God a love that freely moves into contingency, then do we still have God? As Thomas says, following Aristotle: God loves by an operation that is one and simple. In Thomas's synthesis of Aristotle's realism and Neoplatonism's ontology of participation, simplicity means that God is absolute being, with which essence is simultaneous. This simultaneity constitutes pure and unlimited act, utterly uncompounded, devoid of potency, and therefore incapable of the passion that would desire whatever is not itself. We are thus faced with another aporia that needs to be resolved before we can say anything more about the relation between God's love and emergent novelty. For help we shall look at two ancient sources and then return to Rahner's appropriation of Hegel's notion.

Denys

The first ancient source is a fifth-century corpus attributed to Denys, often called the Pseudo-Areopagite. A recent study by Hans Urs von Balthasar has opened a fresh understanding of Denys. Balthasar highlights the important distinction in his philosophical theology between God's self-communication and God's own being. God's self-communication grounds the finite order; God's own being grounds God's self-communication. Accordingly, God communicates being to visible reality through, or by means of, his own being.[48] God's act of self-manifestation is the bridge between infinite and finite being and the ground of the simultaneous similarity and

---

48. Hans Urs von Balthasar, "Denys," *The Glory of the Lord: A Theological Aesthetics,* vol. 2: *Studies in Theological Style: Clerical Styles,* trans. Andrew Louth et al., ed. Joseph Fessio and John Riches (San Francisco: Ignatius Press, 1984), p. 170.

dissimilarity between them. Because God posits the world as a "like un-likeness and an unlike likeness" of himself, God's self-communication constitutes and establishes the analogy of being.[49] At once, God's act of communication flows forth from himself, even as it creates the cosmos, which in its contingency is radically other than God. As a result, God's infinite being is the instrumental cause of the world's contingent being. In other words, the infinite being that is God mediates the origin of the finite being that is the world.

We come now to a key notion in Denys's doctrine of God. The source of being that mediates the finite lies in another perfection of the Godhead — the divine love that Denys names *erōs*. This perfection, he claims, is equally convertible with beauty and goodness, and with light.[50] The divine act of being is thus mediated by these; through them, being proceeds, and in them, being subsists.[51] God's eros (together with beauty, goodness, and light) is thus "the cause of initiation" of being.[52] Eros constitutes "the one cause of all beings," through which flow "both being and well-being to all that is."[53]

From this rich metaphysics of divinity, we can harvest several items important for our discussion. First, because absolute love generates absolute being, being is eternally subordinate to love. Second, because being emerges out of the love that mediates it, being must be infused with love. Third, because God's self-communication is generated in love, the entire order of finite being, human and otherwise, must be impregnated with love. Fourth, if impregnated with love, then the finite order must be immanently dynamic. It must yearn to achieve a purpose, to reach an end or a goal. Consistent with Aristotle's logic, this end or goal must be absolute being. Consistent with Rahner's argument, this absolute being must be the loving person who freely communicates the yearning.

Most importantly, Denys specifies God's absolute love as eros. He thus eschews two other readily available words, *agapē* and *philia*. *Agapē*,

---

49. Denys, *De coelesti hierarchia* (= *CH*) XV.8 (337B); in Balthasar, "Denys," pp. 166, 179-80.

50. Balthasar, "Denys," p. 189, referring to Denys, *De divinis nominibus* (= *DN*), chapter 4. Balthasar does not define "eros" in Denys, but "passionate love" is consistent with Paul's use of it in Galatians 6:14, and with other classical texts (see Bauer, *A Greek-English Lexicon of the New Testament*, 2nd ed.).

51. Balthasar, "Denys," p. 189, referring to *DN*, chapter 5.

52. *CH* III.1 (164D); in Balthasar, "Denys," p. 196.

53. Denys, *De ecclesiastica hierarchia* I.3 (373CD); in Balthasar, "Denys," p. 200.

for instance, is preferred for the divine love throughout the Fourth Gospel. Neither "agape" nor "philia," however, denotes passion, yearning, or desire. "Agape" evokes the universally disinterested love that St. Thomas predicates of God. In using "eros," Denys thus changes what divine perfection means. A high innovator, he supplants the divine love as beneficent impartiality with extroverted engagement. He lodges motion in divinity's core. As a result, being is anything but a static act. On the contrary, being is generated by the motion of love, even as being generates the motion of God's self-communication in the finite order. Moreover, in asserting the divine passion, Denys wishes to posit God's freedom as the ground of his self-communication. In so doing, he poses a counterfoil both to Aristotle, who argues for the eternality of the cosmos, and to Neoplatonism, which posits the necessity of the cosmos.

Nonetheless, Denys's doctrine of God, however seminal and original, returns us to the aporia that we are seeking to resolve. If God's love generates and infuses God's being, then is the essential simplicity of God's absolute nature vitiated? Denys not only posits two principles in God. He makes one subordinate to the other and introduces motion into divinity. Furthermore, if motion is introduced into God, then is God really free? Denys does not solve the problem of the necessity of the finite cosmos. Aristotle is correct in perceiving a certain necessity in love. Because love is motion, it aims at an end, however spontaneously chosen this end may be. As a result, to be truly free, the divine eros must be satisfied within itself. It must entail its own end. Otherwise, if the free motion of love immanent in God does not terminate in God as its own immanent goal, then it must terminate in a goal that is other than God. It must terminate therefore in finite being. In order to avoid this conclusion, God must be seen to communicate his loving being precisely because he is perfectly satisfied. In this case, God's love would be utterly free and gratuitous.

Let us further pursue the relation of simplicity and motion in God by turning to another ancient source, one that is older than Denys: St. Basil the Great (c. 329-379), one of the three Cappadocian Fathers.

Basil

Basil presents us with two important insights. First, he resolves unity and distinction in God by appealing to the analogy implied by the term "one." When one is predicated of God, it means that God's unity is grounded in the simplicity of his nature. By contrast, when one is predicated of finite realities, it means number, definition, limitation, subjection to the conditions of time and space, and the ability to undergo change according to these conditions. The unity of finite realities is thus always compound. Form and matter, the principles of this compound, come together in an ontological harmony that constitutes a substance. Nonetheless, these principles are "really" distinct. They are ontologically heteronymous, in the sense that form confers definition, whereas matter confers specification.[54]

Because numerous attributes are rightly predicated of God, a plurality of entities seems to inhere in him. This appearance is a concession to our finite minds, which cannot objectify the essential simplicity of God. When the term "one" is analogously predicated of God, however, the plurality of God's attributes emerge as only "virtually" distinct from each other and from his nature. God's nature and the distinctions predicated of it are essentially homogeneous. Like the composition of form and matter, God's nature and attributes may be called a substance. Unlike form and matter, however, the unity of this substance is not complex.[55] Any distinction in God, therefore, is not properly countable as a number.

A second important insight is Basil's appeal to the concept of community or *koinonia* to specify God's oneness. The virtual distinctions in God inhere in a unity that is "continuous and uninterrupted."[56] Unlike the complementarity of form and matter that entails a real distinction, "[t]here is nothing which intrudes itself" between the virtual distinctions. "[B]eyond the divine nature," asserts Basil, "there is nothing which subsists that could really divide it from itself."[57] As a result, a paradox obtains in God, whose distinctions constitute a "united separation" and a "disunited connection."[58] God's simplicity of nature resolves this paradox, which therefore vitiates neither God's unity nor oneness.

54. St. Basil, "Letter 8," in *The Letters*, Loeb Classical Library, trans. Roy J. Deferrari, 4 vols. (London: W. Heinemann/New York: G. P. Putnam's Sons, 1926), p. 53.

55. St. Basil, "Letter 8," 55 and note 3.

56. St. Basil, "Letter 38," 209.

57. St. Basil, "Letter 38," 209.

58. St. Basil, "Letter 38," 213.

Denys and Basil

Basil does not explicitly consider the relation between love and being in God, but his insights help to resolve the aporia between motion and the divine simplicity. Love and being can be understood as virtual distinctions that do not vitiate God's essential simplicity. Being emerges eternally from the divine eros, which impregnates it, and thus renders being a constitutive moment within itself. As a result, the distinction between eros and being implies no interval or void but constitutes a continuous and uninterrupted unity. Consistent with God's paradoxical nature, this unity might be called a mediated immediacy. In other words, the divine eros is mediated to itself through being that it generates. Because being is the intrinsic product of eros, it follows that eros is mediated to itself through being.

If being mediates eros to itself, it also follows that eros mediates being, because eros generates being. Being is therefore mediated immediately by eros. Accordingly, the relation of mediated immediacy obtaining between being and eros is reciprocal. As reciprocal, being and eros subsist in God as a community bound together by the immanent motion of virtual distinctions. If love and being subsist in the reciprocal relation of mediated immediacy, then, *pace* Denys, neither love nor being is subordinate to the other. Each is necessary for the consummation of the other, even as their mutual consummation subsists as a function of God's essential simplicity.

Finally, it also follows that God's love may properly be called eros, because it is generative. Its generativity does not compromise God's simplicity, because the fruition of eros as being constitutes the divine unity as *koinonia*. As *koinonia*, God is supremely free. In other words, God is the end, purpose, and goal of his own loving motion. The love that generates being terminates in God, because eros is reflected to itself through being.

God as Real-Symbol

Our synthesis of Denys and Basil in light of Rahner's argument for the intrinsic freedom of being has accomplished three purposes. It has harmonized the divine simplicity with distinction and motion. It has grounded God's supreme freedom. Moreover, it has effectively brought us to an understanding of the simplicity of God's substance consistent with the real-symbol, Rahner's definition of reality that adapts Hegel's notion. Let us briefly explain this. The real-symbol means that reality expresses itself in order to become itself. Reality is thus mediated immediately. It generates its own other and returns through this other to itself. Reality thus constitutes its own symbol that represents itself to itself. In finite substances, form passes into matter, making matter its own other. As form returns through matter to itself, it constitutes a substance as a unified ontological entity. Accordingly, as real-symbol, God may be said to express himself in order to constitute his essential simplicity. The divine love generates being as its own other and returns through being to itself. Being is thus love's intrinsic symbol that, impregnated by love, reflects love to itself. The reciprocity between love and being in God entails no gap or void, because they are virtually distinct within his essential simplicity. Moreover, it entails no subordination of one virtual distinction to the other, because each is necessary for the other's consummation, as well as for the consummation of the divine simplicity. As the essentially simple *koinonia* of reciprocal motion without real distinctions, God is therefore properly called real-symbol by analogy with finite substances.[59]

Emergent Novelty and God as Real-Symbol

Our final question concerns using the understanding of God as real-symbol to explain more fully emergent novelty in the world. We have already seen how the divine love as a final cause partially explains this novelty in both human and non-human substances. What remains to be explained is the existence of ontological potency in these substances that accounts for the emergence of new being when they change. As we saw earlier, this excess needs to be explained by the infinite's immanence in substances as a mode of formal causality. This mode cannot be so construed, however, as to render the finite order the accidents of the infinite substance. The explanation that follows can only offer a sketch that must await a fuller development. It is grounded in exemplary causality.

As the proper subject of eros, God's love can move beyond itself. Nonetheless, because God's eros terminates in himself as its own end, God

---

59. In "ToS," pp. 231-32, Rahner uses the real-symbol to explain the relation between Father and Son in the revealed doctrine of the Trinity. I am not aware of his using it anywhere to explain the philosophical doctrine of God.

is supremely free. As real-symbol, God does not sublate his eros in and through the finite order. God's free intention to create is not driven by the need of his eros to terminate in a heteronymous object. As a result, creation is posited by the divine eros in supreme freedom. As freely created, creation is contingent and therefore radically other than its absolute source. Contingency implies being determined, and being determined implies, as we have seen, negation. Thus an infinite void separates infinite from finite. This void spares the finite from being absorbed as an accident within the absolute substance of its divine creator. Furthermore, because of this void, God and the world constitute, as Denys says, a "like unlikeness."

As Denys also observes, God communicates being to the finite order by means of his own being. As real-symbol, God's being and love are mediated immediately in a reciprocal motion. Because God's being is impregnated with love, the finite order that ensues from it is impregnated with love. Moreover, as Christian Platonism and St. Thomas both affirm, in creating the contingent order, God is the exemplary cause of all that is and can be. An exemplary causality is often called an extrinsic formal causality because of its transcendent independence of that to which it gives meaning and intelligibility. As creation's exemplary cause, God is the absolute archetype of all contingent images. As a principle of being, even pure potency, according to St. Thomas, is constituted as an exemplary image of God.[60] In exemplary causality, the immanence of the cause in its effects obtains by the will or intention of the cause.[61] Accordingly, the existence of all exemplary images, including potency, must be suffused with the divine eros that inspires God's free intention to create them. Because the divine eros is a dynamic motion impregnating potency, the divine eros explains the existence of the excess of potency in finite substances. The divine eros is a motion that, immanent in being, drives substances in change to realize the spontaneous creativity of ontological newness. Driven by love in the potency of being, emergent novelty in the cosmos is nonetheless drawn to its loving end by God as the final cause of all emergent processes. The absolute real-symbol thus initiates and consummates the many real-symbols of the world he freely intends.

Let us conclude by answering the question with which we began. The Ignatian contemplation to obtain divine love, precisely as a product of the

---

60. St. Thomas Aquinas, *Summa contra gentiles* 2, 45, 46; *De potentia* 3, 1, ad 12.
61. *ST* I, 14, 8; I, 15, 1.

religious imagination, makes a credible claim on our philosophical reason. Love alone is credible, because it is the labor of God. God's dynamic and infinite Love, impregnating being, drives the finite order toward himself in a self-transcending motion.

Love and the Organism: A Theological Contribution to the Study of Life

José Granados

Introduction

Does love make the world go 'round? This popular saying reminds us of the last verse of Dante's *Divine Comedy:* "L'amor che muove il sole e le altre stelle," "The Love that moves the sun and the other stars."[1] Dante's verse refers to God as Love, a Love that is the motor of all things. Does the verse apply to spiritual being only, or is it able to embrace all of reality, including the material world, as well?

This second possibility strikes our modern minds as odd. We would tend to think of it only as a metaphor, an example of poetic license, an illicit imposition of human attributes onto the inanimate realm of things. What, then, are the reasons behind this hesitation?

An initial important reason lies undoubtedly in the dualism that is a hallmark of the Western tradition since Descartes. The French philosopher brought about a clear distinction between two worlds: the personal and the cosmological. In the terms of this dualism, concepts that apply to persons (for example, reason or freedom) cannot have any relation to the material or biological realm, and vice versa.[2]

This mindset led to a particular way of understanding the relation

1. Dante Alighieri, *Paradiso*, XXXIII, 145.
2. Cf. Hans Urs von Balthasar, *Glaubhaft ist nur Liebe* (Einsiedeln: Johannes Verlag, 1963), p. 15; for an English translation, see *Love Alone Is Credible*, trans. D. C. Schindler (San Francisco: Ignatius Press, 2004), pp. 25-26.

I would like to thank Carol Brouha and Emily Reilley for their help in editing this article.

José Granados

between the sciences. The positivistic sciences remained the realm of objectivity and truth; the rest of reality became subjective, that is, pertaining only to the individual and not a matter of public debate. There appeared, then, the now-widespread idea that all that is left for us to discuss is the natural sciences alone: decisions having to do with religion and morality are subjective and cannot be brought into the public square. It is, more or less, the image used by Einstein when he compared scientific activity to the longing that pulls the town-dweller away from his noisy surroundings (the realm of the uncertain and the subjective) and towards the silence of the high mountains (the region of objective knowledge).[3]

One consequence has been that objective discussions linked to science are no longer seen as concerned in any way with the moral realm; instead, they are considered pre-moral.[4] But the result is that man's technological power recognizes no inherent ethical principle, no principle that would emerge from within itself. Every attempt to make ethics relevant for science seems to come from the exterior, from a subjective point of view, and is linked in the end to subjectivity and arbitrariness.

This modern dualism has had its effect on the understanding of love, as well. We can refer, for example, to the Kantian distinction between pathological and practical love. The former is merely an affection and is considered irrelevant for morality, something to be studied, rather, in terms of biology and physics. Practical love is an act of the will, an act that

---

3. Cf. Albert Einstein, *Ideas and Opinions* (New York: Crown, 1954), p. 225: "[O]ne of the strongest motives that leads men to art and science is escape from everyday life with its painful crudity and hopeless dreariness, from the fetters of one's own ever-shifting desires. A finely tempered nature longs to escape from personal life into the world of objective perception and thought; this desire may be compared with the townsman's irresistible longing to escape from his noisy, cramped surroundings into the silence of high mountains, where the eye ranges freely through the still, pure air and fondly traces out the restful contours apparently built for eternity." The following comments of Ilya Prigogine, *The End of Certainty: Time, Chaos, and the New Laws of Nature* (New York: Free Press, 1997), on this text are of interest: "But is science as conceived by Einstein — an escape from the vagaries of human existence — still the science of today? We cannot desert the polluted towns and cities for the high mountains. We have to participate in the building of tomorrow's society" (p. 185); "[W]hat is the purpose of science if it cannot incorporate some of the basic aspects of human experience?" (p. 14).

4. Cf. David L. Schindler, "The Significance of World and Culture for Moral Theology: *Veritatis splendor* and the 'Nuptial-Sacramental' Nature of the Body," *Communio* 31, no. 1 (Spring 2004): 111-42; see esp. 111-13.

can be commanded, which makes it part of the moral realm.[5] Because the concept of love seems to have been affected in a special way by modern dualism, a close study of it in particular could prove useful in our attempt to overcome this dualism.

Keeping all this in mind, it is clear that our question of the relation of love to the organism and to physical matter is not simply a speculative one. It carries profound consequences for our culture and for the current problems of our society. A better understanding of this relationship may result not only in a deeper knowledge of nature and how to engage it, but, because a new concept of freedom and love could emerge, in a renewed vision of man as well.

What attempts have been made to overcome this situation, either from the point of view of physics or biology, or from the realm of philosophy?[6] Does Christianity have something to say to us in this regard? In order to prepare our answer, we will (1) begin with a closer examination of the line from Dante we quoted at the beginning; (2) move to the theology of Hans Urs von Balthasar, who will serve as an inspiration for our approach to the problem; (3) enter into a dialogue on this issue with other contemporary philosophers and theologians; and (4) examine some key texts of the Christian tradition that take up our problem. All the above will (5) provide us with the elements for an answer.

The Question Among the Ancients and in Early Christianity

When Dante wrote the final verse of the *Divine Comedy*, he was calling on a rich tradition. Let us examine its two main sources: (a) the influence of the Greek philosophers and (b) the background of Christianity.

a. Dante's thought sinks its roots in ancient Greek philosophy. It suffices to recall, here, Aristotle's doctrine that God moves everything by attracting it: that is to say, by love. This is precisely how God is an unmoved mover.[7] Aristotle understood this love, present in all creatures, as a ten-

---

5. Cf. *Grundlegung zur Metaphysik der Sitten* (Stuttgart: Philipp Reclam, 1967), p. 37.

6. It is interesting to notice how Heisenberg relates the problem of the existence of God with the possibility of addressing the whole universe as we would do with the soul of another man. Cf. Werner Heisenberg, *Der Teil und das Ganze. Gespräche im Umkreis der Atomphysik* (Munich, 1969), pp. 292-93.

7. Cf. *Met* XII, VII; cf. C. J. Vogel, "Greek Cosmic Love and the Christian Love of God:

dency or an impersonal interior force that draws the creature to self-realization through acquiring its form. Later on, Plotinus and Proclus will make another point, which, according to some scholars, was already present in Plato: this love that dwells in everything is understood as love for a transcendent God.[8] This is how the ancients were able to set the movements of the universe into a unified order and to discern within every event a step towards higher levels of reality.

Let us take note that the love in question for these Greek philosophers is the love of creatures for God, not the love of God for the universe. This is because of their conception of love *(erōs)* as something related to a need; love sets out from a lack of something; love is always a movement, it is related to motion and not to being; thus, it cannot be attributed to God.[9]

This last point is especially important in regard to the material world, which is clearly different from God. Plato and the Greek philosophers could reach the point of accepting the love of God for the soul or spirit because of a perceived similarity between them. This would not be a case, then, of love for the inferior, but would be, rather, love for the similar. In the case of the body or material things, any love on the part of God is excluded: it is simply a question of the tendency of all things towards God.[10]

Interestingly enough, we find a different conception in Plato's *Symposium*. Here we find the idea of love as a deity relating to everything, something that moves throughout the entire universe. The idea is attributed to Eryximachus, the physician.[11] Eryximachus' position does not rep-

---

Boethius, Dionysius the Areopagite and the Author of the Fourth Gospel," *Vigiliae Christianae* 35 (1981): 57-81; 59.

8. Cf. Vogel, "Greek Cosmic Love," p. 59.

9. Cf. ibid., p. 63: "since eros springs from a need, it cannot be attributed to a God." Love for the inferior was called *erōs pronoētikos*. Even if this kind of love could be found among humans, it was not considered to be proper to God.

10. There have been attempts at summing up the thought of the Greek philosophers regarding this point, as though Greek love were only selfish. This is a simplification. Greek love does not start only from below, as a love of man for God, but is founded in an attraction from above. The movement towards God has its origin in God. The mystical trend of Platonism finds its foundations here.

11. Cf. *Symposium*, 186 a-b: "If I have learned a single lesson from my own field, the science of medicine, it is that Love does not occur only in the human soul; it is not simply the attraction we feel toward human beauty: it is a significantly broader phenomenon. It certainly occurs within the animal kingdom, and even in the world of plants. In fact, it oc-

resent Plato's thought (indeed the idea that love, *eros*, is a god is refuted later on in the speech by Socrates). It seems to reflect the thought of Heraclitus, which was taken over later by the Stoics. In this way they were able to speak of a love that moved everything: it was the divine Logos, which, however, was not transcendent.[12]

Let us summarize the answer given by the Greek philosophical tradition to our initial question: (1) There is a sense in which we can affirm that love moves everything, whether it is love for the transcendent God (the Platonic tradition), or love for the development of the immanent form (the Aristotelian tradition). The ancients were thus able to see the universe as a cosmos, as something ordered by love towards an end. (2) It is significant that Aristotelian philosophy, which took the lower regions of being more into account, could not accept the idea of the presence in all things of a love for the transcendent God, but stopped instead at the level of a love for the acquisition of form. The Platonic tradition was able to support this transcendent love only at the cost of denying some reality to the *regio dissimilitudinis*. (3) In neither tradition can this love be attributed to God: it is a love that is in no way reciprocal. This is especially clear in the case of material things in their total difference from the divine being. The underlying reason for all of this was the association of love with movement and not with being. (4) There was, certainly, an exception in the doctrine of the Stoics. The Stoics accepted that God, as Logos, was the force that binds everything together, including the physical world. In this way they were able to connect physics with ethics, and matter with love. But the price for maintaining the connection was the denial of God's transcendence.

b. Let us turn now to Dante's second source of inspiration: the Christian tradition, which is able to introduce a new element for our perspective. Let us recall the well-known fact that all three books of the *Divine Comedy* end in the same way, with a reference to the stars. When he emerges from the Inferno, Dante is able to see the stars again; when he finds the way out of

---

curs everywhere in the universe. Love is a deity of the greatest importance: he directs everything that occurs, not only in the human domain, but also in that of the gods."

12. It is from this tradition that the following sentence of the *Consolatio philosophiae* of Boethius seems to emerge: "How happy mortals were, if that pure love did guide their minds, which heavenly spheres does guide!" ("O felix hominum genus,/Si uestros animos amor/Quo caelum regitur regat"): cf. Boethius, *Consolatio philosophiae* II, 8, 28-30; cf. C. J. Vogel, "Amor quo caelum regitur," *Vivarium* 1 (1963): 2-34.

Purgatory, he is purified and ready to climb to the stars; finally he reaches, in Paradise, the Love that is able to move these very stars. Dante's trip is a trip towards God, and the sun and the stars were considered the highest elements of the cosmos. For Dante these stars refer particularly to the saints who inhabit heaven and enjoy the presence of God.

These stars, by reflecting the light that comes from God, enable Dante to prepare himself to see that light directly. When he reaches the point at which he is able to do this, the highest point of his contemplation, he sees the image of man inside the circle of the Divine Essence: the mystery of the incarnation and the union between our nature and the divine: "I wished to see how the image to the circle/conformed itself, and how it there finds place."[13] In the center of the circle Dante finds the image of man, who sums up in himself all of creation and is totally permeated by the love of God. It is through this same vision that Dante is able to be moved by this Love who is God. The material body is included in this movement in a special way.[14] The body belongs thus to these stars, the holy ones, who reflect God's love and are moved by him.

At the basis of this new perspective lies one of the fundamental claims of Christianity: the resurrection of the flesh. If the final destiny of all creation is the resurrected body, which St. Paul calls "spiritual body" (1 Cor 15:44), it ought to form a connection between spirit and body. If this union is the final goal of history, and if, then, this final point has to be thought of in connection with the rest of time, then the body that will become spiritual must be in connection with the spirit already while still on earth. The question we posed at the beginning about overcoming dualism is thus important if we want to account for the very core of Christianity, the resurrection of the flesh.

This union is considered not as something that the flesh obtains by itself, but rather as a being-possessed by the Holy Spirit. "It is the spirit that gives life, while the flesh is of no avail" (Jn 6:63). That means that there is more in the body than simply an inward tendency that pushes it towards God: on the contrary, God the Father himself communicates his own life to the body. Love does not begin, as was the case for the ancient philoso-

---

13. Cf. Dante, *Paradise*, XXXIII, 137-38.

14. Cf. *Paradise*, II, 37-42: "If I was body . . . more the desire should be enkindled in us, that essence to behold wherein is seen how God and our own nature were united"; cf. Guy P. Raffa, *Divine Dialectic* (Toronto: University of Toronto Press, 2000).

phers, in the movements of the world, but in God, who first loved us (cf. 1 Jn 4:10); God is Love, and he establishes *(creatio ex nihilo)* the very being of all things in order to bring them into communion with him.[15]

Let us conclude this first approximation to an answer by reiterating the three points that will be most important for characterizing the Christian contribution. First, the idea of love as reciprocal, that is, as communion. Love for God moves everything because God himself is love and loves the world. It is not only a case of love of things for God, but also of God's love for things.[16] Second, we find the idea that God loves all of creation and not just the spiritual world (that part of the world that could be considered similar to the divine). There is in God not only love for what is equal, but also love for what is inferior. Finally, this love is set in relation to the Spirit of God.

Does this perspective still have something to say to us today? Is it somehow able to resist being totally overcome by our new, modern vision of the world? Balthasar will provide us with important clues for pursuing our investigation.

Balthasar on Spirit and Nature

"L'amor che muove il sole e le altre stelle." The line works well to summarize some aspects of Balthasar's thought. Let us turn to his book

---

15. In these last paragraphs we have begun to speak of the relation between Spirit and body, instead of the relation between love and body. In this regard we can recall the famous sentence of St. Augustine, which shaped Christian thought on love for centuries: "amor meus pondus meum" (my love is my weight). In the context (*Confessions* 9, 10) Augustine is considering the movement of all creation, and especially the weight of things, which inclines them to fall to the earth. This weight that moves everything is used by Augustine to explain love, which is viewed as a force that sets man in motion by attracting him. It is important to notice that the Bishop of Hippo is concerned here with explaining Genesis 1:2, "the Spirit of God moved over the waters." We can thus assume a connection between the Spirit and this weight that moves everything, not only human beings but material objects as well. Augustine gives a reason for this connection between Spirit and the dynamism of creation: the Spirit is Love and Gift and can thus be seen as the link given by God to the world in order to keep it together (cf. *De Trinitate* XI, 11, 18).

16. Vogel, in "Greek Cosmic Love," claims that the newness of Christianity is a personal God who is able to love what is inferior to him *(erōs pronoētikos)*, what is different from him. We do not find this either in Plato or in Plotinus. It comes from the history of Jesus crucified.

Glaubhaft ist nur Liebe [Love Alone Is Credible], which considers three ways of presenting Christianity as credible. Two of them, the so-called cosmological and anthropological reductions, are judged insufficient. They attempt to justify Christianity starting out from the question of the cosmos or the question of man himself. Balthasar argues that it is impossible to reach the mystery of God by setting out from these starting points, and that attempting to do so risks a reduction of God's plan to man's expectations.

It is interesting what Balthasar adds while commenting on the cosmological reduction. This path starts with man's reflection on the cosmos and attempts to present Christianity as a culmination or integration of the fragments of the various worldviews.[17] Balthasar's comment is that this path is no longer feasible, in any case, since the world no longer bears the divine content that it did for the ancients. The physical world is no longer divine; what's more, it is no longer humanized, either — it is experienced instead as mere matter, which means it is experienced as different from and radically alien to man.

Following this critique, the Swiss theologian presents a third way, the way of love and beauty, as the only path that is able to preserve the mystery of Christianity.

Does this mean absolutely precluding the cosmological path from this point forward? Or could it still be possible, after the total disenchantment of the world, to attempt to take up the cosmological path once again? Based on the reasons presented in the introduction, I think that it will in fact be necessary for us to return to this point. This does not mean abandoning Balthasar's intuition and proposal; on the contrary, what we need is a step further in the direction he indicates. The way of love leads us to consider all of creation anew and results in a new understanding of the cosmos and its dynamisms that will permit us, in the end, to propose the cosmological path itself in a new form.

Balthasar himself seems to attempt such an approach in the final volume of his *Theologik*, in a short chapter devoted to the Spirit as soul of the world.[18] He has in mind the meaning of the Spirit as presented by the New

---

17. Cf. Balthasar, *Glaubhaft ist nur Liebe*, pp. 9-10.
18. Cf. Hans Urs von Balthasar, *Theologik III: Der Geist der Wahrheit* (= *TL* III) (Basel: Johannes Verlag, 1987), pp. 383-95. For an English translation, see *Theo-Logic: Theological Logical Theory*, vol. 3: *The Spirit of Truth* (San Francisco: Ignatius Press, 2005).

Testament: the Pneuma is the one who comes from God's love and who is obtained for us through the death and resurrection of Christ. A question now appears on the horizon: Is it possible to transfer this Spirit (and by the same token, this Love) to all of creation? Balthasar proceeds to analyze several proposals.[19] He brings out the dangers of reducing the importance of the event and novelty of Pentecost to the laws of nature,[20] and underscores the difference between the Spirit who swept over the waters (cf. Gen 1:2) and the Spirit given by Jesus.[21] He finishes by suggesting the lines of an adequate method: starting out from the death and resurrection of Christ should shed light on the whole mystery of human history and the constitution of nature. The love that makes the world go around has to do with the suffering love of Christ crucified.[22]

We will try to follow Balthasar's train of thought, which offers the possibility of relating love to the natural sciences, most particularly the sciences of physics and biology. It is important to keep in mind that the love that discloses this proposed vision is the love of God manifested in the cross and resurrection of Christ.

The Philosophical Relevance of the Organism:
Clues Provided by Contemporary Authors

Let us return to our initial question: Is there any link between the organism and love? The question can be reformulated in a more general way: Is there any link between biological processes, which can be measured in a laboratory and determined with precision, and the human realm, where we speak of morality and the good, of freedom and responsibility? Let us examine first the current positions among some representative philosophers of biology. We will move, then, to the work of two contemporary thinkers, Hans Jonas and Wolfhart Pannenberg.

---

19. Especially those of Barth and Pannenberg; cf. *TL* III, pp. 386ff.
20. Cf. *TL* III, p. 394.
21. Cf. *TL* III, pp. 392-94.
22. Cf. *TL* III, p. 395.

José Granados

From the Selfish Gene to Altruistic
Natural Behavior, and Beyond

In current philosophical reflections on biology there exist several attempts
to establish a link between ethics and biological theories, with a special focus on the doctrine of evolution. Several scholars try to explain human behavior, at least in part, by considering the data of evolutionary biology and
natural selection in particular. In the same way that this mechanism attempts to explain the origin of all life, it also attempts to explain the behavior of the highest, most developed forms, among whom we find the human species.

The different theories of natural selection result in different ways of
approaching morality. Of particular importance for our concerns is the
question of the "units of selection," that is, at what level does natural selection take place: at the level of the gene, of the organism, or of the group-
species?[23]

Depending on the answer, we will discover either selfish or altruistic
behavior in nature. If the unit of selection is the gene or the organism, then
selfishness will be at the basis of all animal, including human, behavior.
But if the unit of selection is located within the group, we could see some
organisms ready to offer themselves up for the good of the species, thus revealing altruism as part of natural human behavior. Let us briefly consider
these two options.[24]

1. The first option: egoism is the natural mode of behavior and any
apparent altruism can in the end be reduced to a more or less sophisticated
form of egoism.

The title of a well-known work is significant for characterizing this
position: *The Selfish Gene*.[25] The biology proposed by the author, Richard
Dawkins, has been labeled reductionistic because it explains everything
that happens to the organism solely through a consideration of its parts:
that is, everything can be explained at the level of the gene. Samuel Butler
expressed the same problem thus: "a chicken is just an egg's way of making
another egg." This means that the organism comes to be seen as a survival

---

23. Cf. E. Sober, *Philosophy of Biology* (Oxford: Oxford University Press, 2000), 89-120.

24. For the following, see the account given by Michael Ruse, *Philosophy of Biology
Today* (Albany: State University of New York Press, 1988).

25. Cf. Richard Dawkins, *The Selfish Gene* (New York: Oxford University Press, 1976).

mechanism of the gene. We are able to predict everything about the whole by setting out from the part and its selfish behavior, but, at the same time, there is no way that leads back to the part from the whole.

2. This first position has received criticism from biologists who wish to propose a more balanced point of view. Consider, for example, the work by E. Sober and D. S. Wilson, *Unto Others: The Evolution and Psychology of Unselfish Behavior,*[26] which advances the thesis that natural behavior is at least in part altruistic, and that natural selection does not behave in a selfish way. On the contrary, there are various examples of self-sacrifice in which one member chooses, for the good of the community, not to live any longer.[27] This explanation allows for the possibility of a return from the whole to the part.

These proposals suggest a close relationship between the questions about the organism and those about human moral behavior. They can help us to understand human action, provided that they are not considered an ultimate explanation, which would reduce morality to a natural process.[28] If we set the foundations of ethics within a biological process, we lose the novelty contained in human action and freedom becomes something that is simply mechanical.[29] Either self-love or love for the spe-

---

26. Elliott Sober and David Sloan Wilson, *Unto Others: The Evolution and Psychology of Unselfish Behavior* (Cambridge, Mass.: Harvard University Press, 1998).

27. "[T]he trematode parasite *Dicrocoelium dendriticum*, which spends the adult stage of its life cycle in the liver of cows and sheep. . . . The eggs exit with the feces of the mammalian host and are eaten by land snails, which serve as hosts. . . . Two generations are spent within the snail before the parasite forms yet another stage, the cercaria, which exits the snail . . . and is ingested by ants. About fifty cercariae enter the ant along with its meal. Once inside, the parasites bore through the stomach wall and one of them migrates to the brain of the ant . . . causing it to spend large amounts of time on the tips of grass blades. Here the ant is more likely to be eaten by livestock, in whose bodies parasites may continue their life cycle. . . . The brain worm, which is responsible for putting the ant in the path of a grazing animal, loses its ability to infect the mammalian host. It sacrifices its life and thereby helps to complete the life cycle of the *other* parasites in its group" (Sober and Wilson, *Unto Others,* p. 18).

28. Cf. the discussion as presented by Sober, *Philosophy of Biology,* pp. 206-13. Cf. also Sober and Wilson, *Unto Others,* p. 3.

29. Let us note, in passing, another consequence of this position. It reduces the moral option, in a simplistic way, to a matter of choosing between egoism and altruism. If an intermediate position is found, such as that of inclusive fitness (organisms can grow or develop by judicious donation), it is reduced to a kind of egoism. Any understanding of nature that fails to take the irreducibility of the personal world into account ends up imprisoned within

cies, according to this position, would be the force that makes the world go around. But here love would be little more than a word — it would be reduced to a mere mechanism that is incapable of playing any role in morality as such. Dualism would be overcome, to be sure, but only by eliminating one of the two terms of the problem.

There is another way to explain the relation between ethics and biological science. One representative of this method is the biologist F. J. Ayala,[30] who claims that morality has no foundations in evolutionary biology. It is necessary to make a distinction, he states, between the realm of positivistic sciences and the other, separate, realm of reality, which is that of religion, morality, and the arts. It is in this latter sphere that questions about human life that science cannot answer ought to be posed. Ayala thus manages to resolve the problem of morality, but only by establishing a separation between nature and the world of spiritual values. The result is that God is confined entirely within the higher layer of reality.

This is why Ayala can claim to be in accord with an essay by D. L. Hull, in which the God of evolution is accused of cruelty.[31] If we, following St. Paul's advice to the Romans, proceed from this Creator to his works, then, according to Hull, we will find a cruel God who is careless, wasteful, and abusive of his creation. In sum, the God of evolution, the God of science, is a God who does not care for the world and has nothing to do with the Christian or Jewish God.[32]

---

this dilemma: either an egoism as the contrary of altruism, or an altruism as the contrary of egoism. The possibility of overcoming this perspective by a consideration of the *communio personarum* is closed off if we take any form of mechanism as our guiding principle.

30. Cf. Francisco J. Ayala, "Intelligent Design: The Original Version," *Theology and Science* 1 (2003): 9-32.

31. Cf. Ayala, "Intelligent Design," p. 32; the reference within the article is to D. L. Hull, "The God of the Galapagos," *Nature* 352 (1991): 485-86.

32. Cf. Hull, "The God of the Galapagos," pp. 485-86: "What kind of God can one infer from the sort of phenomena epitomized by the species on Darwin's Galapagos Islands? The evolutionary process is rife with happenstance, contingency, incredible waste, death, pain, and horror. Millions of sperm and ova are produced that never unite to form a zygote. Of the millions of zygotes that are produced, only a few ever reach maturity. On current estimates, 95 per cent of the DNA that an organism contains has no function. . . . Whatever the God implied by evolutionary theory and the data of natural history may be like, He is not the Protestant God of waste not, want not. He is also not a loving God who cares about His productions. He is not even the awful God portrayed in the book of Job. The God of the Galapagos is careless, wasteful, indifferent, almost diabolical. He is certainly not the sort of

But this does not lead Ayala to the conclusion that we must set religion aside. On the contrary, one can accept the Christian God because he belongs to another realm of reality and thus never enters into conflict with science. In the end, the solution turns out to be simply to disconnect God from creation. But in so doing Ayala ends by defending a dualism of which he is perhaps unaware. Nature becomes closed in on itself and is unable to reveal the face of God.

Let us conclude: the explanations touched on so far result either in a) a materialism or naturalism, whether selfish or altruistic, that reduces human action to a natural process, or b) a dualism that separates science and God. This second position seems to be the only one that would justify adherence to religious faith.

In order to consider more rigorous philosophical reflections, we must go back several years and examine the work of a disciple of Heidegger, the German philosopher Hans Jonas. His writings will prove useful in our attempt to arrive at a different approach from those just presented.

Hans Jonas

To understand Hans Jonas's approach we must first take a short look at his biography. Jonas studied under Heidegger and wrote a doctoral dissertation on Gnosticism. Heidegger's behavior during World War II was, for Jonas, an important event in the history of ideas. Existentialism showed its incapacity to maintain the authentic existence it preached. What was the problem? For Jonas, the answer lay in the surprising relationship he discovered between Existentialism, on the one side, and the Gnosticism he studied for his dissertation, on the other. The key for understanding the connection was the dualism within both systems, a dualism between man and nature, between the anthropological mode of existence and the being of the rest of the world; it was a case of a total discontinuity in both systems. Lacking any roots in nature, Heidegger's authentic existence re-

---

God to whom anyone would be inclined to pray." Cf. Ayala's statement: "The defective design of organisms could be attributed to the gods of the ancient Greeks, Romans, and Egyptians, who fought with one another, made blunders, and were clumsy in their endeavors. But, in my view, it is not compatible with special action by the omniscient and omnipotent God of Judaism, Christianity, and Islam" ("Intelligent Design," 29).

mained an absolute freedom that was incapable of opposing the most terrible of atrocities when the time of Nazism came.[33]

Jonas attempted to overcome this dualism by connecting the human
sphere with the realm of all natural life.[34] He started by pointing out the
impossibility of understanding the organism in terms of mere matter,
which he demonstrated through a detailed analysis of the metabolism of
the amoeba. In the metabolic process there is a continuous exchange of
matter between the organism and the exterior world. An external observer
who considered the entirety of the universe in terms of particles and their
movement according to mathematical laws could attempt to explain the
living being as a particular combination of matter; however, considering
the fact that the matter of the organism continually changes, in the end he
would be unable to assign the organism any proper identity at all.

And yet we know that this unity exists. We can be sure, Jonas says,
because one is oneself an organism and thus able to see the organism from
the inside. This is an advantage, or even *the* great advantage, of being a
body. We can conclude, then, that a) because of metabolism the unity of
the organism cannot be reduced to a mechanical one, and b) another explanation exists and is available to us, who are internal observers of the
phenomenon of life.

When asked to give a reason for this unity, Jonas answers that the
identity of the organism is based on the constitution of an inwardness, an
interiority of life, in contrast to a unity of dead matter. This situation can
be described as freedom. It is worth noticing that this freedom has its
foundation precisely in a dependence on matter: the organism must continually renew its matter in order to live, and this very exchange constitutes
its being. The organism must, so to speak, regain its being at every moment, by way of a continuous exchange. Freedom is thus achieved at a
great cost: the cost of being always at risk because of having abandoned the
peaceful state of, say, a dead stone — and the stone will surely outlast the
organism. It is in this way that time, in a different sense from the physical

33. Cf. Lawrence Vogel, "Hans Jonas's Exodus: From German Existentialism to Post-
Holocaust Theology," in Hans Jonas, *The Phenomenon of Life: Toward a Philosophical Biology*
(Evanston, Ill.: Northwestern University Press, 2001), pp. 1-40.

34. For the following, cf. Hans Jonas, "Evolution and Freedom: On the Continuity
Among Life Forms," in *Mortality and Morality: A Search for the Good After Auschwitz*
(Evanston, Ill.: Northwestern University Press, 1996), pp. 59-74, and also his *The Phenome-
non of Life*.

time of matter, comes into play as a fundamental dimension of living existence. For the organism, time means that it must always face the possibility of death.

According to Hans Jonas, then, freedom has to do with the organism and the body. Moreover, it is the primary feature of the organism; it is the feature that allows us to understand its secret. This inwardness, which is always in need of continuous exchange with the exterior world, and the consideration of the stream of time as an interior measure of the organism, together allow for a description of life as an adventure that is always threatened by death. This is why we can call Jonas's attempt an existentialist analysis of all forms of life. This means, of course, an enriched conception of the life even of the amoeba, but it also implies a different concept of existentialism and existentialist freedom.

Let us develop this latter insight. In the case of the organism it is no longer a question of an absolute freedom detached from the material world, but rather a freedom that is dependent on matter and its properties and laws. It is a freedom that needs continual support from the environment, that is always linked to necessity. As the forms of life become more perfect, their freedom increases; so, too, however, does their dependence, so that we can say that the ultimate goal of life cannot be independence as such.[35] The increase in freedom means a simultaneous increase in fragility. And these statements hold for human existence as well.[36] This is the way Jonas overcomes dualism: progressive spiritualization brings about at the same time a progressive dependence on the environment; a progressive materialism, so to speak.

Jonas's examination of the amoeba then arrives at the point of *reductio in anthropologiam:* it affects the way we see man. From this point of view we can say that the question of organism and freedom is not merely a speculative exercise, but remains extremely important for a correct comprehension of the human person. If Jonas's account holds true, hu-

---

35. "[I]nner identity, by being open to what is outside, becomes the subject-pole of a communication with things which is more intimate than that between merely physical units. In this way the exact opposite of isolation emerges from the isolation of the organic structure" (Jonas, *Mortality,* p. 69).

36. "We note here that independence as such cannot be the ultimate good of life, since life is just that mode of material existence in which being has exposed itself to dependence (of which metabolism itself is the prime form) in exchange for a freedom closed to the independence of stable matter" (Jonas, *The Phenomenon,* p. 103).

man freedom always depends on a previous natural order that is the condition for its very existence. The study of nature thus belongs to the study of ethics.[37]

Can we now move forward to speak, not only of a relationship between the organism and freedom, but also of a relationship between the organism and love? Jonas offers us some hints in this direction. In his understanding, freedom implies a mechanism of transcendence. We can thus identify in this freedom an element of love, understood as a tendency towards the higher levels of life in the evolutionary track. This is how Jonas can accept a kind of love in the things themselves, an *eros* already present in mere matter that is a striving towards transcendence.[38]

However, as was the case with the ancient philosophers, this love is by no means reciprocal. In order for freedom to be present, the transcendent God must withdraw from the world and leave it alone. He is in no way present in the normal course of events.[39] This *eros* present in things remains a blind force and not a *logos;* it is not a rule or program with a final destination that could be equated to the design of a divine programmer.

This seems to me to be the greatest weakness in Jonas's account. In his explanation of the organism, the dimension of relationship and association has not been taken enough into consideration. On the human level, this results in singling out self-consciousness as the main prerogative of man, without giving any weight to the communion of persons. Ultimately, this fact has consequences for his conception of God and his action in the world as well. Because freedom is the predominant characteristic of life, and because of the way Jonas understands freedom (based, roughly, in self-consciousness and self-determination), the only way of conceiving of

37. "[E]thics becomes part of the philosophy of nature. . . . Hence would result a principle of ethics which is ultimately grounded neither in the autonomy of the self nor in the needs of the community, but is an objective assignment by the nature of things (what theology used to call the *ordo creationis*)" (Jonas, *The Phenomenon*, pp. 282-83).

38. Cf. Jonas, "Matter, Mind and Creation," in *The Phenomenon*, p. 186.

39. Jonas does not view the natural laws as absolutely closed off to divine intervention. This possibility is opened *de iure*, but Jonas rules it out in order to provide an account for the presence of evil, especially as experienced in Auschwitz, where his mother was murdered. On the other hand, revelation is not excluded, but it is possible only through the divine action in man, and not by divine interference with the material world. Jonas explains his ideas on this subject in his interesting account of the importance of Bultmann's work. See "Is Faith Still Possible? Memories of Rudolf Bultmann and Reflections on the Philosophical Aspects of His Work," in *Mortality*, pp. 144-64.

God's respect for his creatures is in terms of a withdrawal of the divine being from the world. But we will return to these points later.

Wolfhart Pannenberg

We turn now to the work of German theologian Wolfhart Pannenberg, who has attempted to provide an account of the relationship between theology and the natural sciences, especially physics. In a series of texts written over several years, Pannenberg demonstrates the way God is present and at work inside the world.[40] This presence is important to underscore because the failure to correlate theology with the natural sciences can result in a separation of faith and life that leads to practical atheism. Let us ask then: Is there any relation between divine action and natural processes? Pannenberg thinks so, and tries to explain his answer by bringing together two concepts that seem, at first, very different: the concept of "field," provided by quantum mechanics, and the biblical concept of "pneuma."

Modern science has developed the concept of a field of force as a means to give a comprehensive view of all physical phenomena. One important feature of a field is that it is not related directly to matter, but rather to space and time. Particles can be viewed as singularities of a field of force, but the field cannot simply be reduced to matter. This is why Pannenberg claims that modern physics is no longer materialistic.[41]

We can turn then to the second concept: Spirit. For the Bible, Spirit is not primarily synonymous with "mind" (this notion enters the Christian tradition later on, under Origen's interpretation), but rather with "wind" or "breath." It is close to the notion of Spirit found in the Stoics, for whom the Spirit pervaded everything and gave unity to the universe. The Bible maintains a similar notion but with an important difference: according to Scripture, the Spirit is a force that works in creation not only by giving

---

40. Cf. Wolfhart Pannenberg, *Toward a Theology of Nature: Essays on Science and Faith* (Louisville: Westminster/John Knox, 1993); idem, "Faith in God the Creator and Scientific Cosmology," *Communio* 28 (2001): 450-63; Pannenberg, "Gott und die Natur," *Theologie und Philosophie* 58 (1983): 481-500. Balthasar gives an account of Pannenberg's proposal in the third part of his *Theologik,* where he deals with the problem of the Spirit as soul of the world (cf. *Theologik III,* pp. 383-95).

41. Cf. Pannenberg, *Toward a Theology of Nature,* p. 156.

unity to its elements, but also and especially by bringing all things into the dimension of transcendence, that is, into the divine realm.

Pannenberg tries to connect this biblical concept of Pneuma as an all-pervading divine force with the idea of a field. Of course, the meaning the concept acquires here differs from what scientists intend by it. And yet there is a point of connection, for the only thing essential for the concept of a physical field is the existence of space and time, and not necessarily a consideration of matter. This means that we can speak of the Spirit as a field without a material conception; it suffices to relate the Spirit to space and time. Of course, the connection between God and space and time is a transcendent one, but it exists nonetheless and can be related via analogy to the physical concept of field.

Once this is established, it still remains to make an explicit connection between the concept of "field" and the notion of contingency, which is a crucial association for Pannenberg because of the unique compatibility between the contingency of all events and the novelty of the future. It is this contingency that refutes the deterministic assumptions of mechanistic physics and so allows a vision of God as Lord of history. It is in this way that the physical world remains open to divine action, which is a creative action that is analogical to the way a field works and not in contradiction to it (as would be the case between "spirit" and "matter"). That means that the possibility for transcendence opens up inside the very constitution of the physical world.

Let us summarize the most interesting features of this approach for our present purpose: (a) Pannenberg considers the interplay of the Spirit of God not only with the living organism, but with all of creation; (b) he offers a vision of nature that, like that of Jonas, is open to divine intervention, to transcendence, and to the novelty of the future; although Pannenberg does not speak of love, he underscores the newness of the action of God and his creative power, which are important features of love; and (c) in adopting a theological point of view Pannenberg introduces the biblical concept of the Spirit of life into the discussion, which is important because the presence of the Spirit is the usual path Christian theology takes to approach the issue of love in the world, and so of love moving everything.[42]

---

42. Cf. the following sentence by Hans Urs von Balthasar, *Theo-Drama*, vol. 2: *Dramatis Personae: Man in God*, trans. Graham Harrison (San Francisco: Ignatius Press, 1988), p. 356: "The formative spirit in nature, as yet unconscious, presupposes an absolute and real

Pannenberg's attempt, of course, has to be situated within the whole of his theology of history. One important objection can be raised here, which is the matter of the excessive weight Pannenberg gives to the future. It is true that the future is important in human history, but, at the same time, we cannot allow it to obscure the crucial importance of the present. Love is not only a promise, it is also a presence. We are not only projects to be elucidated by our future, but the reverse is true as well: our present determines the future.[43]

The contributions of these philosophers and theologians have prepared the way for us to begin to answer our original question. Before moving on, it is interesting to note that both Pannenberg and Jonas draw connections to the same period of history: the first two centuries of Christianity, when Gnostic doctrines flourished and the Stoics still held a prominent place within Hellenism. Both Pannenberg and Jonas fail to consider, however, the answer that some important Fathers of the Church of this time gave to the same challenges. Our own analysis would be incomplete if we did not first turn to attend to the voices of these Fathers.

A Theological Approach in the Second Century

Let us recall that Hans Jonas began his academic career with a dissertation on Gnosticism. His analysis led him to identify Gnosticism with the existential philosophy he had learned under Heidegger. It is, then, interesting to note that the most important forces in countering Gnosticism were precisely the theological efforts of Justin, Irenaeus, and the Church Fathers of the second century. Just as, for Jonas, Gnosticism shed light on today's philosophical problems by illuminating a negative side, could it not also be the case that the way out of Gnosticism provided by these Christian theologians could point to a way out of today's dualism as well?

For his part, Pannenberg bases his argument on the similarities between the physical concept of field and the Stoic doctrine of the Spirit, preferring the latter to Origen's interpretation (Spirit as mind) because he

---

Spirit that communicates to it the Idea to be aimed at, namely, man, so that this Idea is always approaching, always realizing itself."

43. The same criticism can be made of Pannenberg's *Grundzüge der Christologie.* In Pannenberg's Christology excessive weight is given to Jesus' future, with the danger of not giving enough importance to his present identity as Son of God already during his earthly life.

finds the Stoic doctrine closer to biblical thought. It is interesting that we find a similar doctrine of the Spirit in the Church theologians of the second century, either because Stoicism was still influential or because they were closer to the biblical mindset.

We will therefore examine the answer given to Marcion and the Gnostics by the Fathers of the second century, who will, hopefully, provide us with the theological structure to continue filling out the lines begun by Jonas and Pannenberg.

The Link Between Creation and Redemption

We will begin by highlighting the interconnection between creation and redemption that was fundamental for the early Fathers of the Church, as the following examples will demonstrate.

In his letter to the Corinthians,[44] Clement of Rome speaks of the concord and peace of the created universe. The order of natural things is interpreted in terms of subjection to the Lord, as obedience to his will. This obedience results in peace and love between everything, a bond of love that holds the universe together.

The idea has to be understood within the context of the whole letter to the Christians of Corinth, whom it admonishes to obtain unity through the bond of charity (cf. the hymn of 1 Clem 49). When read in this context, the text shows that there is for Clement a real relationship between Christian charity and the obedience that every creature gives to God's rule. Moreover, for Clement, creaturely love and obedience manifest their total potentiality in the Christian people, because love and obedience are in this case related to the revelation of Christ, who died for us on the cross in order to bring us fullness of peace and reconciliation. An interplay between redemption and the processes of nature is implicit here.

---

44. Cf. 1 Clem 20: "The heavens are moved by His direction and obey Him in peace. Day and night accomplish the course assigned to them by Him, without hindrance one to another. The sun and the moon and the dancing stars according to His appointment circle in harmony within the bounds assigned to them, without any swerving aside. . . . All these things the great Creator and Master of the universe ordered to be in peace and concord, doing good unto all things, but far beyond the rest unto us who have taken refuge in His compassionate mercies through our Lord Jesus Christ, to whom be the glory and the majesty for ever and ever. Amen."

Other authors of the early Christian tradition established the same analogies between the created world and the work of redemption. Tertullian explains the theological significance underlying the analogy:

In His works did God write it, before He wrote it in the Scriptures; He proclaimed it in His mighty deeds earlier than in His inspired words. He first sent Nature to you as a teacher, meaning to send Prophecy also as a supplemental instructor, that, being Nature's disciple, you may more easily believe Prophecy, and without hesitation accept (its testimony) when you come to hear what you have seen already on every side.[45]

Among other authors who drew the same comparisons we find, for example, Theophilus of Antioch. He established a relation between the anointment used in the pagan world and the Christian anointment with the oil of God. Just as many objects in the ancient world (e.g., ships, houses, and some tools) were anointed with oil and thus obtained a dynamic perfection, a final preparation, and an embellishment for their use, so were the Christians anointed with the Spirit.[46] This is not a case of bad apologetics, but of deep theology. Theophilus has in mind a link that unites the created world with the Christian redemption. In the context of biblical tradition, this link is understood as the Spirit of God who gives life to everything.[47]

The first Christians came to the conclusion that there was a link between this Spirit and the Holy Spirit that was given by Christ at Pentecost. The experience of the encounter with the Risen Christ, giver of the Spirit,

---

45. *De Resurrectione,* XII. Tertullian is speaking of the resurrection of the flesh, attested to by all the natural processes.

46. Cf. *Ad Autolycum* I, 12: "And about your laughing at me and calling me 'Christian,' you know not what you are saying. First, because that which is anointed is sweet and serviceable, and far from contemptible. For what ship can be serviceable and seaworthy, unless it be first caulked [anointed]? Or what castle or house is beautiful and serviceable when it has not been anointed? And what man, when he enters into this life or into the gymnasium, is not anointed with oil? And what work has either ornament or beauty unless it be anointed and burnished? Then the air and all that is under heaven is in a certain sort anointed by light and spirit; and are you unwilling to be anointed with the oil of God? Wherefore we are called Christians on this account, because we are anointed with the oil of God."

47. This is clear from the evidence provided by other Christian authors of the same period; see in this regard the important work by A. Orbe, *La unción del Verbo. Estudios Valentinianos III,* Analecta Gregoriana 113 (Rome: Pontificia Università Gregoriana, 1961).

understood as the fullness of the work of God, was able to shed light on the meaning of all of creation.

The Spirit in All of Creation

This is the foundation that allowed Church Fathers such as Justin Martyr and Irenaeus to distinguish two different stages in the work of creation. First, there was the giving of form and structure, a process that was mediated by the *Logos of God*. Second, there was a primeval anointing with the *Spirit of God*, wherein the world acquired the possibility of movement and life. This Spirit was given first of all by the Father to the Logos, his Son, who was in this way constituted Christ (Anointed); it was then communicated through the Logos to all of creation in different measures according to the different grades of being. It was a function of this Spirit, following the biblical tradition, to move everything forward in a process of transcendence that came to fulfillment only in the human being.

In this way the Spirit was understood as a gift present in creation from the beginning, a gift that ensured the constant action of God in the world. The possibility of a gradual donation of this Spirit was linked to the respect due to the very properties of creation. On the one hand, God respected the reality of everything he brought into existence and did not wish to impose his presence; on the other hand, neither did he want to abandon the work of his hands. By means of the gradual gift of the Spirit he was able to stay inside the world and, at the same time, to create freedom, setting in motion a process of transcendence that respected the interior core of every creature.

What was the goal of this process? The freedom that was brought about by the gift was necessary in order to make this gift greater, for through this freedom a communion between the created world and the Creator was made possible. The initial presence was to become a perfect union. St. Irenaeus of Lyons speaks of the flesh "possessed by the Spirit, forgetful indeed of what belongs to it, and adopting the quality of the Spirit, being made conformable to the Word of God."[48]

It resulted, then, that this communion was an initiative of the Father, because the Spirit was his personal gift. "If, however, we must speak

---

48. Cf. *Adv. haer.* V, 9, 3.

strictly, [we would say that] the flesh *does not* inherit, but is inherited."[49] In this way the love that was in the creatures was not only the love of the creatures for God, but also the love of God for the creatures; because of this reciprocity, which only the trinitarian God was able to account for, we can speak properly of a project of communion.

It is important to note that this communion was not offered only within the limits of man's spiritual realm. The crucial point was that communion was offered to all of creation in its material aspect, in precisely that aspect which was clearly different from God. That was the novelty of Christianity, in contrast to the Greek philosophers who had gone before: not only the soul but the body as well, and with it all the created world, could participate in the salvation of God. As one of the oldest texts we have on the resurrection of the flesh, written by Justin Martyr or one of his disciples, puts it:

> For this [that the soul lives forever] we used to hear from Pythagoras and Plato, even before we learned the truth. If then the Savior said this, and proclaimed salvation to the soul alone, what new thing, beyond what we heard from Pythagoras and Plato and all their band, did He bring us? But now He has come proclaiming the glad tidings of a new and strange hope to men. For indeed it was a strange and new thing for God to promise that He would not keep incorruption in incorruption, but would make corruption incorruption.[50]

According to the foregoing, then, the whole movement of creation can be seen as a process in which the Spirit unites, step by step, material flesh with the transcendent God. In this sense the Spirit of life, who gives life to every organism, can be understood as a bond of love between creation and the Father, aiming always at transcending the present stage, while at the same moment patiently respecting the time and particularity of creatures.

The Summit of History

The summit of this process is the center of history, its very densest hours: the death and resurrection of Christ. His filial obedience to the Father cul-

---

49. Cf. *Adv. haer.* V, 9, 4.
50. Cf. *De Resurrectione* X.

minates and sums up his whole life. Christ's gift of himself is understood neither as an act of pure will nor a self-commitment in disembodied free-dom, but as the shaping of Christ's flesh, of his human passions, so that they become totally filial and obedient to the Father. This is precisely the work of the Spirit, of the same Spirit that will be given to the Christians gathered at Pentecost. The act of free self-giving by Christ has to do, then, with his or-ganism, with his feelings and sensibilities, which are shaped during his hours of suffering. All this makes his death very foreign to the moral stan-dards of the Greeks, which were based on activity and self-sufficiency and not on the fundamental receptivity that is proper to the flesh.[51]

In this way, the Spirit that is present in the organism from the begin-ning can be understood as a Spirit of love, of filial obedience to the Father. The action of this Spirit was always to realize this love in fullness; it looked ahead to the perfect image of God, the risen Christ, in which the flesh, in a sense, forgets itself and becomes full of the Spirit.[52] The final goal is then the resurrected body, an organism fully moved by love, in filial obedience and communion with the Creator.[53]

Let us summarize how the foregoing can contribute to an answer to our original question.

1. Love has to do with the organism by means of the presence of the Spirit of God in the world. This Spirit is a gift to all of creation from the beginning, a gift that comes from the desire of the Father to make his cre-ation filial so that he will be able to unite it with himself. This love is not only a love of the world, a cosmic *eros;* on the contrary, it starts first in God, who is in himself Love. The Spirit is, first of all, the love of God for his creation: he is the only one capable of starting a process of communion that will draw everything into the divine realm.

---

51. For further justification of these statements, cf. José Granados, *Los misterios de la vida de Cristo en Justino Mártir,* Analecta Gregoriana 296 (Rome: Pontificia Università Gregoriana, 2005).

52. Cf. *Adv. haer.* V, 9, 3.

53. Taking this into account enables us to understand the doctrine of the Cosmic Cross, which is present in authors such as Justin and Irenaeus. According to this doctrine, there is a small cross inscribed in every being, in even the smallest organism, because the fullness at which every movement aims is the Crucified Christ who appears as the fulfill-ment of all of creation. The same Spirit who will advance the surrender of Jesus inscribes a love in all things that is an anticipation of the love shown by Christ on the cross. On the doc-trine of the Cosmic Cross, see Daniel Wanke, *Das Kreuz Christi bei Irenaeus von Lyon* (BZNW 99; Berlin: W. de Gruyter, 2000).

2. The participation of the Spirit differs according to the different levels of being of the creatures; here we can speak of analogy. The Spirit's action is dynamic, moving all of creation towards a transcendence. The gradual performance of this movement is able to make provision for the properties of all of creation and to respect the freedom of all beings; thus the project of communion allows freedom to find its proper place, thanks to the gradual donation of the Spirit.

3. The final point of this movement, the risen Christ, allows us to interpret the whole process as the communion of God the transcendent Father with his material creation, which is truly different from him. The work of communion is not a fusion of what is similar (God and the human mind), but God's acceptance and union with what is different and what must receive everything from above (God's union with the human flesh).

In this way the relation between the Spirit and the flesh gives us a theological foundation to speak of the presence of love in the organism, of love that makes the world go around. It provides us with a theology that is able to take into account some of the points raised in the first section. Let us consider our initial question, then, in light of what has been said.

The Love That Moves the World:
An Attempt to Provide an Answer

The question of the relationship between love and the organic/physical processes is not just of speculative importance. It is a question of overcoming the dualism typical of our modern time and of enabling a different vision of both nature and the human being. If love has to do with the processes studied by physics and biology, then the natural sciences are no longer closed in themselves as the only place in our society for a common ground of objectivity; on the other hand, if love really is the motor of all things, then human love and freedom are no longer detached from the rest of creation and can be understood in a different light.

A Point of Departure

We have presented the position of a few Christian authors who offer a theological approach to our question. Their faith in the resurrection of the flesh enabled them to have a new vision in contrast to Greek philosophy.

The resurrection of the flesh means that the material world, present in man, enters into total communion with the transcendent God through the life-giving presence of his Spirit who is Love. In this union the creature preserves his dignity and properties as a creature, without being, so to speak, fused with the divine essence. The mortal body becomes a spiritual body.

This idea affirms that at the end of history any dualism between spirit and body will be ultimately unthinkable. But if this union with the Spirit is the final destination of the body, and if this accomplishment is not solely an external one, that is, unconnected to the body's earthly history, then we can say that the Spirit must be present in the body from the very beginning. In other words, if the Spirit is able to become the Lord at the final point of history, it is because he had been in a certain sense the Lord from the very outset.

Thus, starting from the revelation of the destiny of man through Christ's incarnation and resurrection, theology is able to shed light on the entire realm of the human sciences. The final point of all, the Father's love revealed in the risen Christ, can illumine all of creation from its very beginning.[54]

A Challenge to Philosophy: The Possibility of a New Vision

It is by taking its starting point here, at this final stage in which the body is totally moved by the Spirit who is the bond of charity, that theology is able to propose to the philosophies of biology and science a possible understanding of creation as moved by love, that is, as *already* inhabited by this force that will become fully present at the end of time.

This will be important for our understanding of human love, as well. The love we find in the organism is interesting not only as a foreshadowing of human love, but also as an ingredient of it. It will show us how it is possible for the body to be integrated into the human act of love, thus revealing to us in a special way some of the most important features of true love.

This enterprise requires, of course, the proper use of analogy.[55] If we

---

54. According to the same circularity that occurs between philosophy and theology, as stated in *Fides et ratio*, 73.

55. Cf. Schindler, "The Significance of World and Culture," p. 126.

are to speak of love at the physical and biological level, the term must have an analogical meaning. From the perspective of theology, the analogy is supported by the presence of the Spirit, who is able to be given in different measures, respecting the properties of every creature. By means of this analogy the Spirit of Pentecost can be set in relation to the Spirit of Genesis.[56] It is God himself, then, who makes the analogy possible by the gradual donation of his Pneuma. The *princeps analogatum* of this analogy is the presence of the Spirit in the resurrected body of Christ and all the saints.

What sort of credence can a philosopher give to the idea that love is present in all physical and biological motions? If the words "freedom" and "love" are to have any meaning when applied to creation, the first thing to be established is the very fact that nature is not simply the deterministic application of mathematical equations to the movements of particles. This shift has long since taken place in modern science: nature is no longer conceived as entirely deterministic; the possibility of newness and surprise has entered the system.[57] This is a precondition of every discourse that attempts to relate the subhuman world to the human and divine ones.[58]

Inside this open view of nature, the case of life deserves special consideration. It is here that Hans Jonas's analysis of the function of metabolism provides us with a good point of departure. We will now further his reflections towards an understanding of the possibility of love moving the world.

As we have said, Jonas shows that the case of life is unique because an identity of matter is insufficient for giving an account of the unity of the

---

56. As Irenaeus does when arguing against the Gnostics: cf. *Adv. haer.* V, 3, 3.

57. Cf., for example, the words of Ilya Prigogine, recipient of the Nobel Prize in Chemistry: "What is now emerging is an intermediate description that lies somewhere between the two alienating images of a deterministic world and an arbitrary world of pure chance. Physical laws lead to a new form of intelligibility as expressed by irreducible probabilistic representations. When associated with instability, whether on the microscopic or macroscopic level, the new laws of nature deal with the possibility of events, but do not reduce these events to deductible, predictable consequences" (Prigogine, *The End of Certainty*, p. 189).

58. Cf. C. S. Lewis, *Miracles*, in *C. S. Lewis. Five Best Books in One Volume* (New York: Iversen Associates, 1969). This openness of nature is necessary in order to understand human freedom. It becomes essential for an understanding of Christian revelation, for God does not reveal himself only in man's interiority (as could be the case for other religions), but in the reality of the flesh, in the concreteness of salvation history. Compare, in this point, the Jewish position of Hans Jonas, "Is Faith Still Possible? Memories of Rudolf Bultmann and Reflections on the Philosophical Aspects of His Work," in Jonas, *Mortality*, pp. 144-64.

organism: the concept of inwardness is required in order to perceive the particular identity of an organism. This is how he makes it meaningful to speak of freedom even at the very first stages of the development of life, in terms of a detachment from the mere exteriority of dead things. This freedom is not conceived of in a dualistic manner, because the organism always needs the presence and exchange of matter. Jonas maintains that this freedom increases with the complexity of the living being but always in such a way that dependence increases as well; freedom grows at the same pace as dependence and fragility. The more the organism is free and spiritual, the more is it dependent on its environment for survival. In this way the ascent of evolution is not a separation of spirit and matter, but a common increase of both spirituality and materiality.

There is in all this process a striving towards transcendence. How is Jonas able to account for it? It is at this point that the German philosopher speaks of the presence of an *erōs* throughout the process. This *erōs* is a force that is present in everything, a force that strives towards overcoming the present structure and form. This *erōs*, Jonas says, must not be confused with a *logos*. The qualification is important in order to show that there is no global design *(logos)* for the universe, no information present at the beginning that determines the future path.

The absence of a *logos* in nature shows us how, in order to safeguard contingency, Jonas feels it necessary to rule out any intervention of God. God withdraws from the scene of his creation, leaving all the responsibility for the enterprise of evolution in the hands of the world and, ultimately, of man. Any intervention on God's part would either return things to the same dualism that Jonas wants to defeat (for God is pure Spirit, in opposition to matter) or destroy the autonomy of creation (for if God intervenes, the creature has no space; there is no room left for the adventure of life and the risk of its enterprise). Jonas is concerned with the dramatic structure of human existence itself and supposes that God's presence would destroy this structure.

From a Different Freedom to a Different Love

Let us now address a weakness in Jonas's approach: his analysis of the organism takes insufficient account of the interaction between different organisms.

The results of some investigations in the realm of physics and biology serve to highlight the fact that systems are no longer considered the sum of different individual particles, thus granting both the whole's influence over the part and the part's over the whole. Jonas was aware of this, but he did not apply it to the interaction among organisms. As has been demonstrated by some biologists, one important factor by which organisms evolve is the symbiotic association among organisms.[59] In the most developed living beings, we find associations in groups, like bees in a hive or members of a herd, in which each organism subordinates itself to a more complex structure.[60] That holds true even for the most primitive forms of life; we can mention, for example, the recently discovered fact that if an amoeba encounters difficulties in the process of self-division, it "calls" another amoeba who acts as a kind of midwife to assist the first amoeba.[61]

All these facts invite us to conclude that the framework for the emergence of life not only is the interaction of selfhood and the environment, but expands to include the association among organisms and the formation of more complex entities, as well.[62] The organism goes beyond itself by establishing further cooperation with other organisms; this sort of association is an important step in the ascension of life. We can state along with Jonas that every increase in freedom means an increase in dependence with the material environment; but now we can add that dependence on the environment itself mediates a dependence on other exterior forms of life. It is this latter point that better explains the movement of life towards transcendence.

In this regard it is interesting to consider the analysis of animal life conducted by Jonas, with a particular focus on animal emotions and pas-

---

59. Cf. Lynn Margulis and Dorion Sagan, *Acquiring Genomes: A Theory of the Origins of Species* (New York, 2002), who do a fine job of making this point, though its importance is somewhat overstated.

60. Cf. Sober and Wilson, *Unto Others.*

61. Cf. D. Biron et al., "Asexual Reproduction: 'Midwives' Assist Dividing Amoebae," *Nature* 410 (2001): 430: "The 'midwife' cell is chemotactically recruited for this mechanical intervention in what is a surprising example of primitive cooperation."

62. The same phenomenon can be described in the inorganic world, as the introduction of the concept of synergetics by some scientists seems to indicate; cf. the work by A. Ganoczy, *La trinité créatrice: Synergie en théologie* (Paris: Éditions du Cerf, 2003), who gives an account of this theological theory and tries to relate it to the Christian doctrine of the Trinity.

sions. Jonas locates the passions, within his overall perspective, as an increased level of freedom, a new degree of distance from the environment. I think, however, that in so doing he does not fully account for their important role. A more detailed analysis of animal passions reveals the way they enrich animal interiority, especially through contact with other living beings.[63] The passions demonstrate the animal's dependence on others and allow for the building up of an enhanced quality of life that begins precisely because of the living being's vulnerability before other organisms.

Analysis of the passions can help us understand what occurs when we arrive at the human level. What human experience is the continuation and overcoming of animal passions? This experience can only be the experience of love, which includes a relationship with others that leads to self-transcendence. Human love must be considered a forward step in a process that began with the very first forms of life.

The result is that this love cannot be understood as an act of pure will. An essential element of the experience of love is the integration of the world of the passions.[64] That is the way love makes it possible for another person to affect one's own world; this affection sets man in motion towards the achievement of a communion that must be built up in time in a free and active way by the patient integration of all the affective levels.[65] We see, then, that by means of this love, man is able to transcend himself and discover his true freedom via an increase of dependence and vulnerability.

Thus the communion of persons, and not self-consciousness alone, becomes the final stage of this process of transcendence that began with the first manifestations of life. Our proposal is that, through use of the analogy of the communion of persons, we can improve Jonas's approach and better arrive at his goal.[66] For if this communion is present in an analogical way at the origins of life, it is possible to account for the transcendence of the processes of life (which Jonas had difficulties with)

---

63. Cf. Martha Nussbaum, *Upheavals of Thought: The Intelligence of Emotions* (Cambridge: Cambridge University Press, 2001).

64. Cf. José Noriega, "Affettività e integrazione," *Anthropotes* 20 (2004): 163-76.

65. Cf. Angelo Scola, *Hombre — Mujer. El Misterio Nupcial* (Madrid: Ediciones Encuentro, 2001), pp. 96-102. For an English translation, see *The Nuptial Mystery*, trans. Michelle K. Borras (Grand Rapids: Eerdmans, 2005).

66. Cf. the comments on *The Phenomenon of Life* in the review by G. Morgan, *Zygon* 2 (1967): 285-89; here, 288.

while at the same time avoiding the dualistic conception of man (where he succeeded).

On the one hand, the development of life means an increased relationship with and openness to other forms of life that, unlike the surrounding dead environment, are capable of enriching and promoting an organism's life. This increasing openness allows an account of the transcendence of the process. On the other hand, this transcendence is going to be rooted in the body, which allows the living being contact with other forms of life that can enrich his own world. At the human level, the passions manifest in a special way this vulnerability to and dependence on the exterior world.[67] The passions are an integral part of human love, and they show us how the progressive spiritualization is realized through a progressive dependence and fragility.

All of the foregoing opens up the possibility of a new understanding of God's action in the world.

God's Love Inside the World

The use of the analogy of the communion of persons opens up a different understanding of the interplay between God and the natural world.[68] How can God allow his creation to be itself, which means to be contingent, capable of novelty and of different possibilities of free realization? For Hans Jonas, this is possible through the withdrawal of God from all the natural processes in order to preserve their freedom. But recall that, unlike Jonas, we have placed love, and not freedom only, as the interpretive key of all of reality.[69] Once nature has been set in relation to love, it is easier to understand the connection between nature and God. The law of all creatureliness is being opened to an external action that causes the creature to grow

---

67. On the relation between the Spirit and this world of the passions, cf. the recent article by Wolfhart Pannenberg, "Geist und Bewusstsein," *Theologie und Philosophie* 79 (2004): 481-90; 485f.

68. Cf. the discussions on this issue known as "The Divine Action Project"; for a detailed account see Wesley J. Wildman, "The Divine Action Project, 1988-2003," *Theology and Science* 2 (2004): 31-75. Modern physics offers various possibilities for understanding this action.

69. Thus the resurrection of the flesh is no exception, but the fulfillment (in a way, to be sure, that overcomes every possible expectation) of the power already present in creation.

beyond its own limits.[70] If God intervenes in this way, he is not breaking the laws by violence, but rather fulfilling them, for these laws are set in accordance with the supreme law of love.[71]

The concept that allows us to understand God's way of acting in the world, then, is the concept of *synergeia,* a cooperation that is a way towards complete communion. How is this communion possible, given the difference between the transcendent God and the material world? To give an answer, we must consider the Christian, trinitarian notion of God, which claims that God is in himself communion. If God is understood as a communion that presupposes the presence of difference, then he is able to communicate himself to his creatures, respecting their difference as well. This kind of interplay between God and the world is not that of a dualism, but that of a difference that is assumed inside the union of love.[72]

Such a possibility is explained by recourse to the Spirit, as attested to by the biblical tradition (recall, in this regard, our analysis of Pannenberg's contribution). God can respect freedom because he has the Spirit of love. The fact that this Spirit can be given gradually to creatures shows precisely this respect for their properties: God adapts himself to their rhythms of growing. That is why God's presence is not one of an infallible guide directing things to a final point of a static, pre-written script. He is able to partake of the adventure of his creation without destroying the risk and contingency in which, according to Jonas, the very significance of the enterprise of life lies.[73] The presence of the Spirit of God in the world is the key that allows an explanation of the continual divine action in nature.[74]

---

70. Cf. Pannenberg, "Geist und Bewusstsein," p. 483.

71. Cf. Wolfhart Pannenberg, "The Concept of Miracle," *Zygon* 37 (2002): 759-62.

72. Cf. Dennis Bielfeldt, "Can Western Monotheism Avoid Substance Dualism?" *Zygon* 36 (2001): 153-77, who maintains that a sort of dualism is unavoidable if God is to be considered active in the world.

73. The analogy of communion accounts too for all the "waste" in creation, a waste that cannot be understood in terms of a rationalistic account (cf. the objection by Hull, note 32: "Millions of sperm and ova are produced that never unite to form a zygote. Of the millions of zygotes that are produced, only a few ever reach maturity. On current estimates, 95 per cent of the DNA that an organism contains has no function. . . . Whatever the God implied by evolutionary theory and the data of natural history may be like, He is not the Protestant God of waste not, want not"). The meaning of such waste is easy to grasp for one who loves: *da mihi amantem.*

74. Cf. Karl Barth, *Kirchliche Dogmatik* III/1, 60; quoted by Balthasar, *Theologik III,* p. 386.

Through the participation of the Spirit of life, God is present in living creatures, causing them to transcend their own capacities. As already stated, this transcendence is achieved, not in spite of, but through the dependence of the living being on the material realm. There is an ontological meaning to the scriptural citation: "power is made perfect in weakness" (2 Cor 12:9).[75] The flesh, weak and vulnerable, becomes the point where the Spirit touches the creature and moves it towards a wider horizon. At the level of man this flesh includes, especially, the passions and the entire world of human affectivity; moved by the Spirit of God, the passions disclose a horizon of transcendence within which man is able to proceed towards complete communion.[76]

The Highest Point of the Interplay Between Love and the Organism

Before concluding our reflections, let us consider the summit of the presence of love in history: the death and resurrection of Christ, which theology can view as the accomplishment of all the movements of creation.

We will start with a necessary qualification. Any assertion of love as the rule of all creation must take into account Paul's sentence in Romans 8:20-21: "For creation has been subjected to frustration, not of its own choice, but by him who subjected it — with hope — because creation itself too will eventually be freed from its bondage to decay and brought to the glorious freedom of the children of God." Whatever the analogy between the Spirit of Pentecost and the Spirit of life may be, we can never forget that creation is bound to decay because of the existence of sin. The cross of Christ means a fulfillment but at the same time a judgment of all the mechanisms of nature.

Therefore, the redemption brought about by Christ also means a change in the understanding of love as mover of all things. This love cannot be conceived of as an uninterrupted ascension into more perfect forms of communion. In some aspects nature can be cruel and destructive, in sheer contradiction to the love shown by Christ in his final hour.

---

75. The sentence is used in this sense by Tertullian (*De Resurrectione* 9) and Irenaeus (*Adv. haer.* V, 2, 3; 3, 1).

76. Cf. Pannenberg, "Geist und Bewusstsein."

But Paul speaks, too, of the hope that this creation be redeemed. Taking into account all that we have said above, we can interpret Christ's life and resurrection as the confirmation of all of history, as the point where the activity of the Spirit reaches its highest summit. Focusing on this event allows us better to understand how it is that love moves everything.

It was his great love for God his Father that moved Jesus to drink the chalice. But this love was not solely a spiritual one. In the "hour" of Christ the passions of the flesh played an important role and were integrated into this love. The Savior experienced an intense longing for God, together with sorrow and even fear, with all the bodily reactions implied therein. All of these elements formed part of his act of obedience to the Father. All of creation, of which man is the synthesis and summit, was included in the body of Christ. It had been assumed by the Son of God and was transformed into the love of the perfect offering by the action of the Spirit (cf. Heb 9:14). Because of his body's very vulnerability and susceptibility to change, Jesus was able to express in a new form, in the midst of time, his eternal Yes to the Father. "Sacrifice and offering you did not desire, but a body you prepared for me. . . . Then I said: . . . Behold, I come to do your will, O God" (cf. Heb 10:5-7).

Only in this way can the bodily suffering of Christ be understood as a preparation for the bodily resurrection, in which the body is totally moved by the Father's love. St. Paul expresses this idea to the Romans when he speaks of the redemption of the body (Rom 8:23). For the Apostle, this redemption that all of creation seeks is equated to sonship and is related to the resurrection and the spiritual body. The spiritual body is thus conceived by St. Paul as a filial body, a body that is in all things obedient to the will of the Father and docile to the Spirit.[77]

If the resurrection is the most perfect manifestation and realization of love in history, it is so because love has to do with every organism from the very origins of life. After these reflections we know that all of history can be seen as a progressive increase and purification of this love, an increase that has its summit in the Paschal mystery.

All this can be expressed, coming back to Dante, with the verses that

---

77. Cf. J. Ramsey Michaels, "The Redemption of Our Body: The Riddle of Romans 8:19-22," in *Romans and the People of God: Essays in Honor of Gordon D. Fee on the Occasion of His 65th Birthday*, ed. S. K. Soderlund and N. T. Wright (Grand Rapids: Eerdmans, 1999), pp. 92-114; Christian Grappe, "Qui me délivrera de ce corps de mort? L'esprit de vie! Romains 7,24 et 8,2 comme éléments de typologie adamique," *Biblica* 83 (2002): 472-92.

the poet devotes to the Virgin Mary in the last canto of *Paradiso*. In the maternal womb of Mary, the coming of Jesus is not understood as a mere biological phenomenon. Dante saw an interconnection between love and the formation of Jesus' organism. Thus, he was able to say that in Mary's womb love was again enkindled: "Within your womb was lit once more the flame of that love/through whose warmth this flower [the whole Church] opened." "Nel ventre tuo si raccese l'amore" (*Paradiso* XXXIII, 7).[78]

78. The image of love as fire is typical for the consideration of love as a passion, as appears, for example, in the *Aeneid* (cf. IV, 2; IV, 23 *et passim*). This passion will find a final place in the Christian understanding of love, as attested to by Dante when he meets Beatrice at the gates of heaven, with words that echo those of Virgil: "conosco i segni dell'antica fiamma" [I recognize the signs of the old flame] (*Purgatorio* XXX, 48). For an analysis of love in Dante, cf. Nussbaum, *Upheavals of Thought*, pp. 557-90.

Love Makes the World Go 'Round: Motion and Trinity

Simon Oliver

The mystery of motion — particularly the seemingly perfect circular motion of the cosmos and the powerful motions of will and desire — has, of course, been central to reflections on creation and its "motionless" divine origin from the earliest times of the Western intellectual tradition. Aquinas is one of the most prominent among those medieval theologians who deploy the concept of motion widely in their writings, utilizing not least Aristotle's physics. In this essay, I would like to begin with a brief examination of Aquinas's understanding of motion, emanation, and God's relation to a cosmos saturated with change. We find in Thomas that motion is analogically related to the eternal dynamism of the Trinity. Motion is not the means of the disintegration of being, mere flux, or aimless wandering which must be frozen in a kind of parody of eternity (as, for example, in Hobbes), but the means of our participation in the unity of the eternal. I will begin with a consideration of Aquinas's understanding of creation as a motion of emanation from God, before then considering emanation within created beings and its relation to the eternal emanation of the persons of the Trinity. We will see that, in the dynamism of the Holy Spirit proceeding from the Father and Son, we find the principle of natural motion.

Having considered motion in relation to the divine processions, creation, and emanation, I will turn to address Balthasar's development of ideas latent in Aquinas's view with particular reference to trinitarian theology, the ontology of love, and the structure of motion. I will suggest that Balthasar's emphasis on difference within the Trinity as the structure of love implies that motion — which, in its Platonic, Aristotelian, and

Thomist guise, requires difference — is also structured as a kind of kenotic self-donation.

Aquinas: Creation and Emanation

Aquinas is frequently reluctant to describe God's act of creation as any kind of "motion." Given an Aristotelian definition of motion which has at its heart the passage from potency to act and the postulation of a subject that preceded the motion, there is always the danger of compromising the Christian doctrine of creation *ex nihilo*.[1] However, on other occasions Aquinas stretches his use of the term *motus* in such a way that it can be employed at least metaphorically, but without error, of the divine creative act and even of God's immanent and perfectly subsistent intellective life.[2] How can this be so? It is necessary to begin with an examination of the character of emanation, for Aquinas refers to creation as "the emanation of things from the first principle."[3]

Emanation for Aquinas refers to the active self-expression of a nature in relation to others in the production of another self. In the *Summa contra gentiles,* he expounds his understanding of emanation and its hierarchical character.[4] Aquinas begins by noting that "one finds a diverse manner of emanation in things, and, the higher a nature is, the more intimate to the nature is that which flows from it."[5] This is therefore a hierarchy of emanation based on the discreteness of emanation. For example, inanimate bodies are said to have the lowest form of emanation because they are only able to communicate something of their nature through the external action of one upon another — for example, a fire acts on a combustible object and produces another fire. A discrete emanation and complete return to self is first found in the human intellect, for the intellect is capable

---

1. Aquinas, *Summa theologiae* (= *ST*), I, 45, 2, ad 2.

2. For example, see Aquinas, *Summa contra gentiles* (= *SCG*), I, 13, 10. See also *ST* I, 19, 1, ad 3 on the entirely subsistent movement of the divine will.

3. *ST* I, 45: "De modo emanationis rerum a primo principio." For a discussion of divine emanation and motion in relation to Aquinas's understanding of the perfections of being, life, and knowing, see R. A. te Velde, *Participation and Substantiality in Thomas Aquinas* (Leiden: E. J. Brill, 1995), pp. 272-79.

4. *SCG* IV, 11.

5. *SCG* IV, 11, 1.

of self-knowledge and understanding. Thus a human being is able to produce a communication of its nature, an emanation of another self, in such a way that reflection of the self on itself — self-reflection — is possible. Yet the human intellect is imperfect because it must take its first knowledge from without, namely through sense perception, before returning from the external object to arrive at knowledge of itself by its relation to the object in question.[6] Perfect emanation is found in God, whose intellect and act of understanding, unlike those of angels, are identical with his being. Therefore, God's being, intellect, and understanding are one.[7] For the divine to know himself and express himself through that knowledge is the divine essence, the very divine life itself.

Aquinas goes on to maintain that God's self-knowledge, although perfect, unitary, and eternal, still maintains distinction. This distinction consists in the God who expresses his self-knowledge in himself and the God who is expressed or conceived, namely the Son, who is the expression of the self-knowledge of the Father. The former is a perfect emanation of the latter in such a way that the being of both is identical and this emanation remains entirely immanent.[8]

As well as God's knowledge of himself through himself, elsewhere Aquinas outlines the sense in which ideas subsist in the divine mind and are therefore known by him.[9] He claims that these ideas are forms of things existing apart from things, and that the form of a thing can either be the exemplar or pattern of the thing whose form it is said to be, or it can be the means of knowing the thing whose form it is by its residing in the knower. In both of these aspects, ideas subsist in the mind of God. Yet as regards the latter, it can be seen that it is by God's interior self-knowledge, namely the emanation of the Son from the Father, that he knows other things by their proper ideas subsisting in him. In a sense, therefore, all things are known primarily and *per se* as they exist most perfectly in God's knowledge, and as they are therefore known in God's self-knowledge, in God's interior emanation.

Aquinas goes on to describe the place of the Spirit within the divine emanations and creative act.[10] He seeks to make clear what we must un-

---

6. See *SCG* II, 60.
7. See *SCG* I, 45.
8. On the difference between divine and human self-understanding, see *SCG* IV, 11, 11.
9. *ST* I, 15, 1.
10. *SCG* IV, 15ff.

derstand of the Spirit with regard to God's immanent life and act of creation. Initially, Aquinas examines intellectual natures in general and states that there must be a will alongside intellect because such a nature must *desire* to know.[11] Crucially, intellects are not merely passive recipients of "information"; all knowledge is at once *willed* or *desired* knowledge. Just as any natural thing has an inclination to its own proper operations, for "it tends to what is fitting *(convenientia)* for itself," so too an intellectual nature has an inclination, which we call will, towards its own proper operation in knowledge.[12] Aquinas claims that, of all the acts that belong to the will, love *(amor)* is found to be a principle and common root. He describes this in terms of the "affinity and correspondence" *(affinitatem et convenientiam)* between the principle of inclination in natural things and that to which they are moved. An analogy with physics is deployed: "The heavy has such a relation with the lower place. Hence, also, every inclination of the will arises from this: by an intelligible form a thing is apprehended as suitable or affective."[13] Thus it seems that the form of *convenientia* between things, and the principle of the motion one to another, is love, and the motive for their coming together is a teleological desire for fulfillment.

Now, what is loved — the beloved — is in the intellect by reason of a likeness of its species. For example, via sense experience a likeness of an object comes to reside in the intellect of a human soul and in this way it is known by the intellect. However, that which is loved also resides in the will. How? By reason of a proportion and affinity between the term or goal of a motion and the principle of that motion. For example, in the case of the element fire, the upper place to which fire tends is "in" the fire by reason of the lightness of the fire, which gives it "proportion and suitability" *(convenientiam et proportionem)* to such a place.[14] Likewise, in the case of the intellectual nature, we might say that an object is in the intellect by means of species residing therein, while it is in the will by means of a "proportion and suitability" with the object; this *convenientia* then becomes the principle behind the intellectual nature's self-motion towards knowledge of the object. The intellect loves the object and by the will desires to know.

11. *SCG* IV, 19, 1ff.
12. *SCG* IV, 19, 2.
13. *SCG* IV, 19, 3.
14. *SCG* IV, 19, 4.

However, in contrast to intellectual beings such as angels or humans, God is at one with his intellectual nature and, likewise, his will. The first and most appropriate object of the operation of the divine will is the divine goodness, and so God, because God loves himself and is beloved and lover, must be in his will as the beloved is in the lover.[15] The beloved is in the will of the lover by means of a "proportion and suitability" between the two. God has a most perfect proportion and suitability with himself because he is pure simplicity. Therefore, God is in his will with perfect simplicity. In addition, any act of will is, as Aquinas remarks, an act of love, but the act of the will is the divine being. So "the being of God in his will by way of love is not an accidental one — as it is in us — but is essential being," hence the scriptural teaching that "God is love" (1 Jn 4:16).[16]

Coupled with what has been said of God's self-knowledge in the emanation of the Son, we now have a twofold picture of the divine life. On the one hand, God loves himself because, as we have seen, the "proportionate and appropriate" end of God's operative will is himself and his own goodness. Yet this would not be loved if it were not known, and God knows himself through conceiving of himself in the eternal emanation of the Word. Yet it is not quite adequate to say that it is God's knowledge that is beloved, for God's knowledge is his essence. Therefore, coupled to the emanation of the Word must be a love whereby the lover dwells in the beloved, both in God's knowing and in that which is known. The love by which God is in the divine will as a lover in the beloved "proceeds both from the Word of God and the God whose Word he is."[17] It is the Holy Spirit. It is as if the Father is the lover and the Son the beloved, but immediately and in eternity this is returned so that the Son is the lover and the Father the beloved. This introduces a kind of circular dynamism to the inner divine life which Aquinas refers to as a kind of intellectual "motion."[18]

With regard to God's self-knowledge and self-love in the persons of the Trinity, one can now understand how the universe has the divine nature as its cause. Aquinas states that "effects pre-exist in a cause according to its mode of being. Since, then, God's being is his actual understanding, creatures pre-exist there as held in his mind. . . ."[19] Thus Aquinas says "God's

---

15. *SCG* IV, 19, 7.
16. *SCG* IV, 19, 7.
17. *SCG* IV, 19, 8.
18. *SCG* IV, 19, 12.
19. *ST* I, 19, 4 responsio.

knowledge stands to all created things as the artist's to his products."[20] However, in addition to the knowledge of things, Aquinas also notes that an act of will is necessary in the act of creating: creation is not a "necessary" emanation. God is so inclined because his own subsistent goodness wills that other things be in such a way that "by his will he produces things in being" and his self-love thereby becomes the cause of the creation of things.[21] In a similar fashion Aquinas elsewhere states, "It is . . . from the fact that the Holy Spirit proceeds by way of love — and love has a kind of driving and moving force — that the movement which is from God in things seems properly to be attributed to the Holy Spirit."[22] It seems, therefore, that God's knowledge becomes the cause of creation and the ground of the continual subsistence of the cosmos, while the Holy Spirit, which proceeds from the Father and Son by way of love, is properly described as the principle of the motion of nature.[23] This means that what moves all things to their characteristic operation is love, namely a desire for fulfillment in the beloved.

In what sense can this emanation and return to self in God be described as any kind of motion? In answer, Aquinas begins by stating that there are two kinds of action.[24] The first is that which passes to matter outside the agent concerned, for example locally moving another body or the heating of one body by another. The second is that which remains in the agent, for example understanding, sensing, or willing. In the case of the first, the motion is completed not in the agent of the motion, but in another. In the second, the motion is the completion or perfection of the agent of the motion. Aquinas can now stipulate that, since motion involves the actualization of the thing moved, this second type of action or motion, in being the actualizing of the agent, is called movement in a proper sense. However, this is not motion in the strict Aristotelian sense of the passage from contrary to contrary or the actualizing of the potential *qua* potential. In Aristotelian terms, it may be regarded as *energeia* (actuality), a kind of constant similar to seeing, which is not temporally divisible into parts. It is an activity which, at every moment, is the same, not having an end outside itself.[25] Therefore, Aquinas concludes, this "motion" is different from the

20. *ST* I, 14, 8 responsio.
21. *SCG* IV, 19, 12.
22. *SCG* IV, 19, 20, 3.
23. *SCG* IV, 20, 3.
24. *ST* I, 18, 3, ad 1.
25. On Aristotle's distinction between *energeia* and *kinēsis*, see *Metaphysics*, IX.6.

strict Aristotelian definition of the *Physics*. However, he does seem willing to assimilate the Aristotelian view with the self-moving soul of Plato when he writes, "Plato understood by motion any given operation, so that to understand and to judge are a kind of motion. Aristotle likewise touches upon this manner of speaking in the *De Anima*. Plato accordingly said that the first mover moves himself because he knows himself and wills or loves himself. . . . There is no difference between reaching a first being that moves himself, as understood by Plato, and reaching a first being that is absolutely unmoved, as understood by Aristotle."[26] Elsewhere, Aquinas explicitly states that life is especially manifested in motion and specifically in self-motion and those things that put themselves into operation.[27] He states that if love, drive, and motion are particularly suited to the Holy Spirit, as Scripture suggests,[28] it is here that we find the dynamism of the trinitarian life fully expressed and mediated.

Balthasar: Difference and the Dynamism of Trinitarian Love

How does Balthasar develop this Thomist understanding of the doctrine of God and cosmic motion? For Balthasar, motion is similarly grounded in the dynamism of the trinitarian processions. Developing Aquinas's line of thought as expressed in the first part of this essay, it is possible, through the centrality of love in Balthasar's theology, to outline in further detail the nature of the analogy between the dynamic actuality of God's trinitarian life and the motions of the cosmos. Balthasar's doctrines of God and creation, centered on difference, provide further insight into the nature of love and the nature of motion's participation in the divine life.

The life of God, for Balthasar, is characterized by self-donation in the form of kenosis.[29] The revelation of this self-giving is recorded in the hymn to Christ's self-emptying in the Incarnation in Philippians 2. Within the economy of salvation, this kenosis reaches its greatest intensity on Holy Saturday when God, in sovereign freedom, endures the dereliction of godlessness. Yet it is crucial for Balthasar that this kenotic moment is not

26. *SCG* I, 13, 10.

27. *SCG* IV, 20, 6.

28. *SCG* IV, 20, 6. Aquinas mentions John 6:63 and Ezekiel 37:5.

29. Hans Urs von Balthasar, *Theo-Drama: Theological Dramatic Theory*, vol. IV: *The Action*, trans. G. Harrison (San Francisco: Ignatius Press, 1994), pp. 325ff.

an arbitrary act of God, as if the divine had suddenly become subject to godlessness in order to be fully himself (as in the thought of Jürgen Moltmann). Rather, it is suffering and dereliction which are made subject to God, and the godlessness of Holy Saturday is always the economic outworking of God's immanent and eternal kenosis.[30] It is at this moment in the economy of salvation that it is revealed that even that which is *not* God is brought to be subject *to* God. Moreover, as Graham Ward observes, this kenosis is not christomonistic, an act confined to Christ's Incarnation and crucifixion. Rather, divine kenosis, as trinitarian and eternal, is the possibility of God's self-giving within the economy of salvation.[31] As Aquinas refers to the eternal emanation of the Son from the Father, so for Balthasar the Father pours out his life without remainder in the Son's eternal begetting. The Son's response is kenotic *eucharistia,* thus constituting a "eucharistic movement back and forth from the Father."[32] Importantly, the self-donation of the Father is also the self-reception of the Son, thus constituting the relational nature of the eternal divine gift: self-donation and self-reception are one. This love cannot be contained within an enclosed dyad, but opens in eternity in the procession of the Spirit, who maintains the infinite difference between Father and Son. This infinite *diastasis* is revealed in the Son's cry of dereliction on the cross and in the silence of Holy Saturday.[33] Within that hiatus is contained not only sin, but the whole of

30. Hans Urs von Balthasar, *The Glory of the Lord: A Theological Aesthetics,* vol. I: *Seeing the Form,* trans. E. Leiva-Merikakis (San Francisco: Ignatius Press, 1982), p. 461: "God's incomprehensibility is now no longer a mere deficiency in knowledge, but the positive manner in which God has loved us so much that he surrendered his only Son for us, the fact that the God of plenitude has poured himself out, not only into creation, but emptied himself into the modalities of an existence determined by sin, corrupted by death and alienated from God." Crucially, in maintaining that Christ's kenosis on the cross is the economic outworking of God's eternal kenosis, Balthasar is *not* suggesting that there is an eternal suffering in God. Rather, within a sinful world, the cross is the way in which eternal love manifests itself. It is the way in which the eternal love of God, which has always flowed to creation, is maintained in its self-giving in the face of sin. I am grateful to D. C. Schindler for highlighting this point to me.

31. See G. Ward, "Kenosis: Death, Discourse and Resurrection" in L. Gardner, D. Moss, B. Quash, and G. Ward, eds., *Balthasar at the End of Modernity* (Edinburgh: T. & T. Clark, 1999), pp. 44-45.

32. Hans Urs von Balthasar, *Theo-Drama: Theological Dramatic Theory,* vol. II: Dramatis Personae: *Man in God,* trans. G. Harrison (San Francisco: Ignatius Press, 1990), 268.

33. See Hans Urs von Balthasar, *Mysterium Paschale: The Mystery of Easter,* trans. A. Nichols, O.P. (Edinburgh: T. & T. Clark, 1990).

creation, for the "otherness" of creation — the ontological difference — is itself the *imago* of the infinite difference which is being itself, namely the difference of the divine persons. Balthasar writes, "If, within God's identity, there is an Other, who at the same time is the image of the Father and thus the archetype of all that can be created; if, within this identity, there is a Spirit, who is the free, superabundant love of the 'One' and of the 'Other,' then both the otherness of creation, which is modelled on the archetypal otherness within God, and its sheer existence, which it owes to the intradivine liberality, are brought into a positive relationship to God."[34] In fact, for Balthasar, it is only the difference inherent within being itself that makes creaturely difference intelligible — especially the difference within all creatures, that between essence and existence.[35]

The trinitarian difference within the Godhead and the difference of essence and existence in creation indicates, for Balthasar, "both a *similitudo* (insofar as the multiplicity of creatures is one in *esse*) and a *maior dissimilitudo,* insofar as nondivine being necessarily cleaves in two and stands over against the divine identity in the form of non-identity."[36] This is to say that the diversity within creation is not to be interpreted as a fall, but is rather a participation in the trinitarian difference of the Godhead.[37] Yet because of the ontological difference in which the essence of non-subsistent creatures is not one with their existence, the resemblance or *similitudo* is, as Aquinas would say, one of creatures to God, and not of God to creatures.[38] Likewise, Balthasar refuses to mitigate the ontological difference.

So what, for Balthasar, is the nature of the *analogia entis* through which creation is formed as an *imago* of the eternal Godhead? For Balthasar, this must be kenosis, which is itself the form of love. As Ward

---

34. Hans Urs von Balthasar, *Theo-Logic: Theological Logic Theory* (= *TL*), vol. II: *Truth of God,* trans. A. Walker (San Francisco: Ignatius Press, 2004), pp. 180-81. See also Balthasar, *Theo-Drama: Theological Dramatic Theory,* vol. IV: *The Action,* trans. G. Harrison (San Francisco: Ignatius Press, 1994), p. 323.

35. Balthasar, *TL* II, p. 182. This is not to suggest in any way that "difference" is a straightforward concept. It is beyond the immediate purview of this essay to enter into a detailed discussion. For such an assessment of the difficulty of "thinking difference," see R. Williams, "Afterword: Making Difference" in L. Gardner et al., eds., *Balthasar at the End of Modernity,* pp. 173-79.

36. Williams, "Afterword: Making Difference," p. 183.

37. Williams, "Afterword: Making Difference," pp. 184-85.

38. See, for example, *ST* I, 4, 3.

notes, the view that love is kenotic has strong precedent in the early Church: love is self-abandonment and gift, whereas sin is the attempt at self-possession as a rejection of self-donation.[39] Kenotic love is a self-donation, not a "giving-up." This economy of love involves reception and therefore the relationality and difference of the giver and the recipient.[40] In a move seemingly beyond Aquinas, and with an eye on the dangers of sub-ordinationism, it is kenotic love which is elevated to the heart of Balthasar's theology: "But if we reflect once more on the process of the intradivine processions, two approaches are barred to us: the idea of a Father who generates the Son in order to come to know himself as God, and the idea of a Father who, because he has already known himself perfectly, generates the Son. The first position would be Hegelianism, the second, thought through consistently, would be Arianism. For this reason, the immemorial priority of the self-surrender or self-expropriation thanks to which the Father *is* Father cannot be ascribed to knowledge but only to groundless love, which proves the identity of love as the 'transcendental par excellence.'"[41]

As the "transcendental par excellence," it is love alone which is credible as our means of understanding God's revelation of himself and creation's analogical relation to its divine source. Creation bears the marks of its origin: the love of God which is kenotic in nature. So created entities are understood to participate in the eternal kenosis of the persons of the Trinity by continually giving themselves to be seen, known, understood, and delighted in. As Rowan Williams points out, reality is therefore kenotic and ek-static for Balthasar, for all things continually move out of themselves in self-donation.[42] Yet the "watermark" of love in created being is only finally made manifest in the light of Christ's love shown on the cross: "This sign imprinted on nature, however, comes to light only when the sign of absolute love appears: the light of the Cross makes worldly being intelligible, it allows the inchoate forms and ways of love, which otherwise

---

39. Ward, "Kenosis," p. 46.

40. For an exacting theological analysis of the theology of gift, including a critique of Derrida's notion of the "one-way" gift, see John Milbank, *Being Reconciled: Ontology and Pardon* (London: Routledge, 2003).

41. *TL* II, p. 177.

42. See R. Williams, "Balthasar and the Trinity," in E. Oakes and D. Moss, eds., *The Cambridge Companion to Hans Urs von Balthasar* (Cambridge: Cambridge University Press, 2004), p. 41.

threaten to stray into trackless thickets, to receive a foundation in their true transcendent ground."[43]

How might kenotic love at the heart of divine being, and its concomitant image in creation, illuminate the nature of cosmic motion? To answer this question, it is necessary to refer to the specifics of the Aristotelian-Thomist understanding of motion. It must be remembered that motion prior to the advent of modern natural philosophy is a broad category referring not only to the locomotion of bodies in space, but also to the motions of quality and quantity: learning, growing, and maturing in character, for example, are varieties of motion.[44] Central to Aristotle and Aquinas's concept of motion is difference, which is also integral to Balthasar's understanding of love. Whereas the physics of Newton was later to refer to the idealized motion of a single body moving through a vacuum (in which motion is treated as a state that is altered by the more fundamental category of force), for Aquinas, following both Plato and Aristotle, motion is always relational: there is a mover and that which is moved. This is reflected most clearly in the so-called motor-causality principle which has its origins in Aristotle's physics: *omne quod movetur ab alio movetur* (whatever is moved is moved by another).[45] Motion takes place between contraries (for example, black and white, ignorance and knowledge) and is passage from potency to act. It is a necessary condition for motion that there be something in act and something in potency with regard to the motion in hand. For example, for motion from ignorance to knowledge to take place, there must be something in act with regard to the knowledge concerned that draws the ignorant to the actuality of knowledge.

Crucially, therefore, motion requires the difference of mover and moved, and the difference of potency and act. There is also a sense in which motion might also be described as ecstatic and even kenotic. I have already alluded to the distinction made by Aristotle between *energeia* (actuality) and *kinēsis* (motion). The former is constant (that is, not temporally divisible into differentiated parts) and does not have an end beyond

---

43. Hans Urs von Balthasar, *Love Alone Is Credible*, trans. D. C. Schindler (San Francisco: Ignatius Press, 2004), p. 142.

44. For an extensive discussion of motion in the thought of, among others, Plato, Aristotle, Aquinas, and Newton, see Simon Oliver, *Philosophy, God and Motion* (London: Routledge, 2005).

45. See Aquinas, *Commentary on Aristotle's* Physics, trans. R. J. Blackwell et al. (London: Routledge and Kegan Paul, 1963), VII.1.1; Aristotle, *Physics*, VII.1.241b.

itself. Examples include seeing, understanding, and thinking. By contrast, *kinesis* has an end outside itself and is always for the sake of something else and not for itself.[46] The being of something in motion is always constituted by its relation to a mover as it passes "beyond itself" from potency to act. At every moment of the motion, that which is in motion is exceeding itself as it receives a new form and progresses towards actuality. Although there is a constant underlying subject of motion which is often associated with matter, there is nevertheless a genuine transformation. Aristotle states: "For it is not the same thing which at the same time is walking and has walked, or is building and has built, or is becoming and has become, or is being moved and has been moved, but two different things. . . ."[47] Therefore, Aristotle characterizes motion as an *ecstasis* in which a being may receive a new form that is bestowed by its mover. Because nature is identified more particularly with form rather than matter, motion for Aristotle and Aquinas is a genuine transformation whereby something may receive a new form. By contrast, the being of what is energic is self-contained and, unlike that which is in motion, it is at every moment self-identical. However, this is not to say that an energic being is self-enclosed. Quite the contrary is the case, for such actualized beings are the most potent and ready movers of those in potentiality.

In what sense might motion be kenotic in character? In any motion, the mover "donates" the form it already possesses and pours this into that which it moves. For example, in the case of the motion of learning, the teacher donates knowledge or the means of thought in such a way that the student, who is moved to knowledge, receives a genuinely new form. It is not the case that the teacher "gives up" knowledge in order to bring a student from potency to act; rather, this motion is brought about through self-donation. That which is moved receives and seeks a new actuality through desire. Just as in the case of self-donation, this might also be a faint participation in being itself as construed in Balthasarian terms: the self-donation of the mover is at one with the self-reception of a new form by that which is moved. Importantly, for both Aristotle and Aquinas, motion is therefore a reciprocal relation between mover and moved. It is not simply that a creature which is moved is a passive recipient of motion. This is not even the case for inanimate objects. Rather, in the case of natural

46. Aristotle, *Metaphysics*, IX.6.1048b.
47. Aristotle, *Metaphysics*, IX.6.1048bff.

motion (as opposed to violent motion, which takes place contrary to a creature's nature) that which is moved has a natural tendency for the motion and seeks this motion through desire (for example, in the case of humanity, the motion of learning, because, according to Aristotle at the very beginning of the *Metaphysics,* "all men by nature desire to know").[48] It is therefore not the case that creation is simply a series of ultimately passive objects that are moved or manipulated in mechanical fashion by a divine subject. Rather, creation participates in being moved by God, for in its cosmic motion creation exhibits the desire for its natural end in the divine. Where humanity fails of its own power to participate in its motion by God, the divine provides the gift of grace whereby humanity may once again seek motion to the beatific vision.[49]

Motion, therefore, requires difference and is ecstatic and kenotic in character. Rather than being the means of the disintegration of created being or an incidental state of such being, motion is the temporal image of the differentiated, ecstatic, and kenotic self-donation and self-reception that characterize the trinitarian divine life. Cosmic motion is therefore the "watermark" of creation's divine origin, representing a *similitude* — which is yet a *maior dissimilitudo* — of the cosmos to the divine life. This "watermark" is the kenotic self-donation of love which moves the sun and other stars.

48. On the distinction between natural and violent motion, see Aristotle, *Physics,* IV.8.215a.

49. On motion and grace, see Simon Oliver, "The Sweet Delight of Virtue and Grace in Aquinas's Ethics" in *International Journal of Systematic Theology* 7, no. 1 (January 2005): 52-71.

Sources of the Christian Mystery

Balthasar as Interpreter of the Catholic Tradition

Jacques Servais

A Witness of the Wellsprings of Tradition

Balthasar had a chalet in the village of Rigi, perched high in the Swiss Alps where he would spend vacations working, often with de Lubac. One evening, I and another — then young — Jesuit were there with them and, knowing Balthasar to be an aficionado of handmade puzzles, we set out to complete a particularly difficult one, with plenty of blue sky and no two pieces quite the same. As the evening drew on, so did our perplexity: we were puzzled by the heavens, divided out as they were into many tiny pieces on the table before us. Balthasar watched from a distance, tempted to help but holding back, while de Lubac began pacing beside us: perhaps a bit agitated because we were delaying the daily evening get-together. Finally, Balthasar walked up and joined us, picking up a piece, and putting it into place, then the next, and the next, until the whole puzzle was finished, and in less than ten minutes. We, quite frankly, would probably have been there for ten hours.

I tell this story because it is a concrete example of the "Johannine vision of the whole" so characteristic of Balthasar down to its most concrete manifestations, such as seeing the *gestalt* of a clear blue sky even through the jumble of scrambled hand-cut puzzle pieces. Before we consider more exactly how he worked on the basis of the Whole he saw, let us refer to a few circumstances of his life which make evident that he simply wanted to be a witness of the Catholic truth.

Translated by Sylvester Tan.

Jacques Servais

On June 23, 1984, John Paul II presented the International Paul VI Award to Hans Urs von Balthasar, with the following citation: "He is the only prominent contemporary Catholic theologian who has dared to undertake — on his own — the tremendous venture of a theological *Summa*, one whose conceptual unity and impressive scale give it the right to be placed in the line of the other great syntheses that have marked the pace of western theology."[1] Accepting the award from the hands of John Paul II, the Swiss theologian pointed towards the intended center of his work, an "oeuvre plutôt amorcée que terminée," more an inception than an achievement: the *Community of St. John.* What is of immediate interest here is not this community — the secular institute that he founded together with Adrienne von Speyr — but rather the fundamental purpose its initiator pursued. Balthasar makes clear that this, his principal work, "intends to be Catholic in the largest and most theological sense of the word." At the award ceremony Balthasar explained what he had tried to accomplish through the founding of the *Johannes Verlag* publishing house and the many volumes he wrote or published. He sought to "make as concrete as possible the sense of 'catholicity' through the translation of that which, in the great theological tradition, seemed [to him] worthy of being known and assimilated by Christians of this day."[2] All these served but one aim: to prepare the way for communities of lay Christians that would abide in the world in the spirit of the beloved disciple. His works sought to convey a Johannine spirit "deeply rooted in the mysteries of the Catholic faith"[3] that would allow laymen consecrated to the Lord to bear witness through their lives to the organic unity and interconnectedness of the divine mysteries.

The Holy Father's intent to bestow the cardinal's red hat on the Swiss theologian in 1988 only confirmed his continued certainty regarding the catholicity of the theologian's work and highlighted its importance for the Church's engagement in the world today. John Paul II's suggestive gesture goes beyond mere confidence in Balthasar's person; it demonstrates an ob-

---

1. Istituto Paolo VI, Premio Internazionale Paolo VI 1984, *Notiziario,* n. 8 (May 1984) (Brescia, 1984), p. 25.

2. H. U. von Balthasar, "Il discorso di Hans Urs von Balthasar" in *Hans Urs von Balthasar: Premio Internazionale Paolo VI 1984,* pp. 27f.

3. H. U. von Balthasar and Adrienne von Speyr, *Unser Auftrag* (Einsiedeln: Johannes Verlag, 1984), pp. 102-3 (*Our Task* [San Francisco: Ignatius Press, 1991], p. 121). For the ease of the reader, we refer to available translations of Balthasar's works, while reserving the possibility of revising the translated citation.

jective appreciation of his project, which places itself at the service of what is central and enduring in the faith, so as to orient the life and activity of Christians menaced by the neo-paganism that surrounds them.

Henri de Lubac called Balthasar "perhaps the most cultivated [man] of his time."[4] His culture was not something that he pursued as an aim in itself, but rather was an expression of the project of implanting the ecclesial spirit within a sound culture of man. The French Jesuit saw the distinctively catholic outlines of his friend's work from its earliest stages. Highlighting the breadth of the catholic tradition from which the Swiss theologian draws, he exclaimed with admiration: "If there is a Christian culture, then here it is! Classical antiquity, the great European literatures, the metaphysical tradition, the history of religions, the diverse exploratory adventures of contemporary man and, above all, the sacred sciences, St. Thomas, St. Bonaventure, patrology (all of it) — not to speak just now of the Bible — none of them is not welcomed and made vital by this great mind. Writers and poets, mystics and philosophers, old and new, Christians of all confessions — all are called on to make their particular contribution. All these are necessary for his final accomplishment, to the greater glory of God, the Catholic symphony."[5]

De Lubac emphasizes that the return to the sources that characterizes the "Catholic Ressourcement" cannot consist merely in an academic pursuit of historical data under the pretext of finding therein a foundation for "scientific" research. Indeed, Balthasar's own words reveal an altogether different motivation: that of one who has no need to search for the objective in the data, but rather continuously keeps his eyes fixed upon it. "I consider my own theology," he explained to a young disciple, "as a kind of Johannine finger pointing to the fullness of Revelation in Jesus Christ, developed in the huge fullness of its reception in the history of the Church, first of all in the mediation of the saints."[6] "To make known the greatest and most spiritual among our brothers and sisters," he further elucidates, "seemed to me to be in the spirit of him who is known simply as 'the Theologian.'"[7] Balthasar draws from the Greek and Latin Fathers through the

---

4. Henri de Lubac, *Paradoxe et Mystère de l'Église* (Paris: Aubier, 1967), p. 184 (*The Church: Paradox and Mystery* [Staten Island, N.Y.: Ecclesia Press, 1969], p. 105).

5. Ibid.

6. M. Albus, "Geist und Feuer. Ein Gespräch mit Hans Urs von Balthasar," in *Herder-Korrespondenz* 30 (1976): 73.

7. Balthasar identifies a few of these "greatest," saying, "I began with the apostolic fathers: Irenaeus, Origen, Gregory of Nyssa, Maximus, Augustine, passed through the Middle

great medieval Christian theologians and mystics to the Christian culture of Dante and Calderon, and beyond to that of the present day with Péguy and Bernanos. So well does he know Revelation and the clearly delineated figure that shines forth in it, that he even discovers its hidden presence outside of the ecclesial Tradition in every authentic expression of human genius. He assumed all this into his work, seeking nothing else than to serve the most intimate heart of the faith and provide a steadfast beacon that might light the way for truly Christian life and work in the midst of today's neo-pagan haze.[8]

Balthasar has his critics; for example, some Jesuits are concerned by his exit from the Society of Jesus in order to continue his work with Adrienne von Speyr.[9] For these, his convinced avowal of Ignatian obedience through to his very last days seems to ring hollow: Did he not go against the intentions of his Jesuit general in departing from the Society of Jesus? Yet this assessment fails to consider not only that Balthasar had not taken his final vows and that he was legitimately dismissed for the sake of the new Community, but also that obedience is offered to God above all. The Jesuit Peter Henrici[10] has a more considered view of the episode. He cites in particular Balthasar's farewell letter to his Jesuit confrères, a letter that Henri de Lubac courageously published in his *Mémoire* before dying.[11] In the letter, Balthasar explains to his fellow Jesuits that his decision

---

Ages with Anselm, Bonaventure, St. Thomas, and the great English and Flemish mystics, to arrive at Dante, Catherine of Siena, John of the Cross, Bérulle, Pascal, and in our day, Thérèse of Lisieux, Madeleine Delbrêl, Claudel, Péguy, Bernanos, Cardinal de Lubac, Adrienne von Speyr" (H. U. von Balthasar, "Il discorso di Hans Urs von Balthasar," p. 27).

8. The titles of many of von Balthasar's volumes colorfully illustrate this very purpose. For example, *The Office of Peter* (published in German under the even more striking title *Der antirömische Affekt*), *The Moment of Christian Witness* (German: *Cordula oder der Ernstfall*), *In the Fullness of Faith: On the Centrality of the Distinctively Catholic* (German: *Katholisch*), *A Short Primer for Unsettled Laymen* (German: *Kleine Fibel für verunsicherte Laien*), *Credo*.

9. W. Löser, "Karl Rahner and Hans Urs von Balthasar," in *America* (October 16, 1999): 16-20; E. T. Oakes, *Pattern of Redemption: The Theology of Hans Urs von Balthasar* (New York: Continuum, 1994), in particular the last chapter, "Last Things," pp. 300-323.

10. P. Henrici, "A Sketch of Balthasar's Life," in *Hans Urs von Balthasar: His Life and Work*, ed. David L. Schindler (San Francisco: Ignatius Press, 1991).

11. The letter of H. U. von Balthasar can be found in H. de Lubac, *Mémoire sur l'occasion de mes écrits* (Namur: Culture et Vérité, 1992), pp. 371-75 (*At the Service of the Church: Henri de Lubac Reflects on the Circumstances That Occasioned His Writings* [San Francisco: Ignatius Press/Communio Books, 1993], pp. 370-35).

to part from their company was nothing other than an act of Christian obedience to God, who can freely call a man to surrender not only his physical home, but also his spiritual home in an order, to be used for God's own purposes within the Church. At the end of his life, Balthasar would reaffirm the same certainty before the Holy Father: he had left the Jesuits, his "spiritual homeland," with great personal sacrifice only in order to "obey a formal order from St. Ignatius" and "bring about a sort of continuation of his idea in the world."[12]

Today, as we commemorate the immense person and work of John Paul II, we cannot refrain from joining Pope Benedict XVI as he stresses the significance of his predecessor's having nominated Balthasar as cardinal *in extremis*. In the homily pronounced by the prelate at Balthasar's funeral, he explained, on the Pope's behalf, that it was precisely his Ignatian obedience that made the Swiss theologian "a man of the Church for the world."[13] In this context, Joseph Ratzinger alluded to Balthasar's reluctance to accept the cardinalate, which Ratzinger, alongside Wojtyla's mentor de Lubac, saw and praised as the mark of an authentic Jesuit:

> Balthasar had a great reverence for the Petrine, for the hierarchical structure of the Church. . . . But [he] was hesitant in opening himself for the honor intended for him by his being named to the cardinalate. This [hesitance] was motivated . . . by the Ignatian spirit which characterized his life. In some way, his being called into the next life on the very eve of being so honored seems to show he was right about it. He was allowed to remain himself, fully. But what the Pope intended to express by this mark of distinction and of honor remains valid: no longer only private individuals but the Church itself, in its official responsibility, tells us that he is right in what he teaches of the Faith, that he points the way to the sources of living water — a witness to the word which teaches us Christ and which teaches us how to live.[14]

In the school of St. Ignatius and the Spiritual Exercises, we would argue, Balthasar lets himself be taken to the Gospel's very origin. From this surging font, the living Tradition of the Church is continually reborn as the

---

12. H. U. von Balthasar, "Il discorso di Hans Urs von Balthasar," p. 27.

13. J. Ratzinger, "Homily at the Funeral Liturgy of Hans Urs von Balthasar," in *Hans Urs von Balthasar: His Life and Work*, pp. 291-95, here 293.

14. Ratzinger, "Homily," pp. 293-95.

Holy Spirit leads the Church of saints ever again to the gushing wellspring, to the Figure of Revelation in which God portrays himself, to the One, the Uniquely Singular One in whom the entire universe is integrated: Jesus Christ. In him, the eyes of loving faith see — as Balthasar puts it — the "image and figure, Image of all images, Figure of all figures [that], as such, possesses an evidential power of his own which he himself communicates."[15] A living faith burns at the core of Balthasar's great undertaking, which consists in nothing less than an effort to recover the Christian's contemporaneousness with Christ in a new way. By this means, he offers an authentic and immediate interpretation of Revelation that draws directly from the purest and deepest wellsprings of Tradition.

Thanks to the hermeneutical key he expresses in the title of his book *Das Ganze im Fragment* ("The Whole in the Fragment"),[16] Balthasar can penetrate to the heart of the whole-reality and take in the singular event in which God appears and communicates himself in Jesus Christ. One cannot attain the whole of reality by means of outline notes. Only in Christ does the whole present itself, but precisely in Christ, the whole of his person shines forth in every particular aspect. Just as the sun's rays rebound through chips of glass, so the one Light gives itself entirely in each "fragment" that reverberates its rays. The Whole manifests itself through the fragments; but even while the fragments proceed in a well-ordered cadence, they do not allow themselves to be brought down into a system. No: The Whole does not reveal itself to a rationalistic mind but only to a simple glance. Indeed, this alone, paired with an architectonic sense of reality, is capable of gathering together various lines of thought so that they may converge around the unitary Figure implicitly present in each fragment.

The Art of Catholic Symphony

Balthasar explains his notion of Catholic totality using an analogy drawn from the sphere of music: "Symphony means 'sounding together.' First

---

15. H. U. von Balthasar, *Herrlichkeit* I: *Schau der Gestalt* (Freiburg: Johannes Verlag, 1988³), p. 493 (*The Glory of the Lord*, vol. I: *Seeing the Form* [San Francisco: Ignatius Press, 1983], p. 512).

16. H. U. von Balthasar, *Das Ganze im Fragment* (Freiburg: Johannes Verlag, 1990²) (*Man in History* [London and Sydney: Sheed & Ward, 1967]); *A Theological Anthropology* [New York: Sheed & Ward, 1967]).

there is sound, then different sounds and then we hear the different sounds singing together in a dance of sound. . . . In the authentic symphony, all the instruments are integrated in a whole sound."[17] The Figure of Revelation can unfold fully only in the whole of space, the "space between heaven and earth, God and world, Old and New Era." Balthasar continues: "If, in order to be able to unfold, the figure requires such breadth from the beholder, then the latter must allow himself to be stretched until the required space has been created within him. A whole symphony cannot be recorded on a space that is too short."[18] No finite spirit can proffer a complete copy of Christ's figure. One must not succumb to the temptation to isolate certain aspects and take the fragment for the Whole itself, thus running the risk of losing the vision of the Whole entirely. The sight of the fragment without the vision of the Whole can offer only an obscured meaning. "In order to see that each individual aspect in truth receives its full meaning only by its overall relationship to the Whole, that 'art of total vision' is required."[19] "Mozart," the theologian further explains, "had this whole sound in his ear to such an extent that, on occasion, he could write down the single instrumental line of an entire movement because he 'heard' it within the symphony of all the parts."[20] Balthasar himself possessed the ability he observes in Salzburg's "divine" composer; he readily saw every particular aspect within the framework of the greater Whole. In a review of the book *Cosmic Liturgy* in the 1940s, Karl Rahner wrote that in Balthasar's interpretation of Maximus the Confessor, "everything seems to dissolve into an immense unfinished dialectic of views in conflict with one another, and whose synthesis shifts away to an ungraspable distance."[21] The German Jesuit found altogether incomprehensible Balthasar's way of hearing each assertion made by an author in the context of an ungraspable Whole. Rahner's perplexity illustrates the fundamentally different hermeneutical methods adopted by the two theologians. Two years earlier, Rahner had requested and hoped for a collaboration from his Swiss confrère in his project of a new dogmatic theology — what would later evolve into *Mysterium*

17. H. U. von Balthasar, *Die Wahrheit ist symphonisch* (Einsiedeln: Johannes Verlag, 1972), p. 7 (*Truth Is Symphonic* [San Francisco: Ignatius Press, 1987], p. 7).

18. Balthasar, *Herrlichkeit* I, p. 493 (*The Glory of the Lord* I, p. 512).

19. Balthasar, *Herrlichkeit* I, p. 493 (*The Glory of the Lord* I, p. 512).

20. Balthasar, *Die Wahrheit ist symphonisch* (*Truth Is Symphonic*), p. 7.

21. K. Rahner, "Hans Urs v. Balthasar, Kosmische Liturgie," in *Stimmen der Zeit* 138 (1941): 155. Cf. Rahner, in *Zeitschrift für katholische Theologie* 66 (1942): 153-56.

Salutis. Yet, in the same year 1941, Rahner received from him a friendly but unequivocal refusal: "No, I cannot cooperate. . . ."[22]

Balthasar's refusal did not concern Rahner's project as such and its opportuneness in the new era that was dawning. In fact, in the second informal part of the letter, he encouraged Rahner to continue the project with other associates, deeming the new dogmatic theology "absolutely necessary."[23] Nonetheless, he perceived that he was being called by an even more pressing need: "to let the Christian reality radiate from its inmost center, and, thus, in such an irrefutable way that the beacons shine towards the exterior and penetrate into the darkest underbrush before the Church."[24] In order to accomplish his mission, he thought it necessary to renounce constructing a closed system that would fail to do justice to the ever-greater mystery. Certainly, Hegel is right in saying, "the Whole is the Truth." Yet the "Whole" does not open its proper sense up to a dialectical thought that seeks to reconstruct the Truth on the basis of particular fragments. In Hegel's dialectic, Balthasar critically observes, "the opposing points of view are fitted into a thoroughgoing schematic structure": "none of them, however peculiar and eccentric, can drop out of the system of truth." Absolute Knowledge, in the pure "logic" associated with the internal mobility within the dialectic, embraces the One and the Many as two faces of the same Being. As a matter of fact, the theologian continues, this process "yields an inner relatedness of the Absolute, the One, to all its possible prismatic refractions, which can then be reintegrated into the fullness of concrete unity." Balthasar recognizes in this dialectical method the temptation to squelch Christ's event — God's absolute, personal point of contact in the world — into an incalculable mass of other worldly forms. "What has happened here is that the standpoint of God, who freely discloses himself to the world, has been equated with the standpoint of man, who has adopted God's revelation as a universal law of being and now imagines that he can use it as a key to all mysteries."[25]

Balthasar opposed this dialectical approach to his idea of symphonic

22. K. H. Neufeld, *Die Brüder Rahner. Eine Biographie* (Freiburg: Herder, 1994), p. 183.

23. Neufeld, *Die Brüder Rahner,* p. 183.

24. H. U. von Balthasar, in A. von Speyr, *Erde und Himmel* II (Einsiedeln: Johannes Verlag, 1975), pp. 194-95. See J. Servais, "The *Ressourcement* of Contemporary Spirituality Under the Guidance of Adrienne von Speyr and Hans Urs von Balthasar," in *Communio: International Catholic Review* 23, no. 2 (1996): 300-321, at 303.

25. Balthasar, *Die Wahrheit ist symphonisch,* p. 38 (*Truth Is Symphonic,* p. 44).

truth, constantly pointing the listener towards an ever-greater Whole, a figure that is more than the sum of its parts. Such a figure "can be described and seen from every side. Ever anew one perceives something different, and yet it is always the same thing."[26] Every fragment manifests the one unique center, the living figure, the "contingent" determination distinct from every other worldly figure, in which God in his infinite Freedom wanted to represent his love before humanity: Jesus Christ, the "heir of all things" (Heb 1:2), the Son for whose sake the polyphonous orchestra of Creation had been assembled. "As it performs God's symphony under the Son's direction," Balthasar explains, "the meaning of its variety becomes clear."[27] Working from 1961 to 1987 on the basis of this central idea, Balthasar single-handedly erected his Trilogy, the monumental venture that the Paul VI Institute did not hesitate to qualify as an authentic *Summa* for the present time. Indeed, some scholars suggest that with his Trilogy, Balthasar offered the mature fruit drawn from the first outlines of a dogmatic theology he had sketched together with K. Rahner.[28] In any case, Balthasar's own statements suggest that he aimed at something other than a *Summa* in the classical sense of the word. In 1965, he wrote on the brink of finishing the first panel of the triptych: "While the fullness of the Church's tradition has been my only concern, it is only for the sake of preserving what is valuable for the future, since only the best has a chance to survive. . . . Thus the plan for a trilogy matured."[29] Years later, in an epilogue to his threefold opus, Balthasar wrote that in it "the traditional theology of treatises or loci was presented in a completely different way: em-

---

26. M. Albus, "Geist und Feuer," p. 71.

27. Balthasar, *Die Wahrheit ist symphonisch*, p. 8 (*Truth Is Symphonic*, p. 8).

28. M. Löhrer, "Zur Entstehung von *Mysterium Salutis*," in *Mysterium Salutis*, Ergänzungsband (Zurich: Benziger, 1981), p. 13. Cf. M. Albus, "Geist und Feuer," p. 75. However, the authors use significantly different hermeneutical hypotheses to interpret the general plan of Balthasar's Trilogy. See, for example, P. Henrici, "La dramatique entre l'esthétique et la logique," in *Pour une philosophie chrétienne*, ed. P.-Ph. Druet (Paris: Lethielleux, 1983), pp. 109-32; P. Henrici, "La structure de la Trilogie," in *Transversalité* 63 (1997): 17-22; M. Lochbrunner, "Hans Urs von Balthasars Trilogie der Liebe. Vom Dogmatikentwurf zur theologischen Summe," in *Forum Katholische Theologie* 11 (1995): 161-91; K. Wallner, "Ein trinitarisches Strukturprinzip in der Trilogie Hans Urs von Balthasars?" in *Theologie und Philosophie* 71 (1996): 532-46. Critical: E. Biser, "Dombau oder Triptychon?" Zum Abschluss der Trilogie Hans Urs von Balthasars," in *Theologische Revue* 84 (1988): 184.

29. H. U. von Balthasar, *Zu seinem Werk* (Freiburg: Johannes Verlag, 2000²), pp. 67-68 (*My Work in Retrospect* [San Francisco: Ignatius Press, 1993], p. 79).

barking from the transcendentals, in which the passage from a true (and therefore religious) philosophy to a biblical theology of Revelation flows more smoothly."[30]

Balthasar takes for granted in his concept of "Gestalt" (understood, to say it again, as the figurative expression of the Whole that offers itself to be seen) the precedence of transcendental Beauty. Here the Pulchrum — Being as wonder — precedes the Bonum and the Verum. First in the trilogy, then, he develops a *theological aesthetics*. In this "un-Thomistic way,"[31] the Swiss theologian intends to overcome the lure of modern rationalism. The temptation would otherwise be to identify "the standpoint of God who freely discloses himself to the world" and "the standpoint of man, who has adopted God's revelation as a universal law of being and now imagines that he can use it as a key to all mysteries."[32] In the face of this risk, the author underlines the epiphany of divine freedom made manifest as love, as free election, as unmanipulable grace offered to the indifferent and obedient man.

The Sources of Christian Mystery Disclosed by Three Ignatian Notions

Three Ignatian notions undoubtedly assisted Balthasar in disclosing the sources of the Christian mystery. He discerns a threefold center in the method of the *Exercises:* election, indifference, and obedience. The theologian explains that the Ignatian method opens one's vision to revelation by means of these central notions. Revelation can then appear exactly as it presents itself: as an indivisible Whole. Everything within revelation begins with the gratuitous *election* of a God who takes the free initiative of calling man to share in his own life. In order for man to fulfill this vocation — which aims at the salvation of all the nations from the outset — God's elective grace must give rise to an elementary openness within him. The Catholic tradition calls this spiritual stance *indifference,* identifying it as the fundamental attitude of active receptivity towards God's will. Within

---

30. H. U. von Balthasar, *Epilog* (Trier: Johannes Verlag, 1987), p. 7 (*Epilogue* [San Francisco: Ignatius Press, 2004], p. 9).

31. Balthasar and von Speyr, *Unser Auftrag,* p. 82 (*Our Task,* p. 97).

32. Balthasar, *Die Wahrheit ist symphonisch,* p. 38 (*Truth Is Symphonic,* p. 44).

this existential position, which corresponds to his ontological creatureliness, man is enabled to be given God's election in the form of a particular mission for the sake of the world. He can assent to it using his *obedience,* letting the Infinite Freedom make use of his finite liberty.

We will briefly elaborate these three notions before saying a final word about the form of the Catholic *Summa* Balthasar proposes to the Church today.

Election

At the center of his theology stands — by Balthasar's own account — the fundamental Christian idea of election. Balthasar sees Ignatius of Loyola as having reclaimed the full sense of election from where it was languishing in the straits of the Augustinian doctrine of predestination. More than anyone before him, Ignatius brings to the full light of day God's freedom, upon whose acquiescence every finite being depends. The image of Yahweh in the Old Testament was that of the Lord who sovereignly elects and rejects. Almost retroactively, this becomes the image that determines the relationship between the Creator and his world. In his incomprehensible self-abasement of love, God calls and drafts his creature to serve his unforeseeable ends. For his part, man is invited to embrace the opportunity to respond to God's call, which aims to place man in position to fulfill his true end: the praise, the reverence, and the service of God's glory. The grace conferred by this election enables man to renounce his liberty, insofar as it is soiled by original sin, and, as such, marked by estrangement before God. Man now prefers the will of God to his own will by this grace, and thus he receives a new liberty by which he may participate in God's elective liberty.

Ignatius, Balthasar declares, "appears to me as the point in history where the encounter of man with the God who is the Word and has the word, who addresses, chooses and calls, has become inescapable."[33] The Spanish saint places the entire economy of grace — made manifest in the flesh of the Son made man — under the heading of "vocation." Thus vocation becomes, in a strong sense, the essence of human life. Already in salvation history, the image of God and man finds its definitive figure in the

---

33. Balthasar, *Zu seinem Werk,* p. 20 (*My Work in Retrospect,* p. 20).

Word that the Father addresses "to the whole world and to each one in particular within it,"[34] since "in these last days he has spoken to us by a Son" (Heb 1:2). Christ decides freely and sovereignly to meet each man, offering him his pardon and inviting him to follow. By becoming flesh, the Son of God opens up to him the space of the kingdom into which he may be admitted. Christ's proclamation involves something that is going on at the very moment in full force, a "happening" into which each one — from the beginning of time and without exception — is called to enter, freely assuming his part in the event of salvation. The Gospel's proclamation to the world is always its proclamation to every single person individually, since Christ invites each one personally to "not be deaf, but rather ready and diligent in doing God's will."[35] Only one who has first been invited and then freely responds can play a supporting role in the divine drama of salvation. The election of a particular person is always in view of the realization of God's universally encompassing design. By means of the elect, the not-as-yet-elect come to the knowledge of the divine plan of creation and redemption that involves the entire universe. Here Balthasar adopts as his own the social and universal vision that another son of Ignatius, Henri de Lubac, presents in his book *Catholicism:* "Since the divine plan of creation and of redemption is one, and since humanity — insofar as it is created — also forms a unity, God's design through the world's ransom in Jesus Christ cannot but embrace the human race except as an entire whole."[36]

In the Son, St. Paul explains, God the Father "chose us in him before the creation of the world . . . ; he predestined us in love to be his sons through Jesus Christ, according to the purpose of his will," which was that

34. Ignatius of Loyola, *Spiritual Exercises,* n. 95.

35. Ignatius of Loyola, *Spiritual Exercises,* n. 91.

36. H. U. von Balthasar, *Henri de Lubac. Sein organisches Lebenswerk* (Einsiedeln: Johannes Verlag, 1976), p. 31. "The human race is one. By our first nature and still more in virtue of our common destiny, we are the members of one same body. Now, the members live from the life of the body. How, then, could there be a salvation for the members if, *per impossibile,* the body itself were not saved? But salvation for this body — humanity itself — consists in its receiving the form of Christ, and that is possible only through the Catholic Church. . . . Thus this Church, which as the invisible Body of Christ is identified with final salvation, as a visible and historical institution is the providential means of this salvation. 'In her alone mankind is refashioned and recreated' (Augustine)." H. de Lubac, *Catholicisme. Les aspects sociaux du dogme,* in *Oeuvres complètes,* vol. VII (Paris: Éditions du Cerf, 2003), pp. 184-85 (*Catholicism: Christ and the Common Destiny of Man* [San Francisco: Ignatius Press, 1988], pp. 222-23).

"we might live for the praise of his glory" (Eph 1:4-6, 12). In the Son sent to save man, each one is carried by a grace of election that precedes the knowledge that one has of it. The ontological prerequisite of both election and the call (the eternal election's occurrence in temporal life) emerges in the *Spiritual Exercises* as a moral-ascetic attitude of being "disposed" and "indifferent" before the call. The attitude receives the Ignatian label "indifference," and like obedience, which will also be examined, it is already included in election, practically speaking. Nonetheless, each of these constitutes a distinct notion that merits consideration as such.

Indifference

As an ontological prerequisite, indifference constitutes a fundamental act of the creature: the opening up of finite freedom to infinite Freedom. In his most intimate conscience, man knows that he is given to himself as an *imago Dei*, and as such, evokes the free manifestation of God. In the face of this revelation, man always already finds himself in a state of ready availability (a letting-be), which he himself has freely ratified.

Man's spirit is not pure activity, nor is it pure spontaneity, nor again is it pure passivity. St. Thomas considers the problem in the light of the Aristotelian distinction in which man's spirit is at once both "agent intellect" and "possible (or patient) intellect." The agent intellect reveals its universality by abstracting the intelligible form out of matter and causing the intelligibles in potentiality to pass into actuality. The possible intellect yields before the real by receiving the imprint of the form thus extracted. Just as "common being" is a participation in uncreated being, the natural light of the human intellect found in the human soul is itself an active reflection of divine intelligence. "Ipsum . . . lumen intellectuale, quod est in nobis, nihil est aliud quam quaedam participata similitudo luminis increati, in quo continentur rationes aeternae."[37] What Thomas situates on the ontological level as the super-essential and inexhaustible actuality of being has its counterpart on the epistemological level in the light of the agent intellect (which permits judgment in the strict sense). On the other

---

37. Thomas Aquinas, *Summa theologiae* I, 84, 5, resp. "The intellectual light itself which is in us, is nothing else than a participated likeness of the uncreated light, in which are contained the eternal types."

hand, essence finds its counterpart in the intelligible species (by which one apprehends things).

Balthasar sees in Ignatius's notion of indifference a recovery of the profound balance found in St. Thomas's conception, which — alongside unlimited *esse* — assigns a positive value to essence as limitation and capacity to receive. Unlike Eckhart, who tends to dissolve being into God, Thomas firmly maintains the ontological difference and so bypasses a point of view that interprets subjectivity as "pure (mystic) opening in the sense of a receptivity without any spontaneous act of one's own."[38] In the line of this tradition, the Swiss theologian clearly emphasizes the spontaneity of the human spirit that is capable of making itself "quodammodo omnia." The freedom of the person's decision does not derive from the absolute Freedom of the infinite Being, which — as such — is not tied to the world. Rather, freedom is the faculty to choose the elective will of God *in all things*. The human spirit's active spontaneity — that is to say, the capacity to act according to eternal wisdom — is understood as the spirit's contemplative receptivity in the face of that wisdom. Such receptivity includes in itself the necessity of the "finitization" (F. Ulrich) of being (since being does not subsist in itself but rather exists only in created essences).

Hence Balthasar follows Ignatius in proposing a conception of indifference that holds the balance between two one-sided solutions. One ought not consider indifference as merely a function of his decision for the "thing which is more conducive to the end for which I am created,"[39] nor as a passive self-abandonment to God's action in him.[40] The decisionality of the first solution emphasizes — with fairly good reason — the spontaneity of finite freedom and thus highlights the action and the temperance it entails. For modern man, however, this easily leads to a Stoical-

38. H. U. von Balthasar, *Herrlichkeit* III/1: *Im Raum der Metaphysik*, p. 2. *Neuzeit* (Einsiedeln: Johannes Verlag, 1975²), p. 970 (*The Glory of the Lord*, vol. 5: *The Realm of Metaphysics in the Modern Age* [San Francisco: Ignatius Press, 1991], p. 641).

39. "Quod magis conducit ad finem" (Ignatius of Loyola, *Spiritual Exercises*, n. 23). In this direction, see Alfonso Rodriguez, *Ejercicio de perfección y virtudes cristianas* (Madrid: Editorial Apostolado, 1946) (*The Practice of Christian and Religious Perfection* [Dublin: James Duffy and Co., Ltd., n.d.]), and today K. Rahner, *Betrachtungen zum ignatianischen Exerzitienbuch* (Munich: Kösel, 1965), pp. 27-39.

40. "Sume et suscipe" (Ignatius of Loyola, *Spiritual Exercises*, n. 234). In this direction, see Francis de Sales, *Traité de l'amour de Dieu*, IX, chapter 4ff.; cf. A. Ravier, *Francis de Sales: Sage and Saint* (San Francisco: Ignatius Press, 1988), in particular 199-211.

Buddhistic type of interpretation of his activity as a personal conquest (the "self-made man"). What results is a pseudo-ethical air of superiority in the face of the "common" man that stands in stark contrast to the true Christian sense of an intersubjective encounter. The passiveness in the second solution rightly insists on the motions and inspirations of the Holy Spirit in the human subject. However, it overemphasizes Christian transcendence to the detriment of the "conversio ad phantasmata" and the "service of the divine Goodness in all particular things." The second solution thus risks reintroducing the old dualism between action and contemplation.

Indifference should not be interpreted in a one-sided ethical-ascetical key that entails the peril of unknowingly taking one's own will for the will of God, nor should indifference be interpreted in a mystical-quietist key that carries the opposite risk of undervaluing the true font of all engagement: the Creator's personal and active presence in the world and in man. One cannot rightly define indifference as a customary detachment from created things in order to dedicate oneself to contemplation. Nor can one call indifference a temporary distancing from them in view of a more universal engagement. Indifference is the fundamental attitude of active receptivity to the will of the Father that characterizes the Christian existence, the ordinary existence of a healthy and safely intact creature living according to the original divine plan. In his *sume et suscipe*, St. Ignatius interprets this free opening and industrious participation in God's elective mission as the loving disposition of the man who offers his finite freedom, choosing ahead of time that which would be most pleasing to His Divine Majesty. Balthasar bears the merit of having found in this attitude the distinguishing trait of what he calls (like Bremond before him, but in an entirely different sense) the metaphysics of the saints. The equilibrium of Balthasar's theology bears itself out on this decisive point.

Obedience

The third characteristic notion bears the Ignatian label "obedience." Viewed from the central axis of the Balthasarian vision, the *analogia electionis*, the question of obedience might be posed in the following terms: In what sense might finite freedom's self-abandonment to infinite Freedom be a grace; that is, what is the truly positive character it bears for the subject himself? Balthasar turns to consider anew St. Augustine's "totum exigit te qui fecit te," where the free grace of the divine election commandeers finite freedom, incorporating it fully within infinite Freedom. In commending oneself into the hands of God and his elective will, the human subject's freedom intentionally renounces any prospect of actualizing the possibility of being autonomous, of ever separating from God. The creature necessarily appears in his negativity before God's absolute positivity. The creature could repudiate his creatureliness, asserting an autonomous freedom in the face of his Creator, but the rebellious attitude would be in vain. Already the philosophy of the ancients taught that self-realization requires that one accept the Absolute as his uncontestable norm. Balthasar rejects the extreme Platonist suggestion that the creature's *suscipe* is nothing other than its acquiescence to its negativity, to its not-being-God. Rather, the *causa secunda* possesses the authentic positivity of its own proper freedom and dignity. These two qualities — freedom and dignity — find their positive accomplishment in the participation in divine freedom offered to the creature by God in his very person. If the negative aspect draws the most attention, it is only because fallen man sees or understands his personal liberty as a good that exists alongside divine freedom and disposes of a full autonomy before it. This perspective does not correspond with reality. Man finds his own quintessence and genuine autonomy by returning his created freedom to absolute Freedom: his liberation is the grace of his participation in God. Foregoing himself, the creature finds access to himself. In this way, and in this way only, it is given to the creature to, as Ignatius puts it, "approach his Creator and Lord and join [llegar] him."[41] Only to him who detaches from himself — in order to hand over his heart and his entire being — is it given to grasp Him who is essentially ungraspable.

The theology of obedience that Balthasar develops does not revolve around man but rather around Christ, standing before the Father. From the core, a theology of trinitarian obedience radiates through the work. The Son's coming into the world to save it from sin and death is his free act and supreme profession of love towards his Father. All three of the divine Persons decided upon the Incarnation, seen at once to its farthest consequences. As the irrevocable witness of this common deliberation, the Holy Spirit must in some way guarantee its execution (cf. Mt 1:20; Lk 1:35). The Son then passively offers himself to the Spirit's action. "In entering the world" by the power of the Holy Spirit, does the Son not say: "a body hast

---

41. Ignatius of Loyola, *Spiritual Exercises*, n. 20.

thou prepared for me," "lo, I have come to do thy will, O God" (Heb 10:5ff., citing and commenting on Ps 40:7-9 [LXX])? The depth of his will is none other than love and the joy that love contains, which always urges him to accomplish what pleases the Father (cf. Jn 8:29). Recalling the interpretation of the Greek Fathers, Balthasar hears in the words "the Father is greater than I" (Jn 14:28) the revelation of trinitarian obedience.

The Son who "came down from heaven, not to do [his] own will, but the will of [him] who sent [him]" (Jn 6:38) kindles a spousal response. In the face of God's call in the Gospel, creaturely indifference offers itself (actively) in the (passive) docility before God's sovereign dispositions. Because it is made accessible to the world, Christ's objectively manifested trinitarian obedience shows man the way by which he can integrate receptivity and activity, the spirit of a child and an adult responsibility, in a single attitude. Created in the Son and in view of the Son, man does not cease to be an independent and free subject when he seeks to follow the Son. Rather, he lives a voluntary act of total receptivity before the superior thought and will of God, an act that characterizes his genuine but finite freedom and independence. The subject no longer wishes to be anything other than transparent service to the Master who has allotted him a mission. He effaces himself before Him who sends him and whom he represents, "like a viceroy who more perfectly represents the king the more absolutely he places his personal, intellectual and creative powers at the service of the thought and will of his monarch."[42] In metaphysical terms, one would say that self-sacrifice, the subject's self-annulment, does not destroy one's being before the "always greater glory" he wishes to serve. Once again, Balthasar's merit as a faithful disciple of St. Ignatius is to have taken seriously the *analogia entis,* and thus to have taken into consideration the divinely willed consistency of "second causes" and the creature's own activity. Man's *suscipe* does not destroy his nature. It is a voluntary abnegation of his spirit that freely chooses God's choice in his regard, and chooses it such that God acts from inside his activity.

Conclusion

In the school of St. Ignatius, Balthasar caught sight of the highest and most free expression of the divine love present in all created things in Jesus

---

42. Balthasar, *Herrlichkeit* III/1.2, p. 459 (*The Glory of the Lord* 5, p. 106).

Christ. The inconceivable greatness of this love breaches whichever system would claim to be able to contain it. The *analogia entis concreta,* Jesus Christ, "constitutes in himself, in the unity of divine and human natures, the measure of every distance in the relationship between God and Man,"[43] manifesting the "ever-greater God." His incomparable figure verbalizes what God is, beyond merely human concepts and images. Augustine acutely observes, "Semper ille major est, quantumque creverimus" . . . "sub illo majore semper nos pulli sumus."[44] Far from being the end goal of rational effort, the *Deus semper major* that the theologian invites us to hear is in itself "id quo maius cogitari nequit,"[45] the living reality of him who freely reveals himself in his Word made flesh, according to the descending movement of Love. In his work, the Swiss theologian makes heard the symphony God performs in his revelation. Those who hear, discover that they are thus enabled to join in as co-performers in the same symphony.

Balthasar, as interpreter of Catholic tradition, helps us to contemplate Jesus Christ, who is the way and therefore shows the way that leads towards the Father. The way the Son shows is that which he is, and has been before the incarnation, since from all eternity he is the content of the promise. It is the way in which his mother, a creature of his, is given a share by the incarnation. It is finally the way that he represents in his person — and in his body the Church — before mankind. There is no possibility of comprehending the "whole" object of faith, hope, and charity, of comprehending the nature of the Father, the Son, and the Holy Spirit. Balthasar makes clear that the faithful can sense something of it only when they follow along this way.

43. H. U. von Balthasar, *Theologie der Geschichte* (Einsiedeln: Johannes Verlag, 2004[7]), p. 53 (*A Theology of History* [San Francisco: Ignatius Press, 1994], pp. 69-70).

44. Augustine, *En. in Ps.* 62, 16 (in CCL 39, page 804).

45. Anselm, *Proslogion* 2, in *Opera Omnia,* ed. F. S. Schmitt (Stuttgart: F. Frommann Verlag, 1968), pp. 111-12. Cf. *St. Anselm Basic Writings* (La Salle, Ill.: Open Court Publishing Company, 1962), pp. 53-54.

Descensus ad inferos, Dawn of Hope: Aspects of the Theology of Holy Saturday in the Trilogy of Hans Urs von Balthasar

Juan M. Sara

Introduction

> *The twentieth century was marked by a special intervention of God, who is a Father "rich in mercy."*
>
> Dives in Misericordia (Eph 2:4)[1]

In a time characterized by orphanhood and meaninglessness, Pope John Paul II was an authentic and tireless witness of the infinite love of God the Father who is "rich in mercy" and who gives himself in his "two hands" (Irenaeus): the Son, the Redemptor Hominis, whom the Father gives over for the life of the world (Jn 3:16) in the original act of *traditio;* and the Holy Spirit, Dominus et Vivificans, the Lord and Giver of Life. In the midst of a climate of nihilism, sometimes "bestial"[2] and sometimes indifferent (as in the "gay nihilism" spoken of by Augusto Del Noce), John Paul II believed, and bore witness to, the omnipotent mercy of the Holy Trinity. This mercy was, in fact, the first and the last word of his pontificate.[3]

---

1. John Paul II, *Memoria e identità. Conversazione al cavallo dei millenni* (Milan: Rizzoli, 2005), p. 65. For an English translation, see *Memory and Identity: Conversations at the Dawn of a Millennium* (Milan: Rizzoli, 2005).

2. Cf. John Paul II, *Memoria e identità,* p. 26.

3. It is significant that the last writing John Paul bequeathed to us, *Memory and Identity,* focuses on the same mystery of the Trinity to which he dedicated the first trilogy of encyclicals that opened his pontificate. In this joining of beginning and end, the mercy

---

Dedicated to John Paul II; translated by Adrian J. Walker.

Hans Urs von Balthasar and Adrienne von Speyr were also called to bear witness to the Father's mercy before the fragmented world in which we live. In this sense, an essential part of their theological task was the illumination of the mystery of the faith known as the *descensus ad inferos* — an article of the Creed that is generally forgotten, feared, or reduced to insignificance. The theological interpretation of Holy Saturday that the two authors propose seeks to show how Christ's descent into hell is a mystery of the Father's infinitely patient mercy. Holy Saturday, suspended between Holy Friday and Easter Sunday, is a day of silence, on which the Lord remains in the tomb, dead with the dead. On this holy day, the Father so to say finishes the act of *traditio* by which he hands over his Son. He does this by introducing the Son into communion with all who have died "so that, by the grace of God [the Father], he might taste death in place of all" [*pro omnibus*] (Heb 2:9b). Holy Saturday, *in nuce*, is the encounter between two things: the super-luminous mystery of the fontal liberty of the Father, who gives freedom to his creatures and tolerates the consequences of their fall; and of the darkness of the sinful world that rebels against this paternal mystery. "The light shines in the darkness, and the darkness has not mastered it" (Jn 1:5). The light of love penetrates into, and collides with, the darkness of sin and death. Because, however, this light is the light of infinite Love, this encounter serves to increase Love, to glorify it, and to save what is the final moment of man's destiny: "The point of hell is not to kill love. The point of hell is to establish the kingdom of love."[4] As a mystery of extreme mercy, Holy Saturday is also the mystery of the humility of divine love, which not only lowers itself into the good *humus* of creation, but also into the meaningless mud of sin. As C. S. Lewis puts it in *The Great Divorce*, "[o]nly the greatest can make himself small enough to enter hell. Because the higher a being is, the lower it can descend — a man can sympathize with a horse, but a horse cannot sympathize with a rat. Only One has descended into hell."[5] And it is precisely in the folly of his abasement that his divine being is most intensely revealed: "*Non coerceri maximo, contineri*

---

of God — a theme that embraces the whole of John Paul's ministry as Pope — plays a particularly important role. It is no accident that he died on the vigil of Mercy Sunday, a feast that he himself had instituted.

4. Adrienne von Speyr, *Kreuz und Hölle. II: Auftragshöllen* (Einsiedeln: Johannes Verlag, 1972), p. 197.

5. C. S. Lewis, *The Great Divorce* (New York: Touchstone, 1996), p. 121.

tamen a minimo, divinum est" [not to be constrained by the greatest, and yet to be contained by the least, that is divine].

Holy Saturday, the middle day of the Triduum, is a mystery of unfathomable depth and darkness, a mystery of God's love and human sin, from which light pours forth both on Holy Friday and on Easter Sunday, on the Lord's earthly life and on the life of the world to come. Holy Saturday, then, is the sealed center of Revelation. Balthasar's Trilogy, for its part, may be read as an attempt to display the form — the *Gestalt* — of this revelation from an aesthetic, dramatic, and logical point of view, all of which is then recapitulated in its unity in the *Epilogue*. Our task, then, will be to show briefly the centrality of Holy Saturday in the realization of the aesthetic, dramatic, and logical form as Balthasar conceives it and, by the same token, the centrality of this mystery in the Trilogy. We will then conclude with some remarks on the relationship between Holy Saturday and the universality of theological hope.

Glory

Everything begins with the originality *par excellence,* with what Balthasar, following Goethe, calls the *Urphänomen:* the "original phenomenon." Corresponding to, and awakened by, the *Urphänomen* is an equally original decision — an *Urentscheidung* — to let the original phenomenon appear by and from itself. The original phenomenon, corresponded to in this way, is the beauty of being, which opens interiorly to its theological analogate, the glory of God. Beauty-glory has to do with a radiant, intact form whose luminous and attractive wholeness contains both the promise of restoring form to a fragmented theology and a valid response to the nihilistic erasure of being and its transcendentals, the outcome of the logic of modernity.

The origin of Christianity, too, is rooted in the perception of a unique form and in the experience of being enraptured by it. Wonderment over this form is the origin of Christianity and of what is specifically Christian. The name of this unique form is, of course, Jesus Christ. He is the center, the one *"medium tenens in omnibus,"* who holds the center in all things, as Bonaventure felicitously puts it. I would like this claim to be understood radically: Christ really and truly occupies the center of all things: not only of the Trinity (as the middle person between Father and Spirit), not only of the economy of salvation (as the Head of the Church), *but also of the transcendentals themselves.* The incarnate Son upholds the world's being from the inside, from its deepest center and source, even as he never abandons the Father's "bosom," but is always there, his gaze turned ever towards the paternal origin (*eis ton kolpon tou patros:* Jn 1:18). Christ, to put it another way, is the "concrete measure" between God and the creature,[6] the "marvelous accord of man [and of all creation] and of God" in person.[7]

The form or figure of Christ is the universal center of things because he is simultaneously at the center of the Trinity, at the center of creation, and at the center of the redemption that saves creation. By the same token, the form of Christ is not just one more intra-worldly form among others. Rather, it embodies the divine freedom itself and therefore does something that no merely intra-worldly form can do by itself: overcome the opposition, the anti-form of sin, which threatens to undo the fabric of the world's being:

> The One, whose name is Jesus Christ, has to descend into the absolute contra-diction against the Lord's sovereign majesty, into the night of Godforsakenness and the amorphous chaos of sin. He must do this in order to set up and to be, beyond what man can imagine as form, *the* form that overcomes all futility, the intact and indivisible form that unites and reunites God and the world in the New and Eternal Covenant.[8]

It is important to underscore that, according to the *Glory of the Lord,* the *maior dissimilitudo* of the Christ-form retrieves form in general, albeit on a higher level. Form-in-general becomes the mystery of the union of God and man in the new and eternal covenant. At the same time, the perception of the form becomes the unity of seeing with "simple eyes" (Mt 6:22), with "the eyes of one's heart enlightened" (Eph 1:18) — and of life, where "life" is understood as loving, docile, even child-like obedience to Jesus Christ.

---

6. Cf. Hans Urs von Balthasar, "Merkmale des Christlichen," in Balthasar, *Verbum Caro. Skizzen zur Theologie. I* (Einsiedeln: Johannes Verlag, 1960), p. 174. For an English translation, see *Explorations in Theology,* vol. 1: *The Word Made Flesh* (San Francisco: Ignatius Press, 1989).

7. This is the title of Georges de Schrijver's dissertation, *Le merveilleux accord de l'homme et de Dieu: Étude de l'analogie de l'être chez Hans Urs von Balthasar* (Louvain: University Press, 1983).

8. Hans Urs von Balthasar, *Herrlichkeit,* III, 2, 2, p. 12. For an English translation, see *The Glory of the Lord,* vol. 7: *Theology: The New Covenant* (San Francisco: Ignatius Press, 1989).

The *maior dissimilitudo* does not rupture analogy, but founds it from above *and* from below/within — in a catalogical movement characteristic of the God who is *Non-aliud.*

The first part of the Trilogy, then, presents Christ's descent into hell as the last step in the downward movement that is the culmination of the Incarnation: the *Verbum caro* sinks into the *caro peccati* (Rom 8:3). In his contemplation of this last stage in the Incarnation, Balthasar discerns three phases or dimensions, which he designates with the following terms: *Anprall,* roughly "impact"; *Kenose,* "kenosis," a clear reference to Phil 2:6-11; and *Hölle,* "hell." These three aspects form together a unity, inasmuch as they co-constitute what Balthasar calls the *Wucht des Kreuzes,* which might be translated as the "weighty impact of the Cross."

Wucht is itself an aesthetic category corresponding to the *kabod* of the Old Testament. It is the "weight of glory" that accompanies and underscores the imposing presence of the self-revealing God. Now, faced with man's sinful breaking of the covenant, this imposing presence takes the form — as it must in justice — of wrath: *Anprall.* In the New Covenant, the incarnate Son of God himself bears this weighty impact of God's righteous anger within the even greater weight, the greater *kabod*-glory, of the trinitarian love. It is this love that conceives of the cross as a way of condemning the world's sin once and for all, while at the same time saving the world with an embrace so to speak from "underneath" (in an act of what Balthasar calls *"unterfassen"*).

The whole weight of the world's sin falls upon Christ, who made himself available to bear this weight in the attitude of kenotic obedience that prolongs in time his Sonly Yes to the trinitarian decision to save the world in just this way. Here we come to the second of our terms, *Kenose,* which, to repeat, Balthasar draws from the Letter to the Philippians. Following Paul, Balthasar interprets it as the distinctive characteristic of the Son's love, inasmuch as the Son's property is to let himself be generated by the Father and, again, to let this generation be translated into the expressive form of free human obedience. (Balthasar, who pioneered the revival of Maximus the Confessor studies in the twentieth century, held firmly to Maximian dyothelitism throughout his life.) This goal of the Son's economic obedience is to carry and bear at once the world's sin and the Father's judgment on this sin. By bearing both things in obedience, he expresses his real, ever greater love as Son. His double act of bearing, then, occurs within the interchange of love between the Father and the Son in

the Holy Spirit. It is, in fact, a decision of love on the part of the triune God
— a decision of which the Son is a free (super)passive/(super)active subject, just as the Father is a free (super)active/(super)passive subject.[9]

Now, the moment when the soldier pierces Jesus' side and blood and
water begin to flow from his wound represents the consummation of Jesus'
kenosis on the cross. Everything has been given: the Spirit and, together
with the Spirit, Jesus' inmost substance, out of which the same Spirit will
form the sacraments of the Church. From this moment, Jesus remains in
the state of having given everything. The state of being dead. With this, we
arrive at the third and last aspect: *Hölle*, hell, which Jesus undergoes on
Holy Saturday.

Holy Saturday, as Adrienne von Speyr explains, is not an additional
mystery added to the cross, but rather the latter's "obverse." It is the "un-
derside" of the cross, when Jesus' experience of *giving* everything, which is
distinctive of Good Friday, reaches its intrinsic fulfillment in the state of
having given everything. This is a state in which Christ's act of dying is over
and now, having died, he finds himself in the situation in which every man
finds himself at the end of his earthly pilgrimage. In this sense, Holy Saturday completes the descending, "incarnatory" movement of the Word into
the *caro peccati*. The Son has obeyed the Father's saving will to the end, and
his obedience now takes the form of being dead with the dead. This being
dead entails for the Son a real experience of separation from God, the "loss
of glory" that without Christ would have been without exception the fate
of the dead.[10] The *obedience of love* is what expresses here the permanence
of the hypostatic union in the midst of the Son's extreme separation from
the Father and under the crushing blow and incomprehensible weight of

9. This account avoids two extremes. On the one hand, the Father does not damn or
punish Jesus as if he himself were a sinner. On the other hand, the cross is not a mere symbol
of divine love, but expresses love precisely by including a real act of divine justice on sin, an
act that objectively changes the situation of the sinner before God. Jesus shoulders and bears
the whole weight of the world's sin before the Father. In some sense, he makes himself responsible for that sin, but because he assumes this responsibility in loving obedience, and
because he does so within the interchange between the divine persons, he is the personal
"place" in which the whole Trinity swallows up sin in the victory of its ever-greater love.

10. Thanks to the loving obedience of the Son, who remains as the hypostatic subject
of this experience, we can say that what Jesus does here is not to suffer damnation, as if he
were being rejected by God for his sins — of which he has none — but to overcome damnation from within, bearing up under the experience of loss reserved for sinful man out of love
and as a form of filial gift to the Father.

the world's sin. By doing this in absolute purity — and neither before nor after — the obedience of love overcomes the concentrated hatred of sin.

The originality of the contemplation of Holy Saturday in *The Glory of the Lord* (III, 2, 2: 211-17) is rooted in Balthasar's presentation of Jesus' experience in the realm of the dead — to the extent that this experience can be turned into words and images — thanks to the simultaneity of the two central aesthetic categories of perception or vision *(Wahr-nehmung)* and rapture that Balthasar develops in the first volume of the *Glory of the Lord:* being swept up ecstatically and lifted out of oneself (*Ent-rückung* — the word *"Ruck"* means a pull, a blow, a shaking, and so forth). Thanks to Nicholas of Cusa (who speaks of a *visio mortis* by means of a *via cognoscentiae:* a vision of [the second] death by means of an immediate experience) and, in particular, to the congenial insights gained through Adrienne von Speyr's theological experience (in the introduction to *Kreuz und Hölle*, for example, Balthasar says that this is one of the two central themes of Adrienne's theology), Balthasar contemplates how Christ in his descent "sees" the whole sin of the world, separated from the sinner, rejected, and condemned once for all. This vision is the fruit of the suffering of the cross and therefore belongs uniquely to the Lord. This perception of sin as such is interpreted, using categories drawn from Irenaeus and Thomas, as an act that perceives the amorphous mass of sin and, in so doing, assumes it, takes possession of it, and conquers it. This perception is, at the same time, a being enraptured or swept away (one that, by reason of the kind of perception that is in play here, is as harsh and dramatic as possible): Christ, seeing the fruit of his passion, is drawn, "enrapt" through the horror of hell by and towards the Father, in a total, chaotic, and incomprehensible abandonment. Balthasar, basing himself on this second aesthetic aspect, always accentuates the passivity of this experience. He interprets the active verb "he went to preach to *(adveniens praedicavit)* the spirits that were in prison" (1 Pet 3:19) as a passive but no less real preaching with his being, by means of his remaining dead with the dead. He finds support for this reading in 1 Peter 4:6, which employs a passive verb: "the Gospel was proclaimed to the dead" *(mortuis evangelizatum est)*. Christ's lacerating (subjectively: the horror of the experience; objectively: the tearing apart of the kingdom of death) passage through hell is a being placed in, and drawn through, it by the will of the Father, into whose hands he had entrusted himself without reserve.

Now, the principle that underlies the two above-mentioned theological aesthetic categories and unites them in mutual interpenetration is the

(Ignatian) obedience of (Johannine) love. In the unique "space-time" of the descent, in which "vision" and "rapture" coincide in the Son's loving obedience, the majestic splendor of the Father's love shines forth in its opposite, in the loveless night of the anti-divine. Here, in this simultaneity, the Son becomes the "author and finisher" of every creaturely aesthetic form and experience. The Son's obedience of love offers the splendor of the Father's love a right and adequate form from the heart of which it can irradiate precisely in and through the amorphous horror of hell — and so conquer it as a moment of the glory of the mutual love of the Father and the Son in the Holy Spirit. And because this entire paternal-filial event becomes the glory of their mutual love as a circumincession of form and light in the midst of man's second death and sin, the obscure limit that remained in the Old Testament and prevented its consummation falls away from within. There opens, once and for all *(eph' hapax)*, the New and Eternal Covenant between heaven and earth, God and the world.

This covenant, founded and realized in the person of the Son, is, as we saw at the beginning of this section, the aesthetic form *par excellence.* The Son, thanks to his obedience of love in the amorphous chaos of the world's sin, is and becomes the center of the analogy of the transcendentals that obtains between God *(glory)* and the creation *(pulchrum):* the middle that harmonizes and illumines all things, the *medium tenens in omnibus.* This victory, which takes all thought by surprise, sheds light back onto created aesthetic form. This light falls, in the first place, on the metaphysical form *par excellence:* the *distinctio realis,* which can now be perceived and respected as a holy "space" and "time," where the grace of the act of being in its fullness lights up and pours out on the totality of the real. Man, as an artist of being (who is both its son and its father), can perceive and be enraptured by all things, because in them being "re-creates" itself as an image of the form and light of the Trinity. Created reality — in spite of the horror that often threatens existence — is worthy of being loved, welcomed with honor, co-glorified: *pulchrum et esse convertuntur* [being and the beautiful are convertible].

Theo-Drama

In our discussion of the *Glory of the Lord,* we saw that Christ, by his obedience of love, is the aesthetic form *par excellence* that holds together in unity the terms of the analogy of the beautiful within the embrace of the New and Eternal Covenant. The same connection between obedience and love, the transcendentals and the covenant, is central in the *Theo-Drama*. The same convergence founds here the dramatic form, which animates the transcendental *bonum,* understood as "self-gift."

Christ is the covenant, the circumincession of infinite and finite freedom, in person. He is this covenant, however, not for himself, but *pro nobis et pro omnibus.* For the same reason, he is the covenant in the clash, in the dramatic conflict between his obedience of love and the "No" that fallen man sets in opposition to the reciprocity of divine and creaturely freedom in the covenant. In order to realize the covenant in his person, Christ must overcome this "No" without overwhelming, overburdening, or ignoring human freedom. According to Balthasar and Adrienne, Christ does this by means of an act of what they call *"Unterfassung,"* an act in which he bears and embraces so to say "from below" the world's "No." Christ brings his obedience of love into or, better, in obedience to the Father; he lets himself be sent by him *underneath and within* the "No" of man's freedom, in order to be able to open to it from within a way to a renewed assent. This *"Unterfassung"* reaches its climax on Holy Saturday, in the Son's state of *having been* sacrificed:

> Here it becomes evident that the New Covenant is a movement, a dramatic process, in which the light penetrates the darkness and, step by step, conquers a path inside of the night of death. This happens in the Passion, especially in the mysterious third state of suffering in which the Lord, having completed his sacrifice, is entirely the one who has been sacrificed [*der Geopferte*].[11]

Created out of nothing, we are subject to limits, limits imposed on us without any choice on our part. The limit of limits is death. Balthasar speaks of a *"Sterbenmüssen,"* a having to, or being forced to die, which is man's lot.[12] The Old Testament, seen as a whole, considers this "inevitable

---

11. Adrienne von Speyr, *Johannes. I: Das Wort wird Fleisch* (Einsiedeln: Johannes Verlag, 1949), p. 66. Eng., *The Word Becomes Flesh: Meditations on John 1–5* (San Francisco: Ignatius Press, 1994).

12. Hans Urs von Balthasar, *Theodramatik* (= *TD*), vol. IV: *Das Endspiel* (Einsiedeln: Johannes Verlag, 1983), p. 296. Eng. trans., *Theo-Drama: Theological Dramatic Theory,* vol. 5: *The Last Act* (San Francisco: Ignatius Press, 1983).

necessity of dying" to be a mysterious limit placed on man's communion with God. The Psalms tell us that, when man descends into the underworld, he can no longer glorify God. In death, man is incapable of communing with God. But the Son comes into the world in order to "transvalue" death. And he does so precisely by his act of *"Unterfassung."* "Snatching and appropriating to himself all the deaths of sinners in his self-gift unto death, he transmutes into his one death all these deaths, and with them, every life that runs to this death."[13] In this way, Jesus brings about in himself the covenant of divine and human love, the heart of the theo-drama.

Man, as he concretely exists, cannot experience his death as the prolongation or expression of his communion with God. Neither can he suppress or overcome this incapacity because, whether he will or no, he is "thrown" into an existence that is subject precisely to this inability. The Son, on the other hand, is not thrown into earthly existence, but rather allows himself to be sent into it by the Father from the platform of eternity. This is the root of the Son's *"Unterfassung."* The Son is his act of receiving himself from the Father in love. This act contains an infinite letting be and letting be done that make it possible for the Son both to be sent and, within this sending, to assume the total passivity of human existence from conception to death. By the same token, Christ's incarnatory mission thus transforms the experience of the passivity of the human condition into an act of filial love, which he performs *pro nobis.* Because the Son, coming down from heaven, penetrates and remains within our death with his filial letting be, he can meet us in our death, and so enable us to do what we could not do on our own: live our death as a gift of self, as a communion with the God who gives himself away:

> But in Jesus' case, the event . . . of the hour [the final and decisive hour of death] is not a function of his "being thrown" from nothingness into existence, but of something mysterious that takes the places of this "thrownness": his self-dispossession of his divinity [kenosis], which, as such, is an act of obedience to his eternal Father (Phil 2:7). Here, obviously, the power of the cast, of the throw into the mission is more powerful than nothingness. This throw throws — beyond all thrownness — into an end (*telos:* Jn 13:1) that is beyond all ends that

13. *TD* IV, p. 297.

are simply "thrown." While the end of those who are thrown is a withdrawal of movement, the end of the One Sent to this end is always, and is here, too, an act within his being sent: the act of having abandoned himself. This is possible because in his (filial) self-donation there is a correspondence with the [paternal] act of the Sender, who in that action was and always has been the one who gives his most intimate life away. This double self-donation is the expression of absolute love.[14]

This text suggests two aspects that are necessary to complete our sketch of Holy Saturday in the theo-drama. The first is this: man's incapacity to live death as communion with God is not due solely to his being "thrown" from nothingness, but also, in the concreteness of his historical existence, to his sin. The necessity of dying, as we experience it, is a punishment that falls upon man who, having refused to hand himself over to communion with God, finds himself thrown back upon his naked finitude and so bound to an inevitable death. And yet, as Adrienne explains in her book on death, this punishment also includes an aspect of mercy. By imposing death on us, God gives us the opportunity to surrender, haltingly, to him. But in order for this aspect of mercy to become a reality, the Son himself has to redeem death "from underneath" in an act of *"Unterfassung."* This embrace of our being from underneath *(interior intimo meo — superior summo meo)*, must embrace not only our death but also the refusal, the "No," which concretely conditions and shapes our death. And not only that. Christ, embracing death from below, must also take upon himself the solitude of having been separated and cut off from God that is the result and essence of this "No." He must experience what Balthasar calls *Gottverlassenheit,* forsakenness by God in both the objective and subjective sense. This experience culminates in turn on Holy Saturday, when Christ is definitively dead together with the dead:

> The Bible interprets his death, with its embrace from below, in two senses, and it is very important to see that both are inseparable. On the one hand, this death is the substitution for all the deaths of sin, and for this reason Christ gives himself over in dying into Godforsakenness, hence, into a powerlessness that embraces from below every possible Godforsakenness and powerlessness on the part of sinners.[15]

14. *TD* IV, p. 297.
15. *TD* IV, p. 297.

This passage already contains the second aspect. Holy Saturday does not just mark the fact that the Son has died. On Holy Saturday, he completes his entrance into the flesh by being in the state of having died. This is not a mere physical fact. It is an event of substitution in which the Son assumes death as it is concretely burdened by sin: a death saturated with the sinner's "No"; a death, then, that means final separation from God, beyond any ability of ours to uproot. Now, because it is the Son who bears our concrete death as an extreme act of love, he can be dead with the dead and, at that very moment, "transmute" death "from below." And because he takes upon himself the burden of our Godforsakenness in an act of loving obedience, this transmutation happens insofar as he places his filial love at the very point where our "No" has made us completely incapable of any vital movement towards God. In this way, he breaks open from within our ownmost "No," but without any heteronomy. His entrance into the immobility of death on Holy Saturday is the seal of his objective victory over sin, a victory that has already occurred subjectively on the cross. Rising from death, he will show that, from now on, this love has become transparent to trinitarian love: "This is the first aspect, which made such an impression on Paul. But this *action* of God likewise contains the second aspect: the *doctrine* that this action is the proclamation of an absolute love, which reveals itself as such in God's trinitarian essence."[16]

Balthasar, following Adrienne von Speyr, conceives of the Redemption as the consummated "separation of sin from the sinner." This separation depends on the fact that "only One has descended into hell," as C. S. Lewis puts it. In other words, Christ on the cross has taken all sin upon himself, but without the guilt of having committed it, in order that our sin might receive its due condemnation, without our having to go to hell to pay for it. And it is only because Christ shoulders our guilt by his hard and real obedience of love (no insipid play of love with itself, as Hegel said), hence, in perfect innocence, he is not damned (in the sense of Luther's merely formal interchange between *justus* and *peccator*), but rather *unterfasst* within the obedience of his mission the perdition that we have inflicted on ourselves, making it in all truth *his* perdition. In this sense, his obedience of love radically fulfills the justice owed to the Father, transforming it into an expression of ever-greater mercy.

The Son, in other words, makes a reality what, humanly speaking, is

---

16. *TD* IV, p. 297.

impossible: the definitive consummation of the covenant from both sides. By the same token, the Son himself is the "ultimate." "Christ, the Judge, is the *'eschatos.'*"[17] He, not the destiny of sinful man, not Hades, is the last thing. He is the eschatological reality in person, as Scripture itself says: "Do not be afraid! I am the first and the last *(eschatos)*, and the living one, and I was dead, and behold I am alive for the ages of the ages, and I hold the keys of death and hell" (Rev 1:17-18). "For the suffering of death, we see Jesus crowned with honor and glory, so that, by the grace of God, he might taste death on behalf of all" (Heb 2:9).

Christ is the ultimate, then, because, by his obedience of love, he can experience our lostness, and yet, in the midst of this experience, continue to love — to let himself be generated by the Father. For, as Balthasar puts it, the Incarnate Son's obedience, as the supreme realization of freedom, has its transcendent foundation in the Son's eternal generation: "'The Son shares already in performing his own generation; he lets himself be generated, holds himself ready to be generated.'" For this reason, "'the Son prefers nothing so much as doing the will of the Father, because he fully accomplishes it already in the act of being generated.'" Obedience and freedom, independence and dependence, are one in the life of the Incarnate Son because the relationship between the Father and the Son (in the Spirit) is internal to the divine essence as a love that exists in mutual self-abandonment: "'The intra-divine processions occur in an eternal simultaneity,' so that the Father's generative act is already 'an act of donative self-abandonment to the Son, which the Son answers with *his* donative self-abandonment.'"[18] An implication of all this is that, at the moment of death, every man encounters Christ as his only and final judge. And because Christ's own death has "transmuted" death and separated sin at its root from the sinner, this judgment is, at one and the same time, the severest possible condemnation of sin and the offer of an infinite mercy to the sinner. Thanks to the grace that flows from the action of the Holy Trinity in the Son's *descensus ad inferos,* our appearance before our judge becomes the culmination of our *sequela Christi:*

17. Joseph Ratzinger, cited in *TD* IV, p. 329.

18. Hans Urs von Balthasar, *TD* IV, p. 76; the citations within the text of *Theodramatik* are taken from Adrienne von Speyr, *Welt des Gebetes,* 2nd ed. (Einsiedeln: Johannes Verlag, 1992), 57, 59, 223/194.

And in this way, the judgment gathers together in concentrated form everything pertaining to man's redemption, since the judgment is the encounter of the Father's justice with the Son's Cross in the love of the Spirit, an encounter that is at the same time the reunion or reunification of the Father and the Son.[19]

In his descent, Christ founds purgatory and hell in their specifically Christian sense. Purgatory is an aspect of each man's eschatological encounter with Christ, his only judge. Thus, the state of death and the encounter with the God of justice, which without Christ would have been an eternal prison for everyone, now, with and in him, does not have to be for anyone:

> Purgatory comes into being, in the strict sense, on Holy Saturday, when the Son, by means of his passage through "hell," introduces the aspect of mercy into the state of those who had been justly condemned ... "purgatory arises or is ignited under the Lord's footsteps [in his descent]. He brings consolation to this place of [pure] desolation, he brings warmth to this place of infernal cold."[20]

On the cross, Christ becomes a holocaust, a burnt offering totally consumed. Burned, because he himself offers himself in our place to the consuming fire of God, whose sanctity cannot tolerate the slightest evil: "Our God is a consuming fire" (Heb 12:29; cf. Deut 4:24). At the same time, because he has experienced the full impact of this fire — its *Anprall* in aesthetic terms — he becomes the Lord of the eschatological fire of judgment. He thus has the right to apply it to us, not in order to destroy us, but to purify us instead. The fire that burns Christ as our holocaust is transformed into the purifying fire of purgatory as our hope.

The beginning of the process of purification in purgatory is rooted in a mysterious "abandonment of my vision into his vision."[21] Balthasar and Adrienne conceive of judgment and purgatory in terms of an analogy (and not a dialectic or a univocity) with confession. There is, as in all anal-

---

19. Adrienne von Speyr, *Apokalypse. Betrachtungen über die geheime Offenbarung* (Einsiedeln: Johannes Verlag, 1950), p. 681.

20. *TD* IV, p. 331; the citation is from Adrienne von Speyr, *Johannes* IV, p. 173. Eng., *John*, vol. 4: *The Birth of the Church* (San Francisco: Ignatius Press, 1991).

21. *TD* IV, p. 333.

ogies, a fundamental dissimilarity: in purgatory, man does not actively confess to Christ — his life is already finished, there is no longer room for any free decision on his part; rather it is his whole life, already lived, that now comes to light. Better, man finds himself passively before the eyes of the judge, which are like "fire," and so is *confessed* by Christ himself. What man "does" is to let be, to allow this divine fire to burn up everything that does not reflect its love. This process "lasts" until the sinner, "preferring nothing to the love of Christ" in this final vis-à-vis of his personal judgment — recognizes his total lovelessness, acknowledges that he deserves an even greater punishment than what he is receiving, and is ready to pay any price for it . . . until he finally cries out for this "more."[22] At this moment, the fire of God's holiness begins to burn in us in a different sense. The center of our attention shifts — once and for all — from ourselves, from our own suffering, from our own anguish, towards the Lord's suffering and anguish, which is not the anguish of the sinner, but of the Good Shepherd in search of his lost sheep. The cry for "more" now becomes an expression of an offering that forgets itself and mysteriously remains with the Lord in expiation for everything that causes him anguish; and that everything is not only his, the sinner's, personal sin, but also the sin of the world, every offense that ceaselessly rises from the world.[23] This request for "more" is the beginning of God's shining ever more in our state of eschatological confession, in the justice of the final personal and universal judgment. And because it is only in this moment that love begins to burn in the sinner, it is also at this moment that the gates of heaven open for him.

The consideration of the role of Holy Saturday in the *Theo-Drama* and of the connection between Holy Saturday, judgment, and purgatory brings us to the same point in which our consideration of the *Glory of the Lord* culminated: Jesus' obedience of love is the foundation of his being *the* form of Revelation. Transforming our death into the economic enactment of his eternal generation, this obedience can transmute the limit of death into an act of love within the limitless mutual self-gift of God and man.

In this way, Christ realizes, and is in his own person, the dramatic form *par excellence*, the form that now becomes and is (in the *convertuntur* of *esse* and *agere*) the new and eternal covenant and the foundation of all creaturely form. Christ can be and do this because he *is* the Father's self-

22. *TD* IV, p. 336.
23. *TD* IV, p. 336.

gift in the midst of its opposite, of the mortal contradiction against him and against every gesture that "gathers with him," even as this self-gift is held together and promoted by the spiration of the Spirit at this humanly dead point. This divine drama is the ultimate reality that radically cures and transforms the world's tragedy, changing it into a theo-drama. The Father's creation is fundamentally good thanks to the Son's action, and for this reason the self-gift of being in man's free action becomes a fruitful and positive dramatic form. Holy Saturday illumines for us the unity of love and justice that is consummated between Father and Son (not without struggle — see the Garden of Olives) and that embraces and heals the whole of creation and every human drama with it. The light of this consummation "in-fluences" from within, from non-subsistent being in fruitful creativity that we call the good and that "con-vinces" us to realize the convertibility of being, love, and goodness: *esse et bonum convertuntur*. The *Eschatos* of Love suffers and communicates himself *in* every created love:

> The Son has taken their sin away, precisely in order to make out of their distance from the Father the highest proof of his love for the Father. Everything that was, is, and will be thus comes together in the Son hanging on the cross now in the present. He is the whole history of humanity, but also the whole history of God with humanity. And so it is only from the earthly point of view that suffering and death are an end. For God it is a mid-point, which goes right through the middle of the Father. After all, even in his dying, the Son does not stop being generated by him and rendering him thanksgiving, in a love that, precisely at this very moment, is expressing its uttermost. The death of the Son is the display of the highest vitality of trinitarian love.[24]

Theo-Logic

Just as the series of transcendentals begins with beauty, centers in the good, and is sealed in the truth, the third wing of the triptych, the *Theo-Logic*, considers the same event as the first two, but from a new, distinctive point of view. The *Theo-Logic* attempts to show and understand how

24. Adrienne von Speyr, *Das Angesicht des Vaters* (Einsiedeln: Johannes Verlag, 1981), p. 64. Eng., *The Countenance of the Father*, trans. David Kipp (San Francisco: Ignatius Press, 1997).

Christ's gift of self "to the very end" is the *"Auslegung,"* the "exegesis" or exposition, of the Father's love in and for the world, and in this sense the "truth" (in the Johannine sense). Christ is the truth as fullness, and for the same reason as covenant: in him, the Father's whole love is unfolded in the whole incarnate Son in and for the world thanks to the mediation of the Holy Spirit. The Spirit is the exegete of the exegesis of the Father that is the Son. Having given his whole being, Christ is raised from the dead and, at that moment, the Spirit simultaneously seals the exposition of the Father's love performed by the Son and unfolds the wealth of this exposition with creative fidelity as the *"Spiritus Creator."* And only then is the Spirit "released" to explicate Christ's exegesis of the Father in our hearts. Only then is the plenitude of truth accomplished and the New Covenant sealed.

Christ is the *Logos,* the "middle person" (Bonaventure) of the Trinity. As such, he never speaks in the first instance of himself, but of the Father. And, in speaking of the Father, he does not emphasize his own authority as the Father's exegete, but leaves his exegesis in being and act in the hands of the Holy Spirit so that the Spirit may do with it as he wills (and the Spirit wishes only to act in perfect creative fidelity; he wishes to "blow" only in and towards the love of the Father and the Son). Because the *Logos* is the "central person," this double relationality — backwards towards the Father and forwards (with the Father) towards the Holy Spirit — structures his *Logos*-character. Insofar as the *Logos* is the middle person, he has a structure, a logical form, which is at the same time inseparably an exegesis of the living God:

> It is not until Jesus Christ that we arrive at the identity of unity and difference that was described just now, an identity that, for Christian faith, points unambiguously straight into the mystery of the Trinity. Jesus simultaneously posits essential divine unity and opposition [therein], to which he bears witness by speaking about a relational vis-à-vis [within God]. By doing so, Jesus gives us the key to the mystery of the living God, which reveals its mysteriousness never more so than just when an access to it is opened up for us.[25]

According to Balthasar, then, "[c]reaturely logic can be rightly seen for what it is only as an analogous participation in an absolute, *Logos,* which

---

25. Hans Urs von Balthasar, *Theologik* (= *TL*), vol. II: *Wahrheit Gottes* (Einsiedeln: Johannes Verlag, 1985), p. 119. For an English translation, see *Theo-Logic: Theological Logical Theory,* vol. 2: *Truth of God,* trans. Adrian J. Walker (San Francisco: Ignatius Press, 2004).

points into itself back to its (paternal) origin and out of itself forwards to the Spirit of free love who flows from it and its origin."[26] In the ana-logical part of the second volume of *Theo-Logic,* Balthasar explains how creaturely logic reflects the *Logos.* Part of his explanation is negative: Balthasar critiques, that is, a conceptualist logic that closes being in the abstract self-identity of A = A, and so equates the other — B — with the absolute negation of A: A ≠ B. Such a logic, Balthasar insists, cannot capture, understand, and structure reality, in which B, C, etc., are A's "co-constituents, insofar as their otherness positively co-determines A, which has a double presupposition: being-with-others in a finitude (common to all) that in turn is different from, and related to, its origin."[27] This logic expresses the real being of the world: "one *and* the other in a constitutive, differentiated unity."[28] This logical expression is what we call the logical form of created being, the self-expression of this being that at one and the same time captures it, structures it, and illumines it. Balthasar's conclusion:

> Neither "identity" nor mere "difference," Blondel has shown us, can express the structure of real worldly being. . . . In the real, difference, what is "other than myself," is always already overtaken by a third, within which I can notice this otherness in the first place. The antitheses are not mutually indifferent, but each is always for the other — differently.[29]

Returning to our topic in the light of what we have just said, we can say that the *Logos,* descending into the flesh, assures "catalogically" the analogy between worldly logic and trinitarian logic. Concretely, this requires a redemptive action from above, because the creature has rejected the logic of love inscribed in being, contra-dicting, saying "No" to, the other, to oneself, and to the love of the Trinity that is its Original Source. The question of how Christ is the logical form of Revelation thus becomes, *concretissime,* the question of how the *Logos,* the exegete of trinitarian love, can include and tame the "No" pronounced by the creaturely image. How can the *Logos,* who is a pure "Yes" to the Father, take on himself and overcome *(tollere)* the creature's "No"? In accord with the other wings of the

---

26. *TD* IV, p. 57.
27. *TL* II, p. 35.
28. *TL* II, p. 35, italics added.
29. *TL* II, p. 33.

Trilogy, Balthasar's answer will be based on the Son's obedience of love to the extreme of Godforsakenness.

Holy Saturday is the last step in the descent of the *Logos* into the flesh, which is concretely a *caro peccati*. On Holy Saturday, the *Logos* that was in the beginning (Jn 1:1) enters into the darkness that can neither comprehend nor receive him, indeed, *refuses* to do so. The *Logos*, who is the Father's Word (judgment, decision, "diction"), enters into the contradiction, the "No," of the creature to what this "diction" expresses: the Father's love. Because he is the truth *par excellence*, to contradict him is to cooperate with an untruth, with an anti-truth, with pure falsehood. What is at stake is not a failure to understand the truth, but an open hatred of it.

This contra-diction, then, cannot be integrated into the truth. But since it is not simply nothing, where can this hate-filled untruth "end up" if not in hell? Hell is the dark kingdom of naked untruth, shut up in false shadows. But in order for the un- or anti-truth of the creature's contradiction to end up in hell, it has to be uprooted and carried there. This is the main task of the Incarnate Word. This task poses a theological problem, however. How is it that the incarnate *Logos*, who is the truth, can carry and bear the contradiction of sin within his always veridical exposition of the Father, without blessing this contradiction in the slightest as if it were part of the total truth itself? How can he unite the creature's "No," its deep-rooted aggressive negativity, with his simple, pure "Yes," without turning that "Yes" into a "No"? For it is just this union that he must bring about and must bear witness to:

> At this point, it finally becomes clear what "negative theology" is in a Christian sense. No longer the sublime experience that God's majesty transcends all human experience and conceptuality, but that in the cross the contra-diction of sin, its falsehood and unlogic, is taken into the logic of the triune love, not, however, in order to find a place in it, but in all truth to be "damned in the flesh" (of the Son) (*katakrinein;* Rom 8:3). The flesh, "God's enemy" (Rom 8:7), insofar as it is against God, is cast out of the cosmos, which is God's, "into the outermost darkness."[30]

"Behold the Lamb of God who takes away the sin of the world." According to the exegesis of *Theologik II*, Christ, as Lamb of God, literally

---

30. *TL* II, p. 297.

"takes" and "takes away," not only the punishment for sin, but also sin it-self, while at the same time making this action an exegesis of the Father's love. In other words, the redemptive act is an act of substitution in which Christ puts himself in the sinner's place. Here the Latin *tollere* (to take away, to cancel, to overcome, to conserve) joins with Hegel's *Aufheben* in order to give rise to a dense logical play of different, related meanings. Now, this brings us back to the above-mentioned problem. How can Christ take upon himself something that is incompatible with the Father's love without putting himself at odds with that love? Note that what is at stake here is nothing less than the identity of the *Logos* as an expression of this fontal love. How can the *Logos* take on himself what contradicts him without ceasing to be the central *Logos* of the theo-logic? Balthasar's an-swer, once again, lies ultimately in the obedience of love that goes to — and remains in — the extreme of Holy Saturday.

The incarnate *Logos* assumes our sin, not out of an inclination to sin, but out of loving obedience. By the same token, the Son, "bearing up" pa-tiently *(Aushalten)* under the action and consequence of sin, cancels and overcomes sin on its own ground. What does this mean?

We have already seen that Balthasar conceives of truth, or logical form, as a unity embracing distinction and letting this distinction be within itself. As this very formulation suggests, moreover, Balthasar sees the Trinity as the *analogatum princeps* of all truth as such logical form. Seen from this "theo-logical" point of view, then, Christ's assumption of sin can be interpreted as an assumption of fallen difference — the distance the sinner puts between himself and God — within the primordial, posi-tive difference-in-unity between the Father and the Son in the Holy Spirit. This does not mean, of course, that God somehow blesses sin as a part of his intra-Trinitarian life. On the contrary, it means that the Father and the Son, in the unity of the Spirit, make of sinful distance or difference an oc-casion of manifesting, indeed, vindicating once and for all, the logic of love they embody. How so?

Here dry description has to give way to language as vivid as the lan-guage that Balthasar uses in the Theo-drama, which aims to be a reflection of the divine discourse of the Scriptures. The Son lets himself be "loaded" with our sinful distance from God in the infinite patience of his loving obedience. By saying "Yes" to this mysterious transaction, he lets this sinful distance be swallowed up in the ever-greater, positive "distance" between the Father and the Son in the Spirit. Of course, we cannot measure the extent of this divine distance; we can only glimpse its immensity in contemplating the Lord's cry of abandonment on the Cross, which does reveal something of his experience of the Father's silence in the face of sin, which, as Paul tells us, Christ has "become." And yet our faith teaches us that this experience of abandonment, this action/passion of loving obedience, is precisely the Trinity's redemptive deed of swallowing up sinful distance within the difference-in-unity of the Trinity's logic of love. The contradiction of sin is swallowed up within the "Diction," the pure "Yes," of the Word as the exegesis of the Trinity, both in the *theologia* and the *oikonomia.* Indeed, since this Word's loving obedience is the "point" in the *oikonomia* where the Trinitarian logic of love finds its uttermost explication (which does not dissolve the mystery, but underscores it even more), it does not place him outside the structure of the transcendental *verum.* On the contrary, this obedience occurs within, and seals, the analogy between divine and worldly truth:

> The obedience of the Son even in his being dead, even in hell, is his perfect *identity* in all contradiction and so the overcoming also of the last contra-diction through this identity, which infiltrates everything from below [*unterlaufende Identität*]. An obedience, which, christologically speaking, is nothing other than the expression of the Son's trinitarian love, which precisely here, in the absolutely excessive demand, in "impossible obedience" (Adrienne), demonstrates itself to be the Son's hypostatic obedience.[31]

"Father, why have you abandoned me?" This "why" receives (at the moment) no answer but . . . silence. On the other hand, this silence means that the incarnate *Logos* bears the experience of meaninglessness that sin entails in its a-logical contra-diction. On the other hand, by remaining under the a-logical "No" of sin, the *Logos* embodies the answer to the "why" that he himself calls out on the cross. And this answer is the love that has no "point" or "motive" or "why" beyond itself and that exegetes itself as love precisely in the death of the *Logos* in the absurdity of the cross. The incarnate *Logos,* remaining in the midst of the illogic of sin, embraces from below *(unterfasst)* its "gratuity" (its futility, its perverse folly) with the ever-greater "gratuity" (the whylessness, the "folly" of super-positive creativity) of the Father's love. The *Logos,* verifying in his missional being the absolute

31. *TL* II, p. 35, p. 323.

trustworthiness *('emeth)* of the One who sends and in this sending gives himself away (Jn 3:16), is the exegesis, the un-veiling, the illumination of the inoriginate origin *(Grundloser Grund)* of the Father's love. And it is in this way that he is *the* logical form *par excellence.* The Son's obedience of Love makes him once again the form: this time the logical form *par excellence.*

"Life's absurd wound" has been cured at the roots of its being, within the gratuitous wound of the incarnate *Logos,* the center of the Trinity. This means that the rupture, the expressive bursting forth of worldly being in its self-unveiling that we call "truth" *(alētheia),* can be conceived, acknowledged, and said *(legein)* as a light of love — despite all the falsehood and all the anti-metaphysical speculation that attempts to rob it of its evidence and its reliability *('emeth).* This "whylessness" of love as the meaning of being is, then, the foundation that carries truth and gives it sense. This is why, on the creaturely level, the Christian's theo-logical task is to affirm and promote the convertibility, the mutual growth of being, love, and truth: *esse et verum convertuntur.*

The interpretation of Holy Saturday offered in tandem by Hans Urs von Balthasar and Adrienne von Speyr is often criticized for rupturing the unity of the *Logos,* with the lamentable result, supposedly, of a hopeless irrationalism. In reality, Holy Saturday, as the qualitative center of the *Triduum,* is the concrete foundation in the history of salvation of the truth of the world within the truth of the Trinity, of worldly logic within the logic of God. The silence of Holy Saturday is at the center of the transcendental *verum.* This means that the truth is the coming to light and articulation of a foundation that, confirming itself by means of its plenary presence, convinces us with all desirable evidence that it is always greater. The truth, then, is neither rationalist nor irrationalist, it is mystery: a form in which the groundless ground makes itself known as such — gratuitously judging, saving, and giving meaning to all that it grounds. And the thing that guarantees the coherence of this form is not the abstract identity of A = A, but the trinitarian identity of love, which is itself in the fecundity of mutual exchange and mutual gift. This identity can do the impossible: use what is meaningless as an occasion, a means (a middle term), for the manifestation and consolidation of its groundless, because gratuitous, meaning. The point here is not the transformation of all things into the frenetic hostility of contradiction, nor again the false peace of identity without difference, but the mature simplicity of the identity of triune love, that is, its obedience to itself and to nothing but itself — and so its humble service of the creature:

This folly [of the Cross] is not revealed in the essence of God ... but in the One who, in a single act, was able to unite the absolutely divine and the absolutely anti-divine — not in the insanity of a titanic super-human posture, but in the simplicity of his obedience. This obedience alone exegetes God as trinitarian love, and precisely in the fact that the Father delivers his Son to the contra-diction of the anti-divine out of love. Cross and Trinity prove each other mutually, taking the Cross in all its above mentioned, for human logic, difficult to understand dimensions. In this reciprocity (of Jn 1:1 and Jn 1:5 and 14) is present for us that Logos that will not pass away, even if heaven and earth pass away. These die, but in the embrace of the one who also calls himself "the life." A life that has held fast through every death, that possesses the keys of death and hell, but which, being the life *tout court,* also bestows life and light, grace and truth on men.[32]

Dawn of Hope

"Quand tout descend seule elle remonte. . . ."

Péguy

The enemy is conquered by the Lord: "I hold the keys of death and of hell" (Rev 1:18b). The state of death with no hope of return becomes the sealed center of the economic form of God, in which the immanent form glorifies itself and intensifies its grace in the reciprocity of its gratuitous donation as the consummation of the Covenant. The reciprocity that awakened the nostalgia of ancient man and the covenant that nourished the faith of the Jews both find their superabundant fulfillment in the Son's descent.

But what the Father's two hands fulfill in the first instance is the desire of the Father's heart: the creation of the real possibility (real because resting on the foundation of being and of grace) that "all men [and in and through them all creation] be saved and attain the full knowledge of the truth" (1 Tim 2:4). The Son's descent into sin as contra-diction against the Father's love, which he accomplishes thanks to the Spirit's silent and discreet work of unification, brings an absolute novelty: the death laced with sin is transformed into the gratuitous gift-giving in which the love of God

---

32. *TL* II, p. 331.

and the love of man give themselves to each other and illumine each other in an ever-greater reciprocity. Love, then, is worthy of faith and of being, because it is, has become, and has illumined itself as the absolute: by overcoming the final bond that imprisoned creation and oppressed the Father's heart. And that is why Péguy can say *"la foi que j'aime le mieux, dit Dieu, c'est l'espérance"* [the faith I like best, says God, is hope].

> *Love hopes all things.* In love's faith, there is room for all hope. . . . Love has experienced in God that sin has been overcome by means of the death of the Son, and this experience — and every experience — of the fulfillment God has accomplished has given love the infinity of action, for all eternity. Love cannot be placed before any fact and any sin and any alienation without keeping its hope. A hope that is much more alive, much greater, and much truer than what men can invent in order to destroy it.[33]

Holy Saturday, as we have seen, is far from being a rupture of the objective meaning of being or of the creative passion of human subjectivity. On the contrary, it is the absolute triumph of the redemption. By the same token, it is the central point from which shines forth the glory, the goodness, and the truth of the triune God — and, in him, of his creation. The trinitarian exegesis that Adrienne and Balthasar offer of the article of faith that "he descended into hell" shows this item of the Creed to contain a mysterious source of light that shines forth to reveal the full catholicity of the faith. The Son's death out of love, his real solidarity with sinners in their state of being dead, is the origin of the new creation, the beginning from which the Father's will shines out in its unity with the will of the Son and the Spirit, now and for all eternity. It is the momentous day when the Father holds in his hands the Spirit of his dead Son: *"Pater, in manus tuas commendo spiritum meum"* (Lk 23:46). His fatherly hands that created man from the primordial *humus* and that sent his own substance into Mary's womb. On this day, the holy God, and not *l'homme révolté ou dépressif,* achieves the decisive integration between the original goodness of creation ("and God saw that it was all very good": Gen 1) and the body of his Son lacerated by the aggression of the sin of the world that it has borne:

---

33. Adrienne von Speyr, *Korinther I* (Einsiedeln: Johannes Verlag, 1956), pp. 411f.

Through this body of the Son, the Father's hope shines . . . and the Spirit unites the Spirit of the Son's passion and the light of the Father so that the Father's hope might shine in the world, in the Church, and in the Mother.[34]

This light of theological hope pours itself out catalogically on what is the metaphysical question and decision *par excellence:* being's not subsisting in itself, but in what is other than itself, so as to make *it* exist in itself[35] — does it point in the last analysis to God's gratuitous goodness or towards an abyss of nothingness?[36] Christ's overcoming of death as an automatic entryway to Hades is the ultimate, eschatological foundation of the decision for the first possibility. The mortal wound of created being (the death of sin) has

---

34. Adrienne von Speyr, *Das Wort und die Mystik. I: Subjektive Mystik* (Einsiedeln: Johannes Verlag, 1970), pp. 259f.

35. As Thomas Aquinas puts it in a text that is canonical for Catholic metaphysics: "be-ing [*esse*] signifies something complete and simple, but not subsistent" (*De Potentia,* I, 1, ad 1). Creatures' be-ing, their *esse,* is the quintessence of their actuality — hence describable as "complete and simple" — and yet it does not exist in its own right as a substance — which is why Thomas says it is "non-subsistent." Created *esse* is not formally identical with created substances, and yet it never "exists" except as their act of be-ing. By the same token, at the moment in which *esse creatum* makes substances be as their supra-formal cause, it also "depends" on those substances. This moment of dependence in the act-fullness of created *esse* is what makes it, according to Balthasar, a "similitude of the divine goodness" (Thomas, *De Veritate,* XXII, 2, ad 2): the vehicle, that is, of a liberality so generous that it can depend on what it creates — in the sense of giving it a real freedom that counts before the Creator himself.

36. "Being [*das Sein*] does not squeeze entities [*Seiendes*] tightly to itself, but lets them be. In the same way, entities, in the serene confidence of being let be, let being be in their turn, so that being's light might rise like the sun to shine over all things. . . . In the space of the difference that opens for being to let us be and we being, two things can happen. On the one hand, being's lofty elevation over us can make it look alien, indifferent, even terrifying to us, so that we can be assailed by the temptation to perceive it as neutral, as worth-less, as sense-less, and so to prefer non-being. The shadows that darken our own existence because of guilt, sickness, and death; the horror of the world's being as a whole — all this seems to warrant a curse on existence. . . . And yet: in the same distance of letting be, being can also dawn on us in its glory . . . in a glory that sublimely and mysteriously transcends all the beauty and order of the real world, even though the latter are an irradiation and an index of this glory. The worth of this glory is in principle so unsurpassable — the most one can do is unfold it — that all glorious 'power' (in its victory over the impotence of the merely possible), all 'light' (in its victory over the darkness of nothingness), and all 'grace' (in its endless self-impartation) are gathered up in it. The Western metaphysics of light ultimately mean a decision for the second possibility: a homage of being as a whole in the act of letting it be" (Hans Urs von Balthasar, *Herrlichkeit* III.1.2 [Einsiedeln: Johannes Verlag, 1965], pp. 952f.).

been borne and overcome in the Father's heart, inasmuch as the Son has died and descended into hell in the ever-greater unity of the Spirit. For this reason, this death — together with all the suffering that evil inflicts on the world — can no longer be interpreted as the annihilation of all existence. It has become, instead, a mid-point, a source, that traverses the Father's heart in his eternal generation of the Incarnate Son and, therefore, in his re-creation of us as his sons. For this reason — and for this reason alone — the oscillation of non-subsistent being, together with all of its differences (disappropriation in the other; the polarity and potentiality of created being; the finitization that constitutes the essence of created beings), is not the yawning of a dark abyss of nothingness, but the reflection of the gratuity of divine Being, the image of the divine goodness.[37] The theological light that springs up from the mystery of Holy Saturday enables us to read every difference, every otherness, every night — especially the rupture of death — as the expression and concretion of a super-positive meaning, of a power, light, and grace emanating from super-essential being as love. Being and love, in other words, *convertuntur* in each of being's transcendentals. This light of being-as-love transforms the night of nothingness that frenetically anguishes man — transforms it into the "womb" in which "being bathes" (Péguy). This super-luminous ground of being — which is light in its being-given to entities — itself comes to light as the pure image and presence of the Father's abyssal bosom, from whose "fountain of the water of light" the Son will give us to drink without cost (Rev 21:6b). The night of being and its gratuity grow one in the other as an image of the unfathomable gratuity of the Foundation:

> So I want to find in them a sort of gratuity
> Which reflects the gratuity of my grace,
> Which is as it were created to the image and likeness of the gratuity
>   of my grace. . . .
> In a word, I want them to love, says God, not just freely,
> But gratuitously as it were.[38]

---

37. Gustav Siewerth, *Schicksal der Metaphysik* (Einsiedeln: Johannes Verlag, 2003), pp. 390-91.

38. *"Ainsi j'aime à trouver en eux comme une certaine gratuité/Qui soit comme un reflet de la gratuité de ma grâce,/Qui soit comme crée à l'image et à la ressemblance de la gratuité de ma grâce . . ./J'aime qu'ils aiment en fin, dit Dieu, non seulement librement mais comme gratuitement"* (Charles Péguy, *Oeuvres Poétiques Complètes* [Bibliothèque de la Pléaide, 1967], *Le mystère des saints innocents*, pp. 720f.).

Where being bathes
Immersed in the night.
It is the night that continues on, where being bathes, it is the night
    that is one continuous fabric,
A continuous fabric without end where the days are only days . . .
    like windows. . . .
Because it is you who rock all Creation
In a refreshing sleep.
As one beds a baby down on his little bed. . . .
You alone, night, dress the wounds.
The aggrieved hearts. That are broken to bits. Torn apart.
O my black-eyed daughter, the only one of my daughters
who can claim to be my accomplice. . . .
O my starry night whom I created first.[39]

It was then, night, that you came. The same night.
The same night that comes every evening and who had come so
often since the first darkness. . . . The same that had fallen over
    so many crimes since the
beginning of the world;
And on so many stains and so much bitterness;
And on this ocean of ingratitude, the same as came over my grief,
And over this hill and over this valley of my desolation,
it was then you came.
O night, mustn't, o mustn't my paradise
Be one great night of splendor that will fall on the sins
    of the world?[40]

---

39. "*Où se retrempe l'être/En plein dans la nuit/C'est la nuit qui est continue, où se retrempe l'être, c'est/la nuit qui fait un long tissu continu,/Un tissu continu sans fin où les jours ne sont que des jours . . . comme des fenêtres. . . ./Car c'est toi qui berces toute la Création/Dans un Sommeil réparateur./Comme on couche un enfant dans son petit lit. . . ./Nuit tu es la seule qui panses les blessures./Les coeurs endoloris. Tout démanchés. Tout démembrés./O ma fille aux yeux noirs, la seule de mes filles qui sois, qui puisses te dire ma complice. . . ./O ma Nuit étoilée je t'ai créée la première*" (Charles Péguy, *Oeuvres Poétiques Complètes* [Bibliothèque de la Pléiade, 1967], *Le porche de la deuxième vertu*, pp. 662-66).

40. "*C'est alors, ô Nuit, que tu viens. O nuit la même./La même qui viens tous les soirs et qui étais venue tant/de fois depuis les ténèbres premières. . . ./La même qui étais venue sur tant de crimes depuis le/commencement du monde;/Et sur tant de souillures et sur tant d'amertumes;/Et sur cette mer d'ingratitude, la même tu viens sur mon deuil;/Et sur cette colline et sur cette vallée de ma désolation/c'est alors, ô nuit, que tu viens/O nuit faudra-t-il*

The ultimate decision of the metaphysics of being as love is to affirm, to let be, the non-subsistence of being as the gratuity of being-for-the-other, and so to collaborate in the intensification of the beauty, goodness, and truth of reality. In the light of these passages from Péguy we can say that this decision rests on an ultimate decision for hope. For hope means self-gift in the night, at once temporal and eternal, for the salvation, at once temporal and eternal, of all of the Father's creatures. To hope is to give oneself for the salvation *(salvus)*, sanctity *(sanctus)*, and integrity *(sanus)* in body and spirit, in time and eternity of all, that they might all be *"sanctos esse sanos":*

> It is for my little hope alone that eternity will be.
> And that beatitude will be.
> And that paradise will be. And heaven and all.
> For she alone, as she alone in all the days of this earth
> Makes a new tomorrow spring forth from an old evening.
> So also she alone from the residue of the Judgment and the ruins and the debris of time
> Will make a new eternity spring forth.[41]

Hope leads us to abandonment, letting be, poverty, the night that covers man's dream and his creation. The night, the most beautiful of the Father's creatures. Its infinite starry veil covers and cradles the misery and the grandeur of every life. The night of hope pursues the sinner into his darkest hideouts. It is the motor that transforms the nihilism lurking in every human heart (and the heart is the center of creation where the being of the world either lights up or is extinguished) into the gratuity of love, into the light of the transcendentals. It does this by letting the other be in God. Hope, the little sister of the poor who is not afraid to handle the sick and the poor, has a special relation to God's merciful heart, thanks to which it enables us to perceive, to perform, and to unveil within the vain gratuity *(vanitas)* of fallen existence the fontal gratuity *(gratuitas)* of the Father, which changes the old creation into the new:

---

donc, faudra-t-il que mon paradis/Ne soit qu'une grande nuit de clarté qui tombera sur les péches du monde" (Péguy, *Le mystère des saints innocents,* p. 683).

41. "C'est pour ma petite espérance seule que l'éternité sera./Et que la Béatitude sera./Et que le Paradis sera. Et le ciel et tout/Car elle seule, comme elle seule dans les jours de cette terre/ D'une vieille veille fait jaillir un lendemain nouveau./Ainsi elle seule des résidus du Jugement et des ruines/et du débris du temps/Fera jaillir une éternité neuve" (Péguy, *Le mystère des saints innocents,* p. 746).

But it is exactly with those bitter waters that she makes her springs
    of pure water.
And that is why she has never missed it;
But that is also why she is Hope. . . .
How she manages it, how she does it,
Well, that, my children, is my secret.
Because I am her Father. . . .
But it is from bitter waters that she makes an eternal spring.
She knows all right that she will never miss it.
The eternal source of my grace.
She knows all right that she will never miss it.[42]

"Longer than a poor man's hope," says a Latin American proverb. Hope
knows how to relate to the "poor in Spirit." The poor in Spirit, in fact, are
those who do not keep for themselves the gift of being or the gift of grace.
They let the gift flow, and, as they have received it as a free *don*-ation, they
par-*don* in order to be par-*doned* themselves. They let the gift of being
reach the other and, in him, the Non-other who is God. They thus become
agents of reciprocity — between men and between man and God. They allow the Son, the poorest of the poor, to drink their bitter waters, to cleanse
them of this bitterness, and to take their sin into the black depths of hell.
They let him open all that is closed to the paternal Font. They allow the
Spirit to create a reciprocity of hope between them and the Father, so that
God's thoughts become theirs:

> This is why the world's hope lies with the poor: "The world will be
> saved by the poor. . . . And they will save it without trying . . . without
> asking for payment in return, because they have no idea of the price of
> the service they have performed." . . . "To build is always a work of
> love. . . ."[43]

---

42. "*Mais c'est justement avec les eaux mauvaises qu'elle fait ses sources d'eau pure./Et
c'est pour cela qu'elle n'en manqué jamais/Mais aussi c'est pour cela qu'elle est l'Espérance. . . ./
Comment elle y réussit, comment elle s'y prend,/Ça, mes enfants, c'est mon secret./Parce que je
suis son Père. . . ./Mais c'est des eaux mauvaises qu'elle fait une source éternelle./Elle sait bien
qu'elle n'en manquera jamais./La source éternelle de ma grâce même./Elle sait bien qu'elle n'en
manquera jamais*" (Péguy, *Le porche de la deuxième vertu*, pp. 640-41).

43. Hans Urs von Balthasar, *Gelebte Kirche: Bernanos,* 3rd ed. (Einsiedeln/Trier:
Johannes Verlag, 1988), p. 533. Balthasar is citing from Bernanos, *Les enfants humiliés* (Paris:
Gallimard), pp. 248-49, 253-54.

To enter into the Father's hope; to live in the reciprocity between hope for the accomplishment of all things (body and soul; earth and heaven) to which man aspires and the Hope that the salvation wrought by the Son reach all creatures through the Spirit. Such is *the* task of the Christian in the world, *the* integration *par excellence, the* eschatological fulfillment. And this eschatological plenitude is not a future utopia, but the serene presence we feel in the pages of John's Gospel:

> You have to put your hope in God, after all, he put his hope
> in us. . . .
> You have to put your faith in God, after all, he put his faith in us.
> A singular mystery, the most mysterious of them all,
> God took the initiative. . . .
> All the feelings, all the emotions we need to have for God,
> God had them for us, he started it, having them for us first. . . .[44]

The true Christian, who is genuinely "poor in Spirit," obeys the command of grace to enter into the sentiments of the Father, the Son, and the Spirit of which Péguy speaks. He does this on behalf of all, giving himself over into God's own bold hope for the world. The success of this final integration of hope depends, however, on the Christian's willingness to pass through the eschatological fire of Love. The Christian does not purify himself for himself. Rather, he lets the Fountain of life cleanse, nourish, and transform him into a source of love, given *gratis,* for others. The Christian willingly allows Christ's descent to take place again in his despairing heart, giving himself over completely so that this descent might also take place again in each one of the *desperata corda* (Gregory the Great)[45] of his brethren. Following the Son in his descent, letting himself be placed at this "intersection" of abandonment and anguish, the Christian begins to be poor, chaste, and pure like "sister" water, "who," says Saint Francis, "is very useful and humble and precious and chaste":

44. "*Il faut faire espérance à Dieu, il nous a bien fait espérance a nous. . . ./Il faut faire foi à Dieu, il nous a bien fait foi à nous/Singulier mystère, le plus mystérieux,/Dieu a pris les devants. . . ./Tous les sentiments, tous les mouvements que devons avoir pour Dieu/Dieu les a eus pour nous, il a commencé de les avoir pour nous*" (Péguy, *Le porche de la deuxième vertu,* p. 603).

45. Cited in Hans Urs von Balthasar, *Theologie der drei Tage* (Einsiedeln: Johannes Verlag, 1990), p. 169. For an English translation, see *Mysterium Paschale: The Mystery of Easter* (San Francisco: Ignatius Press, 1993).

And to put us at the heart of this axis of distress . . .
And to take the hurt in its full justice. . . .
May we, o queen, keep the honor,
And save for him, him alone, our small tenderness.[46]

This last reality brings us to a final step into the center where the Christian's task lies: the tender, poor, omnipotent heart of the Father. Hope bears us to its own origin. The night, the most beautiful of God's daughters, bears us to that same origin, as does the Son's descent into hell. And that origin is the mystery of the Father's omnipotent heart displayed in creation and redemption. The Father — the inoriginate origin of God, of creation, of redemption; the depth where hope for universal salvation is anchored. The mystery of hope protects us, keeping our worship focused on the heart of God, which is full of tenderness, hope, and patient omnipotence.

It is just here that Péguy brings us back to our two authors. Hell, we said at the beginning, is the encounter between the liberality of the Father who both creates human freedom and bears its consequences *and* the darkness of sin, the perverse chaos of sin caused by human wickedness. Hell is the Father's "preserve," something that he had "reserved" for himself. And the two things — the original chaos that the Father orders and the second chaos that the Son orders — are reflected each in the other. "The chaos of hell, which is a chaos of sin, is like a mirror reflecting the chaos that existed at the beginning of creation."[47] On Holy Saturday, the Father puts this mystery of sin into the Son's hands so that he, the Son, might order it, judge it, and transform it into a straight path to the paternal heart that is rich in mercy. The Father hands over to the Son in the economy of salvation his ultimate "reserve" so that the Son, victim and eschatological judge, might administer it for his greater glory.

Finally, then, the Son, after taking everything down with him into hell, brought up again with him the ultimate mystery of the Father's gratuitous love, accompanied only by "little hope" as his accomplice (cf. Péguy's "*quand tout descend seule elle remonte*"). This is the ultimate mystery that

---

46. "*Et pour bien nous placer dans l'axe de détresse . . ./Et de prendre le mal dans sa pleine justesse. . . ./Puissons-nous, ô régente, au moins tenir l'honneur,/Et lui garder lui seul notre pauvre tendresse*" (Charles Péguy, *Oeuvres Poétiques Complètes* [Bibliothèque de la Pléiade, 1967], *Les cinq prières dans la cathédrale de Chartres, Prière de confidence*, p. 918).

47. Adrienne von Speyr, *Kreuz und Hölle I* (Einsiedeln: Johannes Verlag, 1966), p. 175, cited by Balthasar in *Theologik II*, p. 321.

generates and covers, veils and unveils, earth and heaven, time and eternity. For "it is only the 'chaos' of love (that is, in its unfathomable depth) that makes the chaos [the gift of freedom, which can be misused] of sin"[48] possible. And it is this same "chaos" of love — another name for its gratuitous "whylessness" — that alone holds the power to overcome the chaos of sin in its ever-greater love.

---

48. Speyr, *Kreuz und Hölle I*, p. 107, cited by Balthasar in *Theologik II*, p. 322.

Movement Toward God:
The Relation of Natural and
Supernatural Love, of *Erōs* and *Agapē*

Love, Action, and Vows as "Inner Form" of the Moral Life

David S. Crawford

Introduction

In his *The Christian State of Life,* Hans Urs von Balthasar makes a crucial claim about the nature of love. After reminding us of the strict necessity of an account of love in arriving at any understanding of the meaning of human existence and activity, that is to say, of the fact that *caritatis perfectionem* is not only counseled but is strictly commanded, Balthasar goes on to state the following:

> As soon as love is truly awakened, *the moment of time is transformed for it into a form of eternity.* Even erotic egoism cannot forebear swearing "eternal fidelity" and, for a fleeting moment, finding pleasure in actually believing in this eternity. How much more, then, does true love want [German: *will*] to outlast time and, for this purpose, to rid itself of its most dangerous enemy, its own freedom of choice. Hence every true love *has the inner form of a vow* [*die innere Form des Gelöbnisses*]: It binds itself to the beloved and does so out of motives and in the spirit of love.[1]

This passage might at first strike us as odd. Of course, we are accustomed to thinking of love in terms of eternity, both in popular and in

---

1. Hans Urs von Balthasar, *The Christian State of Life,* trans. Sr. Mary Frances McCarthy (San Francisco: Ignatius Press, 1983), pp. 38-39 (emphasis original; the English translation of this passage omits a sentence: "Liebe auf Zeit, Liebe auf Abbruch ist nie wirkliche Liebe").

theological literature.[2] Love, it would seem, even love that is in reality all too ephemeral ("erotic egoism") — precisely in its pretense of eternity and of giving itself entirely — would seem to disclose at least something of the infinite and timeless. We are also accustomed to the idea that love brings about union with another; love bespeaks a desire on the part of lovers to "bind" themselves to one another.[3]

However, the development of these ideas in the two further claims — viz. (1) that "love has the inner form of a vow," and (2) that love wants to eliminate "its worst enemy," freedom of choice — may strike us as more problematic.

The first claim seems to reverse our instinctive sense of the relation between love and vows. Doesn't Balthasar have it backwards? Wouldn't it be more accurate to say, after all, that a vow has the inner form of love, at least insofar as the cause of a vow is love? A man and a woman exchange marriage vows because they love each other; a religious takes vows because of his love. Moreover, it seems that a vow is only *one* possible expression of love. Even were we to grant that vows are the highest expression of love, they are not necessarily the *only* expression. Rather, love would seem to be the more fundamental (and therefore *form*ative) reality, giving meaning to the possibility of a vow rather than vice versa. To say that something is the "inner form" of something else is to suggest that it makes that something else what it is, gives it its most fundamental character and nature. Thus, if a vow is only one possible expression of love, it cannot be love's "inner form." The question, then, is inevitable: Are vows really so very much at the root of love that we would want to call them love's "inner form"?

The second of these claims, on the other hand, appears to threaten the annihilation of love itself. Isn't love (at least in rational beings) a matter of freedom? Isn't freedom dependent on the possibility of choosing otherwise? In short, then, isn't freedom of choice essential to love, rather than its "worst enemy"? Of course, if we follow out the logic of this position, we may end up concluding that, insofar as vows eliminate freedom, love's culmination in a vow is simultaneously love's death. Thus, if vows constitute the "form" of love, and if they amount to the surrendering of

---

2. See Angelo Scola's discussion of nuptiality as "event," in "The Nuptial Mystery at the Heart of the Church," *Communio* 25 (Winter 1998): 630-62.

3. Aristotle, for example, speaks of friends wanting to spend time together or live together (*Nicomachean Ethics*, 1157b 19-24), and Thomas, of love tending to both affective and real "union" (*ST* I-II, q. 25, a. 2, ad 2; q. 28, a. 1).

the creature's very freedom and autonomy, then its culmination in vows would be at best a kind of Pyrrhic victory.

It seems to me that these initial objections — assuming we are able to offer adequate responses to them — provoke us to explore the importance and profundity of Balthasar's insight. Now, there are two fundamental implications regarding Balthasar's claim. First, there is the question of the way it causes us to think about love's relation to exterior vows, which are a culmination and paradigmatic actualization of love. Second, there is the question of the way we understand love in its beginnings and in relation to human freedom and action generally. I shall touch on each of these in what follows.

Freedom and "Inner Form"

Vows as a Cause of Love?

It is important to bear in mind that the claim that love has the inner form of a vow is made in the context of Balthasar's theology of the Christian states of life, and particularly in the context of his discussion of the three evangelical counsels — poverty, chastity, and obedience. In making this claim, Balthasar is emphasizing love's culmination in self-giving disponibility. Only an irrevocable vow is capable of taking up the whole of a person, including his future, in such an act of open-ended self-commitment. We might say, then, that explicit vows are the "objective" actualization of love itself, because they do not simply lead to but in fact *constitute* love's giving away of self. Love, in other words, is manifested outwardly and becomes a human action in the form of an explicit vow.

Now the significance and depth of this point is particularly well developed in Balthasar's discussion of the role of the "state of perfection" and the evangelical counsels in St. Thomas.[4] Thomas's main discussion focuses on the counsels as a means to the perfection of a charity that transcends them. If perfection is charity, the counsels are only a *means* to or an instrumental cause of that charity;[5] they are not charity itself. This is an important distinction, because it allows Thomas to explain why those who do

---

4. Balthasar, *The Christian State of Life*, pp. 41-65.
5. *ST* II-II, q. 184, a. 3; see also *De Perfectione vitae spiritualis*, cc. 6, 10.

not enter the religious state are not thereby left in a state of *im*perfection.[6] As Thomas famously puts it, *not all* who are in a state of perfection are perfect (Thomas uses the example of wicked bishops and religious), and some of those who are not in a state of perfection nevertheless *are* perfect.[7]

According to this understanding, then, vows given according to the counsels are a sort of regimen that simplifies life, because they take our focus off the multiplicity of objects and direct it toward the one thing necessary. The counsels may, in other words, be the best tools or means of achieving perfection, but they are not the only ones. Virtue may be learned in a variety of contexts and concrete life situations. At first glance, Thomas's answer to the conundrum posed by the disparity between objective state and individual reality seems to recommend itself as eminently reasonable.

Thomas goes on, however, to view the counsels as a personal imitation of Christ's self-holocaust.[8] As Balthasar observes, "the evaluation of the counsels as 'the way of perfection,' as merely a means of attaining a goal toward which all must strive, shifts noticeably to an evaluation of them as a 'degree of love,' as the higher level of love that itself seems to be greater because it proceeds from great self-renunciation."[9] But this second claim seems to have shifted the ground slightly. If the counsels constitute the actual self-holocaust, the giving away of self in love, then they cannot constitute a mere means to an end that transcends them. This further elaboration of the meaning of the counsels is therefore difficult to reconcile with the first; Thomas seems to have undermined his purpose in calling the evangelical counsels merely a means.

We seem to be left with a conundrum. Are the counsels merely a "means" or do they in themselves, in some sense, constitute the actual giving away of self?

If the vows of poverty, chastity, and obedience are simply a means to an end that transcends them, we can easily see how the potential disparity between state of life and personal perfection could occur. But in this first alternative, the vows seem to be merely instrumental, rather than in themselves constituting the self-gift of love. The implication, however, is that they are of secondary importance to Christian moral and ecclesial life; per-

---

6. See Balthasar, *The Christian State of Life*, pp. 44ff.

7. *ST* II-II, q. 184, a. 4.

8. *ST* II-II, q. 186, aa. 1 and 6; *De Perfectione vitae spiritualis*, c. 11.

9. Balthasar, *The Christian State of Life*, p. 46.

haps they are even dispensable. The answer to the so-called vocations crisis might then be simply to allow the counsels to die out as outmoded and inessential.

Alternatively, perhaps the vows are in themselves the self-gift of love, in which case we can see the vows in terms of the fuller reality of an *imitatio Christi*, of the "self-holocaust" of love, and therefore as central to the gospel and Christian identity. This result would suggest that the vows of consecration constitute the actual act of love to which all are called, as it was lived out and embodied in Christ. But this second alternative would also seem to identify the state of perfection with perfection itself; to choose a state of life other than the consecrated state would seem to be the choice of a lesser love. But how can we say that choosing a lesser love is not choosing an "imperfect love"? We would therefore be left wondering about the "universal call to holiness" and whether the majority of the faithful can realistically live up to the new commandment — which comes from the lips of Jesus himself — to "love one another as I have loved you" (Jn 15:12) and, in doing so, to "be perfect as your heavenly Father is perfect" (Mt 5:48).

The Counsels as forma sui et totius

Balthasar's solution is grounded in "indifference," in the Ignatian sense of complete disponibility to God's will.[10] A Christian enters the state of the

---

10. It is important to note that Balthasar employs the word "indifference" in two different and fundamentally opposed senses, both of which are referred to in this article. The first of these is the sense alluded to here. Balthasar draws on the idea of "Ignatian indifference" to indicate the basic Christian stance of readiness for God's call and initiative, particularly as this readiness is manifested in relation to a potential vocation to the consecrated life. For Balthasar, this sort of indifference correlates with love. While it does not reject human desires and inclinations, it does involve a willingness to subordinate them to God's personal call. Indeed, the argument of this essay can be taken to suggest that indifference used in this sense takes up and radicalizes these desires and inclinations. But Balthasar also speaks of "freedom of indifference" (cf. *The Christian State of Life*, pp. 30-31), by which he means a type of freedom that has been reduced to pure "choice" and as such implies an impassive stance that objectifies and holds itself aloof from potential objects of love. As we shall see below, "freedom of indifference" correlates for Balthasar with a lack or at least weakened state of love. See Servais Pinckaers, *The Sources of Christian Ethics*, trans. Sr. Mary Noble (Washington, D.C.: The Catholic University of America Press, 1995), pp. 327-53, for a critical discussion of "freedom of indifference."

counsels only in response to a specific vocation. What is important, then, is not so much the particular state of life one enters as it is one's openness to God's possible call to the state of election. A state of life is therefore most fundamentally a "response," rather than an individual choice between a superior means and a "lesser," albeit still "good," means. In this way, Balthasar is able to account for the possible perfection of those who do not live in the "state of perfection" in terms of their prior and continuing openness to God's call in a particular state. Balthasar is quite insistent that it would be wrong for someone who is not called to the "state of election" to force his way into it.[11] Thus, the state of perfection may be "objectively superior,"[12] but it does not follow that it is subjectively so. Hence, the one who is open to whatever state God calls him to and is content simply to follow God's wishes has at least implicitly and potentially offered love in the form of the three vows of consecration. Because of this openness, his love may be said to carry the "inner form" of the evangelical counsels in the sense that it is ready to give all in the actual and explicit taking of those vows. Given this starting point of disponibility, the vows of the state of life to which an individual is in fact called take on analogously and hiddenly the "all" of the state of election.

The somewhat surprising result of what has been said thus far is that the significance of the vows of poverty, chastity, and obedience is effectively universalized. We can see this first in relation to the other Christian states of life. Claiming that the "inner form" of love is a vow means in the first instance that the vows of a state of life are the objective actualization of this form. The paradigmatic instance is the consecrated state, which partakes more directly in the "supra-sacramental" character of Christ's and Mary's virginity.[13] In an analogous way, the vows of the other states of life also actualize this "inner form" insofar as they take up an initial and continuing Christian disponibility.

Thus, the claim that love has the inner form of a vow serves the basic purpose of showing love's interior ordination to explicit vows, which become the fullest actualization of this "inner form," either directly in the counsels themselves or analogously (*mutatis mutandis*) in other states of life (Balthasar mentions the ordained priesthood, matrimony, and the

---

11. Balthasar, *The Christian State of Life*, pp. 54-55. See also *Vita consecrata*, 30 (1996).

12. *Vita consecrata*, 32.

13. Hans Urs von Balthasar, "The Layman and the Church," trans. Brian McNeil, in *Explorations in Theology*, vol. 2: *Spouse of the Word* (San Francisco: Ignatius Press, 1991), pp. 315-31; 315.

general Christian state of life inaugurated by the vows of Baptism). In other words, the real possibility of perfection outside of the counsels means essentially that the counsels are not only a particular state of life but also constitute the inner meaning and shape (the "inner form") of the whole of Christian and ecclesial life, precisely because this "form" is the form — and therefore "glory" — of God shining in Christ's and Mary's state of life. The counsels are not only one state of life, they are in some sense the inner meaning of the whole Christian life made explicit. As Balthasar puts it, the counsels are *forma sui et totius*. Each state of life, and indeed the entire moral life, must ultimately look to them to see its "inner form," even while each retains its integrity as such.

To speak in this way is also, however, to say something about the beginnings of love. If vows offer the basic possibility for the explicit actualization of love (i.e., a vow is the basic act of love), then this basic act shows us the nature of love's original ordination. We might say that a state of life, and the state of election in particular, shows us the objective structure and order of love as such, a structure and order that is already given prior to any individual, personal act. Indeed, all love, however primitive or seemingly inapt, bears within it this "inner form" insofar as all love is ultimately directed toward the fullness of explicit vows.

In a deep sense, then, vows are indeed a cause of love. They are a "cause," not so much because they are the means or training ground of love (although Balthasar is clear that in a fallen world of very imperfect love they are at least *in part* a "means"), but they are "cause" because they are implicit in the earliest moment of love as its very structure and its deepest meaning as directed toward communion, which is finally only realized in explicit vows. Thus, vows are not only the end or culmination of love, but also in some sense its beginning and formal cause.

The Problem of Love and Freedom

This leads us to our second objection, regarding the claim that the lover desires above all to rid himself of "freedom of choice," that "indifferent freedom" is the death of love.[14] Vows, such as those leading to consecration

---

14. Cf. Balthasar, *The Christian State of Life*, pp. 30-31. See footnote 10, above, regarding the meaning of "indifference."

or marriage, relinquish the possibility of choosing otherwise. Wouldn't religious life or marriage be more loving situations, therefore, if they were freely dissolvable?[15] In fact, this second issue logically follows upon the first insofar as it is precisely the claim concerning the fundamental character of vows that seems to threaten freedom. If love has the "inner form of a vow," we might suppose, it must also have a self-annihilating dynamic built into it. The question of freedom therefore quickly expands into a more general one: viz. the ambiguity inherent in different kinds or senses of love as "need-love" or "gift-love," *erōs* or *agapē*.[16] (I do, of course, recognize that the conceptual range contained in each of the two pairs, need/gift love and *erōs/agapē*, is not simply identical.) A presupposition of our discussion of vows is that love finds its culmination in self-gift and that vows are the means by which human creatures, who are situated in a world of time and movement, can take up and give themselves away.[17] We must ask, therefore, whether the sense of love realized in the desire for perfection or fulfillment, and all of the human values and goods associated with it, is lost by the claim concerning love and vows. This leads to two issues.

15. St. Thomas poses a variation of this basic question in an objection to his discussion of the necessity of religious vows for the state of perfection. The objection quotes Augustine: "The services we render are more pleasing when we might lawfully not render them, yet do so out of love." The objection goes on to argue that since "it is lawful not to render a service which we have not vowed, whereas it is unlawful if we have vowed to render it," it must also be "more pleasing to God to keep poverty, continence, and obedience without a vow." The objection then concludes, "a vow is not requisite for religious perfection." Indeed, the logic of the objection's argument could easily lead to a strengthened version of its conclusion: not only is a vow not requisite, but also it is in fact opposed to the realization of love. Thomas's response is the following: "Religious perfection requires that a man give his whole life to God." "Because that life taken as a whole is not simultaneous but successive," it is impossible to do this except by way of a vow. Hence, "[a]mong other services that we can lawfully give, is our liberty, which is dearer to man than aught else. Consequently when a man of his own accord deprives himself by vow of the liberty of abstaining from things pertaining to God's service, this is most acceptable to God." Thomas's response therefore relies on the idea of love as being most fundamentally constituted in a kind of "self-holocaust" (*ST* II-II, q. 186, a. 6, obj. 3 and ad 3).

16. For a thorough discussion of the "problem of love," see Margaret H. McCarthy, "'Husbands, Love Your Wives as Your Own Bodies': Is Nuptial Love a Case of Love or Its Paradigm?" pp. 291-93 in the present volume.

17. Balthasar seems most especially to have defined love in terms of self-gift: "[p]erfect love consists in the unconditional surrender of self, in the *donum Dei* . . ." (*The Christian State of Life*, p. 59).

First, the question concerning freedom is in part a question about the potential annihilation of the lover through the negation of human goods. Does the characterization of love as possessing the inner form of a vow, insofar as it entails the understanding of love as self-gift, undermine human values or the realization of authentic human goods, which can only be realized in freedom? Does it tend toward an alienating reduction of love, a one-sided evaluation that tends — as P. Rousselot puts it in his discussion of "ecstatic love"[18] — toward the "violent" and arbitrary suppression of what is most human, including natural inclinations and passions as those are so richly elaborated in Thomas's *Secunda Pars?*

Certainly, the significance of human striving for "perfection" in goods cannot simply be ignored. The question, then, is how to understand the authentic and necessary striving for those goods in relation to the objective actualization of love implied in explicit vows and the significance of the claim that the idea of a vow constitutes love's inner form from its very beginning. To put this in positive terms, if love possesses the interior form of a vow from its beginning, this can only be so insofar as vows indicate the interior meaning of *all* love, and therefore of all human striving for goods. This conclusion is, in fact, suggested by use of the idea of "wanting" *(wollen)* in the very passage we have been discussing — "How much more, then, does true love *want* [*will*] to outlast time and, for this purpose, to rid itself of its most dangerous enemy, its own freedom of choice."

The question of freedom's relation to vows is at the heart of the dramatic tension of human action. First of all, it is important to note that behind the goods and values for which human actors strive, and which constitute the ground of the movement of love, is the gratuity of being. The movement toward these goods, therefore, is already in some sense a movement toward their author, as well as toward the persons around us who draw us out of ourselves. It is the mother's smile and all that it discloses that, drawing the child beyond himself, starts him on a movement toward the fullness of love. The *desiderium naturale,* which underlies the movement toward God concretized in a state of life,[19] remains a latent capacity, until it is disclosed to the creature and launched toward its end through God's self-disclosure.[20]

18. Pierre Rousselot, *The Problem of Love in the Middle Ages* (Milwaukee: Marquette University Press, 2002).

19. David S. Crawford, *Marriage and the Sequela Christi* (Rome: PUL, 2004).

20. Cf. Hans Urs von Balthasar, *The Theology of Karl Barth: Exposition and Interpreta-

As a preliminary matter, this primordial *desiderium* ought not to be seen as opposed to human goods and values, since it is quintessentially human. The problem is that we tend to abstract human goods from their concrete meaning, which is always situated within a communion of persons. Thus our pursuit of those goods always occurs within a whole set of personal relations that both give me life and call me out of myself to its fullness. If we abstract them from their origin in communion, we then see the self-donation called for by the presence of the other as a threat to self-realization. We then characterize the goods, and indeed the final good, as if they were simply possibilities for my flourishing abstracted from the original call and gratuity standing behind those goods, and we therefore fail to locate that pursuit of goods sufficiently within the idea of a necessary self-donation entailed in their realization. The *desiderium* turns in on itself, positing others and even (or most especially) God, as occasions for "my flourishing." Such a result is less a grotesque inflation of the role of desire than it is desire's self-defeating enclosure within the bounds of its own solitude. Such a result would finally imply that there are no longer "others" who are not finally reducible to me. Thus, the desire that animates freedom in itself already implies the necessary capacity and need for the self-giving love essential to its perduring in human freedom and action *precisely as* the movement toward self-fulfillment.

Second, these considerations imply a re-centering of our basic presuppositions regarding the underlying freedom at stake. According to Balthasar, "freedom of choice" is the worst enemy of love insofar as it tends toward an objectification of the beloved and therefore a tacit distancing. It may very well be that I choose to remain loyal to the beloved, that I remain in the service of God, and so forth. Nevertheless, such an understanding of love presupposes a basic "indifference" with respect to the beloved, which ultimately degenerates into calculation.

We recoil from the objection that marriage vows, for example, should be freely dissolvable, because we recognize that love does not want to give away only this moment but to give away *every moment in this moment*. Anything less is to betray the essence of love. What is necessary for love to remain true is not only that it give without calculation, but that it

---

tion (San Francisco: Ignatius Press, 1992), pp. 295-99; Balthasar, *The Theology of Henri de Lubac* (San Francisco: Ignatius Press, 1991); Angelo Scola, *Hans Urs von Balthasar: A Theological Style* (Grand Rapids: Eerdmans, 1995), p. 88.

give more than it would ever be able to calculate. For love to be love, in other words, it must simultaneously be an act of faith.

Indeed, to give away only the moment, rather than the whole of one's life, is really not to have given away anything at all, since as Augustine suggests, "this moment," having no duration, fades infinitesimally into the background of an eternity that both encompasses and gives being to the whole: past, present, and future.[21] Thus the giving away of this moment, if it is truly a giving, necessarily also entails the implication and promise of the whole of one's time and eternity. To love for this moment, insofar as it truly is love, is already implicitly to have taken up and disposed of the whole, since the point in time we call the present moment cannot be abstracted from the whole without effectively ceasing to exist.

Hence the "love" that would reject the vow in favor of moment-by-moment gift cannot be the fullness of love, however much it may be filled with a certain passion that mimics and tacitly desires love's fullness.[22] Indeed, the understanding of freedom behind this concept of love is a kind of non-freedom insofar as it is not free — beyond its own alienation — to dispose of more than the fleeting and momentary present, a present nihilistically abstracted from the flow of time and dislocated historically from its part in the movement of the world toward its end.

Some Implications for Human Action

We have argued that a state of life is the paradigmatic actualization of the "inner form" of love and that this actualization offers an insight into love in its beginnings, as it is expressed in freedom and human action generally. Love, in the form of an original aptness for and participation in the good, necessarily always stands at the source of freedom and action.[23] Can the insight contained in Balthasar's formula, "love has the inner form of a vow," offer a deepening of our understanding of human action as a whole, and not only of the definitive action realized in a state of life?

---

21. St. Augustine, *Confessions*, XI.

22. Scola, "The Nuptial Mystery at the Heart of the Church," pp. 646-47.

23. Cf. *ST* I-II, q. 25, a. 2; Livio Melina, *Cristo e il dinamismo dell'agire: Linee di rinnovamento della Teologia Morale Fondamentale* (Rome: PUL, 2001), pp. 24-25.

David S. Crawford

The Radix of Action

One conclusion to be drawn at this point in our discussion is that any discussion of love is necessarily going to refer, sooner or later, to the Christian states of life.[24] My claim goes further, however. It seems to me that Balthasar's formulation of the relationship concerning love and vows suggests that the states of life should have a more prominent place in fundamental moral theology generally. Of course, the basic state of life, membership in the Body of Christ, is brought about in baptismal vows.[25] However, the vows of consecration (and, analogously, the vows of marriage and the priesthood) constitute a further articulation of this basic state of life. If an explicit vow makes the "inner form" of love concrete, then we could also say that a state of life constitutes something like what we might call, along with Thomas, a "radical act" *("radicem")* by which someone dedicates his "whole life to God,"[26] or what John Paul II calls a "decision of faith."[27]

We can conclude from the discussion so far, then, that the vows of a state of life constitute the quintessential moment of the Christian moral life and of its further instantiation in all of the innumerable actions of daily life. All of these actions, we might say, are both a *preparatio* for the love made visible in the "radical act" and, at the same time, an elaboration of the interior meaning of that "radical act."

If the actual vows of a state of life constitute this radical act, then it would seem that every action, insofar as it tends more or less (willy-nilly) toward this actualization, carries within it the implication or structure of such a vow. Now, my basic claim is that moral action always (at least implicitly) constitutes a personal commitment (and hence is "vow-like") to a

24. Thus, the question of the states of life is a central and recurring theme for Balthasar, and one that had profound implications for his understanding of his overall project and mission as a theologian (cf. *Our Task: A Report and a Plan* [San Francisco: Ignatius Press, 1994]). Indeed, the idea of the relation of vows and love is rooted in Balthasar's trinitarian theology and is closely related to his Christology and theology of mission, as well as to the priority he gives to the category of Beauty/Glory. The Son does not continually choose to follow the will of the Father as a possibility for an action toward which his freedom is structurally indifferent or neutral. Balthasar is careful to show that the idea of a vow is latent in the Son's relation to the Father (e.g., *The Christian State of Life*, pp. 35-37).

25. Balthasar, *The Christian State of Life*, p. 39.

26. *Quaestiones quodlibetales*, q. 3, a. 7, ad 6 (cited in *The Christian State of Life*, p. 62).

27. *Veritatis splendor* [*VS*], 66 (1993).

vision of reality as a whole and that this commitment implicitly entails a sacrifice, a certain loss of self, precisely at the heart of human action — viz. its desiring and striving after goods. The implication of these dual claims is clear: the basic inner form of love — the vow — is present in all loves, and therefore in all action, insofar as all action arises from and is a response to love. This is true however detached particular actions may seem from the explicit question of a state of life. Hence, my argument is intended to recuperate the idea of *"inner"* form — insofar as "inner" suggests what is at least initially "implicit" — from love's explicit realization in actual vows.

Let me elaborate two ways in which I think this is so.

Action as a Personal Commitment to the Real

If we consider the discussion of love and freedom above, we recognize that the horizons delineating the arena in which human action occurs are most fundamentally marked out by the movement and aspiration of the creature in relation to God's invitation. As John Paul II tells us, the moral life is a "response of love," which is "due to the many gratuitous initiatives taken by God out of love for man" (*VS*, 10). Indeed, the word "response" already suggests the idea of commitment or "pledge" or vow through its Latin root (*respondere,* which in turn is related to *spondere:* to pledge or vow). A "response" is a "pledge-in-return."

Within this basic character as "response," human action is always a personal commitment to *some* love, to the attachment to some object as good and indeed good *pro me.* However, every action, insofar as in the moment of its realization it necessarily takes up all of my time and eternity, is also a commitment to more than can in fact be known or controlled from within that action. Hence, human action always entails a commitment to much more than it is ever actually capable of performing or grasping. What is utterly unique about human action, what makes it in some sense more fundamental than speculation or contemplation abstracted from action, is that it takes up the entirety of the person in the passing moment of the action's placement in a way that determines and situates this "entirety" in relation to the whole of reality. Action makes the world real for me because it entails the most demanding possible commitment to the world precisely insofar as it puts everything that I am or ever will be on the line.

Indeed, it is on this point that the idea of morality — and the discipline of moral theology — stakes its claim. Without it, the idea of moral responsibility falls by the wayside, and we suffer a slide toward a number of the difficulties that have arisen in recent moral thought, according to which human actions tend to be reduced to simple "happenings" detached from the actor except by way of motivation, or which posit quotidian action as abstracted from a transcendental act of freedom. And yet this taking up of the whole of the actor constitutes a tremendous vulnerability insofar as no actor can predict or control or even know all of the global significance of his action. Hence, moral action is a binding of oneself through a commitment to a certain faith in the underlying character of reality in the implicit knowledge that this action is inadequate to the open-ended character of this commitment. Every action then is a staking of one's life on a vision of the whole of reality. And it is not until there is concrete commitment to reality as a whole, until the human person has committed himself to that vision, that one can be truly said to accept it.[28]

In this sense, then, as an open-ended commitment to a vision of reality as a whole — a commitment in which the risk of my existence is somehow taken up and engaged — genuine human action (actus humanus) possesses the "inner form" or the interior structure of a vow. Now, behind this commitment to reality as a whole, this "response" to the world as it presents itself, there is always the invitation of another who has set my being in motion and who calls me to himself. It is a commitment that takes up the whole of the actor in relation to this other. Hence this commitment is not simply self-referential — a vow to oneself, so to speak — but is implicitly a preparation for or an affirmation of an explicit vow, embodied in the radical act of a state of life.

---

28. Unlike ancient views according to which the Fates dictated a given human destiny, Christianity reincorporates the idea of a human destiny that is given from without, but locates the responsibility for achieving that destiny more solidly within the person himself. Also, the Christian claim is opposed to that of certain trends in modernity in which a kind of absolutizing of freedom as choice is accompanied (ironically) by various forms of determinism (cf. VS, 32-33). At the same time, Christian revelation implies that the idea of human freedom is mediated by God's ever-greater freedom. According to the Christian claim, action is always covering some distance or closing some previously indeterminate or unbridged gap between who I am and who I want to be. And yet this question of who I am and who I want to be is never entirely in our hands.

"Goods for the Person" and the "Good of the Person"

Within this commitment to a vision of reality as a whole, which clearly grounds the possibility of what *Veritatis splendor* refers to as the "good of the person," that is, the goodness of the person as such in his moral development and maturity, the tradition relates particular actions to goods as ends, what *Veritatis splendor* calls "goods for the person."[29] Now, if the argument up to now holds, then these goods have to be considered in relation to the states of life as radical act.

As the phrase "goods for the person" indicates, these goods for the person are not simply goods pertaining to a human nature understood in abstraction from that nature's concrete personal realization. These goods are in some way constitutively and intrinsically related to the complete good of the person, although the good of the person also transcends these goods both in their particularity and in their totality. The goods for the person are ingredient in the good of the person, but the good of the person is not simply their sum.

A basic question, then, is how to characterize this relation. Goods for the person, such as life itself, certainly are ingredient in the fullness of human flourishing. Yet the real possibility of martyrdom tells us that life, at least as such, even when combined more fully with the other goods for the person, is not yet the "good of the person." It is also clear that the moral actor who loves will want his own flourishing and that of those around him in human goods, but he will most of all want the good *of* the person for himself and his beloved.

---

29. John Paul II defines "the good of the person" as "the good which is the person himself and his perfection," while the "goods for the person" or "personal goods" are those goods that are "safeguarded by the commandments, which, according to St. Thomas, contain the whole natural law" (*VS*, 79; cf. *VS*, 13). Hence, the "good of the person" is most especially related to human goodness *simpliciter*, viz. a person's *moral goodness or perfection*, which in turn must be understood in terms of the human vocation in Christ. As *Veritatis splendor* tells us: "Acting is morally good when the choices of freedom are in conformity with man's true good and thus express the voluntary ordering of the person towards his ultimate end: God himself is the supreme good in whom man finds his full and perfect happiness. The first question in the young man's conversation with Jesus: 'What good must I do to have eternal life?' (Mt 19:16) immediately brings out *the essential connection between the moral value of an act and man's final end*" (*VS*, 72, emphasis original). The encyclical later tells us: "The primary and decisive element for moral judgment is the object of the human act, which establishes whether it [a moral action] is *capable of being ordered to the good and to the ultimate end which is God*" (*VS*, 79, emphasis original).

David S. Crawford

John Paul II tells us that "[t]he commandments thus represent the basic condition for love of neighbor; at the same time they are the proof of that love" (*VS*, 13). Later he adds that the goods protected by the commandments give way to their fullness in the Beatitudes, the "self-portrait of Christ" (*VS*, 16). When we situate particular "goods for the person" in this larger context of the "good of the person," we see that particular goods are never simply moments of human flourishing in abstraction from the flourishing-in-self-donation of human destiny itself. Insofar as human action is a response whose inner meaning and final perfection are disclosed by explicit vows, it is also ordered not simply toward achieving fulfillment in goods simply understood as appetible. Rather, particular goods are in themselves and as such occasions for flourishing-in-self-donation. That is to say, precisely in their realization as goods *pro me*, they also and simultaneously entail a kind of kenosis or sacrifice.

The point is not that the realization of human goods requires a prior or additional kenosis or sacrifice, that the goods are good only insofar as I approach them in accordance with the moral limitations imposed on my realization of them in moderation and consistent with the just and charitable relations I owe to my neighbor. Nor is the point that the goods are genuinely goods but that a higher good may be achieved by their sacrifice. Each of these statements is certainly valid. My point, however, is more fundamental, if not paradoxical. It is that each of the goods themselves, precisely insofar as it is good for me, also demands a kind of kenosis in the realization of that good. In short, it is not that self-emptying is the necessary context or precondition for receiving the good in an authentic way. It is that the good itself is intrinsically kenotic. To the extent I try to abstract the flourishing promised by a particular good from the sacrifice it demands, I will invert the good I seek and the flourishing it promises into something other than that to which I had originally aspired.

This may become more concrete if we give an example. We can take the inclinations, and the goods to which they point, on which Thomas bases natural law.[30] Among these is that of union with a member of the opposite sex for the sake of procreation. That there is a natural inclination to union and procreation indicates that it is in itself a good for the person and therefore an enrichment of his being. But it is not only such an enrichment, and therefore not only an aspect of the "good of the person," but also a genuine

30. *ST* I-II, q. 94, a. 2.

258

"good for the person," insofar as it also demands a kind of death or kenosis. In order to give birth adequately, to give to this good — precisely as a good for me — what it demands as a good, I have to abase myself before new human life. I must understand that the inner meaning of really giving birth is that I must decrease so that this new person may increase.

Each of the other inclinations/goods cited by Thomas, it seems to me, could be given a similar construction. Thus, for example, the fundamental good of life itself is not simply the good of existence for myself but — at the same time — the good of existence for another. To live only for oneself is not to have achieved a genuine "human value" or "good." If love alone offers us the explanation of human existence (if love alone is credible), then it is because life and being finally mean the welcoming of another, which itself is to achieve the fullness of life and of being. Anything less is to have failed to have adequately achieved the good of existence and life, precisely as such. Thus, if we think once again of martyrdom, we realize that the genuine sacrifice represented in this witness is not the sacrifice of the good of life per se (to speak in this way is to abstract the good for the person from the good of the person), it is rather to have realized the interior meaning of that good. Again, therefore, implied in the very good of personal life is the reality of "death" for another. Similar statements could be made regarding the human goods of life in society and knowledge of the truth (which is most fully the knowledge of God), although each case of course would naturally take different and analogous forms. To strive for goods in abstraction from this necessary sacrifice that they entail is, in fact, to shy away from the fullest meaning of those goods. Thus, the theme of sacrifice is not a supererogatory addition to the main subject of moral theology in its consideration of human acts.

The implication of this point, then, is that the good of the person (the inner form of a vow as commitment to a vision of reality as a whole) is both contained within and yet exceeds each particular good for the person.

Implications for Action as Elaboration of States of Life

A final implication, whose full elaboration exceeds the scope of our present task, follows from what has just been said about the fulfillment-in-sacrifice implied in human goods. We have seen that the explicit vows of a state of life offer a matrix from which all human action takes its particular

and explicit direction. All action therefore implicitly takes up the prior reality of the vows of a state of life, and all actions therefore relate directly to
that state of life. All of the goods to be striven for in action are goods in relation to the vows of a state of life. The states of life themselves shape human action from the inside, and determine the structure and meaning of
moral action from the beginning. Because the states of life constitute different modalities of the actualization of love, and because as such they take
up particular human goods differently, the different states of life result in
different moral-theological "styles." These "styles" are determined by the
relation of the states to the meaning of the necessary commitment and
sacrifice entailed in goods for the person as ends in relation to the good of
the person. Thus, for example, the good of union with the opposite sex
and procreation is not simply lost in virginity, but it is realized in a different and higher modality and, as Balthasar reminds us, in a way that exceeds the limited bounds and particularity of the natural family. As such,
then, we have a basis for saying that the whole of moral action in its relation to virtues and obligations takes on differing meanings and significance given different states of life.

"Husbands, Love Your Wives as Your Own Bodies": Is Nuptial Love a Case of Love or Its Paradigm?

Margaret H. McCarthy

Introduction

We all think that we know what love is. Whether we refer to it casually or in earnest, we take what "love" means for granted. I love chocolate. God is love. She loves to dance. We ought to love our fellow man. Jennifer Lopez loves her husband. For that matter, I love my husband too! When, however, we have to say what love is, things are not so simple. Concerning the elusiveness of love's meaning, Paul Evdokimov wrote perceptively, "None of the great thinkers or poets have ever found an answer to the question, 'What is love?' . . . If one imprisons the light, it slips through the fingers."[1]

If we look at all that we ascribe to love, we notice that it is by no means easy to draw it all together. There is affection for things and persons we did not choose, and might not have chosen had we been given a choice: a brother, a great-aunt, or a hand-me-down sweater. On the other hand, we also say we love what is purely a matter of preference or "choice": cheesecake, red wine, herring with sour cream. There is the emotion, or passion, of love, which arises in us when the sense of some affinity is kindled in us. Love is benevolence (wanting the good) towards one whom we regard as uniquely precious. There is also that vehement or passionate *erōs*, which transports the lover beyond himself and toward Beauty itself

---

1. *The Sacrament of Love* (Crestwood, N.Y.: St. Vladimir's Seminary Press, 1995), p. 105. Evdokimov echoes Socrates, who, after a long dialogue on friendship, says: "These fellows will say, as they go away, that we suppose we're one another's friends — for I also put myself among you — but what he who is a friend is we have not yet been able to discover" (*Lysis,* 223a).

(though this sort of love can turn in on itself, becoming a kind of vulgar — demonic — imitation of its elevated form). Finally, there is God's love *(Agapē)*, the Love he is and the Love he has for his creatures, revealed to us in the Son's incarnation and cross.[2] And for all of this we insist on using one little word.

In this regard it might seem that the English language is impoverished — although many other languages are every bit as monoglot when it comes to love. Some differences, it is true, present only nuances, such as the terms "liking" and "loving," as when we wish to refer, say, to pleasing aspects of a person as distinguished from the person as a whole. But others appear to have little if anything to do with each other.[3] For better or for worse, the little all-purpose word has its irresistible way of holding together, in a kind of tension, two apparently very different senses of love, which have been described — a little simplistically perhaps — as "need love" and "gift love."[4] The first of these loves would gather up all of those expressions of desire and yearning which human creatures (beggars all) have for happiness and fulfillment. The second would refer instead to more "self-giving" kinds of love, whereby the lover puts himself at the service of the beloved. Clearly, the tension between these two senses of love does not mark a distinction between individuals so much as one that wells up from within every human being. We want to flourish; we want happiness; so we love ourselves. At the same time, we find ourselves to be together with others who aspire to be loved as we love ourselves and want to

---

2. One hardly has to be reminded of C. S. Lewis's masterful presentations of the different meanings of love in his *The Four Loves* (New York: Harcourt Brace, 1960).

3. Josef Pieper takes up this accusation of linguistic "impoverishment" where love is concerned in the introduction to his *About Love,* now published as *Faith, Hope, Love* (San Francisco: Ignatius Press, 1997), pp. 1-8. Anders Nygren is perhaps the most famous for his critique of history's (Augustine's) grievous error of mixing up *Erōs* and *Agapē,* which in his view are "two conceptions which have originally nothing whatsoever to do with one another" (cf. *Agape and Eros,* trans. P. Watson [London: SPCK, 1982], p. 30).

4. These are the terms with which C. S. Lewis first began his exploration of love. As he explains in the preface of his *Four Loves* (pp. 11-21), this division, which at first represented a simplistic division between selfishness and true love, had quickly to be abandoned. The most obvious problem with this division is that one easily misses with "need love" the fact that yearning for that which ultimately fulfills is not simply "acquisitive," but can be very "ecstatic" and self-forgetful. At the same time, a lack or suppression of need is not so easily identified with the "other-centeredness" of "gift love." That love, on the other hand, is itself accompanied by the greatest experience of joy and fulfillment.

be loved, namely "for our own sakes," and not as a mere means to another's fulfillment.

It is generally agreed upon in the tradition, and not less so by those with a more "eudaimonistic" orientation, that a love that ventures out, in a calculating way, toward a loved one only to return, having secured what was previously lacking, is inferior to a love that aims wholeheartedly at the Beloved, at his good.[5] But once this "hierarchy" has been established (even with different emphases) a problem still remains. How is the relation between the love one has for oneself and for one's own happiness or fulfillment, and one's love of another "for his own sake" to be conceived? This problem, which is sometimes called the *erōs-agapē* problem, goes to the heart of the "problem of love."

In his short treatise on love in the Middle Ages,[6] Pierre Rousselot set forth the two medieval solutions to the problem concerning the *relation* between the two loves. As Rousselot notes in his "Preface" to the work, ev-

---

5. In Plato's *Phaedrus,* Lysius's carefully thought-out and regulated, risk-free and, for that matter, love-free, exchange of (sexual) favors in view of one's own self-interests is ultimately trumped by *Erōs,* which for Socrates is something divine, for the reason that it arouses in the lover an awe and reverence for the beloved akin to that for a god (251). Aristotle marks the two loves very clearly with his distinction between a friendship between those who love each other *absolutely* — "for their own sakes" — and one between friends who love each other accidentally on account of usefulness or pleasure (*Ethics* VIII, iii, 6). (St. Thomas resorted often to this distinction with his own between "love of friendship" and "love of concupiscence" [cf. *ST* I-II, 26, 4].) The New Testament, of course, is no less demanding in its implicit ranking of loves: "Do nothing out of selfishness or out of vainglory; rather, humbly regard others as more important than yourselves, each looking out not for his own interest, but everyone for those of others" (Phil 2:3-4); "No one should seek one's own advantage, but that of one's neighbor" (1 Cor 10:24). The Fathers, beginning with the Cappadocians, became explicit in their ranking of the different motives for loving God (based on elements in the New Testament): the slave's love of God *for fear of punishment,* the hireling's love of God *for hope of reward,* the son's or friend's love of God *for his own sake.* (For a good discussion of the "problem of love" in the Fathers, see A. Vincelette's introduction to P. Rousselot's *The Problem of Love in the Middle Ages* [Milwaukee: Marquette University Press, 2002], pp. 70-75.) St. Augustine is noted for his distinction between the love of "enjoyment" (where what is loved is loved for its own sake) and love of "use" (where what is loved is employed in view of obtaining what is loved for its own sake). Cf. *On Christian Doctrine,* 1.4.

6. Pierre Rousselot, "Pour l'histoire du problème de l'amour au moyen âge," *Beiträge zur Geschichte der Philosophie des Mittelalters: Texte und Untersuchungen,* vol. 6, no. 6, ed. C. Baeumker and G. Freih von Hertling (Münster: Aschendorff, 1908), recently published as *The Problem of Love in the Middle Ages.*

eryone in the medieval debate agreed that God was to be loved for himself (and so not merely as a means). There was also agreement that he was to be loved more than oneself. At the same time, however, he was understood to be the author of the unique and final end of the natural appetite. It seemed therefore to all parties that the solution to the general problem of reconciling love of self (wanting happiness for oneself) with a pure ("disinterested") love of another could be found in the question concerning man's love of God. But how was this reconciliation or convergence to be understood? Were the two loves founded on a duality and as such irreducible,[7] or were they the twofold expression of one identical appetite for happiness?[8] Was the love of another "ecstatic" and therefore violently cut off from, or at least radically discontinuous with, self-love (based on the natural inclination to happiness), or was it "physical," that is "natural," and thus an extension of that necessary propensity of beings to seek their own good?[9] Different biblical texts could be invoked in favor of either position. There are the various texts that refer to self-denial,[10] but then in those very counsels is the promise of "finding oneself."[11] On the other hand, there is the commandment to "love your neighbor as yourself."[12]

The following essay wishes to broach the question that was at the heart of the medieval debate, namely, to repeat, how the relation between love of self and love of the other is to be conceived. This essay will do so, however, in view of the specific love (or friendship) between a man and a

7. The most famous of the medieval theologians holding that the love of self (rooted in the desire for happiness) was at odds with a pure love of God was Peter Abelard. See E. Dublanchy, "Charité," in *Dictionnaire de Théologie Catholique,* vol. 2, no. 2, ed. A. Vacant, E. Mangenot, and E. Amann (Paris: Librairie Letouzey et Ané, 1932), pp. 2217-28. More recently L.-B. Geiger, by way of a criticism of Rousselot, claimed the "ecstatic" view as St. Thomas's own in *Le problème de l'amour chez Saint Thomas d'Aquin* (Montreal: Institut d'Études Médiévales, 1962).

8. This position Rousselot claimed as St. Thomas's own in "Pour l'histoire du problème de l'amour."

9. Rousselot, "Pour l'histoire du problème de l'amour," pp. 76-77.

10. Mark 8:34: "If any man would come after me, let him deny himself and take up his cross and follow me." 1 Cor 10:24: "Let no one seek his own good, but the good of his neighbor."

11. Mark 8:35-37: "Whoever would save his life will lose it; and whoever loses his life for my sake and the gospel's will save it. For what does it profit a man, to gain the whole world and forfeit his life? For what can a man give in return for his life?"

12. The text from Leviticus 19:18 is called upon frequently in the Thomistic and Aristotelian theory that all love, even love for God, is caused *in via generationis* by self-love (cf. Aquinas, *3 Sent.,* d. 29, a. 3, ad 3).

woman, a love that has been called "nuptial love."[13] In that particular case of love, as is clear, we have not only two distinct persons, the relation between whom is already problematic enough (according to the aforementioned "problem"), but two who possess their humanity bodily in two distinct and mutually exclusive manners. The difference between the two sexes, which cuts through every level of human being,[14] might seem — to some who would take this form of love seriously — more than merely one sort of love among many, and might seem to validate forcefully the position described as "ecstatic," wherein loving the other requires a radical departure from, or at least a momentary deflection from one's love of self, and therewith from one's search for happiness.[15] On the other hand, when

13. We follow Angelo Scola, who refers to the term "as the inseparable intertwining of sexual difference, love, and fruitfulness" (*The Nuptial Mystery*, trans. Michelle K. Borras [Grand Rapids: Eerdmans, 2005], p. xx). It should be noted that by this term we are not speaking always exclusively of marriage, but include also those relations that are taken up into "virginity for the Kingdom of God." Scola states that "virginity is the culmination of nuptiality — even for spouses" for the reason that it points to the ultimate meaning of indissolubility, namely loving the other as "other," in his or her own destiny ("The Nuptial Mystery at the Heart of the Church," *Communio* 25 [Winter 1998]: 658). For this understanding of virginity Scola is indebted to Luigi Giussani (cf. *Il Tempo e il Tempio* [Milan: Biblioteca Universale Rizzoli, 1995], pp. 11-35). On this broader notion of nuptiality see also Hans Urs von Balthasar (*The Christian State of Life* [San Francisco: Ignatius Press, 1983], pp. 224-49) as well as John Paul II (*The Theology of the Body* [Boston: Pauline Books and Media, 1997], pp. 276-78, 285-87).

14. Commenting on this difference, Hans Urs von Balthasar writes: "The male body is male throughout, right down to each cell of which it consists, and the female body is utterly female; and this is also true of their whole empirical experience and ego-consciousness. At the same time both share an identical human nature, but at no point does it protrude, neutrally, beyond the sexual difference, as if to provide neutral ground for mutual understanding. Here there is no *universale ante rem*, as all theories of a nonsexual or bisexual (androgynous) primitive human being would like to think. The human being, in the completed creation, is a "dual unity" (*Theo-Drama*, vol. 2: *Dramatis Personae: Man in God* [San Francisco: Ignatius Press, 1990], p. 364).

15. Dietrich von Hildebrand, in his book *Man and Woman* (Manchester, N.H.: Sophia Institute Press, 1992), seems to take this view when he begins by separating love "in its authentic sense," namely, "the love for another person, for a *thou*" from "vague analogies of love, such as the desire for self-perfection" (pp. 8-9). Hildebrand would found love not upon appetite, which reduces an object to that which satisfies a need, but upon response evoked by a value that is important-in-itself (pp. 15-17). See also "Prolegomena," *Das Wesen der Liebe*, in *Dietrich von Hildebrand, Gesammelte Werke*, ed. Der Dietrich von Hildebrand Gesellschaft, vol. 3 (Regensburg: J. Habbel, 1971), pp. 13-29.

we consider the natural tendency that the sexes have for each other, and the joy and fulfillment that accompanies their encounter, it is hard to see how the love of the other sex can be so severed from one's own desire for happiness. Indeed, in the so-called "physical" approach, which is the more dominant one in the tradition, this nuptial love would be included among the loves, or friendships for others, which proceed from a love for oneself and help to realize it, even if, or rather, especially, when the beloved is loved "for his own sake."[16]

According to that more dominant account, however, the love between a man and a woman as such seems not only to be one among many cases of love but in fact even one of love's lower forms.[17] And this, it seems, is due to the *differences* that so mark it. In contrast, loves or friendships of a more perfect sort would, in the account to which we are referring, be so in virtue of a certain kind of *similarity*.[18] If, however, nuptial love has been placed by the Christian tradition "front and center" as the first and paradigmatic expression of love among other loves, as it appears,[19] what would

16. For a very thorough exposition of love of self as the cause of friendship for others *in via generationis,* according to the thought of St. Thomas, see D. Gallagher, "Desire for Beatitude and Love of Friendship in Thomas Aquinas," *Medieval Studies* 58 (1996): 1-47.

17. According to his triple ranking of loves (friendships), Aristotle considered the friendship of man and wife as such to be one of utility and pleasure combined — both of which were ranked below friendship based on virtue — insofar as the man and woman, with their different functions, supply each other's wants (*Nicomachean Ethics* VIII, xii, 7). He also notes that between a husband and wife there can be a friendship of virtue if they be of high moral character, but it appears that this possible friendship of virtue is not had in and through the difference of sex which specifies their relation. Where this difference is taken into account, Aristotle identifies the friendship chiefly as one of use and pleasure combined.

18. St. Thomas takes similitude to be the proper cause of love (*ST* I-II, q. 27, a. 3), but according to its twofold expression. A similitude between two things that have the same quality actually gives rise to a "love of friendship" (love in the fuller sense) where the lover takes the friend to be one with him and wishes good to him as to himself. A similitude between two things, one that possesses it actually and the other potentially, gives rise, he says, to an expectation of something that is desired, hence to a "love of concupiscence," that is, a love founded on usefulness or pleasure (*ST* I-II, q. 27, a. 3, obj. 4 and ad 4). It would seem that the difference between man and woman which gives rise to a nuptial love *as such* would be classified as this dissimilar kind of "similitude," giving rise to a "love of concupiscence" (cf. *ST* I-II, q. 28, a. 4, c).

19. So central is this, says Balthasar, that the contemplation of being itself, within the sphere of the Church, is a "being dedicated and taken up into the mystery of the nuptiality between God and the world, which has its glowing heart in the marital mutuality of Christ

this hallowing of nuptial love signify for our understanding of love generally, and more specifically for our understanding of the relation between
the love of one's self and the love of another, on the supposition that these
two loves are compatible? This is the question that this brief essay wishes
to explore.

With that in mind we will proceed by considering the basic features
and rankings of friendships in the Aristotelian account and then the same
in the Thomistic account, looking carefully at the criteria for such ranking
as well as the understanding of the relation or unity between friends (lovers) in the different degrees of love. While doing this we shall note with
particular attention those few places where the friendship between husband and wife is expressly connected to the question of the different degrees of love and friendship. Finally, referring to the work of Hans Urs von
Balthasar and the "theology of the body" of John Paul II, as well as to
Angelo Scola's thought on "nuptial love" (which is indebted to that of
Balthasar and John Paul II), we will consider the nature of the relation between man and woman as expressed in the categories of "original unity"
and "unity of the two" (for John Paul II),[20] "dual unity" (for Balthasar),[21]
and "asymmetrical reciprocity" (for Scola),[22] all with an eye to its implications for the particular problem, in the theory of love, of the relation between love of self and love of other.

Friendship of Pleasure, Use, and Virtue According to Aristotle

Towards the end of his *Ethics*, Aristotle moves to the question of friendship
which, now — a smaller, more intimate community than that of the polis,
in view from the beginning — is the ethos of the virtuous life.[23] There Aristotle outlines the features of friendship. "Friendship" in its most basic

---

and the Church" (cf. *Explorations in Theology*, vol. 2: *Spouse of the Word* [San Francisco:
Ignatius Press, 1991], p. 368).

20. *The Theology of the Body*, pp. 42-48.

21. *Theo-Drama* 2, pp. 365-82.

22. Scola, "The Nuptial Mystery at the Heart of the Church," pp. 643-45.

23. *Nicomachean Ethics* VIII. See Paul J. Wadell, *Friendship and the Moral Life* (Notre
Dame, Ind.: University of Notre Dame Press, 1989), for a discussion of the significance of
Aristotle's "shift" to friendship after a long series of "lecture notes" on the moral life (pp. 44-
69).

sense is between persons who consciously wish each other's good (or "have good will for each other") and who frequent each other's society.[24] This basic meaning is then quickly broken down into three kinds according to the three qualities that arouse liking or love, and in virtue of which friends wish each other good. Such qualities are the pleasant, the useful, and the good.[25] So the good will that friends wish each other is based on one of the three lovable qualities and this, in turn, gives rise to one of three kinds of friendship.

Once Aristotle observes the different kinds of friendship, he ranks them. In the case of friendship of pleasure and friendship of use, friends, we are told, "do not love each other in themselves, but in so far as some benefit accrues to them from each other."

> [I]n friendship based on utility, or on pleasure, men love their friend for their own good or their own pleasure, and not as being the person loved, but as useful or agreeable. And therefore these friendships are based on an accident, since the friend is not loved for being what he is, but as affording some benefit or pleasure as the case may be.[26]

The example provided for the friendship based on pleasure is that between witty people who enjoy each other's society "not because of what they are in themselves but because they are agreeable."[27] These friendships of utility and pleasure, though "accidental," are not to be understood as exploitative friendships, for after all a certain "mutual wishing of the good for the friend's own sake" is implied in friendship as such.[28] In the friendship between two witty men one likes his friend because he is agreeable but also wants to be agreeable in return. It is the same in a friendship of utility, where the friend wants to be useful in return (perhaps in the form of payment). And, of course, to repeat, they enjoy each other's company.

The highest form of friendship which is based on the good exists between the virtuous,[29] and it is the friendship in which friends "wish each

---

24. *Ethics* VIII, ii, 1156, and VIII, v, 1157.

25. *Ethics* VIII, ii, 1155b.

26. *Ethics* VIII, iii, 1156a.

27. *Ethics* VIII, iii, 1156a.

28. *Ethics* VIII, ii, 1156a.

29. Aristotle will say not only that this third friendship is between the virtuous, but that it is the very relationship that is necessary for men to be virtuous. One might therefore note a certain dilemma here. How can the very friendship that is crucial for the moral life be

alike the other's good in respect of their goodness."[30] These friends "are friends in the fullest sense, since they love each other for themselves and not accidentally."[31] Here friendship finds its perfect form;[32] for, as P. Wadell notes, "there is this unity between what is loved and the person who is loved, between the good that is sought and the person who embodies it."[33]

It is not, of course, that such friends are not also pleasant and profitable for each other. They are and abundantly so; but they are so on the grounds of their absolute goodness, which goodness *is the chief object of affection.*[34] We might say that, in the case of this friendship among the virtuous, the pleasure or gain that comes from the friend is never one that bypasses the absolute good of the friend. In this vein, friends are also good for each other;[35] but they are so because the kind of friendship they have is the environment in which virtue can be lived, and more precisely, is the relationship by which men become good.[36] In the friendship between the virtuous, there is thus a unity not only between the good willed and the person who is loved (each wants for the other his absolute good, his perfection, that is); there is also a unity between the good of the person loved and the good of the one loving, for precisely in wanting the fullness or perfection of his friend, one becomes himself more perfect.

---

the preserve of the already virtuous? P. Wadell suggests as a solution that "Aristotle calls these relationships perfect not so much because of the qualities of the friends, though it is partly that, but more exactly because of the moral possibilities of the friendship" (*Friendship and the Moral Life*, pp. 54-55).

30. *Ethics* VIII, iii, 1156a.

31. *Ethics* VIII, iii, 1156a.

32. Aristotle elsewhere calls this friendship "friendship in the primary and proper meaning of the term," comparing it with the other kinds which are only friendships in an analogical sense, "since such friends are friends in virtue of a sort of goodness and of likeness in them; inasmuch as pleasure is good in the eyes of pleasure-lovers" (*Ethics* VIII, iv, 1157).

33. Wadell, *Friendship and the Moral Life*, pp. 52-53.

34. *Ethics* VIII, iii, 1156b.

35. "Each is good relatively to his friend as well as absolutely, since the good are both good absolutely and profitable to each other" (*Ethics* VIII, iii, 1156b).

36. Clearly, for Aristotle, the highest of friendships is itself one of the highest goods for those in such friendships (*Ethics*, IX, ix, 1169b-1170b). Cf. Wadell, who treats Aristotle's response in Book IX of the *Ethics* to the provocative popular dictum: "When fortune favors us, what need of friends?" (*Friendship and the Moral Life*, pp. 61-62).

Margaret H. McCarthy

Once Aristotle has set forth the three kinds of friendship and ranked them, he introduces the distinction between equal and unequal friendships.[37] In his initial exposition of the three kinds of friendship, Aristotle has in mind "friendships of equality," in which both parties "render the same benefit and wish the same good to each other, or else exchange two different benefits, for instance pleasure and profit."[38] The key here seems to be that the friends are both lovable and exchange good will to each other *to the same degree.*[39] Aristotle will refer to this equality as an "equality of quantity."[40] But it is also clear that "equality" indicates, as well, the similarity in the good that is loved and exchanged, be it pleasure, utility, or the good absolutely speaking. This aspect of equality, Aristotle says, renders friendships (between equals) more lasting: "[F]riendship is most lasting when each friend derives the same benefit, for instance pleasure, from the other, and not only so, but derives it from the same thing, as in a friendship between two witty people." When this does not happen, that is, when friends do not derive from each other the same benefit (e.g., pleasure or utility) or, in the event that they do, but not from the same thing, the friendship will be less enduring. The example provided of just such a friendship is that between "lover and beloved"[41] (a sexual love, which by no means should be assumed to be that between a man and a woman, even if it ought to include it), where both find pleasure in each other, but in different things, the lover "in gazing at his beloved," and the beloved, "in receiving the attentions of the lover."[42]

When Aristotle begins to take up unequal friendship explicitly, he indicates quite clearly the superiority of one party over the other. Examples he provides of such friendships are between father and son, between an older person and a younger, between husband and wife, and between any ruler and the persons ruled.[43] From the basic inequality within each of these and other similar friendships, other inequalities are derived, it seems,

37. *Ethics* VIII, vii, 1158b.
38. *Ethics* VIII, vi, 1158b.
39. This seems clear when Aristotle begins to introduce the category of unequal friendship by saying: "there is a different kind of friendship, which involves superiority of one party over the other" (*Ethics* VIII, vii, 1158b).
40. *Ethics* VIII, vii, 1158b.
41. *Ethics* VIII, iv, 1157a.
42. *Ethics* VIII, iv, 1157a.
43. *Ethics* VIII, iv, 1157a.

namely the differences in "function," "motive," "affection," and "benefits."[44] Here then is not only the disparity in "how much" one ought to be loved, due to the fact that one of the parties is more worthy than the other (because more useful, more pleasant, or more excellent), but also a disparity in the good (the "motive") that is loved in the other and the benefits received and given. A father does not love in the son the same as the son loves in the father, for the father loves his son as his offspring, as part of himself, and the son his father as the author of his being;[45] and this in turn explains the difference in what each renders to the other (reverence in the case of the son and care in the case of the father).[46]

As regards the relation between husband and wife as such, it is taken for granted that it is a friendship of unequals in the basic sense, that is, where one of the parties is better.[47] But it is also a friendship of unequals because the man and the woman have different functions by which they supply each other's wants by putting their special capacities into the common stock.[48] This can be seen in both of the aspects that specify the relation between husband and wife, namely, domestic life and the generative act, each of which is good in differing ways. And in these two main aspects of the relation between husband and wife, Aristotle sees a combination of friendship of use and of pleasure, in which the woman and the man are mutually useful and pleasant but in differing ways.[49]

Within the context of unequal friendships, the theme of "opposites" (or contraries) which attract is also raised.[50] Examples of friendships that stem from opposition are those between a poor man and a rich one or a

44. *Ethics* VIII, iv, 1158b.

45. *Ethics* VIII, xii, 1161b.

46. *Ethics* VIII, xii, 1158b.

47. *Ethics* VIII, xi, 1161a.

48. *Ethics* VIII, xii, 1162a. In St. Thomas's commentary he notes: "[t]hese functions — it is immediately apparent — are so divided between man and woman that some are proper to the husband, like external works; and others to the wife, like sewing and other domestic occupations. Thus mutual needs are provided for, when each contributes his own services for the common good" (*In VIII Eth. lect* 12, n. 1721).

49. Aristotle adds that the friendship between man and woman can be based on virtue "if the partners be of high moral character." It might seem that this would be so *in spite of* the difference of the sexes (which seems to be tied to the "supplying of needs," etc.), but then he adds the interesting note: "for either sex has its special virtue, and this may be the ground of attraction" (*Ethics* VIII, xii, 1162a). Cf. note 17.

50. *Ethics* VIII, viii, 1159b.

learned man and an ignorant one, or indeed between the lover and be-loved when one is beautiful and the other plain.[51] Above all, such friend-ships between opposites seem to give rise to friendships of utility; for the rich man and the learned man are clearly loved because they have some-thing that the inferior party lacks and wishes to gain. (The inferior party will, of course, give something useful in return but, as he is inferior, he cannot reasonably ask to be loved or considered useful to the same de-gree.) Interestingly here, Aristotle notes that in these friendships the at-traction is not so much to the opposite as to the mean between them (and therefore to an overcoming of the opposition).[52]

Once all of the "inequities" of such friendships are indicated, it be-comes necessary to explain how such friendships can be possible. They are so, it seems, in virtue of another kind of equality, that of proportion, where each of the parties is loved according to his worth.[53] When Aristotle likens the friendship between husband and wife to the relation between rulers and subjects in an aristocracy, he resorts to the principle of proportion where "the better party receives the larger share of good, whilst each party receives what is appropriate to each."[54] Proportion provides, then, a sort of balance in friendships between unequals. Such balance, or equality, how-ever, can only go so far. In cases of great disparity, proportionate love is in-capable of either bringing together or holding together two "friends."[55] And this is evidence that in friendship "'equal in quantity' is the primary meaning, and 'proportionate to desert' only secondary."[56]

Considering the three kinds of friendship, it is clear that friendship based on the good of the friends (where they are loved for themselves) is superior to the other two, in which the friends are loved in an accidental way (notwithstanding appearances closely resembling their superior rela-tive). Moreover, looking at both equal and unequal friendships, it is clear that as regards the possibility and durability of friendships, equality of

---

51. *Ethics* VIII, viii, 1159b.

52. *Ethics* VIII, viii, 1159b.

53. *Ethics* VIII, vii, 1158b.

54. *Ethics* VIII, xi, 1161a. St. Thomas comments on this, drawing out implications for the governance of the household: "the husband, being more worthy, is placed over the wife; however, the husband does not direct the affairs belonging to the wife" (*In VIII Eth. lect.* XI, n. 1694).

55. *Ethics* VIII, vii, 1159a.

56. *Ethics* VIII, vii, 1158b.

quantity is preferable as is similarity of the good that brings friends together. As regards the friendship between husband and wife as such, it is one between unequals and, when considered according to that which specifies it, is primarily a combination of friendship of use and of pleasure, in which each finds the other useful or pleasant in different manners.

Before we turn to the way in which St. Thomas ranks loves, we shall briefly note a key ingredient in Aristotle's philosophy of love. It appears after the distinctions we have just entertained and we thus assume that it is, for Aristotle, an ingredient in all of the friendships he has outlined, though only analogously in the two lower friendships. This ingredient will assume a large role in St. Thomas's doctrine of love and in fact will be the criterion for his basic distinction. It is precisely this: that the good will one has for a friend seems to be derived from the good will one has for oneself.[57] The very terms of good will, that is, by which one can identify a friendship (e.g., wishing the good of another for his own sake, wishing his existence and preservation, desiring his company, desiring the same things, and sharing his joys and sorrows)[58] are what one has first and most fully for himself.[59] If then they are characteristics of a *friendship*, it is because one "feels towards his friend in the same way as towards himself (for a friend is another self)."[60] As we turn now to St. Thomas's ranking of loves, we will see this conception of unity (identifying a friend with oneself) linked to the highest form of friendship.

Love of Concupiscence and Love of Friendship in St. Thomas

It is within the context of Thomas's discussion of love as the first of all the passions that he introduces us, in a thematic way, to his famous distinction between "love of concupiscence" and "love of friendship," a distinction

57. *Ethics* IX, iv.
58. *Ethics* IX, iv.
59. When treating the question of whether one ought to love oneself or one's friend the most, Aristotle notes: "we admit that one should love one's best friend most; but the best friend is he that, when he wishes a person's good, wishes it for that person's own sake, even though nobody will ever know of it. Now this condition is most fully realized in a man's regard for himself, as indeed are all the other attributes that make up the definition of a friend . . ." (*Ethics* IX, viii, 1163b).
60. *Ethics* IX, iv, 1166a.

that identifies the twofold tendency within every act of love.[61] By way of eliminating one of the obvious difficulties in understanding this distinction, we should say at the outset that the word "concupiscence" is connected here simply with the general idea of desire and in no way has a pejorative sense, nor does it indicate a tendency only to sensible things.

Calling upon the Philosopher's definition of love, namely, that "to love is to want the good for someone," Thomas identifies two objects in the movement of love, *the good* which is wished or wanted for someone, be it himself or another, and *the one for whom* he wishes that good (again, himself or another). Echoing Aristotle, Thomas notes a point that is perhaps missed when we think of ourselves as loving someone: always implicit in our loves is that we want certain "things" for the one we love, be it a box of candy, rest, health, virtue, holiness, and, ultimately, the fullness of being (however we understand such fullness). We wish such things also for ourselves, of course. In loving we are always "wishing good to someone." Now Thomas calls the love for the good "love of concupiscence," and the love for the one to whom the good is wished "love of friendship."[62]

Once Thomas has identified the two objects of love (and their two loves), he shows the order that exists between them. One (the object of the love of friendship) he says is primary because it is loved simply and for itself. The other (the object of the love of concupiscence) is secondary because it is loved not simply and for itself, but for something (rather, someone) else. This order is shown more forcefully with an analogy between the two goods (in the two loves) and the two distinct manners of existing, namely, existing *per se* (substances) and existing in another (accidents):

61. *ST* I-II, q. 26, a. 4. See G. Mansini for a history of the development of this distinction prior to St. Thomas and in St. Thomas's own works ("*Duplex Amor* and the Structure of Love in Aquinas," in *Thomistica,* ed. E. Manning, pp. 137-96, *Recherches de théologie ancienne et médiévale, Supplementa,* vol. 1 [Leuven: Peeters, 1995]).

62. We should note two things here in the use of the term "friendship" in this Thomistic distinction. In the first place, "friendship" here does not mean what it means immediately for Aristotle, and what it usually means for us. In the second place, "friendship" in "love of friendship" does not require that the one loved with such a love be *another person,* as one might easily think. While it is true that man is not "friend" to himself, he is, in Thomas's account (*ST* II-II, q. 25, a. 4c), more than a friend to himself in virtue of the fact that he is one with himself (which, Thomas says, is more than being united to another). Moreover, in that same account, since the unity one has with oneself is the principle of union with another, the love one has for himself is the "form and root of friendship" (*ST* II-II, q. 25, a. 4c). Thus "love of friendship" can indeed be used for one's love of himself.

For just as that which has existence is a being simply, while that which exists in another is a relative being; so, because good is convertible with being, the good, which itself has goodness, is good simply; but that which is another's good, is a relative good. Consequently the love with which a thing is loved, that it may have some good, is love simply; while the love, with which a thing is loved, that it may be another's good, is relative love.[63]

In view of this analogy, it is clear that the ones to whom we wish the good, in a love of friendship, so that they may *have* the good (whatever that may be) are *rational* substances (persons).[64] It is also clear that those goods loved, in a love of concupiscence, so that by them others (or, indeed, we ourselves) may be good, may be subsisting goods, like wine, to use the classic example. What is happening in these cases, as Thomas notes, is that "we do not love them for themselves but according to something accidental belonging to them. So we love wine, wishing to receive its sweetness."[65]

---

63. *ST* I-II, q. 26, a. 4c. Cf. also Thomas's commentary on the *Divine Names*, where he makes this same analogy: "[L]ove implies the first inclination of the appetite towards a thing according as it has the nature of good, which is the object of appetite. But as being is said in two ways, namely of that which exists *per se* and of that which exists in another, so is good. In one way, it is said of a subsisting thing which has goodness, as man is called good. In another way, it is said of that which exists in something, making it good, as virtue is called a man's good, since by it a man is good. Similarly, white is called being, not because it itself is something subsisting in its own being, but because by it something is white. Love, therefore, tends to something in two ways: in one way, as towards a substantial good which indeed happens when thus we love something so as to wish it good, as we love a man, willing his good. In another way, love tends to something as towards an accidental good, as we love virtue, not indeed for the reason that we will it to be good, but for the reason that by it we may be good. Now certain people call the first mode of love a love of friendship, but they call the second a love of concupiscence" (*In Librum Beati Dionysii de divinis nominibus* 4.10 [pars. 427-28]).

64. *ST* II-II, q. 25, a. 3c. One might immediately object to what seems to be for Thomas the impossibility of loving non-personal things with any regard other than a merely accidental one, where one attaches oneself only to one or several of the qualities of a thing and only insofar as someone can benefit from them. Beyond the level of the obvious where "it would be absurd to speak of having friendship for wine or for a horse" (*ST* II-II, q. 23, a. 1c), Thomas seems to base the impossibility of loving irrational things with a love of friendship upon the grounds that they lack freedom by which they can *have* good, and be the master of using the good that they have (*ST* II-II, q. 25, a. 3c). A further, and more ultimate reason could be that the goodwill one has for a friend in love of friendship is ultimately tied to the good of beatitude, which can only be attained by rational beings (*ST* I-II, q. 1, a. 8c).

65. *In Librum Beati Dionysii de divinis nominibus* 4.10 (par. 429).

It is, of course, also true, as we have seen with Aristotle, that persons can be loved *per accidens,* that is, not for themselves, but on account of pleasure or utility.[66] And when this occurs, the person is the object of a love of concupiscence. St. Thomas links his love of concupiscence with Aristotle's friendship of use or pleasure. We should note, however, that, as with Aristotle, such a love of a person is not considered disordered even if it is ranked lower than love of friendship and is not considered to be a friendship in the truest sense:

> When friendship is based on usefulness or pleasure, a man does indeed wish his friend some good: and in this respect the character of friendship is preserved. But since he refers this good further to his own pleasure or use, the result is that friendship of the useful or pleasant, in so far as it is connected with love of concupiscence, loses the character of true friendship.[67]

One might think that the difference between the two loves is that in one case, one has something to gain and in the other nothing at all. But everyone would agree, except for some postmoderns (ready even to crucify the joy they might have at seeing their beloved happy),[68] that it would be strange to think of one of the greatest joys in life as in no way beneficial to us. And, of course, this would be strange in a *Thomistic* theory of love which, after all, has been preceded by a long treatise on the desire for happiness.[69] Concerning the benefit that a person can be for the one loving in both love of concupiscence and love of friendship, D. Gallagher writes:

> I love the other as good for me precisely because of the good that the other has in himself without it first being referred to me. In love of concupiscence, the object is taken as good, not in itself, but *only* in reference to me; its goodness consists solely in its contribution to my well-being. In love of friendship, in contrast, I take the other person

---

66. *In Librum Beati Dionysii de divinis nominibus* 4.10 (par. 429).

67. *ST* I-II, q. 26, a. 4, ad 3. Cf. also *ST* I-II, q. 27, a. 3, ad 4, where Thomas connects the love of concupiscence with the friendship of use and pleasure. Note also the very interesting text where St. Thomas seems to connect Augustine's "enjoyment" of God (because God is the highest good man can want for himself) with love of concupiscence (*ST* II-II, q. 26, a. 3, ad 3).

68. See J. Milbank, "The Ethics of Self-Sacrifice," *First Things* 91 (March 1999): 33-38.

69. *ST* I-II, 1-5.

as somehow good in himself or herself, and *for this reason* as a good for me.[70]

For all of the "other-directedness" or "selflessness" implied by the love of friendship, then, it is not so "pure" that the lover is in no way better off than before.[71]

Having looked at the basic features of the distinction between love of concupiscence and love of friendship, we should look more closely at the conception of unity that accompanies it at every juncture. In Thomas's theory of love, unity can be said to play a part in love in three moments, as love's efficient cause, as love's formal cause, and as love's effect.[72]

We have already been operating at the level of love's formal cause; and at that level love, for Thomas (be it natural, sensitive, or rational love), before it is a movement of desire for and eventual union with what is loved, is what he calls a "complacency" *(complacentia)* in a particular good.[73] This term "complacency," together with a small constellation of synonyms used, expresses the modification that a subject has undergone in the face of that good, such modification being precisely an "affective union" with the object.[74] Now this affective union, or "complacency," is to be considered in a twofold manner. On the one hand, it can be "as to something belonging to oneself," or "belonging to our well-being," if in the case of a love of concupiscence. On the other hand, it can be like substantial union "inasmuch as the lover stands to the object of his love, as to him-

---

70. D. Gallagher, "Desire for Beatitude and Love of Friendship," p. 26.

71. As for how one is better off in a love of friendship, one could refer to the Thomistic doctrine of the common good, according to which a good held in common is more lovable to the individual than his private good (cf. *ST* II-II, q. 26, a. 4, ad 3), even if this goodness (for oneself) of a *companionship in the good* indicates an imperfection, as Thomas says when referring to Divine Love: "The saying that the possession of any good cannot be pleasing without companionship applies when perfect goodness is not found in one person, and so one needs for the full goodness of the pleasure, the good of having someone else as a companion for oneself" (*ST* I, q. 32, a. 1, ad 2).

72. *ST* I-II, q. 28, a. 1, ad 2.

73. *ST* I-II, q. 26, a. 2c. See also *ST* I-II, q. 25, a. 2c and ad 2.

74. The object, as St. Thomas explains in his exposition of love as passion (cf. *ST* I-II, q. 26, a. 2c), "enters into" *(immutatio)* the affections as it were and gives them "a certain adaptation to itself" *(coaptatio)*, which can be more psychologically described as pleasure felt in the face of a perceived good *(complacentia)*. For an in-depth analysis of these terms, cf. H. D. Simonin, O.P., "Autour de la Solution Thomiste du Problème de L'Amour," *Archives d'histoire doctrinale et littéraire du moyen âge* 6 (1932): 190-97.

self," or "as his other self," and "wills good to him, just as he wills good to himself," if in the case of a love of friendship.[75]

The twofold union which love is, is further explained by considering the efficient cause of love. As just noted, love as affective union (or, complacency) is something that is effected in someone by another (thing or person).[76] It is not, as it were, self-motivated. At the same time, the good who "moves into the affections," so to speak, does not do so groundlessly but always as seen, that is, always as apprehended to be in one way or another one with the lover.[77]

Now, this twofold oneness, the seeing of which brings about love between the lover and the thing loved, Aquinas identifies as likeness *(similitudo)*.[78] It is precisely as similar that a known good can bring about love in the lover. And this likeness is, of course, twofold. In the first instance it is between two that have the same quality actually. The most basic example of such likeness between two human beings would be, of course, the likeness in humanity that each possesses actually. One could move then to more particular qualities such as intelligence, profession, interests, etc., to find a likeness of the first kind; and, of course, the intensity of the love of friendship will vary according to the nature and the degree of the similarity between two persons. Where there is a likeness of this kind, it is as though, says Thomas, two had one form (specifically) making them to be, in a way,

---

75. *ST* I-II, q. 28, a. 1c and ad 2.

76. *ST* I-II, q. 26, a. 2.

77. *ST* I-II, q. 28, a. 1c and ad 2.

78. *ST* I-II, q. 27, a. 3. Pieper notes that this "previous union" which arouses love may in fact be found in the etymological link between "love" and "liking." "Love," he notes, is associated with "likeness" not so much on account of a common English root which does not appear to exist, as on account of the Latin *amare,* which is in turn related to the Greek *hama* ("at the same time"). He concludes that this relation between love and likeness "brings to the fore a long suspected and almost consciously known semantic element: that 'love' includes and is based upon a pre-existent relation between the lover and the beloved; that, in other words, no one could love anyone or anything were not the world, in a manner hard to put into words, a single reality and one that can be experienced as fundamentally characterized by unity — a world in which all beings at bottom are related to one another and from their very origins exist in a relationship of real correspondence to one another. In short, we are confirmed in our sensing that love not only yields and creates unity, but also that its premise is unity. Paul Tillich has actually included this state of affairs in his definition of love. Love, he says, is not so much the union of those who are strangers to one another as the *re-*union of those who have been alienated from one another. But alienation can exist only on the basis of a pre-existing original oneness" (Pieper, *Faith, Hope, Love,* pp. 159-60).

"one in that form";[79] and thus "the affections of one tend to the other, as being one with him; and he wishes good to him as to himself."[80]

It should be noted how similarity underscores the way in which, in the Thomistic account of love, the love of another is an extension of one's love for oneself. It is because we find lovable in another the very good that we love in ourselves that we can extend the love we have for ourselves to another, taking him as another self.[81] (It goes without saying that the particular reason for a similarity must be something one considers *lovable*, that is, *good*, and so also lovable in another.) So, similarity is not only the reason we love another but why we love another always as an extension or overflow of our love for ourselves. Thomas will point to the Old Testament text: "Thou shalt love thy friend as thyself" (Lev 19:18) as the authority for such a view (as well as to Aristotle, who held, as we have noted, that "the origin of friendly relations with others lies in our relations to ourselves [*Ethics,* IX, iv, 1166a]."[82] It is, of course, not the case that we are dealing here with some narrow individualism. If the movement of love begins with love for oneself and if love of another is understood in its light, the self in question is clearly a most expansive one.

The second kind of likeness is between one that possesses a quality actually and another having it only potentially by way of inclination. So, for example, between the learned and the ignorant, or between one who wants a promotion and another who has the influence to get it, or between two who seek each other out for the sake of pleasure, there is a "similarity." Where love arises from a likeness or union of this kind, and *where this likeness is the reason for the friendship,* we have a love of concupiscence, because the friend is not being loved, in the ultimate analysis, *for himself* or *for his own sake,* but only to the extent that he can provide or offer something the lover lacks and wants.[83] Thomas associates this

---

79. *ST* I-II, q. 27, a. 3c.

80. *ST* I-II, q. 27, a. 3c.

81. Cf. D. Gallagher on the connection between similarity and love as extension of self-love ("Desire for Beatitude," p. 32).

82. *ST* II-II, q. 25, a. 4c.

83. Though love of concupiscence, for Thomas, does not exclusively refer back to oneself — one can want something with a love of concupiscence, say virtue, for another — in this case where similarity of the second kind is the cause of love between two persons, the person loved is loved with a love of concupiscence and so the love is referred ultimately back onto the lover, as Thomas says when speaking about similarity as love's cause: "in the love of

Margaret H. McCarthy

love of concupiscence with the Aristotelian friendship of usefulness or pleasure.[84]

We turn now, finally, to the union which love as affective union both aspires to and effects. This union Thomas calls "real union" where the lover seeks the presence of the one (or thing) loved.[85] Interestingly, when speaking of this kind of union, Thomas refers to Aristotle where he in turn refers back to Aristophanes, who "stated that lovers would wish to be united both into one," but that since "this would result in either one or both being destroyed" — then Thomas adds — "they seek a suitable and becoming union to live together, speak together, and be united together in other like things."[86] Real union, then, is wanting to be with the other.

Thomas further specifies the effect of love with the notion of "mutual indwelling." Here we will see the extent of the union to which love gives rise (though here the union in question is one in the affections). As is suggested by the term "mutual indwelling,"[87] the lover and the beloved can each be said to be in each other; and this, as we would expect, in two distinct manners corresponding to love of concupiscence and love of friendship.

On the one hand, the beloved can be said to be in the lover (because in his affections); and if the beloved is present, the lover takes pleasure in him, or, in the event that he is not present, the lover either "tends towards him" (with a love of concupiscence) or "toward the good that he wills to the be-

---

concupiscence, the lover, properly speaking, loves himself, in willing the good that he desires" (*ST* I-II, q. 27, a. 3c). On this point, one could refer also to the third effect of love which is "ecstasy" — a being placed out of oneself — which, in the case of a love of concupiscence, is caused by love only "in a certain sense," "in so far . . . as not being satisfied with enjoying the good that [the lover] has, he seeks to enjoy something outside himself. But since he seeks to have this extrinsic good for himself, he does not go out from himself simply, and this movement remains finally within him" (*ST* I-II, q. 28, a. 3).

84. *ST* I-II, q. 27, a. 3c. It might seem that, given the likeness that causes the love of concupiscence, this latter would not have much to do with friendships of use or pleasure between equals. It would be linked only to cases of opposites, such as between rich and poor, learned and ignorant, or beautiful and ugly, but not to friendships of use or pleasure *per se*. G. Mansini explains that friendships of use or pleasure where there is an equality in usefulness or pleasantness are not exempt from the cause of likeness which gives rise to the love of concupiscence. In these friendships each is recurrently in potency for what the other has. The point is that the friend, in these friendships, is not being loved for his own sake, as one, that is, in whom the good inheres as it does in oneself (*"Duplex Amor,"* pp. 185-87).

85. *ST* I-II, q. 28, a. 1c.

86. *ST* I-II, q. 28, a. 1, ad 2.

87. *ST* I-II, q. 28, a. 2.

loved" (with a love of friendship).[88] Furthermore, the beloved can be said to be in the lover in the case of a love of friendship when "he wills and acts for his friend's sake as for his own sake [*sicut propter seipsum*], looking on his friend as identified with himself [*quasi reputans amicum idem sibi*]." On the other hand, the lover can be said to be in the beloved. In the case of a love of concupiscence, this is described as a "seeking to possess the beloved perfectly, by penetrating into his heart." In the case of a love of friendship, it is described in the following manner: "he reckons what is good or evil to his friend, as being so to himself; and his friend's will as his own, so that it seems as though he felt the good or suffered the evil in the person of his friend." Thomas says further that when the lover is in the beloved in this manner, so much so that what affects his friend affects himself, it is "as though he were become one with him [*quasi idem factus amato*]."[89]

In looking at the basic features of the Thomistic distinction between love of concupiscence and love of friendship, we have noted in particular the notion of unity associated with each. Where love is based on the "similarity" of act and potency, where either one has what the other does not yet have or where each is recurrently in potency for (and wants) what the other has,[90] the beloved is being loved as "pertaining to the lover's well-being," that is, accidentally, in such a way that the love ultimately refers back to the lover.[91] Where, on the other hand, a similarity exists between two who each actually possess the same perfection, then the lover takes the other as another self, and wishes good to him as to himself. The highest friendship is associated with the highest form of similarity and quasi-identity between the two friends.

Nuptial Friendship and Its Significance for a Theory of Love

We have now come to look specifically at "nuptial love," the love (or friendship) between man and woman. It is clearly indisputable that between a man and woman, by virtue of their humanity, the highest form of friendship, where each in loving the other wants his or her good, can exist. What is

88. *ST* I-II, q. 28, a. 2c.
89. *ST* I-II, q. 28, a. 2c.
90. Cf. n. 84.
91. Cf. n. 83.

not clear, however, is whether or not this can be said of the love between a man and woman *as such,* that is, taking into consideration the difference between the two which draws them into each other's company and which so specifies the manner of their companionship. St. Thomas seems to connect the love between a man and a woman with love of concupiscence, when, for example, he takes up the last effect of love, namely, zeal, and offers as an example of zeal, in love of concupiscence, the husband's jealousy of his wife.[92] The same seems to be implied in his commentary on the *Ethics,* where he more or less accepts Aristotle's association of the friendship between husband and wife, *as such,* with the friendships of use and pleasure combined.[93] These, as we noted, St. Thomas associates with love of concupiscence.[94] One could, of course, turn to elements in St. Thomas's thought that might weaken this link, such as his theology of marriage, which, to say the least, highly extols the sacramental union between man and wife;[95] or where he points to the equality between man and wife as an argument for indissolubility[96] and monogamy;[97] but our question is whether that friendship, when confronted with the famous distinction, is still not ultimately ranked on the lower end, and, if not, then whether that does not imply in some way a nuancing of the terms of the distinction.

It seems that the difference (of sex) that specifies the relation between man and woman in the conjugal act and in domestic life is invariably read as a difference which, insofar as it is the reason for the relation and that which specifies it, is the element which makes it difficult for that love to be of the highest kind (where the other is loved for his or her own sake and not "accidentally," according to a particular aspect of the other seen as beneficial to the lover). If, on the other hand, the nuptial relation appears to be paradigmatic of love (and friendship) as it seems in Chris-

---

92. *ST* I-II, q. 28, a. 4c.

93. *In VIII Eth,* lect. 12, nn. 1721-23. See nn. 17, 48, and 49 above.

94. *ST* I-II, q. 26, a. 4, ad 3.

95. *ST* III, q. 42. Furthermore, one could identify texts such as the one where, arguing for the indissolubility of marriage, St. Thomas calls marriage the "greatest of friendships" on the grounds that man and woman are united both in body and in a domestic partnership (*SCG* 123, 6). Perhaps one could find elements in such texts that might nuance the association of the nuptial relation with the love of concupiscence, but we do not think that Thomas is consciously attempting to do so here.

96. *SCG,* 123, 4.

97. *SCG,* 124, 5.

tianity, and in its Jewish precursor, might we not be required to account for difference, at least the kind of difference that sexual difference is, in a new way? Following the thought of John Paul II, Hans Urs von Balthasar, and Angelo Scola, we propose to suggest the elements of such an account.

Dual Unity

In the first place, we will consider the phenomenon of man's existence in a "unity of the two," or a "dual unity." These expressions, which come from John Paul II[98] and Hans Urs von Balthasar[99] respectively, indicate a polarity between the identity of human nature, which every individual possesses uniquely (unity), and the fact that that human identity is manifest always and everywhere in two different incarnations (duality).[100] On the one hand, then, is the human identity that every human individual possesses and which, between individuals, is shared, or homogeneous, even if this is not a matter of mere interchangeability.[101] On the other hand, there are always two different "incarnations," as John Paul II says, or two ways of "being a body" of the human being.[102] Balthasar states it thus: "there is always the 'other' mode of being human, a way that is not open to its counterpart."[103] The homogeneous human nature between individuals is always possessed then within a difference that carries with it the idea of a certain mutual exclusivity. Such exclusivity, or "un-openness," means not, of course, that two who exist bodily in these distinct manners are not open to each other — to a communion — but rather that, precisely, for the sake of such a communion, the one can never overtake the other either by exist-

---

98. Cf. *The Theology of the Body*, pp. 45-48, and *Mulieris dignitatem*, 7.

99. "Dual unity" pertains to the third of the three polarities (following body-soul and individual-community) of Balthasar's "dramatic anthropology." Cf. *Theo-Drama* 2, pp. 365ff.

100. John Paul II writes: "Their unity denotes above all the identity of human nature; their duality, on the other hand, manifests what, on the basis of this identity, constitutes the masculinity and femininity of created man" (*Theology of the Body*, p. 45).

101. Angelo Scola, using the polarity "identity and difference," notes that "identity" (or "unity") is not mere "equality" (interchangeability, uniformity), but refers to the "unique and constitutive identity of the I" (*Uomo-Donna: Il 'Caso Serio' dell'Amore* [Milan: Marietti, 2002], p. 21).

102. John Paul II, *The Theology of the Body*, p. 43.

103. Balthasar, *Theo-Drama* 2, p. 369.

ing in the other bodily mode, or, as a way of attempting the same, possessing the other in his or her otherness.[104]

Two things can be said about this polarity of common humanity on the one hand and sexual difference on the other. In the first place, it is not the case that the difference between the male and female manners of possessing humanity suggests, as it were, two partial (deficient) halves who, because of their deficiency, tend towards each other so as to attain wholeness, only to cease tending when united. To be sure, every man is *homo viator*, and why would not his sexual difference be caught up in his movement towards a fuller realization of his humanity? The point is that if the tendency towards the other that sexual difference instigates is caught up in the movement towards a greater possession of one's own humanity, such a tendency is not between two complementary "fractions";[105] nor is such a tendency the temporary state through which each passes on the illusory and therefore always unsuccessful way to (or back to) some kind of an undifferentiated and androgynous identity, the kind that Aristophanes imagines in the *Symposium*.[106] Insofar as the male or female person is each a human "whole," that difference is not the expression of a deficiency or partiality to be overcome. Alongside Balthasar's "dual unity," Angelo Scola proposes the term "asymmetrical complementarity," the first part of which "consists in the fact that sexual difference, in a significant and immediate way, testifies that the other always remains 'other' for me,"[107] even if, or rather, together with the fact that he or she is similar (and compatible).

---

104. Connecting the impossibility of possessing the other (and the attempt to overcome communion) with the mutual exclusivity of sexual difference, Balthasar writes: "as a human being, man is always in communion with his counter image, woman, and yet never reaches her. The converse is true of woman. If we take this man/woman relationship as a paradigm, it also means that the human 'I' is always searching for the 'thou,' and actually finds it ('This at last . . .'), without ever being able to take possession of it in its otherness. Not only because the freedom of the 'thou' cannot be mastered by the 'I' using any superior transcendental grasp — since, in its proper context, all human freedom only opens up to absolute, divine freedom — but also because this impossibility is 'enfleshed' in the diverse and complementary constitution of the sexes" (ibid., p. 366).

105. Prudence Allen calls this view of the complementarity between male and female "fractional sex complementarity," where the male "provides one half and a female one half of a whole human being, or some other combination of fractions" ("Integral Sex Complementarity," *Communio* 17, no. 4 [Winter 1990]: 539).

106. Cf. Plato, *The Symposium*, 189d.

107. Scola, "The Nuptial Mystery at the Heart of the Church," p. 645.

The union towards which sexual difference (duality) tends is further testimony of the constitutive and unsurpassable character of this difference. Such union is not — however much it has been tried in the various ways of taking possession of another — aimed at the elimination of the other (the difference). It is not a romantic fusion of the two, but the welcome or "letting be" of a difference which, paradoxically, the more welcomed in this manner, is ever more different. The fact that sexual union is objectively tied up with and oriented to the possibility of a new life is the evidence that the couple, like it or not, knowing it or not, is not a closed (undifferentiated) circle. "There can be no question of saying that sexual intercourse suspends this contingence and renders the union absolute, makes it something at rest in itself (as Feuerbach thought and as Aristophanes gently suggests in the *Symposium*): for the normal issue is a child."[108] The child issues from a union whose very nature is to welcome the other to such an extent as to wed his or her self, and future, gratuitously, to the other (including all of his or her difference, charming or otherwise, as well as any future changes almost certain to occur). He or she, the new unforeseen future, is the fruit of a love that intends not to "alter when it alteration finds"[109] and the expression of the "risk" taken with an *other,* not to mention the fact that he or she is now yet another with whom to contend.

Original Unity

The second point concerning the polarity of "dual unity" is that the sexual other is not just another option "out there" within a field of "choices." Rather, the nature of the difference is such that prior to any encounter between a man and a woman the meaning of one cannot but imply the meaning of the other. We have not a mere "diversity" between two (or more) things that can be put together or not, but a difference that points

108. Insisting on the indissoluble link between sexual union and fruitfulness, Balthasar wrote: "If, in imagination, we were to exclude from the act of love between man and woman the nine months' pregnancy, that is, the temporal dimension, the child would be immediately present in their generative-receptive embrace; this would be simultaneously the expression of their reciprocal love *and,* going beyond it, its transcendent result" (*Theo-Logic,* vol. 3: *The Spirit of Truth,* trans. Graham Harrison [San Francisco: Ignatius Press, 2005], p. 160).

109. Shakespeare, *Sonnet* 116, 2-4.

one, from his or her inner depths, *constitutively,* to the other,[110] so much so that, as Scola notes, "in order to be able to say 'I' in the fullest sense, *I need to* take the other into account."[111]

John Paul II accounts for the constitutive nature of sexual difference with his term "original unity."[112] Each of the sexes is unintelligible without the other, because each "from the beginning" is in some sense determined by the other. The second creation account (Gen 2) provides an image of "original unity" at the beginning of human history. In that account *Adam,* who is not "yet" specified as a man (male),[113] is, with respect to the other creatures, alone, and this, we are told, is "not good." It is then that "the Lord God caused a deep sleep to fall upon the man, and while he slept took one of his ribs and closed up its place with flesh. The rib which the Lord God had taken from the man he made into a woman" (Gen 2:21-22).

Clearly, as Balthasar notes, the "not good" of this second account of human beginnings "banishes the idea of a primal, androgynous human being (in whom there is no hint of the male-female difference) at peace with himself and only subject to unsatisfied longing after being split into two sexes."[114] Rather, in that text we have one, "Adam," who *from the beginning,* longs for another — it was "not good" — and who also already carries within him, potentially, the woman. Moreover — and this further ban-

---

110. On this point Scola, interpreting "dual unity," proposes that the difference in question here be well distinguished from mere "diversity." This latter, he notes, referring to its etymology (*di-vertere:* turning towards another direction), "has to do with a multiplicity and with the changing of something which puts into play the 'external,' without any reference to the intimate essence of the individual" (*Uomo-Donna: Il 'Caso Serio' Dell'Amore,* p. 21). Our own word "diversion" indicates more clearly, perhaps, the extrinsicism, or in any event the lack of an intrinsic link, between two "diverse" things. "Difference," on the other hand, Scola notes, suggests from its roots (*dif-ferre:* to carry the same thing elsewhere) a "tendency towards" which is intrinsic to that which tends (p. 21).

111. Scola, *Uomo-Donna,* p. 643.

112. Cf. *The Theology of the Body,* pp. 42-45.

113. John Paul II does not see in the text's movement from "man" to "male and female" an espousal of androgyny as more original and therefore more perfect. Rather he reads in the apparent temporal development of things two moments, the first of which considers man in his relation to God ("original solitude"), which sets him apart from the animal world, making him thereby alone in the world, and the second of which further explicates his unique relation to God as well as the resolution of his aloneness in the world. The second moment is not a falling away, but rather a development of what is already implied in the first (cf. *The Theology of the Body,* pp. 35-37).

114. Balthasar, *Theo-Drama* 2, p. 373.

ishes any hint of extrinsicism between the two — the formation of the woman from the rib does not permit us to think of them as having come from "different places" and only then to have encountered each other. Looking at the text, we are told that it is only when woman — *'iššāh* — appears that *Adam* becomes *'iš* (a man),[115] becoming more fully himself. And, of course, it is clear enough that the woman becomes herself by virtue of the man (having come from his "rib"). If, then, when finally the two are turned towards each other in an "encounter," there is fulfillment ("at last!"), this is so because each stands before one who has been there *from the very beginning*, at the very foundation of his or her being.

It is precisely because of this "original unity" that one can sustain the simultaneity of the homogeneous human nature between a man and a woman, on the one hand, and the mutually exclusive difference, on the other, that is implied by "dual unity." The "mythic" account of the woman coming from the rib gives us just such a foundation, for there the common humanity, that basic likeness *(similitudo)* between the man and the woman — "bone of bones and flesh of flesh" — is established by one's coming from the other (each in differing ways). Balthasar notes this unique feature in the creation of man: "God did not simply create mankind male and female as he had created the animals male and female. *He not only created them to be one in the duality of sex; he also created their duality out of their own oneness.*"[116] It was from the oneness of Adam's flesh (poised as it was towards another in its readiness to make of itself a gift), that another with the same humanity came into being. Here we can see in the relation between the first man and woman a homogeneity or likeness which is not first an "abstract" belonging to human nature, standing outside of or alongside difference, but a likeness carried within difference having been derived from the self-gift of one who was always awaiting another (with the "rib").[117]

---

115. John Paul II, *Theology of the Body,* p. 35.

116. *The Christian State of Life* (San Francisco: Ignatius Press, 1983), p. 227.

117. For Balthasar, this unique origin of the duality of human sexuality indicates that the fecundity of the human couple "lies always outside their power and must be bestowed upon them by God" (*The Christian State of Life,* p. 228). That fecundity is "the result of the physical fecundity that God effected in Adam while he slept and that became, by the formation of Eve from the one living body of Adam, a direct physical image of the origin from the Father's substance of the eternal Son who shares his nature" (p. 227). Eve, he notes, recognizes this after the birth of her first son when she says, "I have given birth to a man-child with the help of the Lord" (Gen 4:1) (p. 228).

That the likeness *(similitudo)* between man and woman can be said always to stand within a difference and not alongside it is not without a deeper foundation. The very notion of "the image and likeness of God," in which the man and woman are said to participate, implies as a necessary ingredient, at every point, the creature's being at a remove from God, having come *ex nihilo*. It is because of that remove, that *dissimilitudo*, Balthasar notes, "that the grace that called him into being could also bestow upon him the grace of likeness," by which "he shares in the independence, unity, personality and freedom of his Creator."[118] Moreover, it is on account of the original *dissimilitudo* that growing in the image and likeness of God is never a matter of an identity where the two, God and man, are fused into one — were this possible — thereby extinguishing love. To be sure, the coincidence of similarity and dissimilarity implied in the *imago Dei* doctrine must find its ultimate foundation in a trinitarian conception of unity, but it is enough that we only mention this here.[119] Suffice it to say that it is on those grounds that sexual difference is intrinsic to the homogeneity of nature between a man and a woman.

One might be tempted to dismiss the creation "myth" of human beginnings as hopelessly obscure and remote, as having no possible bearing on relations between other men and women, since, of course, men and women do seem *first* to encounter each other — each having been constituted in his or her humanity independently of the other — and only then to form a union. However, it is precisely to those strange beginnings that Jesus turned when responding to questions posed to him about divorce in his day (at some distance from Eden). It was because God made man male and female, but more specifically, because one came from, or out of, the other that a man and woman join, becoming one flesh. *"For this reason,"* Jesus said, quoting from Genesis 2:24, "a man shall leave his father and mother and be joined to his wife, and the two shall become one flesh" (Mt 19:5).

---

118. Cf. *The Christian State of Life*, p. 68. Cf. also Balthasar's *Theo-Drama*, vol. 3: *Dramatis Personae: Persons in Christ* (San Francisco: Ignatius Press, 1992), pp. 340ff.

119. For a general treatment of the causality of the Trinity in creation where "the procession of Persons in unity of essence is the cause of the procession of creatures in diversity of essence" (Bonaventure), cf. Balthasar, *Theo-Drama* 5: *The Last Act* (San Francisco: Ignatius Press, 1998), pp. 61-109. As regards the bearing of this on the creation of man as male and female, cf. Balthasar, *Theo-Drama* 3, pp. 283-360 ("Woman's Answer"); A. Scola, "The Nuptial Mystery," pp. 655-56; and John Paul II, *Mulieris dignitatem*, 7.

The fact that the first man and the first woman have each come to be by virtue of the other and do not just meet in the middle, so to speak, indicates a relation that is *constitutive,* pertaining, that is, to one's being, and not optional. This is why the "communion of persons," to which the "original unity" of man and woman leads, is a question of nothing less than their *being human persons.*[120] When the Holy Father comes upon the biblical idea of a "helper," he comments that by their mutual existence "one for the other," their reciprocity in existence, the man and the woman "help" each other, in the first instance *to be.*[121] Pieper had already noted the kinship between love, generally speaking, and creation:

> [I]n fact the most extreme form of affirmation that can possibly be conceived of is *creatio,* making to be, in the strict sense of the word. . . . And I am convinced that no one more fully appreciates this, no one is more persuaded of it beyond all argumentation and proof, than the true lover. He "knows" that his affirmation directed toward the beloved would be pointless were not some other force akin to creation involved — and, moreover, a force not merely preceding his own love, but one which is still at work and which he himself, the loving person, participates in and helps along by loving.[122]

Communion of Persons

Given the original state of affairs between man and woman, we have already begun to form a conception of the "communion of persons" they form when they in fact encounter each other. In the face of the other as such, each is helped *to be* according to the terms of their humanity, which exists always as a "dual unity." The second Genesis account does not look upon the expropriation of Adam's rib and its being "carried elsewhere" as a Feuerbachian type of "alienation" of self but rather the completion of a creation that had first to pass through the "not good" of human solitude. The movement of each toward the other, therefore, in no way constitutes

---

120. *Mulieris dignitatem,* 7.
121. *Mulieris dignitatem,* 7.
122. *Faith, Hope, Love,* pp. 170-71. Pieper notes that, of course, "human love . . . is by its nature and must inevitably be always an imitation and a kind of repetition of this perfected and, in the exact sense of the word, *creative* love of God" (p. 171).

an attempt to overcome the difference by repossessing the "rib," but rather the welcome of this *similar* humanity which has now been, so to speak, "resituated."[123]

To think of such a welcoming of another in his or her otherness as anything but alienating can only be said, of course, with a relational or "dual" conception of the unity of the human person. (And, to be sure, this conception has to resist the tug of a certain common experience that would suggest otherwise.) With "dual unity" the conception of union with the sexual other occurs as though with "another self," but not only because one is more oneself by associating his good with the good of another similar to him — the common good being greater for an individual than his individual good — but because one is more oneself when associating his good with that one who is similar ("bone of bones") always in and through his or her difference.[124] John Paul II hints at this when interpreting the text of Ephesians 5:28: "husbands should love their wives as their own bodies. He who loves his wife loves himself," and just a few verses later: "let each one of you love his wife as himself."

> This phrase confirms that character of unity still more. In a certain sense, love makes the "I" of the other person his own "I": the "I" of the wife, I would say, becomes through love the "I" of the husband. The body is the expression of the "I" and the foundation of its identity. The union of husband and wife in love is expressed also by means of the body. . . . The "I" becomes in a certain sense the "you" and the "you" the "I" (in a moral sense, that is).[125]

123. Cf. Scola's note on the meaning of "difference" in n. 107.

124. Speaking on the christological plane of the need for Christ to have the "woman's answer," Balthasar opens up the doctrine of the "mystical body" which relies on the Church's coming forth from his own substance. He notes: "while this complement and partner comes from him and can thus be called his ('mystical') 'Body' — resulting from what his physical body undergoes on the Cross for mankind and from its being 'eucharistized,' seen as a unity — it is not enough for him to see in her *only himself,* his influence, his work. For he *needs* the one who has come into existence from within him" (*Theo-Drama* 3, p. 341).

125. *Theology of the Body,* p. 319. Cf. P. Andriessen, who confirms this sense of "loving one's wife as his own body" by noting that the Hebrew idea of the flesh *(bāśār)* "is a principle of solidarity rather than of individuation," leaving terms such as "my flesh" or "my body" ambiguous, such that they could refer either to the one speaking or to his spouse, and by extension, his kin ("The New Eve, Body of the New Adam" in *The Birth of the Church — A Biblical Study,* ed. J. Giblet [New York: Alba House, 1968], p. 114). Given this wider sense of

Here is the development (on the moral or psychological plane) of the more fundamental (ontological) truth that the "I," being originally marked by a "you," finds himself (or herself) more truly and more completely when "lost" (or re-situated) within the ethos of the "you."[126] To return to the primordial myth, because Eve was originally within Adam, in the sense that he was *from the beginning* ready to hand himself over (in the "rib"), his union with her, after she is presented to him, is as much an embrace of another as it is a finding of himself (in its new and more complete form). Balthasar brings out the paradox of this situation forcefully:

> It is through being overpowered in a "deep sleep" and robbed of part of himself, near to his heart, that man is given fulfillment. . . . At God's instigation, [Adam] steps down from [his primacy] in a kenosis; this results in the God-given fulfillment whereby he recognizes himself in the gift of the "other."[127]

Conclusion

We began by looking at the heart of the "problem of love," namely, how one is to conceive of the relation between the love one has for himself and the love he has for another. Turning to two key moments in the tradition's philosophical and theological thought on love and friendship, we noted that love or friendship is considered to be of the highest kind where what is loved in the friend, and what is therefore the reason for being with the friend, is the good of the friend "for his sake." We noted furthermore that this friendship is possible because of the apprehension of a unity of similarity (resembling that of substantial union) whereby one "feels towards his friend in the same way as towards himself,"[128] and takes him to be an-

---

"body," Andriessen notes that "Eve is shown to be Adam's body (since she issued from it) in order that she might form with him the highest conceivable unity; she is as close to man as his own body. For this reason man will cling to his wife and they become one flesh (2:24) or as Paul will say, one body (1 Cor 6:16)" (pp. 114-15).

126. Balthasar provides the trinitarian and christological grounds for an appropriation of self through expropriation in *The Glory of the Lord*, vol. 7: *Theology: The New Covenant* (San Francisco: Ignatius Press, 1989), pp. 399-415.

127. *Theo-Drama* 2, p. 373.

128. Cf. Aristotle, *Ethics* IX, iv, 1166a.

other self. Finally, concerning this friendship, we noted that it was precisely in loving another in this manner that one becomes more himself (and loves himself) for, by associating with another at the level of his good, one's own good has expanded, becoming fuller.

Ranked beneath that highest form of love or friendship is that love in which "we do not love [the ones loved] for themselves but according to something accidental belonging to them,"[129] looking at an aspect of the persons loved and referring it back to oneself, by-passing their good, as it were. Here one does not love the other "for himself" but according to something accidental in him that is perceived to be a benefit for the one loving. In this love, the "similarity" of the act-potency kind is offered as its underlying cause. One looks upon the other as one who has what the other does not have, whether one does not himself have the same thing actually, as in the case of unequals or opposites — the poor want the wealth of the rich, etc. — or does, but wants and needs it from the other, as in the case of "equals" who are recurrently in want of a certain benefit from the friend, e.g., his wittiness.

We noted the few places in this theory of love and friendship where the love between husband and wife as such, looking at it in those aspects that specify it, tended to be ranked among friendships of the lower kind for the reason, it appeared, that the difference between man and woman suggested a "similarity" of the lower kind, which gave rise to an "accidental" exchange of sorts, in contrast to the kind of friendship in which one stands towards the other "as to himself," or as an "other self," and on that basis loves him "for his own sake."

But if nuptial love is so central to Christian revelation and in its precursor, we asked, might not another account of the difference standing between man and woman be necessary, an account that opens up and deepens the element of similarity long considered to be at the heart of the highest loves and friendships? We suggested just such an opening up in the categories of "dual unity," "unity of the two," and "asymmetrical reciprocity." That opening up could be summarized in the following way.

At the most basic level, what is indicated by these terms is the simultaneity of similarity (most basically that of a common human nature) and difference (male and female), where the former is always possessed in and through the latter. From this we can say that the movement towards the

---

129. Cf. St. Thomas, *In Librum Beati Dionysii de divinis nominibus* 4, 10 (par. 429).

opposite sex is never the movement of a mere aspect of oneself or a movement towards a mere aspect of the other; it is, rather, a movement of and towards a particularity in which the whole of his or her humanity is expressed. Moreover, because sexual difference is this kind of a particular, the movement towards the opposite sex is not *per se* a love of the other *per accidens,* whereby the other person is reduced to an object for the one loving (even if this is abundantly possible when sexual difference *is* taken to be a mere aspect of one's humanity and not the vehicle of its manifestation). It is rather the possibility of an affirmation of the good of the other as other, that is, of his or her (similar) humanity which always exists bodily in a different manner. This possibility is moreover the possibility of one's own fulfillment, for here one encounters "another self," not only because by seeing in the other a common humanity (or some other similarity) one identifies with the other, and so extends his love for himself, thereby expanding his own good (now a larger common good), but also because by associating with this other in his or her difference and leaving one's former place, so to speak, to be resituated, one now has oneself — one now has one's "body" — all the more and is more at home.

In a way, it should be no surprise that the "novelty" of trinitarian love, revealed in Jesus Christ, whose Body became a Bride, opens up and deepens what it means that our love for another be utterly bound up with our love for ourselves, that is, that we love others as ourselves.

Being Fruitful:
Personal Agency and *Communio*

On Moral Theology

Romanus Cessario

That which is mortal of the man whom we commemorate today awaits the resurrection of the dead along a bank of the Reuss, a river that runs through the Swiss city of Lucerne. Over the von Balthasar family crypt located along the cloister of Lucerne's principal church lies a stone slab engraved with names of those interred thereunder. These include "Hans Urs Kardinal." Our centenarian von Balthasar ranks among those theologians that the Church has honored for exceptionally sound expositions of Catholic doctrine. I would like then, first of all, to express my gratitude for the invitation to join this generous celebration that marks the eminent theological achievement of Hans Urs Cardinal von Balthasar (1905-2005).

This panel introduces themes in the writings of von Balthasar associated with ethics and moral theology: "Being fruitful: personal agency and *communio.*" When I observed that the distinguished colleagues on today's panel had managed to accumulate 106 footnotes in the course of preparing short presentations, my thoughts turned immediately toward fellow Thomists. Specifically, I was reminded of research for a book of mine that recently has been published in English under the title *A Short History of Thomism.*[1] These 106 footnotes brought home to me the fact that there exists a body of scholars that now exegetes von Balthasar with as much assiduousness as do Thomists who comment on Saint Thomas, at least since the time of their fifteenth-century *princeps,* John Capreolus.

Inasmuch as there are before us two examples of the commentatorial

---

1. Romanus Cessario, O.P., *A Short History of Thomism* (Washington, D.C.: The Catholic University of America Press, 2005).

instinct that characterizes a new generation of Balthasarians, I have chosen to pursue a modest line of inquiry. This paper includes few footnotes — thirteen in all. One of these comes from the very helpful book by Jesuit Father Christopher Steck, *The Ethical Thought of Hans Urs Von Balthasar:* "Moral action," writes the author regarding what he calls von Balthasar's "aesthetic view" of human agency, "rests on a responsibility grounded in the gift and claim of the other."[2] If I have understood their essays well, both Salesian Father Stefan Oster and Dr. Emmanuel Tourpe develop in diverse ways this general theme. It may come as a surprise to those who have read my 2001 *Introduction to Moral Theology,* as well as to those who have not, that I find the aforementioned description of an individual moral action very satisfactory.[3] "Moral action rests on a responsibility grounded in the gift and claim of the other."

The word "responsibility" is familiar nowadays to students of Christian ethics. In the early decades of the twentieth century, Max Weber sought to distinguish the "ethics of conviction" *(Gesinnungsethik)* from the "ethics of responsibility" *(Verantwortungsethik).* He did so originally in a speech delivered at Munich University in 1918.[4] Weber's distinction, however, is not a clear-cut one. One way of thinking about what Weber means may include the following disjunction: The ethics of conviction belongs to the personal order, whereas the ethics of responsibility belongs to the political. If I understand him correctly, Weber's distinction seeks to justify the

2. Christopher Steck, *The Ethical Thought of Hans Urs Von Balthasar* (New York: Crossroads, 2001), p. 20.

3. Romanus Cessario, O.P., *Introduction to Moral Theology* (Washington, D.C.: The Catholic University of America Press, 2001).

4. The speech was later published in 1919 by Duncker & Humboldt, Munich. For further analysis, see Bradley E. Starr, "The Structure of Max Weber's Ethic of Responsibility," *Journal of Religious Ethics* 27 (1999): 410: "Max Weber's distinction in 'Politics as a Vocation' between the ethic of conviction and the ethic of responsibility is best understood as a distinction between mutually exclusive ethical worldviews. Interpretations that correlate the two ethics with Weber's distinction between value-rational social action and instrumental-rational social action are misleading since Weber assumes that both types of rational social action are present in both ethics. The ethic of conviction recognizes a given hierarchy of values as the context for moral endeavor. The ethic of responsibility acknowledges value obligations, but assumes the absence of any given hierarchy of values and the inevitability of value conflict as the context for moral endeavor. When interpreted in the context of his multilayered understanding of value conflict, Weber's ethic of responsibility emerges as a coherent ethical perspective."

coexistence of deeply held personal decisions, such as conscientious objection to military service in time of war, with the fulfillment of political responsibilities that may run counter to one's personal convictions, such as defense of the homeland. In brief, Weber allows for the pacifist, but not for his engagement in pacifist propaganda.[5]

I think one may safely aver that Weber's use of the term "responsibility" reflects the modern, and perhaps Reformation-inspired, view that ethical choices mainly involve personal decisions, especially those that aim to resolve moments of high conflict between personal values and institutional norms. At the same time, the counterpoint of personal convictions and political responsibility evokes the image of the isolated person in search of refuge from the constraining burden of conformity imposed on him by large-scale societal structures. In his Munich speech, whose title is rendered "Politics as a Vocation," Weber opines: "Luther relieved the individual of the ethical responsibility for war and transferred it to the authorities. To obey the authorities in matters other than those of faith could never constitute guilt."[6] We find ourselves face to face with moral sensibilities that are largely foreign to those that inform a Christian teleology, such as the one that governs the 1993 Encyclical Letter, *Veritatis Splendor.*

Let me say immediately that von Balthasar, as far as I know, was not committed to finding strategies to deal with ethical situations that result from the fact that men and women occupy a bifurcated universe. In fact, we know that von Balthasar gave no quarter to the moral axiom, "*Faut pas chercher à comprendre* — 'You mustn't try to understand.' This formula," wrote von Balthasar in his study of the French novelist Georges Bernanos (1888-1948), "uttered by the *poilus* in a tone of defeatist humor, took on a very humorless form in the German trenches across the way, where a Kantian moral imperative prevailed without which the rise of Nazism would have been unthinkable."[7] Von Balthasar obviously recognized the limitations that distilled responsibility imposes on personal freedom. He

---

5. I am indebted for this elucidation of Weber's distinction to Robert Spaemann, "Conscience and Responsibility in Christian Ethics" in *Crisis of Conscience,* ed. John M. Haas (New York: Crossroad, 1996), pp. 111-34.

6. Max Weber, "Politics as Vocation" in *From Max Weber: Essays in Sociology,* trans. and ed. H. H. Gerth and C. Wright Mills (New York: Oxford University Press, 1946), pp. 77-128.

7. Hans Urs von Balthasar, *Bernanos: An Ecclesial Existence,* trans. E. Leiva-Merikakis (San Francisco: Ignatius Press, 1996), p. 588.

also knew that the Kantian moral imperative ill suits Christian ethics rooted in the gospel command to love God and one another. On the contrary, his understanding of moral responsibility is impossible to interpret apart from this mandate to love. "This I command you, to love one another" (Jn 15:17). Responsibility fermented by love may be one way to express what puts the spring in von Balthasar's action theory.

Father Oster explores the dynamics of love within the context of the aesthetics that we have come to identify with the work of von Balthasar. Real self-acceptance, Father Oster reminds us, is possible only in Christ. Of course, the fact that God in Christ has "radically accepted" us does not eliminate the need for the sacramental and moral mediations that provide the visible structures for Christian *communio*. There is much to ponder in the many claims that Father Oster makes about what is possible only in relation to another.

Emmanuel Tourpe develops the relational character of the von Balthasarian *communio*. A question does come to my mind, however, as a result of one point that Dr. Tourpe makes toward the end of his paper. If von Balthasar does claim that the doctrine of the intellectual generation of the Son is an "anthropological projection," then it seems to me that our honoree is far and away abandoning the doctrine that there are transcendental truths regarding intellect as a pure perfection.[8] This move would, in my judgment, imply a significant devaluation of the role of being, and of metaphysical wisdom, within theology. Sometimes theologians do something similar in accusing Saint Thomas of rationalism when he merely applies to the revealed truths of the Trinity what is already known regarding intellect as a pure perfection. The 1998 Encyclical Letter, *Fides et Ratio*, makes this line of argumentation a difficult one to sustain and defend within the fellowship of Catholic scholars.

The Thomist view is well known: certain truths about intellect as such may be applied to the Word, yielding a fruitful meditation of the Trinity — yet it is not then proven by natural reason alone that the Trinity is such, but rather, a metaphysical truth is brought into conjunction with a truth of revelation and rightly applied to it. This theological move is legitimate inasmuch as pure perfections are not intrinsically self-limiting (as, I might add, the eclectic Thomist Suarez thought), and so apply even to the

---

8. Emmanuel Tourpe, "Dialectic and Dialogic: The Identity of Being as Fruitfulness in Hans Urs von Balthasar," in this volume, at note 54.

content of revelation once it is given (while yet it could not be "proved" from reason alone). The imputations of rationalism and anthropological projection suggest a prior removal of metaphysical *scientia* from theological contemplation, or perhaps more accurately a redefinition of metaphysics as merely the dialectical residuum of revealed theology.

This last proposition is one that I know will be debated among the members of this symposium. I would like to suggest, nonetheless, that it is precisely being as "a Deo" which guarantees that it is never merely anthropocentric and rationalist, but rather ecstatic and analogically transcendent, present even in the revealed mystery of the trinitarian life.[9]

This consideration does not divert us from the realm of Christian ethics. Let me return to the text of Father Steck: "Moral action rests on a responsibility grounded in the gift and claim of the other. . . . Thus we have von Balthasar's repeated claim that the person realizes herself only in the other. . . . We are directed toward others, and this directionality is fundamental to our sense of self; our identities are constructed through relationships with others. The ultimate ground for this self-expressive relationship is the Trinity."[10] Now the question that comes to my mind is the following: If we agree that the Trinity grounds the love-shaped responsibility that distinguishes the moral life of Christians, but the generation of the Son as explained by the theological tradition is nothing but an anthropological projection, then how can the Trinity, or more precisely, our "directionality" toward the Trinity, give specific determination to the moral life?

Veritatis Splendor puts the burden on the moral theologian to announce the primacy of love: "As the Patron of moral theologians and confessors teaches: 'It is not enough to do good works; they need to be done well. For our works to be good and perfect, they must be done for the sole purpose of pleasing God.'"[11] At the same time, the encyclical also requires Christians to decipher the moral quality of particular kinds of actions. Cardinal von Balthasar demonstrates the importance of this teaching when he describes the conspiracy that abets mediocrity: "Indeed, one

---

9. It is, really, the metaphysical dynamic of the fourth way, i.e., the sense in which all act points toward *Ipsum Esse* and is unintelligible save in relation thereto. So that to know act is, properly, to be drawn toward the contemplation of God, specially inasmuch as all things are likened to God by their perfection of being — the metaphysical root of the "trace" of God in all creaturely good of which St. John of the Cross speaks.

10. Steck, *Ethical Thought*, pp. 20-21.

11. Encyclical Letter of Pope John Paul II, *Veritatis splendor*, 78.

comes to see that a real conspiracy exists among these three: *modern Man,* with his tendency to flee from himself; a *Church* that more and more is becoming filled with such men and that, as an organization made up of men, behaves in all too human a manner; and, finally, the *State,* which knows how to profit from this peculiar form of human being and which in fact, being totalitarian, requires nothing better."[12] I suggest that this analysis by von Balthasar, which draws inspiration from his reading the twentieth-century novelist Georges Bernanos, could not provide a more apt warning for the start of the twenty-first century.

We should, of course, hearken to von Balthasar, and not to Max Weber. In order to do so successfully, I respectfully submit, we will require the contemplative ascesis of the metaphysics of *esse* that Cardinal von Balthasar so appreciated. Carrying this further, we will need to complement his refined thoughts on personal agency with those of the Angelic Doctor, especially Aquinas's "insightful analysis" on the object of the moral act, which the late Holy Father authoritatively declared in 1993 is "still valid today."[13]

12. Balthasar, *Bernanos,* p. 348.
13. *Veritatis splendor,* 78.

The Other and the Fruitfulness
of Personal Acting

Stefan Oster

The Human Person Is a Gift to Himself

Hans Urs von Balthasar's essay "Der Zugang zur Wirklichkeit Gottes"
marks the beginning of the comprehensive second volume of *Mysterium
Salutis,* the great dogmatic treatment of salvation history. This article intends to shed light on the question of the possibility of knowing God. It is
characteristic of Balthasar to begin his consideration of this weighty topic
with a simple observation about interpersonal relations: "A little child
awakens to self-consciousness in being called by the love of his mother."[1]
Balthasar is a thinker of love. For him, access to *knowledge* of God does not
come to be in a monological thought exercise; rather, it is grounded in and
radiates from all those original experiences of interpersonal love, experiences in which a loving transcendence arises between one person and another. It becomes clear that there is always a deeper connection between
knowledge of God, the experience of self (and the act of becoming oneself), and the experience of the other. The "I" of a child "awakens in the experience of a 'Thou': in its mother's smile, through which it learns that it is
contained, affirmed, and loved in a relationship which is incomprehen-

1. H. U. von Balthasar, "Der Zugang zur Wirklichkeit Gottes," in *Mysterium Salutis* II
(Einsiedeln/Zürich/Köln, 1976), p. 15. See also idem, *Theodramatik* II, 1 (Einsiedeln: Johannes
Verlag, 1976), pp. 26f. (*Theo-Drama,* vol. II: Dramatis Personae 1: *Man in God* [San Francisco:
Ignatius Press, 1993]): "The fact that no human 'I' can awaken to itself without being spoken
to as a Thou by another 'I' is simply the innerworldly prelude to what we mean here."

Translated by Lesley Rice.

sively encompassing, already actual, sheltering and nourishing."[2] It also becomes evident that what is experienced first — interpersonal love — is not the most original condition for knowledge of God. It is rather the case that what originally bears and makes possible every interpersonal love is the love of God for the world and for man, a love that is recognized after and through the experience of human love. "Thus it is right that the child first catches sight of the Absolute, of 'God,' in his mother, his parents . . . and only in a second and third step has to learn to distinguish the love of God from the love he has experienced."[3]

Balthasar's observation demonstrates that from the very beginning, before a person speaks his first word, he is one spoken to, and is therefore one who answers. As Ferdinand Ulrich says, he is one who from the beginning has *been* himself *with and in another.* And he arrives at himself only in a return from another. Only from the other does he arrive at consciousness and at the experience of himself.[4] Of course, we are not to understand this as though a person owed his existence radically to the other, finite Thou, as though he were not already a whole person from the very beginning but only became a whole person through the encounter with the [finite] Thou. On the contrary, from the beginning, the human person is fully given over to himself. From the beginning he has received his being, which, as Thomas Aquinas says, is the fullness of the real and the "perfectio omnium perfectionum."[5] He always already lives out of the *whole* fullness of being, participation in which does not occur quantitatively or in more or less integral parts, but rather only as fullness.[6] Created being (because it is a *similitudo* of God's goodness, as Thomas says)[7] thus can be understood as a gift that is radically given away to the finite so that the finite can exist, can live in and through being. We can say: God gives being, and thereby gives creatures *themselves.* He *gives (geben)* everything, and this means that he necessarily relinquishes *(freigeben)* creatures to themselves. They belong to

2. H. U. von Balthasar, *Herrlichkeit* III, 1: *Im Raum der Metaphysik: II: Neuzeit* (Einsiedeln: Johannes Verlag, 1965, 2nd ed.), p. 955 (Eng., *The Glory of the Lord,* trans. Oliver Davies et al. [San Francisco: Ignatius Press, 1991], p. 616).

3. Ibid., p. 946.

4. See F. Ulrich, *Gegenwart der Freiheit* (Einsiedeln: Johannes Verlag, 1974), pp. 92f.

5. Aquinas, *Pot.,* 7, 2 ad 9.

6. Aquinas, *Summa Theologiae* (= *ST*), I, 75, 5, ad 1: "primus actus . . . participatur a rebus *non sicut pars* sed secundum diffusionem processionis ipsius."

7. Aquinas, *Ver.,* 22, 2 ad 2: "ipsum esse est similitudo divinae bonitatis."

themselves. But not as though they were static, finished products of God, but rather in such a way that they are relinquished at the same time into the creative becoming of their own self. They are given to themselves in order to be allowed to cooperate in the unfolding of their own selves. In this fashion they may take part in God's own creative act and join in the responsibility for this act. To be given oneself *(sich-gegeben-sein)* thus means also to be charged with oneself *(sich-*auf*gegeben-sein)*. The human person is called to *become* who he *is*. We better understand Thomas's conception of being when we learn to understand the being of human persons, in a deep sense, as *life*,[8] and at the same time, following Ferdinand Ulrich, as *love*.[9] The human person only exists because he has a share in this fullness of life and love, in and through which God mediates creation to itself.[10] The human person has arisen from this fullness, has sprung forth from it.[11] But at the same time, "life" does not exist as an abstract thing alongside the concrete living being. That is, obedient to the Giver, the gift gives itself so radically that creatures for their part live life and are allowed in a certain respect to bring life forth themselves: it belongs to them. For life exists only in and through living beings. To illustrate, Thomas uses the lovely image of a runner: being (and life) *is* not (does not *live*), just as running does not run.[12] This is so even though everything arises from being.

If the being of the human person, as life, is an image of God's goodness, as Thomas says, then "to become alive" means at the same time "to become good" — or, to become one who loves. For this reason Irenaeus of Lyon could say, "The glory of God is man fully *alive*": that "the *life* of man *is* the vision of God."[13] This vision as the end of life is at once and from the

---

8. Of course, being cannot simply be equated with life, for a stone also has being but is not alive. And yet Thomas says: "*vivere* est ipsum *esse* viventibus" (Aquinas, *I Sent.*, 8, 5, 3, ad 3); but he also emphasizes, "esse inter omnes alias divinae bonitatis participationes, sicut vivere et intelligere et huiusmodi, primum est, et quasi principium aliorum, praehabens in se omnia praedicta, secundum quemdam modum unita" (Aquinas, *I Sent.* 8, 1, 1). See also Aristotle, *De Anima* II, 4; 415b113: "For living things, being is living."

9. See F. Ulrich, *Homo abyssus. Das Wagnis der Seinsfrage*. Mit einer Einleitung von M. Bieler (Einsiedeln: Johannes Verlag, 1998, 2nd ed.).

10. Aquinas, *I Sent.* 37, 1, 1; idem, *In De Div. Nom.* 4, 3: "universaliter autem omnes substantias creat, dans eis esse."

11. Aquinas, *ST* I-II, 2, 5, ad 2: "ipsum esse praehabet in se omnia subsequentia."

12. Aquinas, *In Boeth. de Hebdom.*, 2: "sicut non possumus dicere, quod currere curat, ita non possumus dicere quod ipsum esse sit."

13. Irenaeus of Lyons, *Adv. Haer.*, 4, 20, 7.

beginning also its origin: life is created from the love of God, made secure in concrete human love, and summoned to love. "Whoever does not love, does not know God; for God is love" (1 Jn 4:8).

Original Relationality: The Human Person
Comes to Himself Through the Other

"Become who you are" thus makes clear that the being that is given to the human person as a gift is also an abiding task, and, as such, also an abiding promise. If it is true that being as life is also love that is *given as a gift,* then the most original task is *the proper reception of this gift.* Decisive for the success or failure of a man's life is his decision to receive or to refuse being as love.

But what does this mean: the reception of being? On the one hand, we have said that the person has always already received being — indeed, even without his own cooperation in the first place, this reception has happened from the very beginning. From the beginning he is a self-performance *(Selbstvollzug)* grounded in himself;[14] but at the same time, the reception of being is given to him as his innermost task for the completion of his life. Can we then say that in a certain sense he has not yet received being after all? Is it somehow still missing — in part, at least? With Thomas we must reject this notion: he said that being does not admit of participation in parts and thus not quantitatively, but rather as a fullness in accord with its origin in God. But this means that being is given over completely from the beginning;[15] the Giver does not withhold anything. He is not greedy but rather gives radically, so radically that in a certain respect he gives himself with the gift: for because of his being, God is present in his gift.[16]

Here we see clearly that we run into difficulties above all when we think of being either as a concrete object or, on the other hand, when we hypostasize it into an all-encompassing concept.[17]

---

14. In *Met.* 12, 1, 4: "ens dicitur quasi esse habens, hoc autem solum est substantia, quae subsistit."

15. *ST* I, 45, ad 1: "creatio est emanatio *totius esse* ab enti universali."

16. Aquinas, *Ver.* 22, 2, ad 2: "ipsum esse est similitudo divinae bonitatis; unde inquantum aliquae desiderant esse desiderant Dei similitudinem et Deum implicite."

17. F. Ulrich depicts these attempts either to objectify or to hypostasize being in many variations throughout his whole work. See F. Ulrich, *Schriften,* vols. 1-4 (Einsiedeln: Johannes Verlag, 1998ff.).

The reception of being in the dimension we are examining here rather means that the human person is charged with receiving himself as the one who, from the beginning, he has always been. In and through this task, he is allowed, as freedom given over to itself, to assist in effecting his own *self-becoming,* that is, in the language of Thomas Aquinas, his own *perfectio,* toward which every good is finally directed. We see this unusual relationship between completeness (a priori) and present condition (a posteriori), which runs through a person's entire life, in a particularly pronounced fashion at the beginning of life.[18] A child is wholly himself.[19] Everything that he can become, is already within him. And yet from the very beginning the child is given away to the other, surrendered to and dependent upon the other for his very self. The child still needs to grow, to become, to come to himself. And his being-surrendered reveals something: he comes to himself only from another; he receives himself only from what and from whom he himself *is not.* This is true in several respects: first of all, in his mother's womb he is completely secure in another; it is from within this other, this womb, that he grows. Later, as a newborn, the child depends radically on the motherly and fatherly Thous. Moreover, although he is within himself a complete "enfleshed spirit"[20] (wholly and completely, even as a child), he is also given over, completely and from the beginning, to his own bodily-material sensibility.[21] From the first, the child is drawn completely into this dimension, into the world of the many and varied experiences of his touching, seeing, hearing, tasting, and smelling of the world. The dimension of the material world accessible to the senses is the principle in and through which the human spirit comes to itself. The

18. See F. Ulrich, *Der Mensch als Anfang. Zur philosophischen Anthropologie der Kindheit* (Einsiedeln: Johannes Verlag, 1970); see also H. U. von Balthasar, *Wenn ihr nicht werdet, wie dieses Kind* (Ostfildern: Schwaben-Verlag, 1988), p. 12 (*Unless You Become Like This Child,* trans. Erasmo Leiva-Merikakis [San Francisco: Ignatius Press, 1991], p. 15): "The endform, the Omega, toward which [every person's (S.O.)] life is moving cannot be other than the original form, the Alpha, out of which he lives and which provides him the very instruments for his striving."

19. G. Siewerth, *Metaphysik der Kindheit* (Einsiedeln: Johannes Verlag, 1957, 2nd ed.), p. 23, speaks of the "personal perfection" of the child.

20. F. Ulrich, *Zur Ontologie des Menschen* (Salzburg, 1963), p. 24.

21. See F. Ulrich, "Paideia — Logos — Europa," in *Institut international d'études européennes "Antonio Rosmini"* (ed.): L'éducation de l' homme européen: Fondements et limites: Actes de la VIe Rencontre Internationale (Bozen, 1964), pp. 173-222; Ulrich, *Der Mensch als Anfang.*

human spirit needs its bodily-material sensibility: without this capacity, it could never actually come to spiritual knowledge as a human being, for all knowledge begins in the senses and is referred back to them.[22] But because there is an enduring and irreducible difference between the spirit and the senses, for all their unity in man, we understand that, in the act of knowing, it is from his original and foundational position of being drawn into and poured out into the dimension of material sensibility — that is, it is *from the other* — that the human person, as spirit, must turn back again to himself,[23] must gather himself into his own *logos* and in this sense must become, in this movement of returning from the other, *the subject* that in a certain respect he already is. It is an awe-inspiring experience to follow the development of speech in a child, from his first stammerings to the moment when he says "I" for the first time. In this occurrence the return to self happens in a primitive sense: *becoming oneself through the other.*[24]

In the second place, this "becoming oneself as receiving oneself"[25] comes about not just through other things but above all through *another Thou*, as Balthasar emphasizes in the above quote. The child does not yet know who and what he is; he discovers himself first in and through his being-with-the-world, and his being-with-the-other. If this occurs in an atmosphere of original trust, then the child experiences that his own being — as one who is communicated *(Mitgeteilt-sein)* and surrendered *(Preisgegeben-sein)* to the world and to the other — is accepted and affirmed through the other, from the very beginning. The child discovers that his own acting and his neediness elicit a reaction in the world and in his par-

---

22. Aquinas, *Ver.* 12, 3, ad 2: "primum principium nostrae cognitionis est sensus."

23. *ST* I, 14, 2, ad 1: "dicendum quod redire ad essentiam suam nihil aliud est quam rem subsistere in seipsa, forma enim inquantum perficit materiam dando ei esse, quodammodo supra ipsam effunditur, inquantum vero in seipsa habet esse, in seipsam redit." The *anima intellectiva* of the human person is the *forma substantialis* that gives what is flesh its being (life); it is that which in-forms him, for "forma dat esse."

24. In this gathering into one's own *logos*, the person in a sense accomplishes a return to his own essence, because the *anima humana* (as *forma substantialis* of the person) is essentially an *anima intellectiva*. For this reason the human person is that creaturely essence that subsists in the proper sense: *ST* I, 14, 2, ad 1: "redire ad essentiam suam nihil aliud est quam rem subsistere in seipsa." Also see Aquinas, *Ver.* 1, 9: "quia illa quae sunt perfectissima in entibus, ut substantiae intellectualis, redeunt ad essentiam suam *reditione completa.*" Cf. J. B. Lotz, *Person und Freiheit* (Freiburg/Basel/Wien, 1979), pp. 18f.

25. F. Ulrich, *Logo-tokos. Der Mensch und das Wort* (Einsiedeln: Johannes Verlag, 2003), pp. 113, 135.

ents, that he effects change in the living and breathing space of his parents, and vice versa: the parents' acting toward their child elicits and encourages ever new action in the child, toward his discovering the world and himself. The parents affirm the child in his quite concrete situation and historicity. The child acts precisely "this way" and not otherwise, because it is this child and no other, and because it is these parents and no others. In being accepted by his parents, the child discovers that he is given back to himself precisely in and through this being accepted. For accepting a gift in the proper sense always means also affirming the giver in the gift.[26] Looking at this more closely, we thus can say: in his parents' acceptance of his being and essence, the child is given to himself. He discovers *who and what he is;* he thereby encounters himself, as it were, and comes to himself, accepts himself. And the child becomes himself in receiving himself from and through another.

On the other hand, the same goes for the parents (though not simply reciprocally): They too *become* anew what they *are* (in this case, parents), in their life with the child in the unity of giving and receiving. The parents' loving giving toward their child is at the same time a receiving of the child, and their receptivity comes to completion *as* spontaneity toward the child. Becoming oneself transpires through the reception of oneself in the loving encounter with a Thou. In the breathing space of love, of personal encounter, the notions of giving and receiving, spontaneity and receptivity can be used interchangeably.[27] A fruitfulness of love unfolds, making possible the growth and maturation of persons.[28]

26. See "Phänomenologie des Schenkens" in my study *Mit-Mensch-Sein. Phänomenologie und Ontologie der Gabe bei Ferdinand Ulrich* (Freiburg/Munich, 2004), pp. 67-144.

27. This insight into the convertibility of giving and receiving, riches and poverty, spontaneity and receptivity, but also of speaking and keeping silence in the event of loving encounter, arises from Ulrich's fundamental insight into the convertibility of being and nothing in the finitization of being, which, following St. Thomas, is both a "completum et simplex" (fullness) and also a "non subsistens" (nothing). See Ulrich, *Homo abyssus.*

28. Ulrich has demonstrated in many instances how vulnerable this original relationship of love between parents and child is, and how development and maturity are impeded precisely through false forms of love. See Ulrich, *Der Mensch als Anfang,* pp. 47-63, 91-103.

Stefan Oster

The Person Is an "Other" with Respect to Himself — He Is in Himself an I-Thou

The foregoing analysis has shown that the human person always already lives in a relation to himself that, from the perspective of Ulrich's philosophy, can hardly be thought decisively enough. If God's act of imparting being to creation is not just a gift *(Gabe)* but also a generous relinquishing of the recipient unto itself *(Freigabe)* — and thus also its task *(Aufgabe)* — then this communication of being is not simply directed toward an essence that the Giver presupposes (in and through his act of communicating being) as the place of receiving being; rather, the communication of being always has subsistent being itself as its goal. From the beginning, the communication of being "intends" nothing short of subsistence in its own self-actualization, and not merely an objectively graspable, potential essential form (in contrast to the very act of being).[29]

But if the human person is the goal of the communication of being (the event of creation), and is himself also the personal representative of this communication of being, as Ulrich has shown in analyses both wide-ranging and deep, then the task of his becoming himself in accepting himself means that he not only must deepen in and accept responsibility for the essence or nature in which he is already embedded, but beyond this must also accept himself *as a whole person.* We said: The person *arrives* at himself *(zukommen)* as the one who he has been from the beginning. But because this arrival *(Zukunft)* only transpires in and through another, as we have shown, we can say: he comes to himself *as himself, but also as an-other.*[30] In himself he is, in a certain sense, a relationship analogical to the I-Thou relation. Ulrich says, "The person is in himself an I-Thou."[31]

Therefore, the reception of oneself can never be successfully accomplished as with objects, in mere possession, nor simply in self-disposal, achieved in the sense of "I'm going to *make* something of myself," but rather only in a reception that is at the same time a generous relinquishing

---

29. H. U. v. Balthasar, *Theodramatik* II, 1, p. 263: "Essence *(Wesenheit)* is just as much given as actuality *(Wirklichkeit);* the 'I' receives itself *as a whole* from infinite freedom, as one particularly qualified in this way."

30. See also P. Ricoeur, *Das Selbst als ein Anderer* (Munich: Fink Verlag, 1996). Fr. *Soi-même comme un autre* (1990).

31. See my *Mit-Mensch-Sein,* pp. 332-66; in my judgment this insight of Ulrich goes one step beyond Balthasar.

of myself. I can never respond to the other before me by merely disposing of him as of an object; if a true encounter is going to take place, I must rather, in trust and love, generously let him go, in my very reception of him. I must be in relation to myself in this same way, receiving myself as a gift from the loving hand of the Giver. It is only in this way that I am able to affirm my *origin (Herkunft)* and my *future (Zukunft),* as from Another; and it is only thus that I am able to give myself away[32] generously as *present freedom.*[33]

Fruitfulness Within the Horizon of Personal Acting

According to this understanding, what does the "fruitfulness" of personal acting mean? Ulrich distinguishes between "generating," on the one hand, and "making" or "causing" on the other.[34] In this context, "to make" and "to cause" are to be understood as the mode of acting toward objects: we place something here, we work on something, we handle something, etc. This kind of acting is directed toward a material object that is at our disposal. Normally, cause and effect, action and passion, spontaneity and receptivity can be clearly associated with the actor, on the one hand, and the object of the action, on the other. Normally, there is also a difference in the power to exercise the act of being: the actor, in contrast to what is effected, is the one who is free and able to dispose of the other thing — and in this sense, is superior. In addition, we understand acting and handling, both in the sense of "to make," as something that remains extrinsic for the most part, at least for the one who is acting. This kind of action is not able to reach him interiorly and thus is not able to change him.

"Generating" emphasizes what is alive, the aspect of motherhood and fatherhood: in the successful case, we generate our own equal, our own likeness, that is, another person. And this occurs only in a play shared

32. Here we of course recall Kierkegaard's famous definition of the self as a "relation that relates itself to itself" and "in relating itself to itself, relates itself to the one who established the whole relationship." S. Kierkegaard, *Die Krankheit zum Tode,* Ges. Werke, Abt. 24/25 (Düsseldorf/Köln: Diederichs, 1985, 3rd ed.), p. 9.

33. See F. Ulrich, *Gegenwart der Freiheit* (Einsiedeln: Johannes Verlag, 1974).

34. See F. Ulrich, *Leben in der Einheit von Leben und Tod* (Einsiedeln: Johannes Verlag, 1999), pp. 345ff.

by another freedom — over which the other cannot ultimately exercise control — in an act in which giving oneself over to the other and receiving the other are just two sides of the same reality. And the fruit of this unifying act is another freedom beyond the other's control, another person. We cannot say, in the sense discussed above, that we have "made" the child; rather, the child arises from a living union. Through this union (which in the best case is a loving union), a third is generated. And each parent's own contribution, their essential traits and characteristics, manifest themselves in the child in an indescribable way not calculable according to causality. We could never say that the child is *simply* the product of his parents. He is far more: he is a freedom in possession of itself.

In the writings of Thomas Aquinas (but also much earlier in the Tradition, especially in Augustine), there exists an application of the image of generation to spiritual events, especially in his notion of the "interior word" *(interius verbum, verbum cordis, verbum mentis)*.[35] The outer word — what is spoken or written — is, for Thomas, only a sign of the inner word, which is a "child of the spirit," a *proles mentis*,[36] that arises from the "wedding" of the knowing spirit with the known reality. Thomas tends to assign the *res*, the known matter, the active-begetting role, that is, the fatherly role; he tends to see the contribution of the human intellect as the motherly part,[37] because the intellect is formed (particularly as *intellectus possibilis*) through the knowable forms of the real. Thus the inner word arises from a *conceptio* and is at the same time an *intentio*.[38] It is conceived (receptive) and at the same time (spontaneously) formed (it is also a

---

35. Aquinas, *Ver.* 4, 1; *ST* I, 27, 1: "quicumque enim intelligit, ex hoc ipso quod intelligit, procedit aliquid intra ipsum, quod est conceptio rei intellectae, ex vi intellectiva proveniens, et ex eius notitia procedens, quam quidam conceptionem vox significat, et dicitur verbum cordis, significatem verbo vocis. . . ."

36. See *ST* I, 33, 2, 3; see also B. Lonergan, *Verbum: Word and Idea in Aquinas* (London: Darton, Longman & Todd, 1968).

37. Aquinas, *Comp. Theol.*, 399: "quando igitur intellectus intelligit aliud a se, res intellecta est sicut pater verbi in intellectu concepti; ipse autem intellectus magis gerit *similitudinem matris*, cuius est ut in ea fiat conceptio."

38. Aquinas, *Summa contra gentiles* (= *SCG*), IV, 11: "dico autem 'intentionem intellectam' id quod intellectus in seipso concipit de re intellecta, quae quidem in nobis neque est ipsa res quae intelligitur; neque est ipsa substantia intellectus; sed est quaedam similitudo concepta intellectus de re intellecta, quam voces exteriores significant; unde et ipsa intentio 'verbum interius' nominatur, quod est exteriori verbo significatum." *SCG* IV, 11: "est autem de ratione interioris verbi, quod est intentio intellecta."

processio[39] and a *formatum*[40]). It is formed from the unity of the receptivity and spontaneity of the knowing spirit in its encounter with the real. Thus too the spoken word, as a child of the spirit, is what spirit generates, the expression of its fruitfulness.

If the word truly arises from this relationship, then the spoken word in a certain sense bears the signature of the relation of the person to the reality that is known and expressed. In other words, in his every word, a person shows his position in relation to the matter at hand. Does the word live? Does the person's speech draw life from reality truly known? Has the speaker truly given reality a "home" in himself, in order to "wed" himself to it in the act of knowing? Has he made himself so available to the object of his knowing that it can itself show and reveal itself to him? That is, in the act of knowing, was the known reality relinquished to itself in the first place such that it could truly, in the positive sense, take effect in the knower in a fruitful way? Or did the person, by virtue of an unbalanced spontaneity, approach reality with a dominating *ratio* that seeks only to *grasp* it in his "concept," in order to dictate to reality just how he would like to have and use it? In this question we see that there is a speaking that amounts merely to making, and a speaking that draws its life from a deep encounter with what is concretely real; this latter speaking is born from an act of generation.[41] Thus Thomas recognizes an ever-deeper knowing and an ever-deeper union of the knower with the known.[42] This kind of speaking draws life from the knower's loving attention to the known reality, which is not simply something that is "handled" or "treated," but rather something that also was itself able to take effect in the knower, to be fruitful, to generate, because the attention of the knower toward the known was character-

---

39. *SCG* IV, 11.

40. Aquinas, *Pot.* 8, 1: "intellectus enim sua actione format rei definitionem, vel etiam propositionem affirmativam seu negativam. Haec autem conceptio intellectus in nobis proprie verbum dicitur."

41. F. Ulrich shows through various approaches in *Logo-tokos* (Einsiedeln: Johannes Verlag, 2003) that knowing attention to the subject matter succeeds and is "whole" ("heil") insofar as it is a *loving* attention. See also H. U. v. Balthasar (*Von den Aufgaben der Katholischen Philosophie in der Zeit* [Einsiedeln: Johannes Verlag, 1998], p. 35 [first published in 1946/47]) : "To want to understand is love; therefore, outside of love, no true and fruitful thinking is possible."

42. *ST* I, 27, 1, ad 2: "manifestum est enim quod quanto aliquid magis intelligitur, tanto conceptio intellectualis est magis intima intelligenti, et magis unum, nam intellectus secundum hoc quod actu intelligit, secundum hoc fit *unum* cum intellecto."

ized by openness and readiness to give himself over to the real in its ever-concrete and historical essence and being. The knower is ready to receive and not merely to exercise a mighty, even violent, control over the known. Such speech, born of loving attention, has a greater power to take effect, indeed, to be. It has a greater power to refer [to reality — *Trans.*] *(Zeigekraft)* and thus also, with respect to the other who is addressed, a greater capacity for generation *(Zeugungskraft)*. It witnesses to *(bezeugt)* the known reality. Such speech does not want to be seen as itself; rather it wants, in and through its words, the known reality to be known in its own right. Thus in the listener a word conceals itself, in favor of the subject matter itself; the word does not wish itself to perdure; it "dies" in order to rise again in the listener, in his act of knowing, his encounter with the real. This is creative speech.

But while the person, in his being and acting, is always already one who communicates himself, actual speech is simply the special form of self-communication that properly belongs to and identifies the human person. But in fact *everything* about the person is self-communication. His bodily-sensory manner of appearing is the expressive form of his spirit. The person therefore communicates himself in every movement, every gesture, every encounter with the real itself. But in every instant of his life, the human person is one who brings to completion in himself the unity of setting out into the world, on the one hand, and, on the other hand, returning to oneself, gathering up the world and the other; for this reason, the person is charged with enacting this unity also as the unity of giving and receiving. In giving, in communicating himself, he receives the other, and thereby receives himself from the other. Going out of himself to the other, he returns from the other to come to himself. Only in loving can a person achieve this unity. Only as a lover does he give (himself) in such a way that he also receives himself at the same time; only as a lover does he receive in self-giving. Otherwise, his acting splinters into forms of encounter that only superficially resemble what we have described above, but which draw life from the wealth, the spontaneity of an "I" turned in on itself, one that is no longer able to receive and therefore must remain barren.[43]

On the other hand, if this communication of self draws its life from a depth in which the person receives, recognizes, wills, and affirms himself,

---

43. In this regard, see Ulrich's many analyses, such as *Erzählter Sinn. Ontologie der Selbstwerdung in der Bilderwelt des Märchens* (Einsiedeln: Johannes Verlag, 2002, 2nd ed.).

then the person's effecting, as self-communication, is all the more intensely an act of being, the deeper and more truly the person has brought to completion the *reditio in seipsum,* in the sense of self-reception. It is the one who in his acting has lovingly accepted himself as a gift, and who therefore can lovingly give himself away, who can be fruitful.

Let us illustrate what we mean by using an example that most grown-up people can relate to: if we think of the teachers we had in school, we remember, even in retrospect, that those teachers were best who first of all loved their field, had a passion for the subject they taught, and who, secondly, really enjoyed us, their students. We could tell that for these teachers, *we* were important, not just the subject. Having enthusiasm and giving oneself over to the subject matter while attending to another person — these actions are able to call something forth from that other person, in a way that images the birth process. In the first place, in some, an interest is awakened: perhaps the question of why all this is so important to the teacher; perhaps also the conclusion that it is something that somehow enriches *his* life at least, introducing into his life quality, joy, and thus more meaning. And if the teacher's attention to the students is also truly interested in them, is really affectionate *(mögend),* then this attention may be able *(vermag)* to awaken a similar interest in the student, perhaps even a passion. In the best case, this awakening is so deep that the student's future life is shaped, changed, influenced by it. Something new has been born and begins to grow; through the newly discovered love of this subject, one's own life is enriched and deepened. Perhaps a student becomes so enamored of mathematics or Latin or sports that he himself studies the subject and becomes a teacher himself. It may be that we later recall little of the concrete content of the school subject, but there are generally enduring memories of the atmosphere the teacher was able to cultivate: deep interest in the subject and in the person.

If we presuppose all the foregoing, we can claim that this enthusiasm awakened in the other is not something that can be *made* but rather is a child, *generated* by love, which lends life to things and actions. Love is this enthusiasm's *actus* or, alternatively, its *forma formarum.*[44] Love awakens its own image in the other, but not by, so to say, pouring what is its own into the other, but rather by taking for granted that what it has to give is in fact

---

44. H. U. v. Balthasar, *Glaubhaft ist nur Liebe* (Einsiedeln: Johannes Verlag, 1975, 4th ed.); here especially, "Die Liebe als Form," pp. 83ff. (*Love Alone Is Credible,* trans. D. C. Schindler [San Francisco: Ignatius Press, 2005]; "Love as Form," pp. 125ff.).

already present in the other from the beginning. Loving communication of self is always directed toward the other *as other,* in his freedom as other. And if self-communication is able to touch him there, then a birth comes about through a relatedness that is similar to the act of communication *(Mitteilung): con-naissance* is the French expression for knowing *(Erkenntnis):* a shared act of birthing.

The loving presence of the other in me is able to awaken, in the depths of me, my very own act of being as an act of self-performance; it is able to help bring to life what in fact is already there. And in this way this kind of shared personal fruitfulness can be understood along the lines of the old axiom according to which a cause causes something similar to itself ("omne agens agit sibi simile"). Just as the teacher in our example always communicates something of his own interiority (passion, enthusiasm) along with his relaying the subject matter, so too one can become fruitful in this sense only if one has affirmed and accepted one's very self in love — because only such a one can give himself, can communicate himself generously in his action. If he has not done this, then he has to try to conceal himself in the very communication of the subject. In this negative sense he must attempt to remain purely objective, or he must present himself as something he is not — which will lead to his not being experienced authentically by others. Or, using the image of generation: he remains barren and impotent.

The Fruitfulness of the Baptized: To Witness to Christ
(Christus be-zeugen)

The foregoing raises the following question: How do we witness to Christ? We have said that we manage to live being as love only when we receive and affirm ourselves from the loving hand of the Giver of the gift. But we experience ourselves, in our brokenness and sin, as precisely unable to do this: we cannot do this by ourselves because we do not trust that the Giver truly does give the gift. And we do not trust ourselves; we do not forgive ourselves and we are thus unable to recognize and accept the gift. And furthermore, in refusing the gift, we deny the Giver. In our unbelief, we either want, despairing, to be ourselves, or, despairing, we want not to be ourselves.[45]

45. See S. Kierkegaard, *Die Krankheit zum Tode, Ges. Werke,* Abt. 24/25 (Düsseldorf/Köln: Diederichs, 1985, 3rd ed.), p. 9.

The faith teaches us: true acceptance of oneself is possible only in Christ and with him, who radically accepted us ("while we were still sinners," Rom 5:8!), and forgave our *entire guilt* (Mt 18:32!). Only with Christ are we able continually to receive and accept responsibility for ourselves. What he has accomplished gives us the ability to do this, and in our trust in him and love for him, we learn anew to say "yes" to ourselves — but in a way that is at the same time a "yes" to Christ in us: "not I but Christ lives in me" (Gal 2:20). Through him, we have a share in his love. Whenever our loving communication of ourselves has this relationship as its source, we communicate him as well. "Omne agens agit sibi simile" thus means: every Christian whose living and acting originates in the love of Christ, witnesses to Christ himself *(bezeugt ihn selbst)*, whether with or without words. This kind of *witness (Bezeugen)* has creative power: when the other is touched by this love, he discovers and experiences it in himself. As in our earlier example: a person who allows himself to be touched by the love of Christ through another, begins to give more and more time and space to this experience. This in turn leads to a decisive deepening in his life, an increasing joy, new quality, deeper, real meaning. Someone who truly gives the Lord space in his life, becomes in a certain way new. His life takes on a new orientation and a new foundation; he is "born again," as the fourth evangelist says (Jn 3:3). This kind of fruitfulness is the fruitfulness of Christians, of lovers; it is capable of generating and able to awaken faith, new life, in the other.

Dialectic and Dialogic:
The Identity of Being as Fruitfulness
in Hans Urs von Balthasar

Emmanuel Tourpe

> *"The greatest of differences does not violate the unity and simplicity of being."*
>
> Gustav Siewerth[1]

The weary or distracted reader will no doubt have taken the argument that occurs in the course of a difficult chapter of *Theologic* II for a facile formula — at best a play on words, perhaps a quibble: "Love," the Swiss theologian assures us here, "can be recognized as the supreme mode, and thus in this sense as the 'truth,' of being, without our having for all that to exalt it above truth and being."[2]

A strange logic this is, which affirms an elevation of the gift above the *rationes entis,* and which seems at the same time to affirm its equality with the other transcendentals: for, according to this statement, love would dominate over truth, but truth would apparently be reintegrated into its proper place by this very subordination. . . . To say the least, it would seem to be a cavalier way of reconciling, through a cheap linguistic turn, the Scotist *prius* of charity with the Thomist circle of love and knowledge.

---

1. Cited in Hans Urs von Balthasar, *Theo-Logic: Theological Dramatic Theory,* vol. II: *Truth of God,* trans. Adrian Walker (San Francisco: Ignatius Press, 2004), p. 185.

2. Hans Urs von Balthasar, *La Théologique,* vol. II, *Vérité de Dieu,* trans. B. Déchelotte and C. Dumont (Brussels: Culture et Vérité, 1995) (= *TL* II), p. 192 (Eng., *Theo-Logic,* vol. II: *Truth of God*).

Translated by D. C. Schindler.

But ultimately, the hurried reader will scarcely have done anything but stumble over this rhetorical curiosity. He will no doubt have failed to notice that, woven into this unlikely sophism, is one of the purest expressions of Balthasar's thought. It is perhaps the most condensed and powerful of the whole of his work — the moment in which his genius makes itself most manifest.

Dialectic of Fruitfulness

The sequence of chapters within which this passage, which makes love the "supreme mode without forcing us to exalt it above the other transcendentals," occurs, lies at the heart of the *Theologic's* overall project: it is quite simply to elucidate the principal question, which is that of the Logos in God, and to resolve it by demonstrating the identity of being and gift.

While one expected a move to revoke Hegel and the *"identitas entis,"* Balthasar started off this reflection surprisingly by veering sharply, not at all away from the threatening idealism, but, strangely, from Heidegger and Marion — at the place in fact of a certain conception of the ontological difference:[3] the "immanence" in the surpassing[4] of being. In other words, this identity in difference characterizes Balthasar's theology to such an extent that it would be incorrect to reduce it to the schema of a vague polarity, or, even worse, to the juxtaposition of divine love and the difference of being as we see in J. L. Marion. "Being and love" are for the Swiss theologian strictly "co-extensive";[5] there is no "God without being."

It is because Balthasar conceives gift, above all, as "fruitfulness" that he is capable, in contrast to Marion, of understanding their co-extension.

It would be a serious misunderstanding to reduce the Balthasarian doctrine to the side of "intersubjectivity" and dialogical thought alone; to be sure, his most profound concern lies invariably within the wake of Buber, Rosenzweig, and especially Ebner,[6] but he seeks above all to affirm the "emergence of a spiritual subject" that is "manifestly more than a natu-

3. *TL* II, p. 146, fn. 10.
4. *TL* II, p. 146, fn. 10.
5. Hans Urs von Balthasar, "Der Zugang zur Wirklichkeit Gottes," in J. Feiner and M. Löhrer, eds., *Mysterium Salutis* (Einsiedeln, 1967), pp. 15-45: here, 17.
6. Cf. Balthasar, *TL* II, p. 58.

ral process"[7] in opposition to the concept of Hegelian production.[8] Entering unwittingly into the wake of F. Ravaisson's philosophy of marriage, but explicitly following the footsteps of Scheeben, Balthasar conceives the fruitful union of man and woman as the primary analogue of the trinitarian life. Fruitfulness is therefore not only, as Hegel has it, the law proper to organic life, but it is equally the law of spiritual life; it is, moreover, the sole condition that — this time in agreement with Hegel — enables one to understand that the "spiritual 'I-Thou' relation cannot find completion except within a third term."[9]

This "production of a fruit," which can be achieved only by an inclusive triadic logic, is the real canon of being, its fundamental law. That is why it allows us to overcome the abstract spiritualism of classical dialogicism, and to understand the "gratuitous gift of creation through the divine Logos."[10] It above all allows "the parents' relation to the child" to become "the key of the trinitarian logic"[11] in the world.

Thus, Balthasar acknowledges that, as Hegel already understood, "in the identity of God there is already an other,"[12] and the other as an objective third; what Hegel did not understand is the inadequacy of speculative reflection for characterizing the divine life and the law of being: in the identity of the "reflexive" moment there is "the Spirit as free love and as transcending the 'one' and the 'other'":[13] "God's boundless plenitude" "requires the reciprocal ecstasis of the 'persons' in order to unfold itself as love."[14] One notices the vocabulary of "necessity" that Balthasar uses here, which is in search of a "reason" for the life of God, and finds it in the notion that the fullness of God "could never exhaust itself by a single hypostasis."[15] This reciprocal ecstasis, which expresses itself in fruitfulness, is "required" for the unfolding of absolute love "and for that very reason is absolute truth."[16]

---

7. Balthasar, *TL* II, p. 62.
8. Balthasar, *TL* II, p. 60.
9. Balthasar, *TL* II, p. 63.
10. Balthasar, *TL* II, p. 62.
11. Balthasar, *TL* II, p. 59.
12. Balthasar, *TL* II, p. 195.
13. Balthasar, *TL* II, p. 195.
14. Balthasar, *TL* II, p. 194.
15. Balthasar, *TL* II, p. 194.
16. Balthasar, *TL* II, p. 194.

The fruitfulness of the reciprocal love of the Persons, according to which God is "always greater" in his very being, is thus the great "law" of divine being: the Father is in no way obliged to generate the Son, as Hegel believes, in order to know himself; it is rather, reversing Hegel, because gratuitous and "groundless" love is always already true, that the Father generates the Son: "perfected love presupposes a completed understanding,"[17] but this understanding is a fruit of the love which, in this sense, "surpasses being and the knowledge it has of itself."[18]

Such an understanding is not opposed to Thomas's mature trinitarian theology, which distinguishes the common love by which the three persons love, "the love that is God himself,"[19] and the fruit itself of this love, which is the Holy Spirit:[20] "in this way, God subsists in himself through a real identity (God is God), but he also subsists in himself as God known in God who knows (according to the procession of the Word) and as God loved in God who loves (according to the procession of affection or the affection of love)."[21]

Nevertheless, one cannot avoid the impression, which was set in clear relief by L. B. Puntel and then E. Brito, that the *De Deo uno* remains, as it were, juxtaposed to the *De Deo trino*: "Thomas presupposes the unity that embraces the moments of the *verum* and the *bonum*, but he does not thematize their convergence as the very event of the divine being."[22]

It is this lack of systematicity for which Balthasar compensates implicitly by articulating the trinitarian theology of St. Thomas in the light of an insight from Bonaventure:[23] the identity of being is that of *love*, which positively includes difference in itself but does so as a twofold fecundity (similar Word and desiring Impression) in which being transcends itself internally in a mediated unity as love.

Hence the inclusion of the passage taken from Siewerth's *Metaphysics of Childhood*, which affirms that love is "more comprehensive than being itself; it is the transcendental 'pure and simple' which embraces the reality

17. Balthasar, *TL* II, p. 191.

18. Balthasar, *TL* II, p. 190.

19. G. Emery, *La théologie trinitaire de saint Thomas d'Aquin* (Paris: Éditions du Cerf, 2004), p. 273.

20. Emery, *La théologie trinitaire de saint Thomas d'Aquin*, p. 273.

21. Emery, *La théologie trinitaire de saint Thomas d'Aquin*, p. 276.

22. E. Brito, *Dieu et l'être d'après Thomas d'Aquin et Hegel* (Paris: PUF, 1991), p. 129.

23. Emery, *La théologie trinitaire de saint Thomas d'Aquin*, p. 37.

of being, truth, and goodness."[24] What we see here is a following of Siewerth beyond the Thomist doctrine in a non-nullifying but nevertheless real way: if difference is always the non-identity of an identity,[25] it must therefore be thought within the unity of being; for only love understood as the supreme mode of being, as marked by the action common to the Persons (an action that St. Thomas specifies only once as spiritual love and verbal thought), allows such a self-differentiation of being. In this, Bonaventure's insight has to be reintegrated into the Thomist schema, in order to meet the requirement of identity and self-differentiation.

Thus, love is able to be at once the supreme mode and the truth of being, because it is "love that flouts every restriction, and by which in fact the miracle of fruitfulness realizes itself, as this is reflected at the very level of creation, in the child who proceeds from his parents."[26]

The Shadow of Hegel

The Integration of Hegel

As we have seen, Balthasar does not leave unity and alterity "idly" juxtaposed to one another, any more than he finds their resolution outside of themselves in the accretion or the *torso* of being. He is perfectly aware that Hegel was the first to conceive "the other" as "a datum belonging to the fullness of the divine One."[27]

The second volume of *Theologic* has its place thus decidedly within the amphibology of Hegelian love,[28] which could be interpreted either in the dialectical or in the dialogical sense.

To be sure, against the Hegelian reduction of love to logic, that is, against the dialectic, Balthasar erects the statue of Blondel: the French philosopher, who became an increasingly weighty figure for the Swiss theologian, showed that the conceptual contradiction is subordinate to real privation in an integral logic of life.[29] In fact, the Hegelian dialectic is nothing

24. Cited in Balthasar, *TL* II, p. 191.
25. Brito, *Dieu et l'être d'après Thomas d'Aquin et Hegel*, p. 107, fn. 138.
26. Balthasar, *TL* II, pp. 177-78.
27. Balthasar, *TL* II, p. 130.
28. Balthasar, *TL* II, p. 43.
29. Balthasar, *TL* II, p. 48; cf. pp. 28-30.

but a logic cut off from life, constructed upon the principles of identity and difference, which appear as abstract "residues" of "the constitution of the world."[30] The effective contraries "do not stand independently from one another, but different with respect to one another" by virtue of the fact that "in reality, difference, that is to say, 'that which is other than oneself,' is always surpassed by a third term, at the level of which one may posit this alterity."[31]

Nevertheless, if Hegel is thus lacking the true sense of being which is "polarity,"[32] the dialogicians who lead us to the "threshold"[33] of the true logic have forgotten a lesson that the philosopher of Jena did not for his part overlook, insofar as he related love to marriage: that is why generation or fecundity,[34] the "knot" of the entire Balthasarian logic, ultimately lies within the perspective of Hegelian logic. For Balthasar, it is a matter of thinking difference on the basis of the divine identity[35] while at the same time correcting the Hegelian sense of generation,[36] i.e., of love: Balthasar's entire endeavor aims not at dismantling dialectic, but in thinking through the "poverty of abstraction" in connection with the "poverty of the flesh of the Word."[37]

In reality, Balthasar radicalizes the unattained goal of Hegel, for whom the other is "in the end absorbed and dissolved into unity,"[38] by affirming the "contradiction of love"[39] in the place of conceptual contradiction.[40] This contradiction of love is resolved in fecundity and receives its witness in the child, in whom the "*unity* of 'poverty' and 'wealth'"[41] manifests itself. That is why there is in childhood that *simplicitas entis (Einfalt)*

---

30. Balthasar, *TL* II, p. 34.
31. Balthasar, *TL* II, p. 34.
32. Balthasar, *TL* II, p. 48.
33. Balthasar, *TL* II, p. 58.
34. Balthasar, *TL* II, p. 59.
35. Balthasar, *TL* II, p. 198.
36. Balthasar, *TL* II, p. 192.
37. Balthasar, *TL* II, p. 21.
38. Balthasar, *TL* II, p. 130.

39. Hans Urs von Balthasar, *La Dramatique divine*, vol. III, *L'action* (= *DD* III), trans. R. Givord and C. Dumont (Namur: Culture et Vérité, 1990), p. 305. For an English translation, see Hans Urs von Balthasar, *Theo-Drama: Theological Dramatic Theory*, vol. IV: *The Action*, trans. Graham Harrison (San Francisco: Ignatius Press, 1994).

40. Cf. Balthasar, *TL* II, pp. 192ff.
41. Balthasar, *TL* II, pp. 192ff. Italics ours.

that pervades Balthasar's corpus and responds letter for letter to the *identitas entis.*

It is thus fruitfulness that allows Balthasar to think, not the equivalence of the "one" and the "other," but the integration of a living difference in the simplicity of childhood. Made objective in the "common fruit" of the love between the Father and the Son, which is love as Holy Spirit, this simple childhood of fecundity, which is "active unity at the heart of difference,"[42] proceeds from "generative gift" and "grateful receptivity."[43] Child of the Begetter and the Begotten, the Spirit is the identity of the other in God, but as fruitful love.

Thus, corresponding to the reflection of Hegel's absolute spirit, we have Balthasar's fecundation of the absolute Spirit: in other words, in the place of the "I" that possesses itself in reflection there is the birth of the "We." The divine fruitfulness is for all that no less a form of reflection, but of the identical "in" the other, and not "by means of" the other as it is in absolute idealism.

From the Dramatic Structure of Truth
to the Truthful Structure of Drama

Balthasar thus shows quite clearly the "dia-logic" of divine truth, that is, the expressive character of the *verbum mentis* both in the intra-trinitarian procession (Bonaventure)[44] and in the human word (Siewerth):[45] "it is necessary to insist on the fact that the word and the concept . . . are not brought to life without the continual return to the image; . . . detached from it, they become a lifeless structure."[46]

Similarly, following Adrienne von Speyr, he has made strikingly manifest the relationship of Christ's vision (qua *comprehensor*) to his faith (qua *viator*).[47] Everywhere throughout his work, he reveals how the Logos refers the freedom given to itself to the "unreserved truth" "by allowing himself to be spontaneously and gratefully poured out by the Fa-

---

42. Balthasar, *DD* III, p. 302.
43. Balthasar, *DD* III, p. 302.
44. Balthasar, *TL* II, p. 179.
45. Balthasar, *TL* II, p. 277.
46. Balthasar, *TL* II, p. 278.
47. Balthasar, *TL* II, p. 318.

ther."[48] That is why D. C. Schindler is perfectly correct to sum up Balthasar's thought with the notion of a "dramatic structure of truth."[49]

We could nevertheless raise the following question: Has Balthasar given sufficient emphasis to the "truthful structure of drama"? It is not the case, of course, that Balthasar failed to understand the "truth of love,"[50] nor even that he neglected the fact that "every genuine choice, every decision, presupposes a prior knowledge."[51] But it remains the case that one does not always see that "the form of knowledge that is achieved (by transcending itself) in love"[52] is the mediator of the "liberality" common to the processions. The identity or the union of difference in being as love seems at times in Balthasar to be nothing but the final fruit of love — the Spirit himself.

Balthasar leaves one to think that the union of difference is acquired solely in the conspiration of the "We," that is, in the "subjective and objective"[53] will of the self as Love. What one occasionally suspects to be lacking in Balthasar is therefore a consideration of the order of the processions, which he in fact refers to only in passing,[54] or in relation to the trinitarian inversion.

When he faces — at least twice[55] — the Augustinian and Thomist objection, according to which the generation of the Son is intellectual, Balthasar judges it to be an anthropological projection.[56]

That is also why Balthasar is able to give the impression of not sufficiently expressing the in-stance or "reflexivity" of indifference, which is immediately thrown back into the dynamic of gift ("a spontaneity that allows itself to be poured out," "a concept that is expression," etc.).

One might think that a better taking into account of order in the cir-

---

48. Balthasar, *DD* III, p. 305.

49. D. C. Schindler, *Hans Urs von Balthasar and the Dramatic Structure of Truth: A Philosophical Investigation* (New York: Fordham University Press, 2004).

50. Balthasar, *TL* II, p. 192.

51. Balthasar, *TL* II, p. 31.

52. Balthasar, *TL* II, p. 28.

53. Balthasar, *TL* II, p. 153.

54. Balthasar, *TL* II, p. 147, and esp. 178. K. J. Wallner, *Gott als Eschaton: Trinitarische Dramatik als Voraussetzung göttlicher Universalität bei Hans Urs von Balthasar* (Vienna: Heiligenkreuzer Verlag, 1992), pp. 161ff., does not seem to resolve the problem.

55. Balthasar, *DD* III, p. 305, and *TL* II, pp. 175ff.

56. It is remarkable that Emery's conclusion arises directly against such an interpretation of St. Thomas (Emery, *La théologie trinitaire de saint Thomas d'Aquin*, p. 484).

culation of the processions, i.e., a more direct expression of the specification of the common love by the generated Word, would permit the correction of certain apparent tendencies to one-sidedness. Doesn't one go a bit too far by emphasizing the unique "identity of gift" without taking sufficient note of its "speculative" moment *(omne agens agit sibi simile . . .)*?

If Balthasar indeed demonstrates the "background" foundation of divine intellection in the common love, does he make sufficiently manifest the specification by the Word of the common will in the Spirit? Does Balthasar do sufficient justice to Rahner's position, which he discharges in two lines in the *Theologic*,[57] and which aimed precisely at pointing out the reflection of the gift — which Balthasar has a tendency to refer to the spiration of the Spirit. In this, we are asking, in the end, whether Balthasar has sufficiently taken note of the specificity of the generation of the Word *as* word.

These reflections intend merely to carry out the step Balthasar held in suspension, to follow through the path he opened up. In effect, if the desired fruit of the common love, which is the Spirit as personal love, is indeed co-spirated in the order of the generation of the Word, then *conceptio* and *formatio* have a reflexive and coincident value. The form takes its due place in the figure as mediation of the appearing ground, and is thus able to allow the rejection of the "pure rhythmaticians" like Przywara. Love is worthy, not only of faith, but necessarily of the eyes of faith. The Father's kenosis in the Son is not an unmotivated exinanition; it is the gift of itself as motive; it is therefore, in its depths, *manifestation.*

All of these points call for thorough verifications; our purpose in presenting them is heuristic. It must nevertheless be admitted, however, that in order to continue Balthasar's work, there would be something to be gained in developing further what we have called the truthful structure of drama, that is, the manifestative character of the common love. This would be a definitive integration of Hegel, because the reflexive element of fruitfulness would be better noted, love being willed in the word.

It could, moreover, be the case that, in this endeavor, the figure of Franz von Baader, the theosopher of the manifestation and mediation of God, would not be without aid for the work of "integrating" or "reinstating" definitively the *identitas entis* into the simplicity of love. Hans Urs von Balthasar in fact regretted that the "dialogicians" had "completely ignored

---

57. Balthasar, *TL* II, pp. 173ff.

the importance of Franz von Baader, who opposes idealism by founding the 'I' upon the 'Thou' that offers it the space for it to be":[58] "the need for the unity of consciousness [self-preservation] imposes [on it] the law of having to maintain itself in relation to a similar unity, to a Thou, and in a reciprocity of action with it."[59]

Baader is perhaps not only at the origin of "the first attempt ever made to reconcile Thomas Aquinas and Hegel,"[60] as the Swiss theologian had described him, but in fact could perhaps himself succeed in fully bringing Balthasar together with the Angelic Doctor and the philosopher of Jena.[61]

58. Balthasar, *TL* II, p. 49, fn. 49, referring to F. von Baader, *Sämtliche Werke*, vol. IV, ed. F. Hoffmann (Aalen: Scientia Verlag, 1997), p. 227.

59. Von Baader, *Sämtliche Werke*, p. 227, cited in Balthasar, *TL* II, p. 49, fn. 49. "Baader wrote," Balthasar acknowledges, "the philosophy" that would correspond better to the "poetry" by which E. Przywara had expressed the authorization of the "abyssal dramatics" "to a Eucharist and to the wedding feast in which the horrifying hiatus that separates time and eternity will be, not fulfilled, but radiantly illuminated by the trinitarian life" (*La Dramatique divine*, vol. IV, *Le dénouement* [Namur: Culture et Vérité, 1993], p. 437).

60. Balthasar, *Geschichte des eschatologischen Problems in der modernen deutschen Literatur*, 2nd ed. (Einsiedeln: Johannes Verlag, 1998), p. 635.

61. The present paper is in the following series: E. Tourpe, "Esprit, nature et médiation. Un questionnement philosophique de La Théologique III de H. U. von Balthasar," in *Communio. Revue catholique internationale* 1 (1998): 182-98; "La logique de l'amour. A propos de quelques volumes récemment traduits de H. U. von Balthasar," in *Revue théologique de Louvain* 2 (1998): 202-28; "La puissance comme acte suprême. A propos de la 'sainte indifférence' au principe et fondement de la connaissance chez Hans Urs von Balthasar," in A. M. Jerumanis and A. Tombollini (eds.), *La missione teologica di Hans Urs von Balthasar* (Lugano: Eupress FTL, 2005), pp. 151-62; "Sur un mot de Hans Urs von Balthasar. La positivité de l'être comme amour à l'arrière-plan de Theologik III," to be published in *Gregorianum* 1 (2008).

Can a Christian Be a Good Citizen?

Can a Christian Be a Good Democrat, a Dedicated Member of the *Polis,* in a Time of War?

Roberto Graziotto

> *"Election occurs in the womb of eternity, but vocation bursts forth in time. It may be possible, however, to live as one of the elect even if one does not yet know anything about one's own vocation. One lives a hard life without any romantic religious terminology. If someone is a soldier, he wins glory with the sword. If someone is a politician, he weaves his own intrigues. . . . Only a hidden availability of the heart, which may not even be truly conscious, allows Him who elects from all eternity not only to direct the earthly actions of the elect individual insofar as the future is concerned, but also to interpret them in advance as holy actions."*
>
> Hans Urs von Balthasar, *König David*[1]

Introductory Remarks

Allow me to make a brief introductory statement, a simple premise of the sort that is typical of a teacher who is accustomed to reformulating complex questions in simple terminology, so that his students can understand what he is saying.

A Christian is a man. Man, as an individual and as a community

---

1. Hans Urs von Balthasar, *König David* (Einsiedeln: Johannes Verlag, 2004), p. 13.

This paper is dedicated to Ferdinand Ulrich and translated by Michael J. Miller.

(family, nation), was "created to praise, reverence and serve God"[2] in his absolute positivity. What do I mean by the phrase, God in his absolute positivity? In the first place, something obvious and a bit redundant, because to say "God" is to mean this absolute positivity. To say "God" is to express a reality that is inscrutable. The expression "absolute positivity" is also a reference to this inscrutable reality. Every attempt at a linguistic or conceptual determination of God always involves a reduction of this reality, which Adrienne von Speyr and Hans Urs von Balthasar, in the bosom of the Christian tradition, call "the ever-greater God"! I am trying now to express this reality that is always greater — well aware of the limitations of any definition whatsoever of God — as a Yes which is absolute, free, characterized by communion *(comunionale),* indeterminable, and founded solely upon itself.

Man was created to say Yes, to assent to this absolute and communional Yes which is God. If man accomplishes this Yes, if he remains faithful to the purpose of his having been created, then he possesses a power that is the image of this God as absolute and communional positivity.

Democracy, considered not in its adjectival form describing a particular political party, but quite simply as a form of state government and politics, is precisely one political form that expresses this power of man; and if man, as an individual and as a community, is *imago Dei,* then he can exercise his "-cracy," his power *(Mächtigkeit),* in a positive way as a nation as well.

Who Is the Christian?

Who is the Christian? A human being who receives and says Yes to the definitive revelation of God in his positivity — which men had forgotten how to affirm — through the sending, *novissimis temporibus,* of the Lamb who was slain *(Agnus, qui occisus est),* who does not slay in turn; in a word, as the victim who makes a victim of no one. This *Agnus, qui occisus est* is the definitive revelation of God, to which man can assent, because "He who was defeated is the victor."

The Christian is not a man "of this world," even though obviously he

2. *The Spiritual Exercises of St. Ignatius of Loyola,* trans. Louis J. Puhl, S.J. (Westminster, Md.: The Newman Press, 1951), p. 12 (paragraph 23).

is "in this world" and as such is called to assume responsibility for being present in it. Can a Christian be a good citizen of a democracy? The political form of a democratic state is the political form that the Christian, in present-day Western civilization, has to deal with. This is a simple statement of historical and sociological fact. The Christian — unlike someone who thinks that the political form of the liberal democratic state is the definitive form of politics, the culmination of the historical process — now lives out his own membership in this form of government simply and loyally, without thereby concluding philosophically that it is the only possible form. Man also knows that as an individual and as a community he has to act *in angustia temporum* (Charles de Foucauld), if he can regard the positive and the negative aspects of democracy in this way.

A people that has lost existential access to its original purpose in life will no longer be able to exercise its anthropological power of being and of meaning, or (considered within the specific context of this presentation) its political power of liberty, and hence it will presumably travel on paths that are occupied by "the prince of this world," by "the father of lies" who is "a liar . . . a murderer from the beginning" (John 8:44), by the prince of negativity, of a No that is opposed to the absolute and free Yes that we call God. The prince of this world, says Saint Ignatius of Loyola, is the mortal foe of the human creature and wishes to obstruct what is proper to man: he wants to prevent any assent to the communional Yes which is God.

A people that has abandoned the way that leads to the Father, to that source of all positivity which has no origin, no longer has any sense of the logic of what has been revealed definitively about life, about truth, and about the way itself. Individual persons and social groups of any importance whatsoever become in this manner dedicated members of the *polis,* with the word "dedicated" *(devoti)* to be understood here in the mechanical sense of members who are not free, incapable of exercising their power of being and of meaning, who have no recollection of losing their original purpose of assenting to the absolute and communional Yes that is God. Thus, by virtue of their uncritical dedication, they do not contribute to the salvation of the *polis,* because this comes to us only in the figure of the Lamb, the victim who does not make victims of others and who, as I have said, is the definitive revelation of the Father's love.

This non-violent Lamb that has been sacrificed is, as such, the victor and savior, in short, the one who enables man to exercise his original anthropological power of being and of meaning.

The Figure of the Lamb, the Victim
Who Does Not Victimize in Turn

Obviously, one may object that this figure *(forma)* of the immolated Logos, in its radically eschatological character, cannot leave any room for realistic political activity.

In the first place, we have to say that the figure of the Lamb, the victim who does not victimize, is a grace, a gift. The Roman soldier, who in the presence of the cross acknowledges that the Crucified is truly the Son of God, is able to do so only by grace. I believe that a *polis*, also, which considers itself to be a democracy, is rendered dynamic and fruitful by this gift. In this sense it is possible — accentuating in a different way the adjective "dedicated" *("devoto")* — to declare that the Christian is the only person who can call himself a dedicated member of the *polis*, dedicated here in the sense of acknowledging a figure which alone brings salvation to the *polis* itself.

It is not possible in the present forum to demonstrate this in detail, but if indeed the *apocalypse of the American soul* has revealed that its democratic way of life is founded upon principles such as human rights, self-determination, and freedom, the ethos of social responsibility for others, the missionary fight against tyranny, and a theistic orientation, then it would not be difficult to show how these principles are also a revelation of the *soul of the Christian,* who loves and acknowledges the uniqueness and irreplaceability of the individual human being (human rights can be understood and defended only in light of this idea of the uniqueness of the individual person); who defends the anthropological power of being and of meaning in the form of genuine self-determination and freedom; who contemplates the mystery of love in the vicarious suffering of the Lamb, the victim that does not make victims of others, from which mystery springs the idea of solidarity and responsibility for others (without thereby reducing vicarious suffering to solidarity); and who acknowledges and confesses God as the sole Lord against all forms of tyranny!

All this notwithstanding, we must ask ourselves even more radically whether the Christian, this strange worshiper of a sacrificed Logos, might not conceal in his actions and sufferings an apocalyptic tendency leading to the destruction and condemnation *(dannazione)* of all power. This is basically Nietzsche's critique of Christianity. And it is true that we find ourselves here faced with a great temptation, which leftist theological currents have not been able to resist: the temptation of interpreting the anthropological power of being and of meaning as something negative *per se*, to which must be opposed a not-yet-existing positive power. The impotence of the sacrificed Lamb, as it is perceived, is contrasted here with any and all forms of the power of being and of meaning. From this theological-philosophical judgment springs, for example, the disavowal of the post-Constantinian Church (because it is said to have betrayed the powerless and non-violent love of Christ) and also the ontological contraposition of the spiritual Church and the institutional Church.

This radical perspective of the left — I use this term in the archetypal sense, as does Ernst Nolte in his book *Historische Existenz*[3] — which hypostatizes revolution as such, has almost nothing in common with the Jesus of history and of the Church's faith, nor with the reasoning of a human being who is trying to meditate on his original task. This radical ideological perspective is self-generating and remains faithful to itself even when it happens to be in power.

In the political sense, Jesus Christ is not a revolutionary. His non-violent figure — that of a victim Lamb who makes a victim of no one — does not intend *a priori* to destroy human and worldly undertakings, but rather means to shape, educate, and purify precisely these undertakings through the gift of his own figure.

Indeed, I say this as a short digression:[4] God is and remains free to summon and question man in a way that can appear to man, at first view, as destructive rather than formative. St. Augustine, for example, declares that love kills what we were, so that we can be what we were not. Obviously, Augustine does not mean destruction for destruction's sake. *Negati affirmatio*, the affirmation of what is negated. A profound assent takes place in this sort of killing by love.

The Christian who practices obedience in the sight of God and receives from him the radical call to take seriously the Sermon on the Mount could find himself in an existential situation that calls into question this formative and educational aspect of earthly duties that I mentioned ear-

---

3. Ernst Nolte, *Historische Existenz. Zwischen Anfang und Ende der Geschichte* (Munich-Zurich, 1988). Cf. Roberto Graziotto, "How Christians Should Think About Politics: Reflections in a Time of War," *Communio: International Theological Review* 31, no. 2 (Summer 2004): 259-78.

4. I added this digression after Ferdinand Ulrich read and commented on my presentation.

lier; through this questioning the Christian could be considered as the enemy of the *polis* — prophets and saints have often been considered as such. A society that truly lives according to a theistic orientation, regarding God as a free presence and not as an idea of the human mind, would have to remain in an attitude of perpetual openness in its encounters with God, who has revealed himself definitively in Jesus Christ, yet is always free to make us understand in an ever more profound, existential manner the ultimate anthropological consequences of this revelation. A society that considered the *prophets* of God as enemies of the *polis* and did not maintain the attitude of openness to God's ever-unfolding revelation of himself would lose contact with the living God and remain imprisoned by its own ideology, even if that ideology were to have a patina of romantic-religious language.

With regard to God's absolute will, we cannot pick and choose what we want to correspond to and ignore what we feel is exaggerated. We cannot respond to God's call while imposing conditions. The Christian, as a prophet or as a saint, is a radical representation of the will of God. For this reason he has often been considered as a threat to security in society and might be considered today as a destabilizing factor in a modern democracy, whether at the national or the global level.

A temptation lurks even in this openness to God's will, also: the temptation to reduce the presence of God, who is free, to an ideology! What is grace to begin with must remain grace and not become an ideological program.

(Although it is not our intention to deny, at the level of world history, any and all positive results of political action by the left[5] — not even when it happens to be in power, as in the case of some present-day social-democratic governments in Europe — nevertheless we have seen, especially in the twentieth century, the cost in terms of human lives of the revolutionary negation [revolution as such] of the anthropological power of being and of meaning, a negation revealed in political regimes in which the revolutionaries were no longer willing or able to recognize it. The history of Bolshevism as a rebellion against czarist authority, of Maoist com-

---

5. Obviously, to subsume movements such as social-democratic parties and Bolshevism under the heading of "the left" is a risky historical proposition, because the social-democratic movement suffered under the Bolshevist regime; yet at the philosophical level, from the perspective of "revolution for revolution's sake" with which I am concerned here, the social-democratic movement was unable to distinguish itself from the radical historical expression of Communism. This is still the dilemma facing European labor unions.

munism, and of leftist terrorism in the 1970s is an expression of this rebellion for rebellion's sake, which contributed, in the cases of Bolshevism and Maoism, to a dialectical, authoritarian affirmation of a regime that did not recognize the being or the meaning of any form of prophecy. I leave undecided for now the question as to whether, from the perspective that concerns me here, the twentieth-century European Fascist and National-Socialist right was solely a reaction to the Bolshevist left. It is certain that a figure like Hitler, too, is comprehensible only as a negation of that authority which is a gift and a service.)

War as a Duty

How can the anthropological power of being and of meaning be defined with respect to the social task of war? A soldier is a soldier and remains one while doing his duty; an army cannot conduct itself like a humanitarian organization, even though in certain cases it can take on some of the duties of one, as we saw on the occasion of the terrible tsunami in the Indian Ocean.

The figure of the Lamb *qui occisus est,* as the ultimate point of reference for the anthropological power of being and of meaning, does not generally demand that a democratically elected politician and a general who performs his appointed task with political authorization and as a member of a defense ministry should cease doing their jobs, but rather that they perform their duties in the presence of the figure *(Gestalt)* of the sacrificed, non-violent Lamb. In contemplating the actions and the sufferings of the Lamb who was slain and does not slay, the politician and the general, too, must determine as Christians whether their own actions are salutary *(portatore di salvezza)* or not. What happened in Abu Ghraib prison in Baghdad, for example, was certainly not a salvific action.

Contemplation of the Lamb who was defeated yet victorious does not deprive human existence of its difficulty but can help us to understand that life contains the possibility of a disponibility of heart, however concealed it may be, to the salvific action of God.

Conclusion

And so let us repeat the question: Can a Christian be a good citizen of democracy, a dedicated member of the *polis?*

As a Christian, born in our Western civilization, he will be a (more or less good) citizen of democracy, because *prima facie,* by virtue of his assent to God as positivity and to God's creation, he will comport himself loyally in his dealings with the democratic political authority. Presumably he will not be a dedicated member of the *polis* — obviously, one would have to define more precisely the intended meaning of the adjective "dedicated" — because only the figure of the defeated and victorious Lamb can demand his devotion and dedication, but since the Lamb reveals God definitively in his absolute positivity, the Christian will, in the spirit of assent, or, to put it philosophically, in the spirit of the "finitization of being," perfect himself *(finitizzerà),* will take responsibility for a definite task in the building-up or maintenance of the *polis.* In short, he cannot help behaving positively in his dealings with the *polis* itself, without, however, renouncing *his presence as a prophet or a saint,* which will make him an attentive, loyal, but also inconvenient member of the *polis* because he cannot do otherwise than to practice continual discernment as to what brings salvation or damnation to the *polis* itself.

I will interrupt my reflection here, without defining further the difference between the modalities of salvation in the natural order and in the supernatural order. I hope that in this presentation, which is meant to stimulate discussion, I have succeeded in taking into account both aspects of the one salvation offered by God to all men, which is Communion, in these last days *(novissime),* in the form of the immolated Lamb. A salvation that does not deny professional competence and responsibility in fulfilling one's human and earthly duties, but wishes to form and educate these very duties, all the while — or perhaps precisely because — aware of the difficulty of human existence and respecting the relative autonomy of men in their performance of these duties. A salvation, finally, that is not limited solely to confirming what men consider to be salvific. "Your ways, O Lord, are not our ways." The cross is and continues to be the heart in which the natural order and the supernatural order meet! It remains the ultimate modality of assent to the God who reveals himself!

Can a Christian Be a Democrat?
A (Devoted) Member of the *Polis?*
Or, The Common Good and the Modern State

V. Bradley Lewis

Can a Christian be a democrat? A (devoted) member of the *polis?* My answer to this question owes more to the thought of Aristotle, Aquinas, and Yves Simon than to Balthasar, although I doubt it is inconsistent with Balthasar's views. The question posed for this session of the conference (I do not know if this was intentional) suggests Aristotle's question whether the good man and the "serious" or "zealous" *(spoudaios)* citizen are the same.[1] Aristotle's characteristically elliptical treatment begins with the observation that different political regimes take correspondingly different views of virtue — one that seemingly would suggest the obvious superiority of aristocracy, "rule of the best" — and that different virtues must be present in any city, at least the distinctive virtues of rulers and citizens, with rulers having superior virtue. This second point curiously suggests a potentially more positive view of democracy, since there the rulers and citizens are the same. However, all of this is cast into doubt by another suggestion of Aristotle — that the real identity of the good man and the serious citizen is only possible in the "best regime,"[2] the existence of which is beyond any human capacity simply to establish[3] — as well as his later suggestion that the best regime is one most in accord with the best way of life *(bios)*.[4] This only deepens the problem, since the two candidates Aristotle considers are the contemplative life and the political life.

1. Aristotle, *Politics* 3.4.1276b 16-17.
2. Aristotle, *Politics* 3.18.1288a 38-39.
3. Aristotle, *Politics* 1260b 29, 1265a 17-18, 1288b 21-27, 1295a 25-29, 1325b 35-39, 1327a 3-4, 1330a 25-26, 37, 1331b 18-23, 1332a 28-31.
4. Aristotle, *Politics* 1323a 14-16.

In the *Nicomachean Ethics*, Aristotle straightforwardly holds that the contemplative life is best and calls the political life "second-best,"[5] a contrast left discreetly unstated in the *Politics*. This points to the tension between the two lives rather than to any resolution of it.

Nevertheless, the very emergence of philosophy as a human possibility is tied to the emergence of the city, the *polis*, and thus of politics. Aristotle's twin formulations of man as *political* animal and *rational* animal suggest this,[6] as does his account of the development of the city as a complete human community, one that provides not just for the necessities of life but for good life, involving rational discussion about the just and the unjust, the advantageous and the disadvantageous, good and evil.[7] Once the distinctive human capacity for *logos* emerges, of course, it can be applied to things that transcend human affairs, as it was by the first philosophers living in the *poleis* established on the western coast of Anatolia in the seventh century before Christ. Since, as the late and occasionally unintentionally philosophical former Speaker of the U.S. House of Representatives Tip O'Neill once said, "all politics is local," and philosophy strives, as Plato said, to comprehend "all time and all being,"[8] the tension between the two is evident and famously symbolized in the fate of Socrates at the hands of *democratic* Athens, which brings us back to our question, since I suspect that it was precisely the fate of Socrates that Aristotle had in mind in formulating his question about the relationship between the completely good man and the zealous citizen.

Can a Christian be a democrat? A (devoted) member of the *polis*? What is really meant here by "democrat"? Democracy in the classical sense meant rule by the people, the *demos*, and, practically, that meant the poor. It also meant a set of identifiable institutions and practices that included universal qualification for political office among citizens, the selection of public officials by lot, minimal or no property qualifications as a prerequisite for citizenship, short terms of office for officials, and the dominance of

5. Aristotle, *Nicomachean Ethics* 1178a 9-10; cf. 1177b 4-26.

6. See, e.g., *Nicomachean Ethics* 1.7.1097b 11, 1098a 3-4, 7-8, 9.9.1169b 18-19; *Politics* 1.2.1253a 2, 9-10, 3.6.1278b 19, 7.13.1332b 5.

7. Aristotle, *Politics* 1253a 1-18. I have discussed some of this in more detail in "Wealth, Happiness and Politics: Aristotelian Questions," in *Wealth, Poverty and Human Destiny*, ed. Doug Bandow and David L. Schindler (Wilmington, DE: ISI Books, 2003), 241-69, especially pp. 243-51.

8. Plato, *Republic* 486a.

the assembly of all citizens in the making of important decisions.[9] This is radical, direct, participatory democracy, and it exists nowhere in the modern world. "Democracy," in the modern sense, generally refers to governments broadly representative and limited by law with guarantees of basic rights for citizens who are considered, from a political perspective, as equals. When Tocqueville took America to represent the coming democratic revolution, he contrasted it to aristocracy, not in Aristotle's sense, but understood as a political form based on institutionalized inequality between citizens. "Democracy," for Tocqueville, really meant something more like *modernity* — understood primarily as the abolition of hierarchies, natural and otherwise — and here too I suspect that is what is meant.[10] I take "democrat" to mean citizen of a modern political society. But that raises another problem.

Why is the term *polis* in the question? The Greek *polis* was a small political community, small enough that some classical historians understand it by reference to the modern anthropological category of a "face-to-face society."[11] Aristotle is quite explicit that a good *polis* cannot be too large. A *polis* that is too large cannot be ordered by good laws, cannot effectively mold the characters of citizens, cannot properly deliberate, and is difficult to defend from attacks. Indeed, Aristotle states that ordering too large a *polis* is the work of a god and not a human being.[12] The *polis* is a political community commensurate to the natural sensory capacities of a human being. It is not surprising, then, that the rulers of the great empires of antiquity inevitably claimed for themselves divinity. The modern nation-state is very different from the *polis* and is only a real possibility on the basis of what an ancient man might regard as god-like power, that supplied by modern science (mass communications and transportation), which emerged out of the early modern philosophy of nature that took as its point of departure the rejection of Aristotelian natural philosophy.

The aim of the *polis* was said by Aristotle to be the common good or

9. Aristotle, *Politics* 6.2.1317b 17-1318 a3.

10. Alexis de Tocqueville, *De la démocratie en Amérique* (Cambridge, Mass.: Schoenhof's Foreign Books, 1992). See especially the introduction to vol. 1. See discussion in Pierre Manent, *Tocqueville et la nature de la démocratie* (Paris: Fayard, 1993 [orig. pub. 1983]), 13-28; and Francis Fukuyama, "The March of Equality," *Journal of Democracy* 11 (2000): 11-17.

11. M. I. Finley, *Politics in the Ancient World* (Cambridge: Cambridge University Press, 1983), ch. 4.

12. Aristotle, *Politics* 7.4.1326a 8-b24.

common advantage of the citizens.[13] That notion of the common good passed into medieval Christian political theology as the central regulative ideal for politics, as the final cause of human association.[14] A good citizen, Aquinas held, formally wills the common good.[15] So a revised version of our question might be this: Can a Christian be a good citizen of a modern state? Can one will the common good in a modern state? The question seems to suggest its own answer: Why would one not will the common good? But what of its realization? This is less clear. Some recent Christian and classically minded political thinkers have suggested that the notion of the common good is inconsistent with the political realities of the modern state. I have in mind especially Alasdair MacIntyre, and will here consider only his views.

MacIntyre's neo-Aristotelian account of the virtues ties their cultivation to engagement in "practices," defined memorably in *After Virtue* as

> any coherent and complex form of socially established cooperative activity through which goods internal to that form of activity are realized in the course of trying to achieve those standards of excellence which are appropriate to, and partially definitive of, that form of activity, with the result that human powers to achieve excellence, and human conceptions of the ends and goods involved, are systematically extended.[16]

While that work includes harsh criticisms of liberalism and concludes with a quite pessimistic comparison of modern society to the late Roman empire and a call to abandon efforts to shore up this society and in favor of working to create new forms of community that support the life of the virtues, more recently MacIntyre has increasingly turned his attention to political philosophy. Here his most important thesis is that rational claims to authority made by the modern state fail and can only succeed for *local* communities that aim at the cultivation of practices and virtue understood by reference to Aristotle's account.

---

13. Aristotle, *Politics* 3.7.1279a 25-32.

14. See my "The Common Good in Classical Political Philosophy," *Current Issues in Catholic Higher Education* 25 (2006): 25-41.

15. I refer to the interpretation of Aquinas's view here found in Yves R. Simon, *Philosophy of Democratic Government* (Chicago: University of Chicago Press, 1951), pp. 36-48.

16. Alasdair MacIntyre, *After Virtue*, 2nd ed. (Notre Dame, Ind.: University of Notre Dame Press, 1984), p. 187.

More specifically, MacIntyre has argued that modern life is characterized not only by the fragmentation of its moral vocabulary, but also by a corresponding compartmentalization of life reflected in the very structure of the modern state, described as

> a large, complex and often ramshackle set of interlocking institutions, combining none too coherently the ethos of a public utility company with inflated claims to embody ideals of liberty and justice. Politics is the sphere in which the relationship of the state's subjects to the various facets of the state's activity is organized, so that the activities of those subjects do not in any fundamental way disrupt or subvert that relationship.[17]

This is accomplished in part by the state's unwillingness to entertain philosophical questions about first principles and a consequent unwillingness to admit questions about ways of life, even when, as is the case, its decisions, far from being neutral, affect critically the viability of some ways of life, as well as the absence from political discourse of adherence to canons of rational inquiry as distinct from merely manipulative rhetoric. The state's most problematic deficiency is that it provides no opportunity for anything like systematic reasoning about politics and its effect on ways of life, each with corresponding conceptions of virtues and the common good.[18] Indeed, MacIntyre argues that the modern state has a distinct, but thoroughly inadequate, conception of the common good that is characterized by individualism and a minimal commitment to security and utility. The common good is simply the summing of individual goods, the pursuit of which the state claims to make possible.

Against this view MacIntyre suggests a rival Aristotelian-Thomistic view based on his understanding of practices and virtues. It involves reasoned inquiry into particular goods and their relationship to one another by participants in the various practices, both with respect to their own lives and with respect to their common pursuits. Such inquiry and deliberation is intrinsically pedagogical:

---

17. Alasdair MacIntyre, "Politics, Philosophy and the Common Good," in *The MacIntyre Reader,* ed. Kelvin Knight (Notre Dame, Ind.: University of Notre Dame Press, 1998), p. 236.

18. MacIntyre, "Politics, Philosophy and the Common Good," pp. 238-39.

Our primary shared and common good is found in that activity of communal learning through which we together become able to order goods, both in our individual lives and in the political society. Such practical learning is a kind of learning that takes place in and through activity, and in and through reflection upon that activity, in the course of both communal and individual deliberation.[19]

Such a conception of the common good is unavailable to the modern state with its minimal and utilitarian claims, its lack of substantive agreement about goods, practices, and virtues, and its consequent opacity to rational deliberation. This opens it up to two crucial practical defects: the often-discussed "free-rider" problem and its need for some of its citizens to sacrifice, even unto death, for its maintenance and survival. Such sacrifice is demanded, but cannot be rationally justified absent the kind of common good it necessarily lacks. Thus, being asked to die for the modern state is, MacIntyre memorably writes, like being asked to die for the telephone company.[20]

Perhaps the first thing that needs to be said about this last and rhetorically potent claim is too obvious: employees of telephone companies do, in fact, die on the job, as do the employees of other public utilities, not to mention policemen, firemen, and members of the armed forces.[21] Moreover, I think it is fair to say that when employees of public utilities die on the job (knowing something of the risks ahead of time), such people do not think of themselves as potentially dying "for the telephone company." They willingly risk their lives as necessary to providing the goods and services they do provide to the community. One might suggest that matters are otherwise with police officers, firefighters, and members of the armed forces. However, I think this is only true to a degree. They are certainly

19. MacIntyre, "Politics, Philosophy and the Common Good," p. 243.

20. See Alasdair MacIntyre, "Poetry as Political Philosophy: Notes on Burke and Yates," in *On Modern Poetry: Essays Presented to Donald Davie*, ed. V. Bell and L. Lerner (Nashville: Vanderbilt University Press, 1988), p. 149; MacIntyre, "A Partial Response to My Critics," in *After MacIntyre*, ed. J. Horton and S. Mendus (Notre Dame, Ind.: University of Notre Dame Press, 1994), p. 303; MacIntyre, "Politics, Philosophy and the Common Good," p. 236.

21. According to the federal Centers for Disease Control, the number of occupational deaths in the transportation/communications/public utilities sector of the workforce between 1980 and 1997 was 17,489. http://www.cdc.gov/mmwr/preview/mmwrhtml/mm5016a4.htm.

asked to take risks that are ordinarily much greater, and such appeals are often made in terms of patriotism. When there is conscription, the asking is replaced by orders backed by the threat of coercion.

What do such citizens think of themselves as doing? First, consider the young men and women who voluntarily enlisted in the armed forces after the attacks of September 11, 2001. Most, I take it, saw terrorism as a threat to their families and friends and to institutions (however imperfect) that they valued. They may have seen threats to their communities too, some of them perhaps not unrelated to the sorts of local communities of mutual learning that MacIntyre takes as genuinely instantiating the common good. Were they deceived?[22] Were they operating on the basis of some kind of false consciousness? Is defending modern countries like the United States, Great Britain, or Australia unreasonable, as imperfect as all three no doubt are? Local communities cannot defend themselves against terrorism and, however innocent they may be of the crimes alleged of the countries they are in by terrorists, cannot prevent becoming targets. MacIntyre does say that local communities cannot avoid cooperating with the state for some necessary purposes,[23] but if one such purpose is warfare, then arguments against the state's justification in asking soldiers to risk life and limb lose their force. If the state can be justified in that, it could in principle be justified in claiming the legitimacy to perform most of its other characteristic tasks.

That the modern state has performed those tasks imperfectly is obvious, but what kind of alternative can one articulate that really does answer to contemporary problems? To concede, as MacIntyre seems to, the unavoidable presence of the state and its utility for genuine communities seems in some respects paradoxical: if we need such a community and cannot do without it, is there not some need to support and improve it? One need not invest it with any kind of mystical or ultimate significance for such purposes. Indeed, the notion of the common good seems just the sort

---

22. I leave out consideration of the claims about any specific *casus belli* made by allied governments to concentrate on the issue of principle. Of course, one might argue that modern governments cannot but make false claims in justification of military action, but for purposes of my argument it is only necessary that such claims have been (in some cases) and can be true — even if they might in fact usually be false. I assume the usual principles of the doctrine of just war and that just wars are possible in modern times.

23. MacIntyre, *Dependent Rational Animals*, 133; "Politics, Philosophy, and the Common Good," 252.

of idea one needs to explain the need for and legitimacy of state institutions without investing them with exaggerated "meaning."[24] In many parts of the world today, the most pressing social and political problems are likely to be solved only by the successful construction of states with sufficiently strong capacities to control violence and provide a framework for solving interaction and coordination problems.[25] States are "vertical silos" for ordering such functions that need adequate capacity but also limits on scope precisely to allow the sorts of activities that MacIntyre associates with local communities to go on unthreatened.[26] While "nationhood" has, since the eighteenth century, often provided a kind of affective cement for loyalty to the state,[27] developed political societies now see their political unity in more generic terms, with increasing importance attributed to the principle of subsidiarity, well-known to Catholic social thought.[28]

One can, then, think of the "state" as a kind of instrument without thinking there is no common good as its final cause. Moreover, the fact that a community lacks agreement on fundamental matters does not automatically prove that there is no common good, any more than lack of agreement about any matter of fact proves that there are no facts of the matter. For one thing, even though it seems reasonable to demand some measure of agreement on principles and goods pursued by the political community, it is less clear what *degree* of agreement one needs to keep a modern political community, with great scope for internal pluralism, together. Certainly disagreement, even on important matters, is nothing new—Aristotle gives ample testimony to its presence in the classical *polis* in the third book of the *Politics*.[29] Disagreement may well mean that what the state as instrument can do is limited in various ways, and this, I suggest, would be no surprise to

24. Russell Hittinger argues that the modern papacy has adopted a much scaled-down view of the theological significance of state power in "The Problem of the State in *Centesimus Annus*," *Fordham International Law Journal* 15 (1991-92): 952-96.

25. See Francis Fukuyama, *State-Building: Governance and World Order in the 21st Century* (Ithaca, NY: Cornell University Press, 2004).

26. Fukuyama, *State-Building*.

27. See, e.g., Ernest Gellner, *Nations and Nationalism* (Ithaca, NY: Cornell University Press, 1983).

28. See Fukuyama, *State-Building*, 67-76; Andreas Føllesdal, "Subsidiarity," *Journal of Political Philosophy* 6 (1998): 190-218; Pontifical Council for Justice and Peace, *Compendium of the Social Doctrine of the Church* (Vatican City: Libreria Editrice Vaticana, 2004), §§185-187.

29. See also *Nicomachean Ethics* 1.3.1094b 24-26, 5.7.1134b 24-27.

Aristotle or Aquinas, nor would it constitute a reason to deny that the state's authority can be justified by the common good.

Recall the earlier point from Aristotle about the relationship between the size of the *polis* and its substantive aim of leading citizens to the good life. In the course of the discussion in Book Three that follows the discussion of the relationship between the good man and the good citizen, Aristotle distinguishes a city "truly and not verbally so called," from what he calls an alliance *(symmachia)*. The latter is a community for the sake of mutual security, exchange, and utility. A true city, however, is aimed at the good life, has magistrates in common, and manifests a concern for the character of citizens.[30] The contrast looks very much like MacIntyre's account of the two rival conceptions of the common good. Should one think of the modern state as merely an Aristotelian "alliance," not intelligible by reference to the common good and thus the source of unjustified and unjustifiable authority?[31]

This conclusion would, I think, be rejected by Thomas Aquinas.[32] I cannot go into the matter in the kind of detail needed here, but I think two aspects of Aquinas's political theology are important here. In his discussion of whether or not some men should be allowed to exercise authority over others, in the *prima pars* of the *Summa theologiae*, Aquinas writes that such authority is justified by the necessity of directing and coordinating the actions of many wills with a view to the common good.[33] Moreover, the main instrumentality of such coordination is law, which Aquinas famously defines as "an ordinance of reason directed to the common good by those who have the care of the community, and promulgated."[34] However, Aquinas's view of law is less ambitious than that of Aristotle. He repeatedly stresses the limited aims of law, writing that laws must be framed

30. *Politics* 3.9.1280a 25-1281a 11.

31. This suggestion is made in Peter L. Phillips Simpson, "Making the Citizens Good: Aristotle's City and Its Contemporary Relevance," *Philosophical Forum* 22 (1990): 149-66, especially 160. Simpson does not argue for the conclusion that the authority of the state cannot be justified, however. He rather emphasizes the aspects of the true city now manifested by smaller communities within the modern nation-state. See also his "Liberalism, State, and Community," *Critical Review* 8 (1994): 159-73.

32. For a number of other questions about and criticisms of MacIntyre's account of the common good from a Thomistic-Aristotelian perspective see Thomas S. Hibbs, "MacIntyre, Aquinas, and Politics," *Review of Politics* 66 (2004): 357-83.

33. Aquinas, *Summa Theologiae* (= *ST*), I, 96.

34. *ST* I-II, 90, 4.

"for a number of human beings, the majority of whom are not perfect in virtue," that they neither command all virtues nor forbid all vices, but "only the more grievous vices, from which it is possible for the majority to abstain; and chiefly those that are to the hurt of others, without the prohibition of which human society could not be maintained; thus the human law prohibits murder, theft, and such like."[35] The notion of law and state in Aquinas's view suggests a more general limitation on the ambitions of law as an instrument of formation. This aspect of law is not completely abandoned, but it is clearly attenuated, and this already in the medieval period. I suspect that this thinning out — not elimination — of the notion of the common good and the aims of the political authority is a function of two things: the increasing size and complexity of the political societies that eclipsed the Greek *polis* and that are the ancestor of the modern state, but also the eclipse of the political community itself as guardian of man's highest good. The rise of Christianity meant that the city could no longer constitute the moral and spiritual horizon for man. The first factor is one that we might conclude does not alter any of the theoretical points made by Aristotle, not his judgments about the political good. Rather, it limits the possibilities available to modern political societies. I think one could make the argument that from an Aristotelian perspective that the modern nation-state still possesses more in the way of formative ability than a mere alliance. It is, I would suggest, somewhere between the city and the alliance, perhaps closer to the latter, but retaining some of the character of the former. The second theological issue is more theoretically important and returns us to where we began.

The tension that existed between the two paradigmatic ways of life, the contemplative and the political, was left unresolved in Aristotle's most immediately political work, but resolved in favor of the contemplative life in the *Nicomachean Ethics*. The background to both discussions is, I suggested, the life and death of Socrates, and the thought of Plato, for whom the same tension was treated in the *Republic*. The claims of the gospel transcend both classical ideals in such a way as to recontextualize them. But since grace does not destroy nature, but rather perfects it, I see no reason why a Christian cannot formally will the common good of modern societies, even as directed by the modern state, so long as its limited spiritual, moral, and even physical possibilities are acknowledged.

35. *ST* I-II, 96, 2.

Heartfelt Grief and Repentance in Imperial Times

William L. Portier

> "Save my soul from evil, Lord, and heal my soldier's heart.
> I'll trust in Thee to keep me, Lord, I'm done with Bonaparte."
>
> Mark Knopfler, "Done with Bonaparte," 1996

We begin with this question: Can a Christian be a (devoted) citizen of the polis (even in time of war)? When I first read the terms *citizen* and *polis* in our question, they reminded me of Aristotle. But then I thought of the early Christian work, the *Letter to Diognetus*. In its most frequently cited sections, the terms *polis* and derivatives of *citizen* also appear. Christians live in both Greek and barbarian cities but are said to have no cities of their own. "They live on earth but their citizenship is in heaven." "Every foreign country is their fatherland, and every fatherland is foreign."[1] John Courtney Murray cited this last sentence in the Introduction to *We Hold These Truths*. Though he noted the Christian difference or novelty implied by *foreign*, he chose not to dwell on it.[2]

---

1. *Letter to Diognetus* 5.
2. John Courtney Murray, S.J., *We Hold These Truths* (New York: Sheed & Ward, 1960), p. 15. In discussing religious pluralism, Murray compares our situation with Aristotle's. "For us today man is still a citizen; but at least for most of his life is not absorbed in the City, in society and the state. In the citizen who is also a Christian there resides the consciousness formulated immortally in the second-century *Letter to Diognetus:* 'Every foreign land is a fatherland and every fatherland is a foreign land.' This consciousness makes a difference, in ways upon which we need not dwell here. What makes the more important difference is the fact of religious divisions." Why he does not dwell on the difference, Murray never says.

349

Perhaps the most often cited sentence from *Diognetus* comes at the beginning of paragraph 6: "What the soul is to the body, Christians are to the world." *Lumen gentium* 38, speaking of the witness of lay people in the world as "a sign of the living God," cites this line from *Diognetus*.[3] George Weigel's 1996 *Soul of the World* took its title from this sentence. Weigel gave it what he called an "eschatological" reading.[4] One might reasonably interpret Weigel's title as a pre-emptive strike at another book that appeared later in 1996 from the same publisher, David Schindler's *Heart of the World*. More recently, Michael Baxter has challenged Richard Neuhaus's use of *Diognetus* 6 to defend U.S. foreign policy. Neuhaus uses the text selectively, Baxter argues, to understate the difference, the *alien* quality, of Christians as the "soul of the world."[5]

And so, this piece of pre-Constantinian Christian literature has become a contested site in contemporary discussions of the meaning of Christian citizenship. The contest has to do with Christians as "resident aliens" in the polis. How alien are we? I shall return to *Diognetus* at the conclusion of this paper, and to Balthasar's more "incarnational" reading of Christians as "soul of the world."

We can begin to approach our question by saying that, since the time of St. Augustine, the answer has tended to be "yes." A Christian should give the polis the devotion it deserves even in a time of war. Augustine's "yes" was not unmindful of the alien character of Christians in the earthly city. Nor did he forget the peace tradition that had preceded him.[6] But in the centuries since the *City of God*, this affirmative answer has tended to come

3. The *Catechism of the Catholic Church* also cites *Diognetus* 5 on the duties of citizenship. See 2240. See also 2271 and 2796.

4. George Weigel, *Soul of the World: Notes on the Future of Public Catholicism* (Grand Rapids: Eerdmans, 1996), chapter 2. Weigel's "eschatological" take on American economic and political business as usual means that Christians, "knowing that he [the Son], not we, will build the City of God, . . . can relax a bit about the world and its politics," at p. 34. He adds the requisite cautions against indifference, but his emphasis is clear. For a review, see William L. Portier, "Democracy at the Democratic Crossroads," *Washington Times,* July 20, 1996, A13.

5. Michael J. Baxter, "Why Catholics Should Be Wary of 'One Nation Under God,'" *Houston Catholic Worker* 25, no. 1 (Jan.-Feb. 2005): 8-13.

6. On Augustine's relation to the peace tradition of the martyrs and early Church Fathers, see Ronald Musto, *The Catholic Peace Tradition* (Maryknoll, N.Y.: Orbis Books, 1986), chapter 4, at pp. 48-50. See also David A. Lenihan, "The Just War Tradition in the Work of Saint Augustine," *Augustinian Studies* 19 (1988): 37-70.

more easily. Passing historical periods have seen an increasing forgetfulness of St. Augustine's "heartfelt grief" over the human misery even of just war. We find his own struggle with our question, among other places, in Book XIX of the *City of God*. It is the hope of retrieving for the present this Augustinian notion of grief and its connection to repentance that drives these reflections.[7] But first, in order to explore just how alien we are, we must ask about our particular polis.

Which Polis? Desacralizing the United States

From a theoretical "yes" to our opening question, we often slide to a prudential "yes" to a particular war such as the one my country is presently fighting in Iraq. It is, therefore, most important to ask: Which polis? Many of us live in the United States of America. Looking back to John Winthrop's fateful identification of the new land and covenanted people with the gospel "city upon a hill," there has been a strong tendency for citizens of the United States to sacralize their country, to see it as chosen by God. *God's New Israel* and *Redeemer Nation* are titles of historical standards that chronicle this tendency. It is associated with the Puritan or Pilgrim fathers and comes with a built-in sense of contrast between Old World and New

7. Michael Hanby's christological reflection on the occasion of the U.S. invasion of Iraq, for example, urges a return to an Augustinian lament of virtue, or "having the courage to lament our virtue." He refers to "the 'regret' of virtue, or the entailment of grief within theological virtue," which he associates with St. Augustine's critique of pagan virtue in *City of God*, XIV.8-9 (connecting grief and repentance) and XIX.4. See Michael Hanby, "War on Ash Wednesday: A Brief Christological Reflection," *New Blackfriars* 84 (April 2003): 168-79, at 175 and 178, n. 33. Augustine speaks of "heartfelt grief" at XIX.7. "And so everyone who reflects with sorrow on such grievous evils [the context makes clear that he speaks not only of the injustice that makes war morally necessary, but also the evils entailed in the actual conduct of war he would consider just], in all their horror and cruelty, must acknowledge the misery of them. And yet a man who experiences such evils, or even thinks about them, without heartfelt grief, is assuredly in a far more pitiable condition, if he thinks himself happy simply because he has lost all human feeling." I cite Henry Bettenson's translation from the Penguin edition. "Heartfelt grief" is Bettenson's rendering of *animi dolore*. Jacques Maritain retains this lament of virtue with reference to contemporary means of war. "[I]t is clear that force and . . . the carnal means of war are not intrinsically bad, because they can be just. . . . The worst anguish for the Christian is precisely to know that there can be justice in employing such horrible means" (*Integral Humanism*, trans. Joseph Evans [1936; New York: Charles Scribner's Sons, 1968], pp. 246-48, at 248).

351

World. New is clearly better than old. This mythical contrast often plays out politically and historically in "American exceptionalism," a fervent belief in the virtuous uniqueness of our political institutions and way of life.

This tendency to look upon our country as providential entered Catholic thought in the United States with Orestes Brownson. His 1856 essay, "Mission of America," founds what is sometimes called the tradition of Catholic "Americanism" and gives classic expression to the notion that there is a providential fit between Catholicism and American institutions. Think of the heroes of American Catholic historiography. They are the heroes of the Catholic Americanist tradition: Isaac Hecker, John Ireland and James Gibbons, John A. Ryan, and John Courtney Murray. The idea that Catholics have what America needs has increasingly had its counterpart in the idea that the Church needs America to do its work in the world.[8] In some Catholic quarters since the Council, American exceptionalism has been applied to the Catholic Church in the United States.

Such judgments about the providential status of the United States must always be contingent. They are at best readings of the signs of the times that go far beyond the normal devotion we have to our people and our place. A salutary beginning to answering our question would be to admit that, if these judgments about our exceptional status in God's sight were ever true, they are surely not true now. Reading the signs of the times requires discernment and time is short, so I will simply assert the following. If American exceptionalism means only that we have our own historical circumstance, then who could argue with it? But if it means that we are paradigmatic, the model for the world or the Church to follow into a "democratic" future, then it is a self-deceiving story. The United States is not God's New Israel. It is not Christendom. This is neither a Christian nation nor a Christian culture. Whatever Christian aspects it exhibits are best described with Jacques Maritain's metaphor of the "cut flower." There is no unique fit between Catholicism and America. The Church does not need America to do its work.

The United States of America is simply the place where I live. Nevertheless, it is my home, my country, my *patria*. If we follow in the tradition of Aristotle and St. Thomas, as the term *polis* in the question suggests, we

---

8. For bibliography and an account of the various senses of "Americanism," see William L. Portier, "Americanism and Inculturation, 1899-1999," *Communio* 27 (Spring 2000): 139-60.

have to say that human beings are social rather than individualistic by nature. Political community, therefore, is to be expected as natural. Its end is to serve the common good. But it is another long slide from this philosophical affirmation to practical judgments about how good our present national political community might in fact be, and how well it in fact serves the common good. Is the United States, we must ask, the kind of *patria* that we might reasonably expect to wage what have been called "just wars"?

As a Christian and a citizen who, in the words of the Council (*Apostolicam Actuositatem* 5), has only one conscience, do I have the wherewithal to make informed judgments about whether my political community requires my devotion in a time of war? Do we? If Emmitsburg, Maryland, the town of 2400 or so where I have lived for a good chunk of my life, were contemplating a defensive war with the neighboring Pennsylvania town of Gettysburg, I think I would answer "yes." Emmitsburg is close to a polis. The United States is more like a Hobbesian Leviathan than an Aristotelian polis. It is more like a bureaucratic Weberian cage than a Jeffersonian republic.

As the question about Iraq's possession of weapons of mass destruction illustrates, the United States is a national security state that has a monopoly on the information that citizens would need to make the sort of judgments just war theory should require of individual conscience.[9] Not only do we lack information, but the "news" we do get is suspect. "The ability of governments to employ state-of-the-art methods for shaping public perception of an enemy is so potent that in the end it is capable of overpowering any Catholic opposition even to the use of weapons of mass destruction."[10]

The United States is the only remaining superpower. The publication of *The National Security Strategy of the United States of America* by the

---

9. For those who take just war theory to be a form of statecraft and just war teaching as addressed primarily to national leaders, this lack of information is not a serious problem.

10. Robert Dodaro, O.S.A., "Pirates or Superpowers, Reading Augustine in a Hall of Mirrors," *New Blackfriars* 72, no. 845 (January 1991): 9-19, at 10. "Modern war 'is more than war fought with modern weapons'; it is also, says Szura, 'war that is advertised, marketed, . . . supported by shaped public opinion, public relations, propaganda, and disinformation,'" citing John Paul Szura, O.S.A., a social psychologist who studies processes of enemy dehumanization. Dodaro's title comes from *City of God* IV.4, where St. Augustine uses a story about Alexander the Great's encounter with a captured pirate to make an analogy between pirates and unjust empires.

White House on September 17, 2002, gave a very specific shape to our imperial posture in the world. With one stroke and barely a peep of debate, the United States shifted from its Cold War strategy of containment to a new international strategy of unilateral pre-emption.[11] The invasion of Iraq followed within months. Suddenly Pope John Paul II became a dangerous "multilateralist." Imperial theologians rushed to revise "just war theory" to accommodate the president's new doctrine of pre-emption and its seeming inclusion of morally dubious "preventive" wars. The voices of more conventional proponents of "just war theory," including the pope's, have been drowned out in the national fever that preceded and accompanied our invasion of Iraq.[12] Given the strategy of unilateral pre-emption, our government's decisions about going to war are, on their face, untrust-

---

11. For the complete text of *The National Security Strategy of the United States*, see *Anxious About Empire: Theological Essays on the New Global Realities*, ed. Wes Avram (Grand Rapids: Brazos, 2004), Appendix, pp. 187-215. The president presented his new doctrine as a response to the attacks on the United States in the previous year. But the new strategy had been hatched nearly four years before by a group known as the Project for the New American Century. The twenty-five signers of its 1997 statement of principles included three prominent members of the present administration, the present governor of Florida, and one ubiquitous court theologian. Subsequent communications to President Clinton and congressional leaders strongly urged the removal of Saddam Hussein, lest "a significant portion of the world's supply of oil . . . be put at hazard." On the Project for the New American Century, see Daniel E. Martin, "The Sources of American Conduct," unpublished paper in possession of the author. The point here is not to deny the threat of "terrorism." Nor is it to deny that, as the only superpower, the United States may find itself obliged in justice to intervene militarily in such places as Bosnia, Rwanda, Sudan, or even Iraq. Rather, the point is that, under the threat of "terrorism," and as a response to the U.S.'s new role in the world, the agenda of the Project for the New American Century became national policy with minimal debate. Further, it took an exaggerated unilateral form that places those who would reason from just war principles in the unprecedented position of having to defend preventive war. Superannuated leftists are no longer the only ones who call the United States of America an empire. As Robert Bellah argues, the question is: What kind of empire will the U.S. be? See his opening essay, "The New American Empire" in *Anxious About Empire*, pp. 21-26.

12. For a discussion of the theological framework from which Pope John Paul II responded to situations of international conflict, see William L. Portier, "Are We Really Serious When We Ask God to Deliver Us from War? The Catechism and the Challenge of Pope John Paul II," *Communio* 23 (Spring 1996): 47-63. There is every indication that in the months before March 2003, he responded to the impending invasion of Iraq from within the same framework. See, for example, Cardinal Joseph Ratzinger's remarks of 25 September 2002, as reported in *Avvenire* and picked up by the Catholic News Service, accessed from usccb.org/sdwp/international/cns-1-ra.htm on 2 April 2003.

worthy because they are not subject to debate in just war or any other terms. While I shall not deny that in some truncated and minimal form the United States is still a political community, it is not easy to be devoted to a *patria* that looks more like an imperial plutocracy than a polis.

Heartfelt Grief and Repentance

St. Augustine's thinking about war is often said to be more concerned for the moral status of the soldier who fights than for the innocent victims of war. When I read him, I often think that the only people who could possibly fight a just war as he understands it would be members of an order of monk-knights, analogous to *jedi* perhaps. Their ascetical practices might give them at least some hope of mastering the *libido dominandi,* characteristic of the earthly city (*City of God*, e.g., XIV.28). Augustine did not break completely with the peace tradition that preceded him. Rather, he interiorized it. A Christian soldier kills his people's enemy with peace in his heart. And because he has peace in his heart, he feels grief.

Augustine's concern for the moral status of the soldier who fights has long since faded from most contemporary forms of just war thinking. Many now understand just war reasoning as an impersonal form of statecraft rather than as a form of casuistry that helps individuals know whether to accuse themselves of sin. As long as Augustine's concern for the soldier's interior state remained part of Christian thinking about war, repentance was important too. Christian soldiers feel heartfelt grief at the concomitant evils that go along with even a just war. This is the "lament of virtue," and it can lead to repentance. A soldier who has been swept up in the terrible force of the *libido dominandi* has even more need to repent, as do those in whose name he fights.[13]

13. In *The Truce of God*, a series of Lenten meditations on peace, Archbishop Rowan Williams takes as his controlling metaphor the seemingly quixotic "experiment in conciliation" encouraged by the monastery of Cluny in the early Middle Ages. According to the "truce of God," feudal neighbors would agree to restrict their fighting to Monday, Tuesday, and Wednesday. Williams finds the combination of "naïve earnestness and cynicism" (p. 25) in this proposal both comical and theologically profound and takes it as a kind of type of Christian peacemaking in the world. For his thoughts on repentance in this context, see Rowan Williams, *The Truce of God* (Grand Rapids, Mich./Cambridge, U.K.: Eerdmans, 2005), pp. 32-35.

We find a chilling anatomy of the *libido dominandi* in Chris Hedges'
2002 bestseller *War Is a Force That Gives Us Meaning*. A veteran war corre-
spondent who survived El Salvador and Central America in the 1980s and
Kuwait and Bosnia in the 1990s, Hedges takes Wilfred Owen's *Dulce et decorum est* as his thematic epitaph. Its last lines introduce the book: "The
old Lie: Dulce et decorum est, pro patria mori." In chapters with titles like
"The Destruction of Culture," "The Seduction of Battle and the Perversion
of War," "The Hijacking and Recovery of Memory," and "Eros and
Thanatos," Hedges paints warfare as a mad lie. Those who live through
battle are never the same.

Hedges begins with a chapter on "The Myth of War." We find an example of it in a patriotic song that Willie Nelson and Toby Keith made
popular at the time of our invasion of Iraq. Here is the *libido dominandi* in
its more banal early stages. I quote this verse from memory: "Well, justice
is a thing you can always find, you gotta saddle up your boys, you gotta
take a hard line. When the gunsmoke settles, sing a victory tune, and we'll
all meet back at the local saloon." And then the chorus: "We'll raise up our
glasses against evil forces, singing whiskey for my men, and beer for my
horses, whiskey for my men, beer for my horses." Hedges opens his Introduction with a line from Plato: "Only the dead have seen the end of war." If
the boys who saddled up make it back to the local saloon, Hedges reminds
us, they will bring the war with them.

Students of medieval history in the United States are more likely to
learn about forced conversions and crusades than about the monks and
bishops who protested the violence of Frankish kings and the third-order
Franciscans who outnumbered medieval crusaders. We all need to read
Ronald Musto's much-neglected *The Catholic Peace Tradition*. Rather than
a simplistic narrative in which the witness of early Christian martyrs and
peacemakers disappears in a rush of Constantinianism, Musto tells a more
complex story. It is a story of tension and interplay between Christian
peacemakers and Constantinian rulers. Central to this dialectic are the Augustinian notions of heartfelt grief and repentance. They survive in various forms through the early and later Middle Ages in the practice of soldiers doing penance for what they have done in battle.[14]

"Down to approximately A.D. 1000," Paul Ramsey wrote in 1961, "a
private soldier had to do forty days' penance for fighting in any war, how-

---

14. See Musto, *The Catholic Peace Tradition*, chapters 5 and 6.

ever just."[15] With the Holy Spirit being "more than the odd man," Ramsey urged the churches to debate questions such as "a Christian's action as a soldier during wartime in refusing to participate in the use of immoral means" and whether the just war "doctrine," as he called it, was addressed primarily to national leaders or to individual private citizens. He interpreted modern Catholic just war thinking to emphasize national leaders over private citizens. Ramsey seemed a bit dubious about the value of penance. Nevertheless, he reached an extraordinary conclusion that we would do well to recall.

> If the decision is reached that the church's doctrine of just or limited war is *not* addressed to private citizens and soldiers, then, if also penance is good for anything, consideration should be given to reviving the requirement of forty days' penance following participation in any war.[16]

Reviving Medieval Liturgical Penitential Practices

Ramsey made his proposal nearly fifty years ago in a Cold War setting. With more faith in the goodness of penance than he might have had, the contemporary Church should return to his proposal for reviving in some form medieval penitential practices. Such liturgical practices of penance would have to be moral sanctuaries, safe from political co-option. Some-

---

15. "I suppose," Ramsey continued, "this was for any private animosity that may have arisen in him, and also as a precaution in case he had been involved in doing an injustice which, however, he had not to determine." There follows a note explaining the axiom "the Church shrinks from bloodshed." The penances imposed by ecclesiastical synods for killing in war "had plainly more of a purifying than any special punitive character. . . ." Ramsey underscores the need for purification as underlying the medieval practice of penance for returning soldiers. Paul Ramsey, *War and Christian Conscience: How Shall Modern War Be Conducted Justly?* (Durham, N.C.: Duke University Press, 1961), p. 115, n. 1. For a contemporary example of how the Church in Northern Uganda has worked with ancient tribal "cleansing rituals" to help heal and reconcile former child soldiers, see G. Jefferson Price III, "Seeking Redemption," *Baltimore Sun*, August 28, 2005, 1C, 6C.

16. Rather than on the Augustinian "lament of virtue," Ramsey's shocking proposal is based on the presumption of the likelihood, if just war doctrine is addressed primarily to national leaders, that soldiers will have used immoral means. But heartfelt grief and repentance, as understood here, need not presume that returning soldiers doing penance acted immorally. For Ramsey's conclusion, see *War and Christian Conscience*, pp. 132-33.

how the community to which soldiers return would have to be part of such liturgies. Their purpose would be the purification and healing before God of both returning soldiers and those in whose names they fought. All of this would require historical knowledge of medieval penitential practices and the history of their abandonment, pastoral and liturgical sensitivity, and a more careful account of what repentance and penance mean than I can give here.

But if Plato was correct to say that "only the dead see the end of war," imagine how salutary it might be if returning soldiers and veterans could do penance in a liturgical setting offered by the Church. Whether their penance was an Augustinian lament of virtue or for the sake of immorality in Ramsey's sense, only returning soldiers would know — and perhaps even they would not. We hear and know enough about the suffering of re-turning soldiers and veterans to make us think that Hedges is closer to get-ting it than Willie Nelson and Toby Keith.

In addition to its salutary effect on returning soldiers and their com-munities, such liturgical practices of penance would present a powerful witness in the midst of American society. For just this reason, such a pro-posal might be difficult to enact. It would require just war thinking to be-gin to move away from a primary emphasis on statecraft and back in the direction of an Augustinian concern for the interior state of the soldier who fights. The moral ambiguity acknowledged by widespread penitential practice would dim the glory of war. It might be more difficult for states to go to war. What would soldiers make of this proposal? A lot would depend on who proposed it. We can only imagine how national leaders and mili-tary authorities might respond to such a proposal from church leaders or military chaplains. If they dismissed it out of hand as unpatriotic or im-practical, that would tell us a lot about our opening question of whether a Christian can be a devoted citizen of the polis even in a time of war.

Diognetus in the Empire

Thoughts such as these are usually dismissed as "sectarian." Over the years, I have learned that this is a very bad thing to be in America, perhaps the worst. Its heinousness seems to consist in a lack of concern for and with-drawal from the political community. Sectarians are politically irresponsi-ble. If they are pacifists, they are parasites and worse. Even Hedges, who denounces the horrors of war as immoral, takes the Niebuhrian position that pacifists are irresponsible. In concluding, and by way of addressing the charge of irresponsible withdrawal, I want to return to the *Epistle to Diognetus,* and Balthasar's comments on it.

J. B. Lightfoot called *Diognetus* "the noblest of early Christian writings." It is a Christian apology in epistolary form written in elegant Greek. Its context is the world of the Roman Empire some time between the second century and the early fourth century. It is eleven pages long and divided into twelve paragraphs or sections. Most haunting and memorable are paragraphs 5 and 6 with their provocative images of Christians as homeless and alien even in their own *patria.* These images have stayed with me from the time I first read *Diognetus* as a college student more than forty years ago.

Paragraph 6 begins: "In a word, what the soul is to the body, Christians are to the world. The soul is dispersed through all the members of the body, and Christians throughout the cities of the world."[17] Balthasar cites this text at the beginning of "The Council of the Holy Spirit." This essay is programmatic for his interpretation of the Second Vatican Council as a "theological breakthrough" and "re-discovery of the true essence of the Church" as the means by which the love of Christ is imprinted on all worldly order.[18] The passage from *Diognetus* does a twofold work for Balthasar. Most importantly, it places Christians at the "heart of the world." But it also relativizes, to some extent, whatever place in the world, whatever polis, if you will, Christians happen to inhabit. It is the interpretation of this relativization or Christian difference or novelty that makes *Diognetus* a contested text. It is well to recall that *Diognetus* is an apology written in an imperial setting.

Here is how Balthasar uses *Diognetus* to illustrate the "theological breakthrough" of the Council:

> The "reform" of the ever "imperfect" Church offers the opportunity for the Church to understand herself more deeply in the mirror of revelation and of her mission. If the Letter to Diognetus (ca. 190 A.D.)

---

17. *The Apostolic Fathers: Greek Texts and English Translations,* edited and revised by Michael W. Holmes (Grand Rapids: Baker, 1992), p. 541. This is the 1891 edition of Lightfoot and Harmer.

18. Hans Urs von Balthasar, "The Council of the Holy Spirit," in *Explorations in Theology,* vol. III: *Creator Spirit* (San Francisco: Ignatius Press, 1993), pp. 245-67, at 247.

could say, "What the soul is in the body, Christians are in the world," then this image today is brought to its inevitable consequences, free from all the Platonic anxiety about the body that existed at that early period; while it is true that the soul is preeminent over the animal body, it is through the body that it attains to God and to its own spiritual being, and it is in the body that the soul portrays itself. Thus the Church, too, is preeminent over the world, but she attains to God and to herself only by carrying out her mission, by the self-portrayal of Christian love in the orderings of the world.[19]

In Balthasar's "incarnational" reading of the soul image, embodying, displaying, or dramatizing Christ's love in the world is what Christians do. This is the "self-portrayal of Christian love." It is inevitably a witness to the world in what Balthasar calls the world's various "orderings." But it is difficult to see how such witness, such self-portrayal of Christian love, can take place anywhere but in the world. Nor can I see how such witness fails to be "public," even when it has nothing to do with public policy questions. To take the example that I have proposed, liturgically enacted penance on the part of soldiers, and the rest of us as well, a display of heartfelt grief, even if done in church, would affect the polis in countless ways. We would be acting as the "soul of the world."

In his christological reflection on the U.S. invasion of Iraq, Michael Hanby argues that liturgical repentance is the most fitting Christian response to national liturgies that sacralize the dead and the state:

[I]f the capacity of sovereign power to inflict war depends upon its command of symbols that underwrite its power, the church's best weapon in response is the only one at its disposal: the truth, performed in liturgies of repentance, of the God who empties himself unto death, even death on a cross.[20]

19. Balthasar, "The Council of the Holy Spirit," p. 247.
20. Michael Hanby, "War on Ash Wednesday," p. 170.